WORKING THE BOUNDARIES

WORKING
THE BOUNDARIES

RACE, SPACE, AND "ILLEGALITY"

IN MEXICAN CHICAGO

NICHOLAS DE GENOVA

DUKE UNIVERSITY PRESS

DURHAM AND LONDON 2005

© 2005 DUKE UNIVERSITY PRESS

ALL RIGHTS RESERVED

PRINTED IN THE UNITED STATES OF AMERICA ON ACID-FREE PAPER ∞

DESIGNED BY REBECCA GIMÉNEZ

TYPESET IN MINION BY KEYSTONE TYPESETTING, INC.

LIBRARY OF CONGRESS CATALOGING-IN-PUBLICATION DATA APPEAR

ON THE LAST PRINTED PAGE OF THIS BOOK.

FOR MY PARENTS, **DONNA** AND **WALLY**

CONTENTS

ACKNOWLEDGMENTS

There is a saying, *Dime con quien andes y te diré quien eres*: Tell me with whom you roam, and I'll tell you who you are. Over the years through which this book has emerged, I have wandered and roamed with many people along many different paths, with diverse itineraries and sometimes divergent destinations. As with any book, there is never any adequate way to acknowledge all of them. Yet it is impossible not to try to express my appreciation to those for whom I feel an enduring gratitude and affection.

In the first place, the ethnography that supplies the foundation for this book emerged from innumerable conversations and controversies, dialogues and disputes, interviews and interruptions, in which countless people shared with me their poignantly critical perspectives as well as their most sincere and heartfelt prejudices. I am confident that what ensues in the chapters of this book will provide some modest testament to the many lessons that they variously taught me with their intelligence, ingenuity, humor, and resilience. I am hopeful, furthermore, that this book may make yet another contribution to the unresolved quarrels and vexing dilemmas with which we struggled together. Now as then, we must "make the road by walking."

This book first took shape as my doctoral dissertation at the University of Chicago. I was fortunate during my career as a doctoral student to have had several outstanding teachers, each of whom made his or her unique contribution to the ultimate formulation of this study in its earlier incarnation as a Ph.D. thesis. The members of my doctoral committee—Raymond T. Smith, Jean Comaroff, Michael Kearney, Claudio Lomnitz-Adler, and Terence Turner—should each be able to see traces of the respective paths that we walked together. In particular, what I have sought to do in this study—the questions that I have posed, and the manner in which I have sought to explore those questions—would never have been possible had it not been for the enduring and critical influence of my adviser, Raymond Smith. My thinking has also been deeply inspired by the late Bernard Cohn. My years in the Department of Anthropology at Chicago would have been unfathomable without Barney Cohn's incisive wit and iconoclastic wisdom, surpassed only by his singular kindness. I must also honor the memory of a host of illustrious antagonists at the University of Chicago, too numerous to mention by name. In the face of adversity, Arjun Appadurai, Barney Cohn, and Claudio Lomnitz gave me their decisive support at critical junctures, for which I remain truly grateful. Finally, a special note of appreciation is also due to Mike Kearney, who found the strength to support me in the midst of two tremendous personal tragedies.

Among my best colleagues and most engaged interlocutors at the University of Chicago were many of my fellow students, including Oswaldo Alfaro, Bill Bissell, Neil Brenner, Nahum Chandler, Deborah Cohen, Susan Gooding, Manu Goswami, Josh Price, Gary Wilder, and Judith Wise. Early drafts of chapters 1, 3, and 6 were read and discussed with exemplary care and attention by the Red Line Working Group, whose critical insights over the years continue to be a rich source of intellectual sustenance for my work.

The Spencer Foundation for Research Related to Education provided crucial material support for this project, first with a dissertation-writing fellowship, as well as the nurturing intellectual environment created under the direction of Catherine Lacey, and then again with a very generous small research grant during the early phases of revising the book manuscript for publication.

During my visiting appointment in the Department of Cultural and Social Anthropology at Stanford University, many colleagues and outstanding students contributed to my thinking while I brought the first incarnation of this study to its completion. The enduring support of my colleagues Sylvia Yanagisako and Renato Rosaldo, in particular, has been especially important. Among so many excellent students whom I taught and advised, Alejandro Amezcua, Carole Blackburn, Kathy Coll, Raúl Coronado, Rozita Dimova, Nejat Dinc, Bakirathi Mani, and Victor Pablo White were especially valuable interlocutors for this project. Above all, a special note of appreciation is due to Martha González-Cortés, whose deep personal, intellectual, and political engagement with the central concerns of my work and rigorous reading of an earlier draft of the manuscript were truly extraordinary and have made a lasting contribution to this book.

During my appointment at Columbia University, I have deeply appreciated the generous support and encouragement of several cherished colleagues in the Department of Anthropology, especially Lila Abu-Lughod, Partha Chatterjee, Val Daniel, Nick Dirks, Mahmood Mamdani, Brink Messick, and Sherry Ortner. Likewise, in the Center for the Study of Ethnicity and Race, the support of Gary Okihiro has been greatly appreciated, and Nicole Marwell has been a precious colleague and ally in our efforts to launch and sustain the fledgling program in Latino Studies. A special note of appreciation is likewise due to Sherry Ortner and Steven Gregory, who took the trouble to read portions of the manuscript. Nick Dirks provided crucial assistance, and Janaki Bakhle offered invaluable advice at a decisive moment in the life of this book. Furthermore, Partha Chatterjee, Hamid Dabashi, Mahmood Mamdani, and the late Edward Said have not only provided enduring inspiration as colleagues during my time at Columbia, but also have been the source of decisive support, precious mentoring, and much cherished solidarity, for which I will always be profoundly indebted.

I am grateful, likewise, to have been challenged, motivated, and supported by many outstanding students at Columbia, including Gajendran Ayyathurai, Khiara Bridges, Liz Capone-Newton, Michelle Chan, Yogesh Chandrani, Ryan Chaney, Ayça Çubukçu, Danielle DiNovelli-Lang, Adriana Garriga-López, Nell Geiser, Nadia Guessous, Ron Jennings, Patience Kabamba, Anush Kapadia, Mario Lugay, Nauman Naqvi, Nima Paidipaty, Kristin Ruppel, Shahla Talebi, Yakira Teitel, Steve Theberge, and Antina von Schnitzler. In addition to those already mentioned, a further note of gratitude is due to those students who have worked as my research assistants—Soraya Batmanghelichi, Daniela Gandolfo, Ashley Greene, Kimberly Seibel, and especially Mahesh Somashekhar, who was remarkably devoted, resourceful, and resilient in his preparation of the map for this book.

In addition to so many friends and colleagues already noted, still others have supplied vital intellectual and political sustenance at various junctures during the writing of this book, including Micaela di Leonardo, Juan Flores, Marcial Godoy-Anativia, Alejandro Grimson, María Lugones, George Marcus, Tami Nopper, Suzanne Oboler, Mary Pratt, Ana Yolanda Ramos-Zayas, Rayna Rapp, Rossana Reguillo, Mérida Rúa, Arlene Torres, Howie Winant, and Pat Zavella.

Early drafts of assorted portions of the chapters of this book were presented in a variety of academic settings. Among the more memorable venues were the Department of Cultural and Social Anthropology at Stanford University, as well as the Latino Studies Workshop and the

"Bastards of Imperialism" conference at Stanford; the Department of Ethnic Studies at the University of California, San Diego; the Department of Politics at the University of California, Santa Cruz; the Departments of Anthropology at Columbia University, the New School for Social Research, and the University of Oregon; the Chicano Studies Department at San Jose State University; the Center for the Study of Ethnicity and Race at Columbia; various annual meetings of the American Anthropological Association; the University of Illinois, Chicago/Colegio de Michoacán Project Conference on Mexico and Chicago; the Methodologies of Resistant Negotiation Research Group conference at SUNY-Binghamton; and the Translocal Flows conference in Santo Domingo, sponsored by the Social Science Research Council and the Facultad Latinoamericano de Ciencias Sociales (Dominican Republic). I am very grateful to have had these opportunities to share my work with such a variety of fine audiences and interlocutors, appreciate the contributions of all who served as discussants, and am likewise thankful to all who attended, posed questions, or offered comments on these many occasions. Although they must regretably go unnamed, they have nonetheless been an essential part indeed of this book's community of argument.

During the life of this project, Ken Wissoker has truly accomplished great things at Duke University Press. This book has been blessed with his remarkable and enduring support from the very beginning. I am very grateful to Ken for his abiding energy in cultivating our relationship, as well as his keen intelligence as an editor.

An earlier and considerably more abbreviated version of chapter 3 appeared in 1998 as an article in *Latin American Perspectives* (25[5]), and an abridged version of chapter 6 was likewise published in 2004 in *Latino Studies* (2[2]), in Spanish translation in *Estudios migratorios latinoamericanos* (no. 52), and in Italian translation in the anthology *I confini della libertà: Per un'analisi politica delle migrazioni contemporanee* (Derive-Approdi), edited by Sandro Mezzadra.

Although I am of course solely responsible for any errors of fact or interpretation, the legal analysis in chapter 6 would not have been possible without the practical expertise and insightful reflections of Kalman Resnick, to whom I am enduringly grateful.

Febronio Zatarain did an exceedingly artful job of transcribing tape-recorded interviews, and I will continue to appreciate and admire for years to come his remarkably detailed and loving attention to language and precision with my ethnographic interlocutors' ways of expressing themselves.

In addition to many friends and colleagues directly associated with this book's more narrowly academic context, my work has also been thoroughly enriched by the engaged dialogue and critical insights of a variety of friends and comrades over the years, including Cristina Buena, Pancho Buena, Valeriano Buena, Vicki Cervantes, José David, Gabriel Díaz, Simmi Gandhi, Miguel Jiménez, Ramiro Landa, Alexy Lanza, Emilio Maldonado, Luis Montenegro, Peter Putnam, Abel Rodríguez, Pete Rodríguez, and Gustavo Sánchez. Furthermore, Tannia Goswami, Nav Jhaj, Frank Maugeri, Michael McCabe, Cecilia Novero, and Mario Picayo each provided generous support at crucial moments in the history of this project.

In addition to having struggled with me as a valued friend and most trusted comrade for more than half of our lives, Chris Wright also struggled through an earlier, more arduous draft of the manuscript in its entirety with characteristic devotion and care; his always rigorous criticisms and thoughtful suggestions, as well as our more open-ended and ongoing dialogue, have been simply indispensable.

Both the original research for this project in Chicago and the completion of this book in New York were very deeply interwoven with the love and passion that I have shared with Magdalena, as well as the life that we have made together with our daughter Silvia, and the sheer enchantment that we have come to know with the birth of our baby Artemisia. The news that the book was finally going to the copyeditor came only days before Artemisia's monumental arrival. In addition to her constant companionship and affection, Magdalena has likewise been one of this project's most enduring and cherished critical interlocutors, from our earliest conversations about my research, to her engaged reading of the manuscript, to her loving insistence that I get it finished.

Finally, I deeply appreciate the faithful support of so many people in my family. Above all, I am thankful for the love of my parents—my mother and stepfather, Donna and Wally. Without their hard work and sacrifice, my work would never have been possible. I dedicate this book to them.

PREFACE

When we consider the connections between the United
States and the rest of the world, we are so to speak *of* the
connections, not outside and beyond them. It therefore be-
hooves us as intellectuals . . . to grasp the role of the United
States in the world of nations and of power, from *within* the
actuality, and as participants in it, not as detached outside
observers . . . The imperial contest . . . is a cultural fact of
extraordinary political as well as interpretive importance, because it is the true defining horizon, and to some extent, the
enabling condition of such otherwise abstract and groundless
concepts like "otherness" and "difference." The real problem
remains to haunt us: the relationship between anthropology
as an ongoing enterprise and, on the other hand, empire as
an ongoing concern.**—Edward Said,** "Representing
the Colonized: Anthropology's Interlocutors"

Writing a book is a horrible, exhausting struggle, like a long
bout of some painful illness. One would never undertake
such a thing if one were not driven on by some demon whom
one can neither resist nor understand. . . . I see that it is invariably where I lacked a *political* purpose that I wrote lifeless
books and was betrayed into purple passages, sentences
without meaning, decorative adjectives, and humbug
generally.**—George Orwell,** "Why I Write"

This book arises from the extensive connections between the United
States and Mexico and must account for itself from *within* the actuality of
global capitalism, U.S. imperial power, and white supremacy. This book
also arises from *within* the ongoing intellectual enterprise of U.S. anthropology. Thus, it inevitably bears many of the unseemly but indelible
stains that tell of its long and contradictory gestation and delivery, the

distinctive birthmarks that betray the systemic inequalities that have supplied its material and practical conditions of possibility. It is likewise "from within," therefore, that this book seeks to make its modest contribution to the disruption, subversion, and ultimate transcendance of these same systems of unequal wealth, privilege, and power in which it was incubated.

My interest in the lives and labors of Mexican/migrant workers in Chicago first emerged during several years of intense political involvements, and so, as a doctoral student in anthropology, I came to formulate a research project that reflected my prior experiences and sought to continue grappling with those political concerns. In some sense, the realization of my research was also intended to be an intrinsically political engagement with people like those who had taught me much about my own politics and the centrality of their transnational Mexican/migrant experiences for understanding the transformations of Chicago's working class, as well as the U.S.-dominated imperial order of global capitalism at the end of the twentieth century. While the imprint of those preoccupations and ambitions is still manifest, this project nevertheless was profoundly shaped, in ways that were subtle and insidious, by the particularities and peculiarities of its location within the institutionalized academic discipline of anthropology. In short, more than one demon drove me on in the struggle to produce this work, with divergent goals and conflicting purposes, some vital and others rather more decorative.

It is my sincere hope, nonetheless, that the contradictions of these conflicts themselves serve to animate this text, such that it may seem less the result of a long bout with a painful but elusive illness and more a testament to the relentless struggle of a participant in the sheer restlessness and irresolution of everyday life: an immanent and self-reflexive critique, operating from within—and against—both the disciplinary constraints of anthropology and the defining horizon of empire as an ongoing concern.

INTRODUCTION

WORKING THE BOUNDARIES

This is a book about the laborious condition of working men and women, and about the borders and boundaries that have meaningfully framed their lives and labors, but above all, it is about the everyday struggles that go into producing those boundaries. It is not a book that pretends to be a complete or comprehensive scientific account of fixed and finally knowable objective truths. Although it is very much a book about social realities, it is less about how a *thing* called society really is than about how social *life* comes to appear so thinglike, and about how people immersed in those processes seek to make sense of them. In other words, this book is about the inherently contradictory messiness of ongoing social dynamics and conflict, and the always unresolved processes of social becoming and transformation. It takes as its fundamental starting point the premise that "things" could have been different, and that nothing has to remain as it presently appears. Thus, this is a book about how specific people in a particular place have inherited the manifold consequences of a complex history but also have been and continue to be vital participants in the making of that history and their distinct location within it, in a manner that necessarily leaves them ultimately situated at the center of an open-ended historicity. Therefore, this book is more about questions than conclusions, and the critical formulation of problems that ought to be even more vexing by the end of the book than they were when it began. In this sense, this is a book not only about the ways that the significant boundaries that define social life get elaborated in everyday practice, but also about working and reworking the boundaries of how we even begin to understand and think about those lines of difference and division that impose their dreadful order on the sheer restlessness and creative ferment of living and historical becoming.

More specifically, this book examines the everyday *processes* of transnational migration, racialization, labor subordination, and class formation, as well as the historical production of the structures of citizenship and immigration law that have defined the relationship of Mexican migrants to the U.S. nation-state as its iconic "illegal aliens." Emphasizing processes, all these analytic categories refer precisely to the vital *movement* of social life itself. Migration, by definition, is about movement across space, and transnational migration is best understood as a movement of people across the borders that differentiate nation-state spaces. By the term *racialization*, likewise, I emphasize the dynamic processes by which the meanings and distinctions attributed to "race" come to be *produced* and continually reproduced, and more important, are always entangled in social relations and conflicts, and thus retain an enduring significance because their specific forms and substantive meanings are eminently historical and mutable. This study presents an ethnographic account of the ways that Mexican migrants in the United States become embroiled in a reconfiguration of what it means to be "Mexican" in relation to the dominant U.S. racial polarity of whiteness and Blackness,[1] and thus examines how their experiences of racialization provide a crucial standpoint of critique from which to interrogate the racial economy of the U.S. nation-state. Furthermore, when I refer to *labor subordination* and *class formation*, these terms specifically signal the always unresolved and contingent *struggle* intrinsic to the labor-capital relation due to the necessary and constitutive role of labor within, and simultaneously against, capital. Finally, when I suggest a legal *production* of citizenship and migrant "illegality," historically, my aim is to denaturalize the commonplace notion that migratory movement can be equated with transgressing that "thing" we know as the law, and to underscore instead the deliberate and calculated interventions by which particular laws have effectively generated undocumented Mexican migrants' "illegal" status.[2]

Among those whom I have designated in this book as "Mexican/migrant," there was inevitably a remarkable heterogeneity of experiences and conditions, ranging from seasonal migration to long-term settlement, and from undocumented legal status to U.S. citizenship. When the category *migrant* is deployed here, it should not be confused with the more precise term *migratory*. Rather, the term *migrant* is intended to do a certain epistemological work, to serve as a category of analysis that disrupts the implicit teleology of the more conventional term *immigrant*. The terms *immigrant* and *immigration*, in other words, imply a one-directional and predetermined movement of outsiders coming in and thus are conceptual categories that necessarily can be posited only from the standpoint of the (migrant-receiving) U.S. nation-state. Throughout this book, therefore, unless referring specifically to U.S. immigration law, policy, or politics, I rely on the category *migrant* and systematically reject the term *immigrant* in order to retain a sense of the *movement*, intrinsic incompletion, and consequent irresolution of social processes of migration. I use the term *Mexican/migrant*, furthermore, to refer specifically to people who had migrated from Mexico to the United States. Regardless of their various legal statuses and heterogeneous migration histories, Mexican migrants in Chicago virtually never used terms such as *Mexican American* or *Chicana/o* to identify themselves; they pervasively referred to themselves simply as "mexicana/o" in Spanish, and "Mexican" in English. Similarly, Mexicans born or raised in the United States also predominantly identified themselves simply as "Mexican," rather than either "Chicana/o" or "Mexican American." Although there were often substantive differences in their citizenship statuses as well as other meaningful divergences that were the consequence of having been raised in either Mexico or the United States, both migrants from Mexico and U.S.-born Mexicans nevertheless tended to identify themselves the same way in Chicago (see Davalos 1993; Guerra 1998; Valdés 2000). Thus, in this book, the term *Mexican* refers to both and is generally modified as "migrant," "U.S.-born," or "raised in the United States," as required by context. This inherent ambiguity and heterogeneity about being "Mexican," regardless of one's place of birth, citizenship status, or cultural orientations and tastes, is instructive; it reflects an expression in everyday practice of the resignification of Mexicanness as a specifically *racialized* category within the U.S. social order.

Ever since Mexican migration to Chicago began during the first decades of the twentieth century, there has always been a preponderance of migrants who come from the central-western Mexican states of Michoacán (perhaps singularly accounting for one-fifth to one-quarter of the total), Jalisco, Guanajuato, and Zacatecas (Gamio 1930 [1971]; Jones 1928 [1971]; Taylor 1932; and see Año Nuevo Kerr 1976; Rosales 1978; Weber 1982). The small neighboring state of Aguascalientes likewise provided a noteworthy number of migrants, historically, but this has become relatively insignificant numerically. In addition to these primary "sending" states, substantial numbers have migrated from Durango and San Luis Potosí (further north) as well as the central state of México (including the Federal District), and Guerrero (further south). Finally, there are also smaller but noteworthy numbers of migrants from the central-eastern states of Querétaro, Hidalgo, and Puebla, from Morelos (south-central), as well as from Nuevo León and Chihuahua (northern border states). As of 2002, there were more than 160 Mexican hometown associations and seven state federations—Durango, Guanajuato, Guerrero, Jalisco, Michoacán, San Luis Potosí, and Zacatecas—organized in the Chicago metropolitan area (Cano n.d.). But beyond all the diversity of their origins—beyond village or city, province, and region—Mexican migrants to Chicago are incorporated into the U.S. social order in a way that is, from the start, incorporation into a racial order, where they are reracialized—as "Mexicans."

The research for this book relied upon ethnographic techniques, but it is not an ethnography in the conventional sense. It does not presume to be an all-encompassing study of a discrete and identifiable community or the authoritative representation of a "culture." Rather, this study builds upon an ethnographic engagement with the everyday lives and struggles of transnational Mexican migrants in Chicago (now the second largest urban concentration of Mexican residence in the United States after Los Angeles), in order to analyze the social productions of race, space, and migrant "illegality,"and how they intersect as decisive features of class relations in the United States. By investigating the actual dynamics of racialization and illegalization through ethnographic methods, this book foregrounds the emergence of a transnational Mexicanness that is distinctly reracialized in the United States in a way that exposes the concomitant production of a racialized "American"-ness. Rather than giving an exhaustive case study of a particular Mexican/migrant neighborhood or workplace, then, this book presents an ethnographic critique of U.S. nationalism as a racial formation and seeks to contribute to the formulation of a radically transnational paradigm for the study of migration, citizenship, and the production of nation-state space.

The research for this study was primarily located in a variety of industrial workplaces and urban spaces throughout the Chicago metropolitan area. During the primary research period, over two and a half years from May 1993 through December 1995, I was employed as an instructor of English as a Second Language and basic mathematics (in Spanish) in ten industrial workplaces (predominantly metal-fabricating factories), located throughout the city and some of its industrial suburbs.[3] Factory classrooms thus emerge in this book as uniquely dialogical and highly politicized sites where Mexican migrants explored questions about labor subordination and class formation within a global division of labor, their experiences of racialized conflict and discrimination related to employers' divisive labor recruitment and workplace organization strategies, as well as the racialized politics of language, "assimilation," and nativism. During this same period, I was living in the almost exclusively Mexican neighborhood known as Pilsen, or *La Dieciocho* (the Eighteenth Street barrio), on Chicago's Near Southwest Side (a.k.a. Lower West Side), which has historically been the city's most prominent site of Mexican community organizing. Later, I again resided in Pilsen during a second yearlong period of research (August 1999–August 2000).[4] During the primary research period, I also worked, to a much more limited extent, as a teacher in nonworkplace settings, including three community organizations in the Pilsen neighborhood and a voluntary vocational training and job-placement program in the majority-Mexican working-class suburb of Cicero. In addition to factory-based ethnography, then, this book draws from participant observation in the communities where I lived and worked, as well as approximately two dozen semistructured, open-ended "life-history" interviews conducted in people's homes in neighborhoods throughout the metropolitan area.[5] Thus, the research was also situated in a wide array of Chicago's urban and suburban working-class and poor communities, where Mexicans commonly found themselves inhabiting either notoriously segregated interstitial Mexican or mixed-Latino zones between impoverished African American communities and working-class white neighborhoods in flight, or ghettoized enclaves within deteriorating, historically white working-class areas. However, this book explores the apparently local workplace conflicts or struggles over racialized urban space in Chicago in relation to experiences of undocumented border crossing, the everyday practices of migrant "illegality," and innumerable productions of a transnational social formation linked to countless communities throughout Mexico.

The racialization of Mexican migrants is located in this book at the center of broader discourses of nationalism and nativism that have been elaborated in historically specific ways since the late 1960s and became remarkably pronounced during the period of my ethnographic research in the mid 1990s. This more contemporary history of Mexican migration and racial formation in Chicago is likewise situated within the deeper historical framework of conquest and colonization in the U.S. Southwest, and the subsequent proliferation of interwoven ensembles of transnational social relations between the United States and Mexico. My ethnography is further contextualized in relation to the long history of racialized prerogatives underpinning U.S. citizenship, immigration law, and naturalization policy that chart an institutional nexus linking U.S. citizenship, white supremacy, and the racialization of Mexican/migrant "illegality."

Mexican migration to the United States and the social status of Mexican/ migrant workers are distinguished by an irreducibly singular historical specificity that has been racialized, spatialized, legislated, and enforced. Thus, Mexican/migrant transnational social formations in the United States must be situated at the intersection of three integrally related and mutually constitutitive features. First, transnational Mexican migration has historically been and continues to be primarily a *labor* migration, and so it is necessary to examine its preponderantly proletarianized class composition within and against global capitalism. Furthermore, Mexican migration comes to be *racialized* as specifically "Mexican" in relation to the hegemonic polarity of whiteness and Blackness within the space of the U.S. nation-state. Finally, the specific transnational character of Mexican migration is constituted across the nation-state border between the United States and Mexico and thus must be considered in specific political relation to the legal economy of the U.S. nation-state. Its precise migrant status is profoundly implicated in the production of nation-state space and the *spatialized* difference between "American"-ness as a national identity and Mexicanness as a racialized transnationality. By exploring the social productions of race, space, and "illegality" for Mexican labor migration, and the particular transnational social formation constituted by their conjuncture in Chicago, therefore, this book does not seek to make authoritative anthropological claims about Mexicans or their supposed "culture," but rather deploys ethnographic techniques in order to focus a critical lens on the significance of racialized and spatialized difference and the unequal politics of citizenship as constitutive features of class relations within the space of the U.S. nation-state.

A forceful politics of anti-immigrant restrictionism and nativism, distinguished by its specifically anti-Mexican racialized content, prevailed in the United States during the the the mid-1990s, when this book's research was conducted. Rather than treat this nativism as a transhistorical and presumably always latent political impulse in the United States, however, this book emphasizes the specificity of late-twentieth-century immigration restrictionism in light of an unprecedented and expansive legal production of "illegality" for Mexican migration in particular, beginning in the late 1960s. Further, the book locates nativism as a crucial feature of nationalism that helps to resolve the problem posed for any nation-state by the contingency of the nation through a kind of hegemonic identity politics that promotes the priority of "natives" over "immigrants," simply on the basis of their being native. Thus, nativism appears to be necessary for the productions of national identity. In this light, nativism tends to ground claims not only against immigration but also in favor of it, by always evaluating migration from the standpoint of citizens who authorize themselves to debate the question in terms of what is good for "the nation." Similarly nativist conceits are likewise pervasive in hegemonic U.S. discourses concerning migration, which subsume diverse and distinct migrations into the teleological discourses of *im*migration and assimilation and thus are posited always from the standpoint of the migrant-receiving U.S. nation-state. Through a critique of such nationalist premises, this book lays a groundwork for a more rigorously transnational paradigm for the study of migration.

This counternationalist paradigm and its critical standpoint on the U.S. nation-state are embodied in the formulation of *Mexican Chicago* as a transnational conjunctural space—a Chicago that is practically and materially implicated in Mexico and thus, a Chicago that can be understood to belong meaningfully to Latin America. Locating Mexican Chicago as its unique standpoint of critique, the book makes a critical intervention aimed at a transnational reconceptualization of the theoretical paradigms that ground Chicano studies, Latin American studies, and American (U.S.) studies.[6] The research that is the basis for this book emerged from a multiplicity of sites across a metropolitan space that is not at all delimited by a bounded geographical locale, and moreover, is not reducible simply to a population of Mexican people contained in such a place. Not merely an "ethnic enclave" or an "immigrant" ghetto, then, Mexican Chicago is a conjuncture of social *relations* and thus comprises innumerable places. Understood as a conjuncture of the national and the transnational, furthermore, Mexican Chicago is constituted through the everyday social relations and meaningful practices of a racialized labor migration, capitalist enterprises, and the U.S. nation-state. Thus, Mexican Chicago emerges in this study as the conjuncture of an urban ethnographic site (comprised of a multiplicity of particular places across the metropolitan region) and a set of specific questions about class formation, racialization, and the transnational politics of space.

Migrant "illegality" proves to be a decisive feature of the distinctive racialization of Mexicans in the United States. Rather than naturalize this "illegal" or undocumented condition, however, the book demonstrates empirically how U.S. immigration law has generated the juridical categories of differentiation among various migrations, defined the parameters of "legality," and continually revised the possibilities for "legal" migration in ways that have been disproportionately restrictive for Mexicans in particular, and increasingly so. The U.S. nation-state's enforcement of immigration law and policing along the U.S.-Mexico border, notably, have long sustained the operation of a revolving-door policy—simultaneously implicated in *im*portation as much as (in fact, far more than) deportation (Cockcroft 1986). This study contends that the legal production of migrant "illegality" has never served simply to achieve the apparent goal of deportation, so much as to regulate the flow of Mexican migration in particular and to sustain its legally vulnerable condition of *deportability*—the possibility of deportation, the possibility of being removed from the *space* of the U.S. nation-state. It is deportability, and not deportation as such, that has historically rendered Mexican labor to be a distinctly disposable commodity. "Illegality" is thus lived through a palpable sense of deportability whereby some are deported in order that most may remain (undeported) as workers. In other words, "illegality" provides an apparatus for producing and sustaining the vulnerability and tractability of Mexican migrants as labor. In this way, migrant "illegality" is a spatialized social condition that becomes inseparable from the particular ways that migrant workers from Mexico are racialized as "illegal aliens" within the United States, and thus as "Mexican" in relation to "American"-ness.

The intertwined racializations of Mexicanness and "American"-ness, furthermore, expose the workings of U.S. nationalism itself as a racial formation for which "American" national identity is inherently racialized as white. This book's ethnographic research reveals how Mexican migrants in Chicago tended to systematically infer and consistently recapitulate a socially ubiquitous equation of "American"-ness with racial whiteness, to the exclusion of African Americans as well as U.S.-citizen Latinos (including Mexicans born in the United States).[7] Mexican migrants thus negotiated their own reracialization as Mexican, always in relation to both a dominant whiteness and its polar opposite, a subjugated and denigrated Blackness. While this book is indeed centrally concerned with the production of Mexicanness in the migrant encounter in the United States, therefore, this is *not* a study of something that might be called "Mexican culture." Rather, this book explores the social production of a "Mexican"-ness that is always doubly produced at the conjunctures of race and space, as an "illegal" transnationality, reracialized between whiteness and Blackness within the space of the U.S. nation-state.

PART ONE

POLITICS OF KNOWLEDGE/

POLITICS OF PRACTICE

We realize all the more clearly what

we have to accomplish in the present . . .

a *ruthless criticism of everything*

existing.—**Karl Marx,** ''Open Letter

to Arnold Ruge''

CHAPTER ONE

DECOLONIZING ETHNOGRAPHY

Representation becomes significant, not just as an academic
or theoretical quandary but as a political choice.—**Edward Said,**
''Representing the Colonized: Anthropology's Interlocutors''

"¿Por las buenas o las malas?" So responded Celso in a manner that was
light-hearted but not without a certain measure of suspicion, upon learning from Emiliano that I was interested in learning and eventually writing
a book about the experiences and problems of Mexican migrants in the
United States.[1] My friend Emiliano, whom I had known during several
years of political collaboration, first introduced me in the spring of 1992
to a group of men who had migrated from his rural hometown in the
Mexican state of Morelos—the supporters and members of a soccer team,
whose weekend matches I too would later attend fairly regularly.[2] "¿Por
las buenas o las malas?" Demanding in a jocular tone, "[Are you going to
do it] with the carrot or the stick?"—literally, "by good means or bad?"—
Celso immediately expressed his reservations that I might intend to force
it out of them, as in an interrogation. With this concise and poignant
question, he ironically registered his sense that the very act of trying to
make people or their lived experiences into an "object of study" was
something invasive, and even potentially coercive. Questions concerning
the politics of representation have been a persistent preoccupation, literally from the outset of the research that was the basis for this book.
As evidenced by Celso's skepticism, moreover, that quandary was never
merely mine alone. Beginning with the very first preliminary research
notes that I ever scribbled, and throughout the history of my ethnographic endeavors, there was ample and recurrent evidence of the salience of questions about who I was and what exactly was my purpose,
followed by diverse expressions of a skeptical spirit and an engaged critical sensibility that frankly challenged my intention to write about the
social situation of Mexican migrants.

On the same occasion, another team member, José Luís, asked if what I had in mind would resemble the Hollywood film *The Border*, whose protagonist is a white Border Patrol agent. By citing this rather high-profile, mass-mediated depiction of Mexican "illegal aliens" and the purported crisis they represent for U.S. border policing, José Luís was clearly suggesting that there were already abundant representations of "Mexicans" in the United States, indeed, images that contributed to the racialized stigma of their "illegality" and foreignness (Chávez 2001; Johnson 1997). The extent of his skepticism about my ethnographic interest to represent the experiences of Mexican migrants, however, was truly revealed only once I myself began to denounce the film for its transparent racism. Perhaps somewhat encouraged by my reply, José Luís then went on to ask me to explain why the U.S. Immigration and Naturalization Service (INS)—*la Migra*—was known to have sometimes strip-searched undocumented migrant workers when they were apprehended during factory raids, emphasizing that they obviously could not have been concealing narcotics if they were arrested on the job. José Luís's expectation, reasonably and rightly enough, was that I was a U.S. citizen, an "American," and ought to have an answer for such gratuitously degrading and dehumanizing practices on the part of what we both knew was certainly not *his* government. From the very inception of my attempt to conduct ethnographic research, then, it was abundantly manifest that my "anthropological" aspirations were inextricable from the politics of my social location—as a U.S. citizen, as someone racialized as white, as an intellectual educated in elite schools, with the luxury of having the pretension to write books, and thus, regardless of my working-class family background or my radical politics, as an objectively privileged and effectively middle-class person.[3] Who was I, after all, to want to write about the experiences of Mexican migrants in the United States, and more important still, *how* would I do so?

A critique of the discipline of anthropology and dominant forms of anthropological representation, furthermore, was articulated forcefully and explicitly when I first met Efraín, a man in his late forties who had migrated to Chicago from Honduras in the late 1960s. We met in a nightclub in May of 1994 in Chicago's Pilsen neighborhood, where I was living. I was there with my friend Anselmo, a migrant who was twenty-three and had been in the United States for only three years. When Anselmo introduced me to Efraín, he included the fateful mention that I was affiliated with the University of Chicago. "The University of Chicago?!?" Efraín immediately exclaimed, "In Latin America, we know all about the fucking University of Chicago!" The mere mention of the notorious place inspired him to launch into an impassioned denunciation of "los Chicago boys," the University of Chicago economists who had engineered the austerity programs that intensified the misery of the Chilean working class under Pinochet's dictatorship. Efraín concluded as he had begun, reaffirming, "We already know all about the University of Chicago." Anselmo was probably a bit embarrassed at having unsuspectingly subjected me to all this unforeseen adversity and tried to defend me, now by insisting that I was an *anthropologist*—not like those Chicago economists at all! Efraín continued unabated, "You know, anthropology has really fucked us over! I went today to that fucking Field Museum [of Natural History] to see the exhibition 'Visiones del Pueblo'—it was an infamy! What a horror! People are stupid, and the museum increases people's stupidity—that's its function." Clearly, for Efraín, the global inequalities of power and wealth created and perpetuated by U.S. imperialism undergirded and unified the diverse capacities of a broad continuum of U.S.-based academics in a range of distinct intellectual disciplines to nevertheless participate in the domination of the peoples of Latin America. Some devised neoliberal economic policies for Latin American dictatorships; others, such as anthropologists, authoritatively represented indigenous Latin American "cultures" in museums and textbooks that located their presumably discrete cultural visions within Eurocentric social evolutionary schemes of "natural history." Indeed, the very notion that the history of pre-Columbian civilizations (or contemporary Latin American "cultures") belonged in a natural history museum that houses dinosaurs signaled a whole legacy of colonial anthropology that evaluated and cataloged the "traditions" of "primitive peoples," depicting them as living analogies to Stone Age cavemen, trapped somewhere in humanity's ascent from apes, apparently incapable of progressing to the self-styled "modernity" of "Western civilization." Thus, some U.S. academics worked on the economics of "underdevelopment" in the so-called Third World, and others rationalized such "backwardness" in relation to "cultural" difference.

I was laughing along with Efraín's robust disdain for such imperial and racist arrogance and agreeing with his passionate denunciations while Anselmo persisted on my behalf. In his own fashion, affirming with Edward Said that representation is finally not merely an intellectual problem but also a *political* choice, Anselmo declared in my defense, "But

Nicolás is a communist!" Once some semblance of my political credibility had been established after further discussion, Efraín nevertheless warned me ominously, "Just be careful that you don't let the University of Chicago seduce you!"

Even when people became fairly confident that my politics were sure to be critical of the racial oppression and exploitation that Mexicans confront in the United States, there often remained a healthy skepticism about my purported plan to write a book. In a small taquería in the predominantly Mexican/migrant working-class suburb of Cicero, where I regularly ate lunch and passed the time between teaching assignments at a nearby factory, I would often have long conversations with the owner and the other workers. The owner Arnulfo, himself formerly a factory worker, rented the store and worked full-time behind the counter, cooking and operating the cash register. In his late thirties, Arnulfo had migrated from a small agrarian town in Zacatecas eleven years earlier, and he dreamed of returning to Mexico to open a restaurant there. Discussing my stated intention to write a book, Arnulfo objected, "But the government knows about all this, they understand very well—and they're not going to want you to tell people about all of this; they might not let you say these things, because I know that what you'll say will be critical of what the government does!" Implicitly, Arnulfo challenged me not to subscribe to such a naive faith in the duplicitous liberal promises of U.S. democracy. Even if I presumed to write a book that might tell the truth, Arnulfo reasoned, why should I imagine that I could get away with it?

It was not as if the Mexican/migrant communities of Chicago had not already been subjected to the various investigative techniques of academic researchers from local universities. In February of 1995, I was planning to interview my friend María, a single mother in her late twenties who had grown up in both Mexico and California as a result of her family shuttling back and forth every year or two, and who then had migrated from Mexico to Chicago about seven years before I met her. María told me that she was already having regular interview visits with another friend, a Mexican/migrant herself, who was a college student collecting data on welfare programs for some anthropologist or sociologist who had employed her as a research assistant. María laughed at the almost perverse absurdity of how, for the purposes of the "social scientific" documentation of her poverty and "welfare dependency," she was expected to report all of the various ways that, as a "Latina single mother collecting public assistance," she received goods or services free of charge through "informal networks." Later that year, María poignantly criticized my own "anthropology": "I'm slowly facing the reality that you're not Mexican and that you're only living in Pilsen to do your *research.*" She emphasized the word *research* with a tone of disdain and estrangement. When I asked her what she meant, she explained, "Well, I think to myself —that's such a *white* thing to do—come here from outside to do research for some university; then you're just gonna leave to go live in Hyde Park to be close to that Chicago University." María confronted me bluntly with the complex web of racialized class inequalities that not only made it possible for me to be conducting research in Mexican/migrant communities like her own but also would implicate my subsequent life choices in a career trajectory that seemed inseparable from white middle-class communities and elite universities. She also forcefully asserted that university studies of racially oppressed communities were inevitably linked to white power.

My friend Jaime communicated similar concerns when he imparted to me a rather memorable warning. Jaime had grown up in Chicago since the age of five in a Costa Rican family comprised of a widowed mother with ten children, in predominantly Puerto Rican communities on the city's North Side; as Jaime liked to put it, "We weren't working class, we were welfare class." Jaime had gone to college and was working for a Pilsen-based, Latino-identified social service agency. In 1997, when we crossed paths after having not seen each other for several months, I mentioned that I was no longer working as an ESL teacher because I was now being supported by a doctoral dissertation-writing fellowship to work on my thesis full-time. With a mischievous grin and a sparkle in his eye, Jaime cautioned, "You better be careful—next thing you know, they might want you to set up a Department of Cucaracha Studies." Reminiscent of Efraín's stringent warning about the seductions of the university, Jaime reminded me that the enticements of money and prestige associated with an academic career could subtly distort and subvert the aims of my research, implying that I had to be vigilant against the ethical and political dangers that would accompany my professional advancement. Furthermore, he made it plain that I was responsible, ethically and politically, to the Mexican migrants and the broader Latino community with whom I had been working. One of the central burdens of that relationship concerned, precisely, the politics of representation—the ease with which Mexican or Latino studies might be disfigured by elite educational institutions into the kind of scholarship that objectifies people and represents them as something akin to so many miserable and filthy cockroaches, lined up for "scientific" scrutiny.

As my friends persistently and provocatively reminded me, I had a responsibility not to transpose my research into the kind of dehumanizing study by which a white social scientist, bolstered by the power and privilege of credentials and funding from elite universities, presumes to make authoritative pronouncements about "the Mexicans" and some ossified thing called "their culture" (see Fanon 1956, 29–44). With all of these cautionary dialogues as a guide, I have sought to produce this book and its ethnographic representations of Mexican/migrant perspectives and experiences, not so as to presume to demonstrate "this is what they're like," or "this is their culture," but rather in a manner that serves the ends of a critique of global capitalism and the U.S. nation-state, its nationalism, its racial order, and its imperial projects, which, taken together, are the defining and also enabling horizon of the research that informs this work. My purpose in this study has been precisely *not* to "study Mexican immigrants," whose "culture" could be objectified and rendered intelligible to the dominant institutions of the U.S. nation-state. Rather, my aim here is to interrogate the U.S. nation-state and its nationalism from the critical standpoint of Mexican migration—as a particular racialized, transnational, working-class social formation—as I have come to understand its vital movement, in dialogue with some of the people whose everyday struggles have produced and sustained that dynamic.

OBJECTIVITY AND OBJECTIFICATION

If the role of anthropology for colonialism was relatively
unimportant, the reverse proposition does not hold. . . . It is not
merely that anthropological fieldwork was facilitated by European
colonial power . . . it is that the fact of European power, as discourse
and practice, was always part of the reality anthropologists sought to
understand, and of the way they sought to understand it.
—**Talal Asad,** "From the History of Colonial Anthropology to the
Anthropology of Western Hegemony"

There is, of course, a myth of fieldwork . . . but as a means for
producing knowledge from an intense intersubjective engagement,
the practice of ethnography retains a certain exemplary status.
—**James Clifford,** "On Ethnographic Authority"

> The by now massed discourses, codes, and practical traditions of
> anthropology, with its authorities, disciplinary rigors, genealogical
> maps, systems of patronage and accreditation have been
> accumulated into various modes of *being anthropological* . . . .
> And if we suspect that as in all scholarly disciplines, the
> customary way of doing things both narcotizes and insulates the
> guild member, we are saying something true about all forms of
> disciplinary worldliness. Anthropology is not an exception.
> —**Edward Said,** "Representing the Colonized:
> Anthropology's Interlocutors"

Anthropology's disciplinary preoccupation with "cultural" difference has a defining historical relationship to what Partha Chatterjee has called "the rule of colonial difference" (1993, 16–27; see Chatterjee 1986, 10–17). The practical means, furthermore, by which sociocultural anthropologists seek to understand social reality and produce knowledge—that complex of methodological procedures that make up the practice of ethnographic research—were colonial-era innovations that have hardly relinquished the racializing imprint of colonial power relations. The practice of ethnographic research, therefore, poses what appears to be an intractable problem: it is the singular means of formal social research that enables a production of the textured knowledge of human perspectives and structures of feeling in the present that emerges only through extended engagement with the everyday lives, labors, and struggles of living people, yet it seems to be simultaneously an inherently objectifying methodology.

This contradiction between ethnography's "exemplary status" and its colonial character summons a critical consideration of the relationship between ethnography's "objectivity," as a means of (intellectual) production, and the political problem of objectification. At the most general level, this contradiction manifests the social division of intellectual and manual labor that is a fundamental precondition of academic knowledge production itself, whereby the very possibility of research is posited only as the professional activity of a privileged minority. As Peter McLaren (1995, 275) points out, the status of the researcher as such is "both a discursive fiction and a social practice." The ethnographic researcher's own identity and subjective outlook come to be premised upon the particular investigative techniques and analytic tools that comprise what Said (1989, 213) calls "modes of *being anthropological*," the "customary way of doing things" within the anthropological "guild." The researcher or ethnographer becomes so only by operating according to the conventional disciplinary protocols that define what an ethnographer is supposed to do. Thus, a person's participation and observant practice as an actor in a particular social setting are bestowed with a special status that is apparently removed from the immediacy of those interactions and seemingly transcends that particular social engagement. That special quasi-transcendent status is the status of researcher. Most important, such status is achieved not simply by engaging in some kind of preconceived research practice, but rather—as Efraín, María, and Jaime all emphatically reminded me—by doing so through the *institutional* channels that enable it to be officially sanctioned and credentialed, after the fact, as having indeed been valid as "research."

It is precisely the *institutional* contexts that underwrite the anthropological disciplinary mythology of "fieldwork," and authorize the ethnographic fiction by which the putative researcher can produce the intended effect that what he or she did was genuinely research. Research, in short, is a social practice that has to follow certain rules or conventions in order to be officially recognized as legitimate. Those rules and conventions, as well as that legitimation, however, all emanate from disciplinary institutions. Even James Clifford, one of ethnography's premier critics, has had to recognize its "exemplary status" as a means for producing a particular kind of knowledge—its exemplary status, that is, as an intellectual means of production. When the critique of ethnography remains confined to its *textual* form, however, rather little critical energy is devoted to the institutional framework that organizes such knowledge production, and which is required to anoint it as the discipline's methodological signature. The exemplary status of ethnography, in other words, is not an intrinsic virtue but rather is itself an *effect* of disciplinarity (see Trouillot 1991, 38).

The contradiction between ethnography's exemplary status and its colonial character has to be situated, therefore, in relation to the material conditions of its own possibility as a social practice and has to be accounted for politically in terms of the variety of institutionally embedded social relations of domination and subordination that supply its "true defining horizon" (Said 1989, 217; see Asad 1973a; Cohn 1996; Wallerstein 1997b). In this light, ethnography is intrinsically problematic, and the politics at stake is not at all reducible to the merely epistemological subjugation inherent in textual representation (Fabian 1983; Gupta and

Ferguson 1992, 17). Epistemological questions and problems of textual representation are always embroiled in the operations of larger-scale structures of inequality and domination and thus are indisputably crucial. However, it is a fallacy to try to rectify practice from within its product (e.g., the ethnographic text). Theorizing ethnographic practice itself, therefore, becomes an urgent and long overdue demand. In order for ethnographic research to *not* serve the ends of domination (however inadvertently or haphazardly), it is necessary that deliberate and diligent efforts be made toward its decolonization (Mignolo 2000; see Arvizu 1978; Blauner and Wellman 1973; Harrison 1991a; Ladner 1973 [1998]; Stavenhagen 1971). Much as the project of decolonizing anthropology may prove to be futile, it is certainly not unthinkable that ethnographic practice may finally be recuperable despite its disciplinary genealogy.

At the edge of the soccer field, when Celso asked ironically whether, in order to arrive at the knowledge of Mexican/migrant experience that I was seeking, I was going to use the carrot or the stick, good (persuasive or enticing) means or bad (intrusive or coercive) ones, he was incisively affirming that methodological questions—always concerned with the means of producing knowledge—are at once preeminently epistemological *and* political. They are epistemological, of course, in that they involve definite premises about truth and how it may be known and understood, but also political, because they involve *how* one goes about acquiring that knowledge. In short, the means of producing knowledge always also imply the *social relations* necessary for that process of production. Here, then, is the critical problem of examining social science methods' purported objectivity in relation to practices of objectification—not only at the level of representation, but also in terms of the social relations of the research itself.

In the work of anthropologists and other ethnographers, the claim of expertise has conventionally been based upon rigid inside-outside dichotomies that presuppose and reinforce essentialist notions of discrete bounded "cultures" and "cultural" difference. The authoritative knowledge of the ethnographer has often derived from an anthropological fantasy about unlocking the apparently esoteric truths of an exotic "culture" that one accesses from an imagined outside. This anthropological conceit reserves scientific objectivity as a privilege of the ethnographer, as an intrepid outsider. The palpable analogies with gendered themes of masculine adventure and sexual domination, and the equally masculinist but also racialized themes of colonial discovery, penetration, exploration, and conquest, of course, are not accidental (see Bederman 1995; McClintock 1995; Trexler 1995; Young 1990 and 1995). As if from an imagined standpoint outside of the social relations under scrutiny, the ethnographer—despite the direct and immediate involvement and participation in those social relations required for ethnographic participant observation —can purportedly know most comprehensively what all the so-called natives inevitably know only partially from their respective locations *within* the "culture" or "social structure" being studied. This founding myth of "fieldwork" emphasizes the subjective limitations of all involved, with the singular exception of the ethnographer, as scientific observer, who is implicitly supposed to be capable of transcending his or her own particular subjective perspectives in the course of objectively and systematically observing and intellectually mastering the "object" of study.[4] Here, to be sure, I have sketched a caricature that exaggerates a naïveté about ethnographic knowledge that few contemporary anthropologists would endorse. Nonetheless, such pervasive notions as "going to the field" in order to "study the culture" of some circumscribed group of people reveal the strong residue of this inside-outside premise about anthropological study, and its enduring importance for disciplinary mythologies about "fieldwork."

Such conceits about ethnographic expertise, and about the very possibility of social "science," require an epistemological stability of the subject-object relation. The anthropological subject makes knowledge claims that implicitly reaffirm the stability of an essential and irreducible otherness of a circumscribed group of people through purportedly objective accounts of what their "culture" consists of—their distinctive ways of being, doing, and knowing. The active and fundamentally open-ended engagement of living people with their social circumstances and their efforts to transform their own history, therefore, get reduced to the delimited object of study of an institutionally credentialed researcher who fashions him- or herself as intrinsically outside of their meaningful concerns and struggles.

THE DIALOGICAL IMPERATIVE:
TOWARD AN ANTI-ANTHROPOLOGICAL ETHNOGRAPHY

I came into the world imbued with the will to find a meaning
in things . . . and then I found that I was an object in the midst of
other objects.—**Frantz Fanon**, *Black Skin, White Masks*

"The real danger," Paulo Freire forewarns, "lies in shifting the focus of the research from the meaningful themes to the people themselves, thereby treating the people as objects of the investigation" ([1968] 1990, 99).[5] Freire's *Pedagogy of the Oppressed*, from which this quote is excerpted, is an extremely provocative, widely influential, and seminal work that holds very little currency (indeed, is almost entirely neglected) in anthropological theory or practice.[6] Freire's pedagogical polemic has important implications for reconceptualizing and transforming the practice of ethnography, but it is not at all surprising that ethnographers have largely overlooked his potential insights for their craft.[7] Freire himself was never really concerned with the generic quandaries of social science, nor even the specific conundrums of ethnographic method. His work is concerned, instead, with teaching and learning. In particular, Freire is interested in adult literacy education for workers and peasants, and he is specifically devoted to formulating an explicitly politicized pedagogical method that might serve as "a practice of liberation."[8] For me, there was a peculiar inevitability to this linkage between pedagogy and ethnography, as my research was intricately entwined with adult education.[9] There was no time during my principal period of research when I was not working as a teacher, nor was there ever a moment when my teaching was not also a major facet of my ethnographic work, as I was mainly teaching Mexican/migrant factory workers. Hence, pedagogy, ethnography, and politics together constituted a restless triangulation at the practical core of my research. Freire's inspired appeal for *dialogue* as the centerpiece of his method, therefore, has proven quite productive in my efforts to theorize the practical decolonization of ethnographic research.[10]

Dialogue is the hallmark of the critical pedagogy to which Freire aspires. When Freire formulates his conception of dialogue, it is posited as a moment in the collaborative, collective practice through which human beings create and transform the world and thereby create and transform themselves. For Freire, dialogue is the encounter between human beings, educating each other, mediated by the world, in order to name the world ([1968] 1990, 67, 76–77). Dialogue "imposes itself as the way by which men [*sic*] achieve significance" as human beings; because significance is thus always emergent, "dialogue is thus an existential necessity." It is not an act of consumption; it is an act of production, "an act of creation and re-creation" (77).[11] When Freire warns against "shifting the focus of the research from the meaningful themes to the people themselves, thereby treating the people as objects of the investigation," the investigation to which Freire refers is, specifically, a preliminary research that he posits as necessary to identify the "thematic universe" of the people to whom an educational project purports to address itself. Freire proposes this thematic inquiry as necessary in order for educators to become acquainted with the actual "cultural" situation of the prospective learners. For Freire, it is crucial that a collaborative and liberatory pedagogy start with an identification and critical exploration of the meaningful concerns that demarcate the specific "thematic universe" of those to whom the educational project addresses itself (86). Notably, the investigation itself is likewise instrumental in initiating a dialogue and thus establishing the overall dialogical character of the educational encounter as a whole (86). For our purposes, such thematic investigation can be productively glossed as an "ethnographic" mode of inquiry, but only with the caveat that such an ethnographic encounter itself be thoroughly dialogical.[12]

The ethnographic situation is always inherently, and inevitably, dialogical, for this is intrinsically true of all social life (Bakhtin 1981; see Fabian 1990, 763–66; 2001, 11–32; Mannheim and Tedlock 1995).[13] Furthermore, as all ethnographic situations are necessarily dialogical, they are inherently problematic and contested—and thus political (see Page 1988).[14] Thus understood, intersubjective dialogue directed toward an interrogation of the wider sociopolitical world potentially enables an ethnographic account to emerge from the critically engaged collaboration of people who are becoming conscious, together, of their own roles in the production and reproduction of their social realities and the making of their own histories. Objective contexts are nonetheless decidedly salient for Freire, in that they present human actors with concrete circumstances in which to go about producing, reproducing and most importantly transforming their world of social relations as historical subjects ([1968] 1990, 67).

Freire's vision of a critical pedagogy requires—in its own terms—that it be inaugurated through a quasi-ethnographic investigation of the meaningful themes that will otherwise provide the content of the educational encounter. That preliminary research effort itself must be dialogical, however, as it pivotally serves to initiate the more extended dialogue of the collaborative learning process. It is hardly an implausible conceptual leap to suggest that the extended pedagogical dialogue Freire outlines can itself be deliberately reconfigured as an extended ethnographic research dialogue. Adapted in this way, Freire's conception of dialogue would therefore mandate that the researcher struggle to engage the ethnographic encounter in a collaborative, self-consciously political manner. Rather than simply domesticating Freire's critique as mere methodology (Aronowitz 1993; Giroux 1993), dialogue might inform the possibility of "concrete collaborations" (Harrison 1991b) and the reworking of participant observation into "the methodological and political stance . . . of an observing and communicating actor" (Turner 1991, 305), as an open-ended partisanship (Sanadjian 1990) that is unabashed about its "taking sides" (Peña 1997), toward the ends of a radical decolonization of ethnographic practice (Stavenhagen 1971, 337). As a colearner and a coworker, the ethnographer would not aspire to reify a circumscribed group of people as an other and objectify their "culture," but instead would aspire, with his or her ethnographic interlocutors, to meaningfully engage the world and collectively act within it. This process is possible only through dialogue, and it is oriented not to fixing the differences between ethnographic interlocutors but rather to intersubjectively collaborating in the meaningful mediation of the world. Thus, an ethnographic dialogue can become the encounter between human beings, educating each other from the respective sociopolitical standpoints of their historical specificities, mediated by the world, in order to name the world and transform it. Again, "the real danger . . . lies in shifting the focus of the research from the meaningful themes to the people themselves, thereby treating the people as objects of the investigation." In this sense, the ethnographic encounter would be, precisely, *not* anthropological.

HISTORICITY: AGAINST "CULTURE"

Freire's indictment of objectifying research culminates in an explicit critique of the notion of objectivity: "The researcher who, in the name of scientific objectivity, transforms the organic into something inorganic, what is becoming into what is, life into death, is a man who fears change. . . . [and] betrays his own character as a killer of life" ([1968] 1990, 99–100). The conventional subject-object relation presupposed by social science "objectivity," then, by treating people as the objects of study, thereby treats the living as mere things, and therefore, as dead.[15] Thus, Freire's critique of objectivity also entails a theory of methodological objectification. Ultimately, these are inextricable from one another and confirm that all methodological problems (interested in the procedures for producing a knowledge of social life) are fundamentally epistemological in character (framed by questions of how we know and, moreover, what we *do* in order to know), and thereby, have directly political ramifications.

Freire's critique of objectivity indirectly confronts and rebukes the presumptions of ethnographic "expertise." Such claims to expertise are an example of what Freire calls "sectarianism" ([1968] 1990, 22–23), by which he refers to all forms of fetishistic thinking that aim to fix reality into something static by imagining a well-behaved present that can be encircled by certitude. This sectarian objectivity is, in short, a hopeless effort on the part of the social scientist to enclose him- or herself in invented truths, a kind of myth-making. Incapable of recognizing and embracing the dynamic character of the present, such objectivism seeks to domesticate time, treating history as a kind of property that can be possessed and held in check and guarding its knowledge claims against the precariousness of an always unknown and indeterminate future. By seeking to domesticate time, in fact, this sectarianism sets itself against change and against the future (whatsoever it may entail). It thereby establishes itself squarely against the vitality of human beings *as historical subjects*, preferring to domesticate living people and enshroud them in its own myths of the real, the objective, and by implication at least, the immutable (22–23). Hence, living human beings—constitutively incomplete, always becoming—are methodologically detached from their own *historicity*, domesticated and fixed in an artificial, mythified reality outside of time, and reduced to objects—effectively inert, inorganic, dead (45–46; see Fabian 1983). And so it is that the researcher who hankers for scientific objectivity comes to uphold a sectarian dread of history, time, and change, and thus of subjectivity itself, opting instead to treat people as objects, and wittingly or unwittingly serving the ends of their domestication and oppression.

Freire's insistence on the constitutive incompletion of human subjectivity is a plea to radically posit human historicity as a conscious condition, in which historically situated human subjects in objective social contexts deliberately appropriate their own incompletion as an ongoing project ([1968] 1990, 27, 71). Notably, Freire proposes a debate around "the anthropological concept of culture" as an indispensable starting point for the pedagogical encounter as a search to know more (117). "The important thing," Freire maintains, "is for men [*sic*] to come to feel like masters of their thinking by discussing the thinking and views of the world explicitly or implicitly manifest in their own suggestions and those of their comrades" (118). In this light, Freire's conception of "culture" is never depoliticized; it is "a field of struggle over meaning" (McLaren 1994, 200). Freire's dialogical imperative, therefore, enables a critical reconceptualization of a central category of anthropological theory. Notably, the anthropological concept of "culture," for Freire, is indispensable not as an organizing framework for the essentialist objectification and cataloging of human differences (whereby people are reduced to culturalized objects, encircled in anthropological certitude), but rather as a pedagogical theme to be debated among historically situated subjects in dialogue (117).

For my own purposes in this book, in light of the accumulated and ossified connotations of "culture" as a fetishized analytic category within anthropological as well as popular discourse, I reject the usefulness of the concept of "culture" altogether. Likewise, I regard with general suspicion all social theories or descriptions that rely on notions of self-enclosed, bounded, thinglike "cultural" realities posited as separate, distinct, and relatively autonomous spheres of sociopolitical life. I characterize such approaches as *culturalist*. Indeed, for Freire, the "culture" concept serves merely as a preliminary, open-ended standpoint from which to arrive at a more profound sense of people's historicity, the social specificities that human beings produce collectively through historical practice. The displacement of human historicity by an essentialist fixing of "cultures" and the objectification of "cultural difference" on the other hand, is what Freire disdains as "sadistic" (because it deprives the living of the freedom to make their own history and transform their world and themselves) and "necrophilic" (again, because it knows human realities only by possessing them in the form of objects to be domesticated, owned, and controlled, and thus, prefers to turn life into death) (45–46).[16]

Against methodological objectification and sectarian objectivity, Freire's dialogical imperative recognizes research to be a socially situated form of political action and deliberately intends for his own to be a critical practice of liberation. Freire cites Maria Edy Ferreira, who declares that "thematic investigation," which I have glossed as ethnographic research, "is only justified to the extent that it returns to the people what truly belongs to them, to the extent that it represents, not an attempt to learn about the people, but to come to know with them the reality which challenges them" (quoted in Freire [1968] 1990, 102n23). Here we arrive at the necessary conclusion that corresponds to Freire's whole line of argument for dialogue and his impassioned appeal against the veritable perversity—the necrophilia—of objectification and social scientific dogmatism about objectivity. Ethnography that simply seeks "to learn about the people" is illegitimate; it is only justified insofar as it is a collaborative (dialogical) endeavor to learn *with* people about an objective reality so as to transform it. Here, education and the ethnographic investigation of its themes are "simply different moments of the same process" (101). Ethnographic practice potentially becomes more candidly what it has always been—an exercise in *learning*, and more important, one which is not merely one-sided, instrumental, and extractive.

It is noteworthy that even before I had ever actually read Freire's work, I had already become roughly acquainted with the basic tenets of his pedagogy and his ideas had already influenced my approach to teaching adult workers. Remarkably, on January 23, 1995, after I had been teaching in factories for about a year and a half—but still had not yet gotten around to reading Freire—a Mexican worker at Die-Hard Tool and Die[17] confirmed that the time had come. On this particular occasion, I was conducting individual spoken English tests with Latina/o migrant workers whom the company had scheduled for me to see. When Néstor arrived for his "assessment," however, it became immediately apparent that he was an exceptionally fluent English speaker, although he had migrated from Morelia, the capital of Michoacán, only some five years prior, when he had already been in his mid-thirties. We congenially dispensed with the exam altogether and enjoyed the opportunity to talk casually for the allotted half-hour. As someone from an urban middle-class background with a comparatively high level of formal education relative to most of his co-workers, Néstor took an extraordinary interest in *how* I would be undertaking the task of teaching ESL to the other Latina/o migrants in the factory. After hearing me describe my general approach to workplace literacy, and upon learning that I was also working on a doctoral thesis in anthropology concerned with Mexican/migrant themes, Néstor became visibly curious (and even enthusiastic) about my project and immediately identified the relevance of Paulo Freire for my combined pedagogical and ethnographic pursuits. "You know, there's a book you should read," he recommended with confidence, "There's a Brazilian anthropologist who has been very influential in all of Latin America; I'll find out his name for you. I think the book is called 'Anthropology of Misery' [*Antropología de la miseria*]—do you know it? I know a bookstore where you'll be able to find his book; I'll bring you the address next time you come." Néstor could not recall the author's name, the title he suggested was inaccurate, but he was certain that there was something of profound relevance for my work that he wanted to impress upon me. Perhaps to ensure that I would do a decent job of it, he would even go out of his way to track down the more precise information. Whereas our encounter had begun with the official mandate that I assess Néstor's language, now what was being evaluated was the extent and fluency of my own education, and the conceivable gaps in my own training, my own preparedness for ethnographic dialogue. More revealing still, Néstor had effortlessly transposed *pedagogy* into *anthropology*. It has indeed been one of my central preoccupations to conceptualize how exactly one might move from an "anthropology of misery" to a "pedagogy of the oppressed."

The dialogical imperative of his methodology distinguishes Freire as a formidable interlocutor for anthropologists committed to the prospective decolonization of their research practice. But this imperative, finally, offers little more than a critical *starting point* for reformulating ethnographic practice. In reality, of course, dialogue itself never ceases to be problematic. Freire insists, idealistically, almost preemptively, "at the outset . . . the teacher-student contradiction [must] be resolved. Dialogical relations . . . are otherwise impossible" ([1968] 1990, 67). This desire for the instantaneous elimination of the inequality that divides teachers and students is profoundly utopian. Indeed, wagered against the outright impossibility of dialogical relations, this unrealistic demand even threatens an absolute disillusionment. Such a desperate all-or-nothing proposition reveals a fundamental tension in Freire's argument: he refuses to acknowledge the persistent social inequalities between educational professionals (or intellectuals) and their working-class students and appears to simply deny the prestige (if not also material privileges) that accompanies the social status of the educator (Weiler 1994). The aspiration to realize an egalitarian, dialogical collaboration within the always-hierarchical structure of the teacher-student relationship is probably an inescapable and irreconcilable contradiction in Freire's work. In professional ethnography, the social and political inequalities between researcher and researched, indubitably, are even more pronounced.

Ethnography remains a truly intractable problem—especially because it is primarily a professionalized, institutionally embedded methodological artifact of anthropological disciplinarity. Dialogical ethnographic practice, as I have attempted to formulate it, therefore remains problematic as well, but it may nonetheless provide a critical framework for formulating practical alternatives to the standard procedures of an oppressive status quo. It would certainly be naive, however, to imagine that such alternatives could automatically accomplish the effective decolonization of ethnographic techniques. The politics of ethnography can surely never be resolved at the merely formal level. Instead, it is necessary to critically examine the continuum between the politics of ethnographic dialogue and the specific institutional settings and particular social relations that supply the preconditions for actually putting the research into practice. There is an institutional mediation of the research relation that is always material, practical, and historically specific, to which the more general theoretical critique of objectification must be anchored. "The problem," Freire indeed affirms, "is not at the level of conceptualization but, rather, in making the process concrete" (1978, 23). What is required, therefore, is an ever more exacting assessment of the constitutive contradictions that inhere in the very conditions of possibility of the ethnographic encounter.[18]

CONDITIONS OF POSSIBILITY OF ETHNOGRAPHIC KNOWLEDGE

In the context of racially subordinated migrant labor, second-language learning is itself a highly politicized terrain. The labor-power of Mexican/migrant workers fulfills a dire need in important sectors of capitalist production in the United States because their labor is conceived to be easily exploited and tractable; commonly, this is associated with the historically specific ways that Mexican migrants have been maintained in a protracted predicament of legal vulnerability as well as spatial and linguistic segregation. As these workers are typically among the most exploited in an absolute sense—that is, they tend to work inordinately long hours—there is not very commonly any easy recourse to learning the second language except in the framework of the workplace itself. Yet, in most cases, Mexican/migrant workers in Chicago had minimal or no occasion to learn any English at work because it was often perfectly viable for a workplace to depend on the bilingual capabilities of a rather small personnel of supervisory intermediaries who oversaw operations that otherwise took place entirely in Spanish. Thus, for my purposes, a preliminary task is to outline the circumstances under which English as a Second Language became a concern on the part of the management of the workplaces where I was employed.

The politics of English as a Second Language and literacy in the workplace has to be evaluated through an account of workplace "training" itself as a disciplinary process beginning with what Karl Marx called "the technical subordination of workers to the uniform motion of the instruments of labor" ([1867] 1976, 549; see Chakrabarty 1989, 65–115; Foucault 1977, 135–228). Literacy education, harnessed within the technocratic and instrumentalist constraints of workplace "training," is furthermore inseparable from the imperatives for a factory to generate documentation and produce specific types of knowledge of the conditions of production (see Chakrabarty 1989). In the Chicago-area factories where I worked, management-driven imperatives for workplace literacy were entangled with typically contradictory, potentially irreconcilable compulsions for high productivity and mandates for standardized "quality" and precision (which command more sophisticated measurement as well as qualitative specifications and regulation). Some balance of these divergent demands for both quantity and quality became, in each particular production process, a working quotient of efficiency. In contexts involving large numbers of migrant workers, second-language learning can be a greater or lesser prerequisite of the subordination of labor to these regimes of productivity, efficiency, and quality control.

My practical ethnographic engagement with workplace literacy as an ESL teacher involved an incursion into a complex terrain of contradictions that commenced under the sponsorship and initiative of management. I was generally employed as an ESL instructor in small- to medium-sized factories (employing from fifty to five hundred production workers), which relied extensively on deskilled labor processes and almost entirely on low-paid, migrant workforces—especially transnational Mexican/migrant workers. There were unions at half of the ten factories where I was employed. Most of these were metal-fabricating manufacturers, although I also taught in a plastics factory, a corrugated paper company, and an industrial container–cleaning and chemical waste–disposal operation. Nearly all the companies principally made parts for, or otherwise serviced, larger industries (such as producers of capital goods, automobiles, and various durable consumer appliances)—which is to say that their customers were frequently transnational corporations whose fields of operations were construed on a global scale. Increasingly, these employers had become acutely anxious about their capacities to meet their customers' "global standards" of quality control and simultaneously maintain production quotas that could reliably secure their profit margins.

Notably, these companies conveniently enjoyed the encouragement of both federal- and state-level government funding, which at least at that time was readily available to underwrite and dramatically subsidize their workplace training projects. While the state funding that was available for workplace ESL might have retained some more classically Fordist notions of the factory as a "modernizing" pedagogical apparatus in the service of nationalist assimilation (see Feagin 1997, 25–26; Peña 1997, 36–37), it is significant that the English language that was being promoted had little to do with any explicit "Americanization" project. This late-twentieth-century workplace ESL had much more to do with the global standards by which these small-scale firms could legitimate themselves before their (U.S.-based) transnational corporate patrons. On one occasion during the summer of 1994, nonetheless, at the graduation ceremony marking the completion of an ESL course that I had taught at the factory of Czarnina and Sons, my supervisor in the workplace literacy program, Elaine, delivered a brief speech about "the American Dream" and "new Americans in pursuit of a better life." Although she celebrated these "new Americans" as "hard-working people on shop floor," who were also "hard-working in English class," Elaine's speech was certainly incomprehensible to most of the workforce at Czarnina, which was comprised of a variety of predominantly Polish, Vietnamese, and Mexican migrants, few of whom spoke much English. Indeed, in what was perhaps a sincere expression of her own U.S. nationalist beliefs as the daughter of Polish migrants, Elaine was probably addressing herself primarily to the Polish American management of the factory and reaffirming what she presumed to be their "immigrant Americanism" in a strategic effort to reiterate the legitimacy of the workplace ESL endeavor. While Elaine's assimilationist invocations of an "immigrant America" still have a tremendous ideological purchase for liberal U.S. nationalism (see chapter 2), the managements of these factories were impelled by less idealistic motives for reshaping the language competencies of their workers. They simply imagined that a more English-proficient workforce automatically translated into a more efficient production process, and thus heightened global competitiveness. Memorably, alongside Elaine's ideological performance, Zbigniew, one of the Polish workers who had participated in the ESL course but could still barely manage a sentence in English, amused himself and his Mexican coworkers by practicing not his English but his Spanish. "¡Mucha chinga, poquito dinero!" croaked Zbigniew playfully, boisterously rehearsing an aphorism that the Mexican workers had taught him, which may be roughly translated as "Much fucked over, very little money!" Thus, Zbigniew bluntly proclaimed the Polish and Mexican migrant workers' shared derision for what they deemed to be their employer's truly most cherished strategy for enhancing the factory's competitiveness.

A related expression of the managerial anxiety about enhancing their companies' answerability to global standards was a ubiquitous preoccupation with "total quality management" (TQM) and the "team concept" —overlapping expressions of a pervasive pseudohumanistic mantra of contemporary capitalist managerial organization theory (see Grenier 1988; Moody 1988, 187–91; Peña 1997, 39–44, 345–46n66). In a euphemistic effort to dispense with the conventionally more hierarchical idioms of old-fashioned industrial relations, TQM's putative goal is "empowering" workers to "take ownership" of their respective locations in the production process. The TQM movement aspires toward a reconfiguration of factory discipline, premised upon the prospect that workers might embrace it as a liberalizing reform that would nonetheless rationalize and enhance their subordination to the imperatives of efficiency and quality. As the supposed "owners" of their jobs, and sometimes as participants in superficially nonhierarchical quality circles, workers are held more accountable for the "quality assurance" of their own production and are supposed to relate to other workers (as well as supervisors) who are implicated in subsequent operations in the production process as their "customers." All of the relations of production are semantically inverted as relations of exchange, in order that workers may come to inhabit the standpoint of their employers, as owners with a vested interest in maximizing the profitability of their own production. Such strategies entail an enhanced disciplining of all workers, not only by augmenting their actual responsibilities in the labor process to include various quality control and inspection tasks, but also by intensifying their accountability for every aspect of the production process that involves them.

With this newly exaggerated emphasis on answerability, a prominent object for reformatory discipline would now be the English-language fluency and literacy of the migrant workers, who had, in some instances, labored over fifteen- and twenty-year periods for these same employers, previously having had to speak barely a word of English. After all, how could these employers "empower" workers to produce "total quality" and be able to answer their "customers" if they could not communicate effectively in the language of their bosses? Personnel managers (now, more typically called human resources managers) sought to redress what increasingly appeared to be an urgent necessity. Thus, these companies came to enlist the services of a university-affiliated workplace literacy program that employed instructors such as myself and dispatched us to teach in its corporate clients' factory classrooms. Our task was, in effect, to produce in the workforce an obscure target called English proficiency, customized to the particular character of each workplace.

This kind of customization of literacy education to the particularities of each workplace began with the implementation of what my employer called a Literacy Audit. This meant administering written tests of basic mathematics and reading in English to the entire workforce and conducting oral tests to assess all of the workers who were not native speakers of English, in each factory where our program would be newly initiating "training" courses. During the Literacy Audit at Die-Hard Tool and Die during the summer of 1994, the management was concerned that many of the older workers, and the Appalachian whites in particular, were feeling an acute anxiety about being tested. This inspired Elaine, the literacy program director, to encourage everyone involved to self-consciously and ubiquitously adopt the euphemistic term *assessment* instead of *test*. In part, this educational jargon lent itself to the management's own positivistic cult of quantitative measurement—assessment would merely measure and objectively reveal what was presumed to be a natural truth. In her presentation to the workers at Die-Hard, Elaine explicitly compared the testing to taking their blood pressure or shoe sizes. This approach, likewise, accentuated the production of a naturalized discourse of "needs"— "If you don't need a size 10-D shoe," Elaine appealed, "I'm not gonna try to put it on your foot!"

This production of needs, of course, implied a hierarchy of neediness. The Literacy Audit at Die-Hard was somewhat extraordinary in its superficial egalitarianism: the company president and all other management personnel were tested alongside the production workers. Among the latter, there was a majority composed of a variety of Latina/os (with Mexican migrants comprising the largest single constituency)—few of whom could read much English, and some of whom could barely read in Spanish, either; in addition, there was a sizable minority of Appalachian whites from West Virginia, some of whom were themselves not very able to read. Thus, with the paternalistic outward appearance of egalitarianism, the testing process made quantitative (and seemingly measurable)— and thus, reified—all of the actual inequalities of the factory. As Beatriz stated plainly, "I don't like taking the test with all these people, with the owner and all the bosses—because we don't know this stuff, we weren't able to go to school—but them, they went to school, even university, and they can do it. It's not equal, we're much lower than them [*No es igual, somos mucho mas bajitos que ellos*]." Beneath such a chummy, humanistic surface, inequality was supposed to assume the semblance of a simple matter of innate "intelligence" or educational "hard work." More pragmatically, this quantification procedure also enabled the workplace literacy program to conjure a certain urgency for the management about their newly discovered (indeed, newly manufactured) needs—which of course would require remediation if the company was going to be able to compete in the global marketplace.

Within this confining framework of management-mandated workplace training, therefore, English as a second language had a colonizing, deauthenticating, and domesticating character, predicated in the politics of labor subordination and racialized relations of oppression. Each worker would be ideally trained in the particular language uses that served to give voice to his or her role as an appendage of the machine or as a functional moment in the work process, but little or nothing more. The requirement to speak English, therefore, was generally dehumanizing, as it displaced the full extent of communication and creative expression possible in the workers' first language with a narrow, stigmatized, and stultifying means of merely giving voice to the division of labor. This kind of functional service to the labor process is precisely the meaning embedded in the concept of "vocational ESL" (one of the standard synonyms for workplace-based ESL). Indeed, on one occasion when my own ESL courses were perceived to defy these imperatives, one supervisor at the DuraPress factory began to sarcastically refer to the course as "vacational English," insinuating that production was being interrupted for frivolous reasons, and that the workers in the class seemed to be enjoying a holiday away from their duties on the shop floor and simply having too much fun. From the workers' point of view, on the other hand, there was always potentially reason to be apprehensive about anything in the ESL course that appeared to stray from the presumed aim of teaching them something useful for their own purposes, both within and beyond the workplace. When I first started teaching at the chemical waste–disposal plant Caustic Scrub, for instance, Leonardo and Mario expressed their suspicions about what seemed to be a peculiar and rather excessive interest in the most tedious details of their work, when they complained to me about the previous instructor: "The teacher who was here before couldn't decide whether he was here to interview us or teach us English. It was always an interrogation about *everything*, as if he were the police . . . all stupid nonsense! [¡*puras babosadas!*]."

THE PRODUCTION OF LANGUAGE

Early in my experience as an ESL instructor—indeed, during the first workplace course I ever taught in 1993—the participants in a class at Imperial Enterprises taught me a memorable lesson about the politics of workplace ESL. It was an evening class that straddled the second and third shifts, so that those who worked midnights were required to come to the factory early, before starting work for the night; the second-shift workers came to class at the end of their workday. I was unpacking my materials and shuffling papers while a handful of the third-shift people had already gathered and we all waited for the course participants from the second shift to quit work and come to the training room. The alarm bellowed and the booming of the huge punch-press machines came to a halt, signaling a coffee break that was likewise the cue that the rest of the class would soon shuffle in.

Alfonso was seated at the far end of the room—as far as possible from me, but also directly in front of me, squarely in the center of my field of vision. Alfonso worked midnights, but his mandatory attendance in English class was hardly sufficient to deprive him of his sleep before starting work; he had pulled the brim of his baseball cap down over his eyes, nuzzled his chin into his chest, and began to nod off in his chair. I was still absorbed in my paper-shuffling routine as the second-shift people began to stroll into the training room. Suddenly, Ramón, one of the two Puerto Rican workers in the group, boisterously announced his entry, comically mimicking a supervisor: "Hey, wake up! Time for school! Come on, let's go! Get to work! What do you think this is? You have to make production!"

We all laughed, and Alfonso grumpily retorted, "Production?!? What are you saying?"

Assuming a greater semblance of seriousness, Ramón replied, "Well, this is production," and glancing in my direction, he added, "Right, Teacher?" Returning his attention to Alfonso, he continued, "You're getting paid to be here—so it's production." And again, he invited me into the dialogue, while remarking nonetheless upon my official role and playfully signifying my putative authority—"Right, Teacher?" In my turn, somewhat disconcerted by the playful irony of Ramón's equation of the classroom and the factory, I invited the rest of the class to take up this theme as a matter for discussion—I reposed the question, "Well, I don't know . . . What do you all think? Is it production or not?"

A lively debate ensued, and I continued to try to facilitate by posing the question repeatedly to various people in the group. Victoria, the only woman in the class, was fairly adamant, "No, this is not production; this is studying and practicing." Alfredo weighed in similarly, affirming, "Production is working on the machines."

Tomás, however, was skeptical, and began with an analogy: "You have to make 100 percent production," he pointed out, reminding his co-workers of the production-rate quotas that regulated their work routines, "and you have to make 100 percent on the exam . . . so it's the same." He then introduced another, more grim line of reasoning to support the analogy, suggesting that "maybe Morris [the owner and president of the company] will fire us later for not speaking English." In support of this hypothesis, Tomás then offered a personal anecdote: "There was one time last week when I called Howard [the personnel manager] and I spoke to him in English, but he didn't understand me, so I called Jorge." Jorge was a shift supervisor; although he was also a Mexican migrant, Jorge hailed from a middle-class background in Mexico City and was college-educated and fluently bilingual. "I explained it to Jorge in Spanish and wanted him to translate for me," Tomás related, "but then Howard asked me, 'You're in the class—why can't you speak English?' "

Fernando, who was otherwise exceptionally enthusiastic about English class, seemed to find Tomás's argument persuasive and was now ambivalent about whether or not English class was "production." Pedro concurred, but posited, "This is a different kind of production."

The original object of Ramón's teasing, Alfonso, dismissed so much silliness, now with greater irritation: "This is school; it's not production!"

Finally, a sly grin and a glimmer in his eye foretold that Guillermo, who had until that moment been quietly observing the debate, sitting alongside Alfonso, was now prepared to settle the dispute: "Es producción de lengua."

We all broke into laughter again.

Producción de lengua—Guillermo's phrase could be taken at least three ways. This was indeed a kind of "production of language." It may also have been a production of *lengua*—"empty talk," "gossip," or "bullshit," as in the colloquial expression "es pura lengua" ("it's all tongue," or a lot of tongue-wagging), meaning that the person in question is a big talker but will not act on what he or she says. Thus, Guillermo's contention that this was really a *producción de lengua* suggested a question about whether these English classes amounted to anything of much use or importance— perhaps a question about whether management's interest in their learning English was serious and sincere, or a question about whether the discussions in class were really something to take seriously. If what transpired in English class was literally the production of language, however, and if moreover it may also have been a production of a lot of "hot air," it was also possible to gloss Guillermo's pun as the tongue's production, production by the tongue. In English class, even the workers' tongues would have to go to work and meet a production quota—*producing* language. Production by the tongue, as instantiated by the company's new imperative that workers attend English classes for which class time would be (at least partially) remunerated as labor-time, seemed to signal the advent of a still more invasive form of labor discipline that might aspire to the integration of every part of workers' bodies into the production circuit. And as Tomás suggested, ESL in the factory could conceivably be accompanied by unanticipated punitive repercussions. The production of language is itself a form of production, a production of language that could not be separated from the language of production: the language of "making production" (meeting the production quota), the language of the factory, the language of exploitation and labor subordination, the language of oppression. On the other hand, "production"— understood here in a manner too narrowly equated with alienated labor —may also be counterbalanced by a broader concept of production as purposeful praxis, by which producers of language can be recognized as properly historical subjects in their own right. After all, as Johannes Fabian argues, "social communication is the starting point for a materialist anthropology . . . *Production* is the pivotal concept of a materialist anthropology" (1983, 162; emphasis original). Even in this effectively disciplinary context of workplace literacy training, it was necessary to recuperate a sense of the possibility that these workers could be producers in and for themselves, and not only in the service of their employers. Yet the language of "production" that haunted the production of language in these workplace ESL courses tended to be a language already constrained by the circumstances of exploitation and labor subordination.

The critical pedagogical problem to engage dialogically, therefore, was how this foreclosure of the meaning of a production of language had come to pass, and whether *production* might viably come to mean something else, which is really to say, whether *production* could viably be infused with other (contrary, oppositional, or even counterhegemonic) meanings. In 1995, for example, I was teaching an ESL course at Die-Hard in which I was expected to integrate the managerial language of "quality" into the curriculum. Thus, I sought to transpose the theme of quality into one that would need to be specified in relation to the potentially conflicting needs and desires of the company and the workers, respectively. On one occasion, I posed the question, "Does English affect quality on the job? (And if so, how?)" Catarino's reply was poignant: "Well, I think it's only when they're giving you orders, because you're not using your tongue to do the job." Physically demonstrating, with his arms and hands and tightly braced shoulders, how the labor process subordinated his body, he continued, "You're using your whole constitution, your body, but you're not talking to run the machine—you can bring someone from the university with very high skills, but he can't do the job; but maybe someone who never went to school and can't speak English does it better —so that's what I think, it's only for when they tell you what you have to do." Catarino's perspective confirmed that the entirety of the institutional apparatus of the workplace—objectively, materially—as well as the entirety of the managerial ideological apparatus, operated decidedly to contain and confine the substance of workplace literacy to the managerial prerogatives of efficiency, discipline, and command.

The actual language that predominated in the daily practice of production—the language of everyday life in virtually all of these factories— was, in fact, Spanish. The introduction of ESL courses in these factories was designed precisely to change that fact and bolster the rationale for implementing a new language, English. Thus, it becomes possible to appreciate just how much the introduction of ESL training in the workplace was, effectively, a disciplinary reform. If much of my own ethnographic research was enabled by my position as a workplace instructor, then the immediate material and practical conditions of possibility of this ethnography must be critically situated in relation to the politics of labor subordination.

MANAGERIAL "ANTHROPOLOGIES"

It is a matter of widely acknowledged historical fact that the institutionalized academic discipline of anthropology came about and came to flourish in relation to European and U.S. colonial projects of rule and the consequent global racial order of white supremacy. Likewise, throughout the period of its historical formation as a distinct mode of inquiry, anthropology's specific intellectual task was the description and analysis of nonwhite societies, conducted by white practitioners for white audiences (Asad 1973, 14–15; Trouillot 1991; see L. Baker 1998; di Leonardo 1998; Michaelsen 1999). Yet, as Michel-Rolph Trouillot has argued (1991, 17–18), there has long been a wider symbolic field of effectively colonial and racialized meanings and significations upon which the formal discipline of anthropology was historically premised, and with respect to which anthropology is simply devoted to professionally filtering and ranking various contested arguments, legitimating some themes over others, and truly disciplining particular organizations of meaning. In this sense, "anthropology" can be understood less narrowly—as a metaphor. Thus, anthropological ways of constructing notions of the differences between "self" and "other" can be identified and distinguished for the diverse ways they mediate a wider field of racialized meanings that characterize the substantive social relations of domination that continue to shape our global capitalist society, as our universal colonial heritage.

It is in this sense that I will now examine some expressions of a variety of anthropologies that proliferated among the white management personnel of the factories where I was employed, in their own efforts to sort and rank the significances they attached to the racialized differences between themselves and the Latina/o migrant workers whom they daily sought to supervise and discipline for the sake of production within their respective capitalist enterprises. During a Literacy Audit in the fall of 1994 at Liberty Carton, a manufacturer of cardboard boxes, my "consultations" with the management were revealing. I met with Ron, the vice president of operations, and Kevin, the production manager, together. Both of them were white men, born in the United States—like myself. Ron explained to me the "core objectives" of production at Liberty: "Safety, delivery, quality," he proclaimed, "for the company and the individual." With this characteristic gesture of managerial humanism, I knew that I was about to be subjected to a familiar sermon about Total Quality Management (if not for my sake, then at least for his colleague's and his own). These objectives, Ron explained, were being implemented through department meetings as well as crew meetings, and the company was actively promoting the peculiar idea of each crew's "ownership" of their machine. The Liberty management also had a great stake in "cross-training" within work teams, which required that a worker could bid for a different job only if he or she was also already prepared to be moved into the next job up. In this manner, each worker would be required to learn and perform and be available upon command for multiple jobs before enjoying any access to a promotion. Furthermore, each worker would be required to train his or her own replacement (and thus, render him- or herself potentially redundant, and hence, more vulnerable). Ron admitted that this scheme "doesn't always work," so I asked him to explain why that might be. "Well," he posited, "some individuals don't want to move up, they don't want more responsibility (even though there's more money in it)—they just don't want it, it scares them." His theory about "some individuals" was then summarily rearticulated—in terms of what was, in effect, a managerial anthropology:

> With the Hispanic group, there's a lotta macho—if they feel they're gonna fail, they'll say they just don't want it 'for personal reasons,' and just won't do it. Given the area we work in, or 'live' in (at least most of the time!), much of the population we have is Hispanic and don't know English. A lot of times, they pretend they understand you . . . they wanna please, and—there it goes again—they don't want to fail—so they tell you they understand when they don't.

Ron's account, in this instance, retreated from his earlier methodological individualism and explained the behavior of the group with recourse to the explanatory device of a "cultural" trait—"macho." "The Hispanics," as a group, became apprehensible to the company's white (male) vice president of operations through their purported preoccupations with, and insecurities around, masculine honor. (Thus, in another classically anthropological move, Ron thereby elided all of the Mexican/migrant women who worked at Liberty.) The "macho" inhibitions of "the Hispanics," however, were coupled in Ron's managerial anthropology with another putatively "cultural" characteristic of the group—their presumed desire to please. By ironically suggesting that everyone at Liberty worked such inordinate amounts of time that it was as if they lived in the factory, furthermore, Ron also alluded to the plant's geographical location near the Pilsen and Little Village neighborhoods on Chicago's majority-Mexican Near Southwest Side, where many of the workers in the plant (and also, I myself) did indeed live, but where the factory's white management most probably could have never fathomed actually residing.

"They're comfortable in their job and what they do," added Kevin, the company's production manager, "but when ya move 'em out of their element, then they have a problem!" Ron continued, "Two years ago, I really put my foot down and said, 'No more Spanish—everything's gonna go out in English!' I told the union, 'Look, this is America.' But I guess I was a little macho myself, because I realized they weren't understanding half of it, and we had to drop back." In a moment of self-reflexivity, Ron now ironically conceded that his own behavior might have been "a little macho." He could not get past his own "native's point of view," however: the U.S. nation-state was equated with "America," and it was presumed to be self-evident that the "American" national community should be uniformly English-speaking. The apparent "problem," plainly enough, was that the whole place functioned largely in Spanish, which itself had been a grudging managerial concession to what seemed like the more fundamental "problem" of the so-called Hispanics' "culture" and, by implication, the inflexible traditionalism that manifested itself in their alleged resistance to change ("when ya move 'em out of their element, then they have a problem").

Ron also suggested that the workers seemed stubbornly inclined to suspicion with regard to management and its attempts at "reforming" the workplace. "There's still a lot of people who think—no matter what we do, no matter how much money we pour into the place, try to improve their jobs, their skills—they think, 'They're trying to get me,' they think, 'It's trying to get rid of our jobs.'" The workers' distrust of management seemed, in this account, to border on paranoia. I asked Ron how all of this, in his estimation, might pertain to the planned ESL classes. On this score, he seemed somewhat more hopeful that the workers might indeed be more favorably responsive: "I'd say the majority of people out there [in the factory] really want to better themselves—I may be naive, but I really think they do." Although he anticipated the cynical retort that corresponded to his own prior assessment of the Latino workers' disaffection for management's ostensibly good intentions and conceded that it might be mere naïveté to imagine that those people "out there" in the factory would actually desire their own "improvement," Ron nevertheless optimistically affirmed his liberal faith in their basic capacity for "progress." From this managerial perspective—which was likewise a white, middle-class, U.S.-born "native's point of view"—learning English was an unequivocal good—it was quite simply about the Mexican/migrant workers "better[ing] themselves."

The white management of other factories articulated similar viewpoints. Around the same time, Howard, the personnel manager at Imperial Enterprises, complaining about the workers, insisted, "They don't know how to reason!" In the same meeting, George, the production manager at Imperial, added, "They're incredibly poor at problem-solving —there might be some culture issues going on there." In order to explain what both men deemed to be basic intellectual deficiencies among the workers, George's recourse to anthropological speculation—relying upon an explicit discourse of "culture" that could naturalize social inequalities as distinctive group differences—was revealing. Two months later, George decided to observe a mathematics course in Spanish in which I was teaching many of the workers whom he had himself tried to "train," abortively, in English. Afterward, I met briefly with both George and Howard (who was directly responsible for contracting the workplace literacy program at Imperial). George, for his part, was simply shocked at the discovery that most of the workers in my class were still learning about decimals and fractions. He was flabbergasted, as he reflected on his own previous mathematics "training" efforts: "They must think I'm a real jackass! Because I'm up here tryin' to teach 'em things, and now I see that there's no way they can understand it—they have no idea, but they sit there and give me all the right body language like they understand, and here I'm tryin' to teach 'em this stuff that must be way over their heads! So they're smilin' at me, thinking I'm a total asshole!" (For my part, I did not attempt to detract from George's epiphany with any kindly reassurances.) Rather than presume, as Ron at Liberty Carton had done, that "the right body language" signified that "they wanna please . . . and they don't want to fail," George projected his own insecurities onto the Latina/o workers and simply detected deviousness and a subtle, smiling subversion.

During this meeting, although I could not admit that I myself objected to the management's intrusions into the classroom when I was teaching, I wanted to impress upon them both, nonetheless, that when management personnel appeared in this manner to "observe" the classroom, the work-ers might not feel comfortable, and thus, the learning process might be disrupted. Howard acknowledged that this could be true; he explained: "I know how it is—they [the workers] never want us to know that they don't understand something, because they're afraid we'll fire 'em—especially with the Mexicans, because it's part of their whole socialization process in coming to this country: they went to second or third grade, then they were farmers, then they came here . . . It's still true, but it was even worse ten years ago because they were all illegal then—that was before the amnesty."[19]

Then, referring to a bulletin board in the entrance to the factory offices that included photographs of all the employees, under the heading

"The Imperial Enterprises Team," Howard continued, "This board in front with people's pictures on it—ten years ago, we would have had a mutiny if we did that! Because they were all illegal; any policeman or INS officer could have looked at it, said, 'This is the one we want,' come inside the plant, and grabbed 'em. Some of 'em still don't like it, because they have bad credit and they don't want anyone to know where they can be found." Notably, since Imperial's workforce had a sizable number of Puerto Rican workers in addition to the Mexican/migrant majority, Howard's managerial anthropology generated more subtle distinctions than that of Ron at Liberty Carton. Whereas Ron had made cruder claims about "the Hispanics" (referring to a workforce comprised almost entirely of Mexican migrants), Howard was more certain that he was speaking specifically about "the Mexicans" (in contradistinction to Puerto Ricans) and their particular "socialization process in coming to this country," especially their socialization into "illegality." Whereas Ron had imagined that "the Hispanics" simply wanted to please their superiors and hypothesized that their machismo made them fear and disdain failure, and likewise in contrast to George's sense of their sly duplicity, Howard interpreted the workers' perceived will to conceal their lack of understanding in terms of power inequalities ("they're afraid we'll fire 'em"). Furthermore, Howard traced the outlines of a different kind of vulnerability and tractability that was particularly characteristic of Mexican workers, linked to a rather caricatured sense of them as uneducated farmers, but rooted above all in their experiences of undocumented migrant labor.

What frequently was foremost for Howard's managerial purposes, however, was merely to identify who among the Latina/o workers could be relied upon to "competently" take orders and dutifully carry them out, which he consistently glossed as "she's pretty smart" or "he's fairly intelligent." While he differentiated in terms of how much and how well individual Latina/os spoke English, Howard did nonetheless have a way of describing "the Hispanics" as a general racial category. Howard's crude judgments of various workers' English language proficiency never made any apparent distinction between Latina/os raised (or even born) in the United States and those who had migrated as adults. In addition to his own purely instrumental managerial considerations about efficient communication on the job, therefore, and in spite of his attention to substantive differences between the sociopolitical circumstances of Mexicans and Puerto Ricans, what was clearly operative as well was Howard's sense that

Latinos were, in effect, all the same as a *racialized* category (see De Genova and Ramos-Zayas 2003b). He simply perceived their different degrees of English fluency as transparent indicators of their individual "intelligence." On one occasion, when I was discussing the question of testing some workers who had been recently hired (for the purposes of including them in future courses that we were planning), Howard explained, "I really don't think we have too many [among the recent hires] that speak broken English. I think almost all of them have at least a high-school-level education; we've been hiring a higher class of people." Revealing precisely how these educational euphemisms figured in his own hierarchical thinking, he then immediately corrected himself, "Or maybe we could say, 'a higher *literacy level.*'" In Howard's estimation, lower educational attainments simply signified deficient intelligence. Thus, the hierarchical rankings he assigned to workers on the basis of language were readily translated into the rigid calibrations of higher and lower classes, and migrant workers who spoke "broken" English were evidently people of lower quality. When I mentioned a recently hired Polish worker who barely spoke any English (but who happened to be a highly skilled tool-and-die maker), Howard assured me, "Oh, but he's very intelligent!" and smiling with admiration, added, "He understands a lot—you tell him what to do, and he does it!"

THE RACIALIZATION OF LANGUAGE

The presumption on the part of white bosses that Latina/o migrant workers' Spanish language was merely a "deficiency" articulated the more general Anglo hegemony of the U.S. nation-state and signaled the pervasive ways that Spanish was racialized (see De Genova and Ramos-Zayas 2003a, 145–74). Many Latina/os experienced the racialization of their language as a palpable feature of the discrimination against them. Indeed, one afternoon when I was first beginning my work at Imperial Enterprises, I spoke casually with a young white worker who, upon discovering that I was there to teach English, smugly declared, "They need that! In fact, my opinion is they should learn English *before* starting a job." He volunteered with satisfaction, furthermore, that he was acquainted with taverns where the owners had installed placards, announcing an overtly discriminatory policy of "No English, No Service." To this, he added with a certain admiration, "Ya own yer own place, you can do whatever you want." Not only did he believe that speaking English should be enforced as a prerequisite for employment, he openly condoned discriminatory and punitive practices against people who could not speak English well.

At Liberty Carton, where the Vice President of Operations had equated the prospect of the "Hispanic" workers' learning English with "bettering" themselves, at least one of the workers, Antonio, who was thirty-nine years old and had migrated from the Mexican state of Guanajuato eighteen years earlier, was decidedly not interested in "bettering himself" on his bosses' model: "I think I don't want to be in a class—it's a form of discrimination against us because we're Latinos—because it's only going to be for some people and not everyone has to go . . . I told them I don't want to go to school, but they told me that I have to do it. Why?!? That's discrimination!" For Antonio, obligatory ESL classes in the factory were clearly being imposed only on the Latina/os, and that seemed discriminatory in itself. Insofar as English was the language of the management, it was the language of power. Among Antonio's coworkers was a twenty-five-year-old woman, Sylvia, who was an exceptionally fluent English-speaker among the Mexican migrants who worked at Liberty Carton. After migrating to the United States from Mexico City with her first husband only five years prior, Sylvia had been remarried to a white "American" and was raising her small children in a home where only English was spoken. "I learned English," she explained quite plainly, "because I don't want to be stuck like this forever and I don't like to feel lower than other people—not higher either, but not lower." For as long as she was identified as someone who did not know English, Sylvia seemed to posit, she was made to "feel lower than other people" and felt "stuck" in that subordinate status.

These sentiments—that not speaking English, and speaking Spanish in particular, became the objects of discrimination—were expressed to me in innumerable ways by countless people, but predictably, they were most commonly articulated on the part of people who did not speak much English. Alfredo, who worked at Imperial Enterprises, was a Mexican migrant in his fifties, originally from the state of Jalisco, who had been in the United States eighteen years when I interviewed him in his home in 1995. Speaking explicitly both as a Latino and specifically as a Mexican, he explained how he experienced his lack of fluency in English to be an object of routine discrimination and racial contempt.

> I tell you one thing: that . . . as a Latino, Nico [. . .] we as Mexicans, I as a Mexican, yes, I have felt some discrimination [. . .] in workplaces, on buses, in government offices, in hospitals, in, you

know, Nico, so many things [. . .] I at times have even felt that . . . they have even made fun of you right there to your face, because of not understanding the language [. . .] One feels that . . . that it's not equal, it's not equal—yes, one feels the discrimination. And it will be because of . . . everything—because of the language, because of race or color, as we say, but . . . it's difficult, Nico, difficult.[20]

Through a variety of more specific examples, Alfredo expressed his certainty about having often been the object of discrimination and explicitly characterized these abuses as a *racial* matter, but the inability (or presumed inability) to communicate effectively in English was granted a central importance within this particular racism.

Similar themes arose when I conducted an interview in the home of Carlos (who, like Alfredo, worked at Imperial Enterprises) and his wife Rosario, whom I was meeting for the first time. Carlos and Rosario were in their midforties and, like Alfredo, had migrated from a rural town in Jalisco. Rosario was especially concerned with the issue of language and its centrality to her particular experience of racism. Rosario explained:

Here, I have noticed that they don't want a person to speak Spanish, they ignore that person [. . .] they even go so far as to make a mean face at a person. [. . .] Including when I call the factory by telephone, they don't pay me any attention because I speak Spanish. No, sometimes although they understand, they hang up on me. Sometimes I need to speak to the husband for no less than an emergency. [. . .] I tell [Carlos], "Oh, how one is made to feel that English is lacking when one needs it most!" Because yes, yes, yes, in reality, they *ignore* a person in a really ugly way! . . . And I tell him, "Ay, Carlos! How truly, in reality, how much one notices here, right? The racism, I tell you!" [. . .] You notice that they're doing it to you, really a lot, and it makes you very angry, because we're human, right, we're all human—not because one might speak Spanish and the other might speak English, no, that could be different, but as people, we're all equal, right? [. . .] The least they could do is be friendly, right? But no. . . . [Referring to her toddler son] This boy, he's very friendly with all the kids, and sometimes he wants to play or something, and then one notices, right, after a while the parents take them away for nothing more than they figure out that we're Mexican, right, and little by little one notices the discrimination.

At that point, Carlos only half-jokingly addressed himself to their young son, who was playing restlessly on his lap: "You're getting yourself straightened out with your English, aren't you, my son? [*Te arreglas del inglés, ¿verdá m'ijo?*]." Rosario and Carlos both had rather light complexions and fair hair in comparison with most Mexicans in Chicago. In this regard, it is particularly noteworthy that Rosario's experience of discrimination on the basis of her Spanish language was so inseparable from her specifically *Mexican* identity, and so readily apprehensible for her, explicitly, as *racism*.

DECOLONIZING LANGUAGE

To speak means . . . above all to assume a culture, to support
the weight of a civilization. . . . Every colonized people—in other
words, every people in whose soul an inferiority complex has been
created by the death and burial of its local cultural originality—
finds itself face to face with the language of the civilizing
country.—**Frantz Fanon,** *Black Skin, White Masks*

Teaching English as a Second Language to Mexican/migrant workers, for whom their own Spanish language was itself one of the objects of their racialization, clearly involved teaching what was, in effect, the language of their oppression, and thus playing a rather active role in the mediation of that larger process by which their own language was rendered "inferior." From the very beginning, during the first workplace ESL course I taught at Imperial Enterprises in 1993, I had become acutely aware of how stigmatized participation in an ESL course often was for the workers. I had heard one white (U.S.-born) worker say that the classes were for "the fuckin' rejects," and I had found white (European-origin) migrant skilled workers referring to the course as "kindergarten." On one occasion, Carlos likewise reported in class, "Some people in the factory say school [ESL class] is only for dumb-asses [*burros*, literally 'donkeys']."

Beyond the particular complexities of my institutional location teaching ESL in factory classrooms, moreover, the contradictory repercussions of my status as an English teacher were still further underscored by my more general social location—as a native speaker of English, as someone born into U.S. citizenship, and as someone racialized as white. Indeed, these more elemental and profoundly salient indices of my sociopolitical position during the course of my research always framed important conditions of possibility (and also impossibility) for my ethnographic practice. This is a crucial standpoint from which to assess what often appeared to be a troubling inclination among some Mexican/migrant course participants—for both ESL and math, in workplace classes as well as courses I taught in community organizations—to frequently deprecate their own intellectual capabilities. The phrase that was most ubiquitous was simply "Somos burros"—we are stupid, we are dumb-asses, we are donkeys. The term *burro* also connoted the idea of labor through the image of a beast of burden—in effect, "we are pack mules." I had become so accustomed to people seeming to disparage their own intelligence in this fashion that I came to have a ready response; I would reply with a saying that had become popularly attributed to Subcomandante Marcos, the prominent spokesman of the Zapatista insurgency in the Mexican state of Chiapas. "As they say in the Lacondón jungle in Chiapas," I would begin (catching people somewhat by surprise and typically eliciting the amused question, "What do they say?"), " 'Somos un chingo—¡y seremos un chingo más!' "—We are a fuck of a lot, and we're going to be a fuck of a lot more! My reply simultaneously rejected the predication of my "students" about themselves (*somos burros*), and included myself in the *we* that had previously referred only to them (in contradistinction to me). *We* now became inclusive (and overtly politicized) as I insisted upon my own collaborative participation with them in the classroom.

What was more profound by far than my pirating of the critical ingenuity of the Zapatista leader, however, was that the apparently self-deprecating declarative statement—*somos burros*—was, in fact, not that at all. Indeed, the apparent declarative form was always followed with a question, demanding my response—"isn't that true?"—*¿verdad, Nicolás?*, or more intimately, *¿verdad, Nico?*, or more revealingly addressing me with the title "teacher," *¿verdad, maestro?* This question, then, invited me, dialogically, to either confirm or invalidate the proposition that the Mexican/migrant participants in my courses were "dumb" (and thereby either confirm or reject the racist contempt or condescension that could otherwise be suspected or expected of me, as someone racialized as white). Thus, what at first might have appeared to be self-deprecating operated instead as a dialogical invitation to at least symbolically subvert the status hierarchy that was inherent in our unequal social positions (see Díaz-Barriga 1997, 55). Similarly, another seemingly self-deprecating expression that I heard repeatedly in my work as an ESL instructor was: "Tengo la cabeza de Teflón, no me pega nada"—I have a head (brain) made of Teflon, nothing sticks to it. With this remark, the speaker could appear to be disparaging his or her own intellect, as if to provide a preemptive excuse for not really comprehending the English language. But the verb *pegar* means not only "to stick" but also "to hit," or "to punch." From the critical vantage point that identifies English as the language of oppression, it becomes possible to detect a double-entendre—"nothing hits me," and hence, "nothing can hurt me." In effect, English cannot reach me, cannot touch me, cannot harm me; it will not stick. In this way, rhetorically, the integrity of Spanish was guarded; it could not be destroyed.

The dialogue that is central to the kind of pedagogy that Freire advocates and I sought to reinvent, and that was likewise central to the kind of ethnographic encounter to which I aspired, could not have taken place in my research, in most instances, except in Spanish, or at least, with free and easy recourse to Spanish.[21] The extensive use of Spanish in my English classes, however, directly rejected a self-serving dogma prevalent in much of the professional sphere of adult ESL education—that is, the stubborn insistence that "students" should be as thoroughly as possible "immersed" in the English language. The "immersion" metaphor is telling. Indeed, it might be more appropriately (more honestly) glossed as a "drowning" technique, or perhaps, something more akin to water torture. Such an "immersion" strategy is methodical, really, only in its authoritarianism, whereby an all-powerful instructor inundates the class of relatively captive ESL learners with a mind-numbing repetition of formulaic, arbitrary, and ultimately meaningless English-language catchwords and phrases. By implication, second-language learners are incapable of playing a purposeful and decisive role in their own education because they are presumed, in effect, to know nothing—to begin from a position of total neediness and pure lack.[22] The pedagogical result is the total dependency of the students on the paternalistic pseudo-omniscience of a teacher who supplies them with communicative baby food and imposes on them a packaged knowledge with which they have no conscious, deliberate, or critical relation. This so-called method presents no challenges, cultivates passivity, and thus, when it is most effective, serves to accommodate people to their oppression. Indeed, when I had just begun to work as an ESL instructor in the summer of 1993, my friend Pancho, a Mexican migrant whom I had known for several years through my previous political work at a food-processing factory where he was a skilled machinist, was quick to give me a stern but simple recommendation (grounded in his own experience of English classes where immersion had caused only frustration): "You have to speak Spanish when you teach—it doesn't help anyone if they don't understand what you're saying."

Teaching the language of oppression, I had to sustain an independent dialogue with the Mexican/migrant participants in these courses that would refuse to abide by the presumed imperative that their own language be subordinated. Thus, an immediate protocol for any further engagement with the problem of learning English was the necessity of debating English itself. English had to be subjected to critical scrutiny, rendered problematic, destabilized, and decentered. To critically engage the challenge of learning a second language that was itself the language of oppression required a dialogue that could disrupt the naturalized power that English represents in the United States. Hence, I began every ESL course that I ever taught: "Why should you bother to learn English?"

"Why should you bother to learn English?" On virtually every occasion, the most immediate reply to this question was one or another approximation of "It's very important; it's necessary because we are in this country; English is the language here." English was enshrouded in importance and necessity; it appeared to have an inseparable relationship with the U.S. nation-state and the space it claims for itself, "here"; it seemed that English was truly hegemonic—*the* language, the one and only. I would follow with some further questions: "With whom do you have to speak English? When? Why?" Without recounting here the wide array of specific replies, two general truths would emerge: the great majority of these workers, regardless of how many years they had been in the United States or in the same workplace, did not truly "need" to speak much English at work or in their daily lives outside of work, and generally did not do so. In practical terms, in their everyday experiences, Spanish—and not English—was the language "here." In the space that I designate "Mexican Chicago" (see chapter 3), Spanish was spoken—and, to paraphrase Coco Fusco (1995), English was broken.

This fracturing of the hegemony of the English language has to be qualified, however, by adding that something else emerged from the typical replies to my provocation, which testified in a different way to the importance and necessity of English for Mexican migrants "in this country": they had to speak English with the police, in court, and in a myriad of other institutional contexts such as public schools and hospitals. Indeed, these sites referenced precisely the same contexts that Mexicans frequently cited as places where they had experienced discrimination in forms that directly made an object of their language. At work, notably,

English was most needed when Mexican migrants had to defend themselves, concerning disputes or problems on the job for which they were held accountable, which frequently required them to communicate with higher managerial authorities than was customary for their daily routines, as suggested by Néstor from Die-Hard Tool and Die when I interviewed him with his wife Julia in their home in 1995. When I asked Néstor how it happened that he spoke English so well, he replied, "With the bosses, [. . .] sometimes one really has a lot of problems with them, and . . . and one has a special feeling against them." Néstor now paused and smiled: "and you don't have enough vocabulary to tell them off!" In short, Mexican migrants had to speak English in their confrontations with power—because in the United States, English is the language of power. It was precisely in light of this fact that we would arrive in our classroom dialogues at a new conclusion about why it was indeed necessary to learn English: *para defenderse*, to defend yourself.

Whereas the hegemony of English had previously been naturalized and seemed self-evident, now it became more plausible to name and expose that hegemony as such. So began the dialogues in which I could collaborate with course participants in devising a realistic curriculum that corresponded to their needs as they formulated them, based upon their experiences and the problems that they articulated. The participants posed practical problems for their own second-language learning, consciously and critically apprehended the English vocabulary, expressions, and syntax that would serve them, and collectively generated much of the language themselves—in both Spanish and English. The ensuing dialogical encounters, moreover, thus occasioned the kind of ethnographic engagement by which people might not be reduced to mere objects of the research but instead locate themselves in their proper place as the subjects of their lives, struggles, and historicity.

"WITHOUT US, YOU'D HAVE NOBODY"

None of the foregoing is to presume to have resolved any of the constitutive dilemmas of ethnography. My own position never ceased to be problematic. During the first ESL course I ever taught at Imperial Enterprises in 1993, the more that my critical pedagogical efforts came to facilitate classroom dialogue about the upcoming contract negotiations, the possibility of a strike, and the workers' complaints about the bureaucratic unresponsiveness of their union, then so much the more did the contradictions of my own institutionally embedded material position raise obvious questions about my trustworthiness. Enrique, a Puerto Rican worker in his early sixties who had worked at Imperial Enterprises for over thirty years, posed the question to me directly: "Who pays you—the company or the government?" Although I was directly employed by neither, the university-affiliated workplace literacy program that did employ me was funded through grant money from the government. Although some workers may have taken some comfort from the knowledge that I was not really paid by their bosses, the notion that I was operating through the auspices of the state could hardly be reassuring. On another occasion, in late 1995 at Caustic Scrub, in one of the last ESL courses I ever taught, Manuel, who had migrated from a small rural town in Jalisco thirteen years prior, made a rather stringent evaluation of the class difference between us. Upon discovering that I would not be returning to teach at Caustic because I would be traveling to Asia, and after asking the distance and cost of the flight, Manuel simply smiled sarcastically, and said:

> Well, you have a lot of money, I can tell. I can see it. I've been around and I know, I know someone with a lot of money when I see it—speaking casually about going off to so many faraway places —"I'm going to India, I'm going to London." Me, where do I go? Chicago, East Chicago, maybe Long Beach [California, where his sister was living]. We look at a map and say, "Wow! From Mexico to Chicago is a long, long way!" We almost can't imagine how far it is, and here, you're going off to the other side of the world—I don't even know where it is, really. Yes, I'm sure you have plenty of money—it only figures, you speak two languages, you're a teacher, a professional person, you don't drink—you have a lot of money to go traveling all over. I know it's true, I can see it!

For Manuel, it mattered little who was paying my salary. There was a harsh and irreducible fact that had become bluntly apparent in this instance: everyday, routinely, Manuel and the rest of the workers at Caustic literally risked their lives with lethal chemicals for miserable wages, while my education and professional status insulated me from such extreme physical hardships and hazards, remunerated me relatively well, and ultimately would ensure class privileges for me that he and his co-workers were systematically denied.

Neither was the problematic status of my ethnographic location so simply dispelled when, instead of teaching in a workplace, I was teaching at Casa del Pueblo,[23] a community organization located in the Pilsen neighborhood where I was living. During a discussion in 1995 of the significance of California's passage of the anti-immigrant ballot initiative Proposition 187, the Mexican/migrant course participants supplied a variety of critical characterizations of the new law and the nativist impulse behind its passage. Claudio said it was "anti-immigrant." "It affects all of us," added Andrea. Luís specified, "It affects all Latinos." "More than anything," Luz María added, "it affects all Latino *children*." Esmeralda said plainly, "It's racist." Gerardo added, "It's unjust." Lupita declared further, "The illegals are the ones who work the most, but they're the ones who are discriminated against." "It has nothing to do with anything the immigrants have done," Memo clarified, "because the owners of the fields need the immigrants and they go to the government asking for us to do the work—it's because the politicians can use it to get votes, because it's good for the Americans [*los americanos*], it's to their benefit, although it's bad for us." Then, Memo joked, "It's good for *you*, Nico!" but he reconsidered his charge. "Well, maybe not for *you*—because without us, you'd have nobody to teach!" Indeed, Memo was remarking upon a constitutive contradiction of my research—that Mexican migrants like himself and the rest of the group, many of whom were undocumented, supplied me with a condition of possibility for my own sustenance. Indeed, this was at least doubly true, in that this was not only a job in which I had a material stake, it was also the basis for my ethnographic research, in which I had a much more substantial and long-term professional stake. Furthermore, it was also a frank identification of the materiality of my being an "American," a "native" English-speaker, and a U.S. citizen racialized as white. Beyond the immediate contexts of the workplaces where I operated as a teacher, and likewise beyond even the institutional mediations of the academic discipline of anthropology, these broader features of my social location were also institutionally embedded conditions of possibility for my ethnographic practice. The substantive sociopolitical differences of race, citizenship, and national identity gave particular shape to the broad differences of social class that Manuel had indicted and reinforced the fundamental and protracted inequalities between my Mexican/migrant interlocutors and myself.

Indeed, as the discussion at Casa del Pueblo recalls, a predominant characteristic of the immediate historical context of my ethnographic research (conducted from 1993 to 1996) was an aggravated and increasingly aggressive political climate in the United States of anti-immigration restriction and regulation. The nativist campaign in California for the punitive "Save Our State" ballot initiative, better known as Proposition 187 (approved by referendum on November 8, 1994), was a crisis-mongering catalyst that had repercussions on a national scale and ultimately heralded the passage in 1996 of some of the most punitive anti-immigrant federal legislations to be seen in U.S. history: the so-called Immigration Reform (signed September 30, 1996), as well as the extensive anti-immigrant stipulations of other laws that preceded it (see chapter 6). Throughout the research for this book, the issues of "immigration" and "immigrants"—and undocumented Mexican migration in particular—were extraordinarily high-profile mass-mediated objects of public debate and political struggle. Thus, the racialized politics of immigation, citizenship, and national identity supplied a momentous ideological backdrop for the lives and struggles of the Mexican migrants with whom I worked. I now turn, therefore, to the politics of nativism that defined the terms not only for these political debates, but also for the dominant modes through which scholars have conducted research on the subject and produced their various authoritative representations and "expert" knowledge. Far from merely academic or theoretical quandaries, then, my own representation of Mexican migrants in this book has involved strategic choices that inescapably participate in the political conflicts that situate "the immigrant" as a central ideological concern of U.S. nationalism.

CHAPTER TWO

THE "NATIVE'S POINT OF VIEW":

IMMIGRATION AND THE IMMIGRANT AS

OBJECTS OF U.S. NATIONALISM

American studies runs the risk of functioning as just
another technology of nationalism, a way of ritually repeating the
claims of nationalism by assuming [a national subject]
as an autonomous given inevitably worthy of scholarly study.
—**Janice Radway,** "What's in a Name?"

Let us begin by considering the effects of shifting critical
paradigms in American studies away from linear
narratives of immigration, assimilation, and nationhood.
—**José David Saldívar,** *Border Matters: Remapping
American Cultural Studies*

Public discourse and debate as well as much of the scholarly study concerning historically specific migrations and distinct migrant experiences in the United States seems to be almost always hijacked by a fixed agenda of generic and transhistorical questions about "immigrants" and their "assimilation." There is something quite peculiar about the pervasive assumption that what is most meaningful or interesting about the dynamics of migratory movements, and the experiences of people who move, is the cessation of their movement—their presumed settlement and assimilation as "immigrants." By privileging these particular questions, scholars seem to reveal that movement—and thus, change and indeterminacy—are really intolerable. Therefore, what matters most for such approaches to migration is, precisely, *not* migration so much as its presumed completion or predictable closure. Conventional narratives of immigration, as José David Saldívar suggests, are customarily characterized by a taken-for-granted linearity.

A radical doubt and a critical stance toward such narratives of the presumed one-directional linearity of immigration, however, has become greatly emboldened with the rise to prominence during the 1990s of social theoretical paradigms of transnationalism. The analytic framework of transnationalism (especially as specified for the purposes of anthropological inquiry) has largely foregrounded the ways in which radically expanded and relatively accessible means of communication and transport, often in concert with macroeconomic and state-driven political processes, have contributed to a proliferation of diverse sociocultural interactions of a new order and an unprecedented intensity that reconfigure space by traversing, sometimes defying, and potentially destabilizing or even transcending national boundaries (see Appadurai 1990, 1991, and 1996; Basch, Glick Schiller, and Szanton Blanc 1994; Glick Schiller, Basch, and Szanton Blanc, 1992; Kearney 1991, 1995, and 1996; Ong and Nonini 1997; Ong 1999; Rouse 1991, 1992, and 1995; Sassen 1996a). Frequently with a particular emphasis on migration, theorists of transnationalism have raised vital questions about the formation of new claims to citizenship and rights to place facilitated or accelerated by the contemporary "globalization" of capital and the rescaling of nation-state authorities. My own work, of course, has been significantly enabled by these various prior formulations of transnationalism and is partly motivated by the dialogical desire to critically advance these debates and sharpen the critical perspective by way of an emphasis on the centrality of racialization, nativism, and migrant "illegality" for the transnationalization of labor within the fractured class politics of global capital.

In spite of the insights and concerns of the emergent transnational paradigm, however, the assumption that migration processes are basically one-directional remains quite ubiquitous and reveals the fundamentally teleological conceits that continue to animate immigration discourse in the United States. This enduring persistence of the immigration teleology and its obsession with assimilation expresses a central article of faith of U.S. nationalism: that "America" and "American"-ness comprise something desirable, choice-worthy, and indeed inevitably embraced by immigrants who abandon an Old World and ultimately repudiate its lifeways in order to come to a Promised Land of Opportunity, irresistibly settle permanently, and seek to reinvent themselves as "Americans" (see Chock 1991; Honig 1998 and 2001). When U.S.-based scholars of immigration and immigrants ritualistically preoccupy themselves with teleological questions of settlement and assimilation, therefore, they reaffirm these nationalistic assumptions. Such a teleology, elaborated in terms of outsiders coming *in*, presumably to stay, could be posited only from the epistemological standpoint of the migrant-*receiving* U.S. nation-state, on the parts of those who authorize themselves to speak as its natives—what I will call, with deliberate irony, "the native's point of view." Thus, such research becomes complicit with the project of U.S. nationalism, enacting what Janice Radway (1999, 30n27) calls "a practice helping to create an 'American' nation poised both to 'contain' and 'include' those who would challenge it from within, and to interact with and dominate those defined as different on the far side of the border." A critical examination of the categories of "immigration" and "the immigrant" (and the specific problematic of "assimilation"), then, becomes a necessary starting point for any viable transnational paradigm in U.S.-based migration studies. Therefore, whereas in chapter 1 I was primarily concerned with a consideration of the material and practical conditions of possibility of my own ethnographic research, here I interrupt my ethnography in order to foreground the more discursive predicament of my work by situating it within the nativist politics of its specific sociohistorical moment as well as the broader ideological terrain of U.S. immigration discourse.

To produce a critique of the U.S. nation-state through an ethnography of the distinctive transnational conjunctural space that I have designated "Mexican Chicago" (see chapter 3), I have had to interrogate the various ways in which the very idea of immigration and the figure of the immigrant are cherished native categories of U.S. nationalism. From this standpoint, whereas much of sociocultural anthropology has long been directed toward the interpretive evocation of the so-called native's point of view (Malinowski [1922] 1984, 25; see Geertz, 1971), it may be instructive to consider the following question: What precisely is at stake when an anthropologist does *not* go out from the imperial metropole to some more or less faraway and "exotic" place to conduct research among people in their own native place, but rather, when the people with whom the anthropologist conducts research come to the place where it is the anthropologist who is a native? Here, moreover, the social location of "the native" is no longer a simplistic and groundless abstraction about geographically inflected "cultural" difference. Instead, the researcher's position as native is, above all, significantly substantiated in his or her juridical status as citizen and so entails a social relation to the U.S. state; as such, it is a preeminently *political* identity. To conduct research related to the migrant (especially undocumented) noncitizens of the U.S. nation-state from the unexamined standpoint of its citizens clearly would involve the kind of uncritical ethnocentrism that is, by definition, a perversion of anthropology's putative aims as a distinctive mode of inquiry. Beyond such more narrowly anthropological protocols, furthermore, the U.S. state has conferred upon me, in quite material and practical ways, the sociopolitical status of "citizen," while it simultaneously produced my Mexican/migrant interlocutors as "aliens"—whether "legal residents" or "illegal"—and thus, all, to one degree or another, deportable. Especially during a historical period of heightened nativism and anti-immigrant racism, without seriously taking stock of these constitutive inequalities and also critically destabilizing the conceptual presuppositions that accompany them, this study would risk becoming, in Radway's memorable phrase (1999, 12), "just another technology of nationalism."

This book seeks to formulate new kinds of questions in the study of migration and the social relation of migrants to the U.S. state by systematically sustaining a rigorous critique of the premises and presuppositions of U.S. nationalism itself and repudiating its conceits. Thus, it is necessary to identify the distinctive ideological field concerning "immigration" in relation to which any research on contemporary migrations to the United States ought to be able to account for itself. This chapter aims, therefore, to critically assess the whole problematic of immigration as such—to identify and examine the epistemological problem and interrogate the tacit question through which the questions of immigration are themselves organized and orchestrated.

It will first be necessary to consider the production of U.S. nationalism's "natives." If, in the previous chapter, I was primarily engaged in a critique of the discipline of anthropology, in this chapter I am more concerned with the inevitable and necessary intersection of any critical ethnography of the United States with the broader interdisciplinary fields of American studies and its presumed subsidiary ethnic studies.[1] U.S.-based research about the United States often presupposes its own epistemological object. In other words, such American studies presume to already know in advance the elemental meaning and implications of the category "American" and everything to which it refers. Likewise, as I have already suggested, this scholarship often operates from the epistemological grounds of the U.S. nation-state and thereby recapitulates (wittingly or unwittingly) the imperial conceits of U.S. nationalism.[2] That is to say, researchers commonly produce their studies in an unproblematized way *as* "Americans." One rather telling manifestation of this conceptual trap is the failure to distinguish between invoking a *we* that refers to an imagined intellectual community of scholars conducting research on the U.S. social formation, and invoking the *we* that refers to an imagined political community of U.S. citizens, which is to say, the *we* of U.S. nationalism. This latter *we* is comprised of those who authorize themselves (however much unconsciously) to speak as U.S. "natives." In an effort to clarify something about the discourses of immigration and the immigrant, therefore, it is useful to begin with a consideration of the standpoint of the native. And it is crucial to underscore that this "native's point of view," so to speak, is likewise the animating impulse of nativism itself.

NATIVISM

In his landmark historical study of anti-immigrant politics in the United States before 1925, John Higham ([1955] 1988, 4) contends that nativism "should be defined as intense opposition to an internal minority on the ground of its foreign (i.e. 'un-American') connections."[3] However, while the opposition of "native" and "foreign" is surely crucial, what is ultimately decisive in defining the anti-immigrant politics of nativism is precisely *not* a preoccupation with the foreignness of any particular migrants or other internal minority so much as with the "native"-ness of U.S. citizens, and the promotion of the priority of the latter—exclusively on the grounds of their being "native." Nativism, therefore, is not at all reducible to the sort of aversion to or distrust of foreigners that tends to be called xenophobia, much as it may be typically entangled with it.[4] More important, nativism may be overtly disarticulated from both xenophobia and racism. Some forms of nativism, in other words, may even be fashioned as antiracist and promote their politics of immigration restriction on the presumed basis of a commitment to racial justice. It is decisive here to emphasize this point because what is at stake is not only the more predictable right-wing nativism but also a nativism from the left, which calls for immigration restriction in the purported interests of "native" workers in general and "native" minorities in particular.

What nativism is, then, is precisely native-ism—a preference for the native exclusively on the grounds of *being* native; thus, it is a premier exemplar of identity politics (Michaels 1995, 13–14).[5] "The power of nativism," Walter Benn Michaels argues persuasively, "depends upon its pluralism, its transcendence of questions about superiority and inferiority. The point of suspending the question of America's goodness is to make clear the fact that our attachment to it is based only on our identity with it" (77). Rather than making claims for the superiority or inferiority of one's "nation," "culture," or "race," therefore, nativism rejects the validity of a common hierarchical scale of comparison in favor of a politics of "identity" that assumes the existence of a plurality of irreducibly distinct and essentially different *groups*. Once the differences among such groups are posited as mutually exclusive and absolute, these differences serve to define them—*as groups*—in terms of their respectively incommensurable "identities." The mere plurality of such group differences is presumed to be sufficient, then, to sustain the basic divisions and effectively permanent antagonisms among them (see R. T. Smith 1996, 101–9). In this respect, nativism's pluralist commitment to essentialized difference—difference as such—is antiassimilationist; it refuses any basis for overlap or intersection among those apparently fundamental differences. Thus, nativism tends to render each identity, in and of itself, as unrelated, immeasurable, incomparable, and finally incompatible (Michaels 1995, 66). In the nativist project, therefore, a conception of identity (based on the assumption of a plurality of discrete groups) may be variously posited in terms of "culture," or "race," or "nation"—and it ultimately makes very little difference to its more elementary politics of *identitarian* difference.[6] "In pluralism," Michaels contends (1995, 67), "one prefers one's own race"—or one's own "culture" or "nation"—"not because it is superior but because it is one's own."

Nativism can ultimately relinquish not only overt references to race but also explicit commitments to particular claims of "culture" as well, but what nativism cannot do without is the more elementary pluralism that both racialist and culturalist understandings of difference share. Nativism must always privilege one or another notion of "identity" against the rest. Indeed, this is precisely what nativism serves to do for nationalism—it produces an identitarian *we* that can appear to resolve a fundamental problem of all nationalisms, namely, that there is nothing natural or objective or intrinsically necessary about any "nation." Nativism thus serves to mediate the more or less accidental character of the nation. Whereas Benedict Anderson ([1983] 1991, 7) has discerned the necessity for every nation to have limits—the requirement of imagining any nation as a unity defined by boundaries—the contingency of all nations derives from their fundamental lack of any organic unity or natural boundaries (Habermas 1998, 114–17; see Appadurai 1998b, 444).

Thus, nativism's pluralism supplies nationalism with a politics of identity. More precisely, nativism equips the nation-state with a "national identity" in the image of which to fashion its people. It posits a *we* whose identity is simply incommensurable with everything external and "alien" to it. Higham has incisively observed ([1955] 1988, 4), "through each separate [nativist] hostility runs the connecting, energizing force of modern nationalism," but the more pertinent concern may be to identify how nativism is indeed a unifying and animating force within nationalism itself. Nationalism is certainly something more complex than its nativist moment, but in this respect, the identity politics of nativism can never be fully excised. No nationalism is ever truly recuperable from its nativism.

Returning, then, to the politics of immigration in the United States, all discourses of the immigrant are ultimately unified by what I call the "native's point of view." The native's point of view is an effect of the nativist presupposition of U.S. nationalism by which both liberals and conservatives produce themselves as its natives and thereby authorize themselves as U.S. citizens to debate the questions of immigration policy. Disagreements notwithstanding, these questions that unite both sides in discourse are systematically concerned with what a native *we* should do with a foreign *them*, and the answers are defined around a variety of contending interpretations of what might be best for "the nation" (*our* nation) and its citizens (*us*). In this regard, both liberal and conservative discourses of immigration collude in the shared presumption of their own nativeness.

U.S. NATIONALISM AND ITS NATIVES IN THE LATE TWENTIETH CENTURY

The anti-immigrant legislations of the 1990s were not simply a response to growing nativist sentiments in the U.S. electorate; rather, these laws and the political campaigns that nurtured them were instrumental in the *production* of what was then being called "the new nativism" in the United States (e.g., Acuña 1996; Calavita 1989; Perea 1997). The aggravated nativism of the mid-1990s, with its acute preoccupation with "illegal aliens," pervasively bore the particular imprint of a distinctly anti-Mexican racism. Already by the beginning of the twenty-first century, however, the distinctive nativism of the 1990s has been largely eclipsed, though not extinguished. In the aftermath of the attacks on the World Trade Center in New York City and the Pentagon in Washington on

September 11, 2001, a still newer nativism directed primarily against Arabs and Muslims suspected of "terrorism" and religious "fundamentalism" has arisen in concert with remarkably repressive anti-immigrant policies—including dramatically expanded surveillance, mass arrests, and indefinite incarcerations, frequently followed by deportations (see Cole 2003). While the most visible targets of this nativism clearly have not been undocumented Mexicans, the repercussions for all migrants have been manifold. Notably, in addition to predictably intensified policing along the U.S.-Mexico border, workplace raids against undocumented Latina/o workers have likewise been rationalized, all the same, in terms of "antiterrorism" and "homeland security," in defense of an "America" assaulted by nefarious transnational networks unconstrained by the bounded sovereignties of nation-states.[7]

While there certainly is a long trajectory of recalcitrant nativism in U.S. history (Higham [1955] 1988; R. M. Smith 1997), the critical task of historical contextualization requires that one account for what precisely is new and distinctive about each conjuncture of nativism—how it is produced and comes to assume a particular form, with particular sociopolitical effects (see Calavita 1989; Schneider 1998; Stefancic 1997; Tatalovich 1997). The restrictionist legislations of the 1990s were a culmination of anti-immigration impulses and efforts that were evident throughout much of the 1970s and 1980s (Cornelius 1982; see Chávez 2001; Johnson 1997). Indeed, those earlier efforts had already led to the passage of the Immigration Reform and Control Act of 1986. Taken together, they reveal the outlines of a more extended nativist conjuncture that is comprehensible only in relation to the particular operations of the 1965 amendments to the Immigration and Nationalities Act (see chapter 6). While nativist agitation against Mexican migration (Balderrama and Rodríguez 1995; J. García 1980; Guerin-Gonzáles 1994; Hoffman 1974) and distinctly anti-Mexican forms of racism (Acuña 1981; Barrera 1979; Montejano 1987; R. Paredes 1977) were not in themselves new, a central feature of what was characteristic and historically specific about the nativism of the late twentieth century was, indeed, precisely the obsession with "illegal aliens" and "border control," and the prominence of anti-Mexican racism that animated it (see Acuña 1996; Cockcroft 1986; Dunn 1996; Johnson 1997; Nevins 2002; N. Rodríguez 1997; Rosaldo 1997). More generally, however, and especially by the mid-1990s, the nativist fervor in the United States, while reserving a special animus for undocumented Mexican migration, had increasingly expanded its scope beyond "illegal immigration" and became preoccupied with "immigrants" in general. As migration since 1965 had been disproportionately comprised of Latin Americans and Asians, and also significant numbers of non-Latino Caribbean Blacks as well as Africans, this more generic nativist discourse deployed the terms *immigration* and *immigrants* as the plainly racialized figures of an amorphous nonwhiteness and commonly expressed a more or less explicit white racial panic.

NATIVISM FROM THE RIGHT

During the early- and mid-1990s, there was no shortage of unabashed expressions of rather alarmist nativism predictably articulated from the more conservative sectors of the U.S. political establishment. The most vociferous expression of the politically right-wing nativist upsurge was surely Pat Buchanan's America First campaign for the presidential nomination of the 1992 Republican Party primary convention, and his subsequent presidential bid in 1996. Perhaps the most audacious and forceful intellectual elaboration of this nativism from the right, however, was Peter Brimelow's book, *Alien Nation: Common Sense about America's Immigration Disaster* (1995).[8] Directed toward a broad reading public rather than a narrowly academic audience, furthermore, Brimelow's book sought to make a significant intervention in the wider debates concerning U.S. immigration policy.

Nativism, and right-wing nativism in particular, commonly operates erratically across the unstable, frequently incoherent terrain that always conjoins the pluralist essentialisms of "race" and "culture," in order to produce a pluralist *we* that can stand in for a national identity. Within the U.S. nation-state, that national identity is called "American." It is telling that the infamous nineteenth-century nativists, known as the Know-Nothings, organized their political movement under the banner of the American Party, characterized their philosophy as Americanism, and described their work as the vindication and protection of "the principle of nationality" (Higham [1955] 1988, 4). It is even more revealing that these nineteenth-century nativist positions were forcefully resurrected at the end of the twentieth century. In *Alien Nation*, Brimelow reclaims the heritage of the Know-Nothings and reaffirms their mission: "The nativists were genuine American originals . . . [the Know-Nothings] *were nationalists*—culturally and politically" (1995, 12–13; emphasis original). Despite his elite credentials as a senior editor for both *Forbes* and the

National Review, Brimelow articulates his nativism in a populist register: "Today, U.S. government policy is literally dissolving the people and electing a new one" (xv). Indeed, it is precisely through this distinctly reactionary populism that Brimelow juxtaposes "the people"—the nation of "genuine American originals"—with the menace of an "alien nation," a mob of immigrant intruders poised to usurp their sovereignty and patrimony. Notably, Brimelow makes explicit that his particular nativist politics upholds an "American" *cultural* nationalism. Brimelow's cultural propositions about the "American" nation, however, are entirely incomprehensible in any terms other than racialized ones. "The American nation has always had a specific ethnic core," Brimelow confirms. "And that core has been white" (10).[9] Citing the Naturalization Act of 1790 (in which the first U.S. Congress legislated the requirement that an applicant for naturalization as a U.S. citizen be a "free white person"; see chapter 6), Brimelow further demands, "How much more specific can you get? . . . Americans . . . are being tricked out of their own identity" (15). The "American" national identity, for Brimelow, is therefore a definitively white racial identity, and the "cultural" project of his nationalism is inseparable from the racial chauvinism of his nativism.

Brimelow's articulate promotion of an explicitly nativist and overtly racist argument in *Alien Nation*, notably, aimed toward a bold reconfiguration of the boundaries of permissibility in official political discourse around race and immigration in the United States (see Feagin 1997; Kanstroom 1997; Roberts 1997). Similarly, during his 1992 presidential campaign, Pat Buchanan, on a nationally televised news broadcast, projected that, although "God made all people good," it would be radically "easier" and "would cause less problems" for the state of Virginia to assimilate a million immigrants if they were "Englishmen" rather than "Zulus"—and insisted that "there is nothing wrong with . . . arguing that issue, that we are a European country" (quoted in Bosniak 1997, 297n33; also in Feagin 1997, 36). Significantly, while deploying transparently racialized figures only thinly veiled by their national/tribal labels ("Englishmen," "Zulus"), Buchanan advanced a *culturalist* argument about the possibilities and impossibilities of assimilation in order to facilitate more overtly *racist* premises and conclusions ("we are a European country"). Indeed, on a related note, asserting that "Americans" were more shocked by massacres in the former Yugoslavia than in Africa, Buchanan asserted plainly that it was because Yugoslavians "are white people. That's who we are. That's where America comes from" (quoted in Feagin 1997, 36). The continuities of the culturalist and the racist logics, of course, are not trivial. Neither are they accidental; both rely on an identitarian pluralism that prioritizes incommensurable "difference" over the comparative but universalist criteria of superiority and inferiority. Buchanan contended that "we" ("Americans") care about "white people" because "that's who we are"; in other words, it is a simple matter of identity. For Buchanan (as for Brimelow), "American"(national) identity is coterminous with (racial) whiteness. For this species of nativist racism, there was simply no need to sustain claims of white superiority; identity was sufficient. Buchanan's racial nativism was explicitly disarticulated from white supremacism: although all people are equally good and no group is intrinsically better or worse, he reasoned, an immigration of Englishmen would be preferable to an influx of Zulus because the former are more "like us" and the latter are simply too "different." While articulated in an idiom apparently preoccupied with "cultural" difference and the question of assimilation, Buchanan's intervention plainly aimed to re-legitimize fairly overt racist discourse in debates construed around the problematic of immigration. Notably, though, nativist recourse to debates over assimilation in terms of "culture" need not be explicitly racist, and in fact, may operate in nominally race-neutral terms. Thus, immigration restriction may be advanced as a means for preserving or promoting a unitary and cohesive "national culture."

Brimelow nevertheless audaciously advances openly racial criteria as the bulwark of his nativist argument for the prerogatives of "the American people." "Race and ethnicity," he confirms, "are destiny in American politics. The racial and ethnic balance of America is being radically altered through public policy. This can only have the most profound effects. *Is it what Americans want?*" (1995, xvii; emphasis original). In this manner, he clearly establishes that the *immigration* question is fundamentally a *racial* problem. Brimelow proceeds by elaborating his articulation of race and ethnicity with "nation": "There is confusion nowadays about what it means to be a 'nation,' and a 'nation-state' . . . But, essentially, a nation is a sort of extended family. It links individual and group, parent and child, past and future, in ways that reach beyond the rational to the most profound and elemental in human experience. The mass immigration so thoughtlessly triggered in 1965 risks making America an *alien nation*" (1995, xix; emphasis original). In these introductory remarks, Brimelow thus supplies the rationale for his book's alarmist title and appeals to a nationalist "common sense" of white racial estrangement. Race is destiny, he proclaims, and nation is so elemental as to be beyond the reach of reason. By recourse to such an avowedly meta-rational, essentialist notion of "nation" as virtual family, Brimelow affirms that national identity can only be a kind of primordial kinship of shared blood.

This kind of nationalist extended family, however, while it implies a sense of birthright entitlement to the national patrimony, must also renounce birthright citizenship as one among many "institutional accidents . . . [that have] essentially robbed Americans of the power to determine who, and how many, can enter their national family, make claims on it . . . and exert power over it. The heart of the problem: immigration" (Brimelow 1995, 4–5). Brimelow's target is the way that the institution of birthright citizenship—confronted with the racialized specter of immigrant fertility—becomes an affront to the "majority" status and prerogatives of the legitimate "national family."[10] In this sense, Brimelow's nativism not only elides the substantive differences between "legal" and "illegal" migrants, but also refuses to sustain any meaningful distinction between migrants and their U.S.-born citizen children. He clarifies his position: "It's not just illegal immigration that is out of control. So is legal immigration. *U.S. law in effect treats immigration as a sort of imitation civil right, extended to an indefinite group of foreigners who have been selected arbitrarily and with no regard to American interests.* Whether these foreigners deign to come and make their claim on America—and on the American taxpayer—is pretty much up to them" (5; emphasis original). Thus, Brimelow construes birthright citizenship (which, of course, pertains to the U.S.-born children of migrants, and *not* the migrants themselves) as an undeserved entitlement for self-selecting and self-interested "foreigners" (see Balibar 1991d, 221). Moreover, the "immigration" problem becomes akin to a "civil rights" problem, whereby the "majority" loses control over "minorities."

In his carefully modulated introduction of the racial premises of his "immigration disaster" thesis, Brimelow invokes the example of Colin Ferguson. Ferguson was a Jamaican migrant (of well-educated, upper-middle-class origins) who had found himself reracialized as "Black" in the United States; after having been fired from his job, Ferguson went on a shooting spree against white fellow-commuters on the Long Island Railroad in 1993. Brimelow deploys the specter of Colin Ferguson to insinuate that migration only aggravates the already stark menace of racial otherness that threatens to engulf and terrorize an innocent and helpless white "American majority." "Ferguson's own writings showed him to be motivated by hatred of whites," Brimelow argues. "*Is it really wise to allow the immigration of people who find it so difficult and painful to assimilate into the American majority?*" (1995, 7; emphasis original). Here, Brimelow's racism requires recourse to a logic of culturalism that, like Buchanan's example of "Englishmen" and "Zulus," is hinged upon the question of assimilation. By this logic, nonwhite migrants are plainly inassimilable to an "American"-ness equated with its (white) "majority," and it would be in the best interests of the "American"nation (as well as those migrants themselves) to simply keep them out. Moreover, the migrants' "pain" and "difficulty" of assimilation (at first glance, a kind of personal psychological trauma) produce in Brimelow's account a corrosive if not explosive kind of collective social pathology, "motivated by hatred of whites." Indeed, it is only *after* Brimelow has consistently treated immigrants as nonwhites and, with such examples as Ferguson, presented immigration as a specifically racial problem, that he ultimately proclaims explicitly that the "American" *national* family is in fact a *racial* family.

In the wake of such trenchant hostility to immigration, it may be especially jarring to learn that Brimelow himself is a British migrant and naturalized U.S. citizen. What is especially instructive in examining Brimelow's case for nativism, therefore, is how he ultimately authorizes himself, in spite of his immigrant status, to speak to "Americans" as an "American" against immigrants. That he has naturalized as a U.S. citizen is, in itself, insufficient. Brimelow is able to accomplish this counterintuitive feat solely on the basis of his racialization—as a white man. By embracing his whiteness with a vengeance, Brimelow's legal naturalization as a U.S. citizen is supplemented by a racial naturalization. Brimelow's whiteness naturalizes him as an "American" native, genuinely belonging to "the American majority," and thus finally authorizes his right-wing nativism to boldly promote the priorities of "American" citizens as synonymous with the primacy of racial whiteness for U.S. national identity.

NATIVISM FROM THE LEFT

Nativism is ubiquitously associated with the kinds of politically conservative and frequently antiforeign or candidly racist projects that I have characterized as nativism from the right. The opposite end of the spectrum from racist nativism in debates over immigration policy, as Linda Bosniak has quite persuasively demonstrated, is congested with a quibbling over numbers—what she calls "cost arguments" (1997, 287–91; and see Bosniak 1996). These cost arguments concern the purported economic impacts of immigration, positive or negative, for the material well-being of citizens and "the nation" generally. Bosniak shows clearly that while such cost arguments may be controverted with empirical refutations, the presumptive legitimacy of their concerns is seldom disputed (see Chock 1991, 280). As Bosniak explains (1997, 288): "What I wish to emphasize about the debate over costs is its unspoken normative backdrop: it presumes that determining who is right in empirical terms on the cost question is dispositive of the immigration policy issue. It presumes, in other words, that if immigrants could somehow be definitively determined to cost more than they contribute, then restrictionists' efforts to curtail immigration would be basically unassailable on normative grounds."

Further, Bosniak demonstrates that the operative assumption is that national immigration policy should above all promote the interests of citizens, and that this "national priority thesis" is the normative crux of any principle of national sovereignty (1997, 288–89). Thus, she underscores a fundamental divergence between this "legitimate" promotion of the priority of citizens and the more dubious racial or xenophobic undertones of conventional nativism. However, there is really no rigorous way to distinguish between the "national priority thesis" that Bosniak identifies as a fundamental premise of modern nationalism, and nativism, as I have formulated it, whereby priority and preference is reserved for "natives" on the basis of their identity, howsoever construed, as members of a national polity or citizens of a particular state. In this manner, both liberal and conservative discourses of immigration collude in the shared presumption of their own nativeness. The challenge, therefore, is not to presuppose a stark disjuncture between the more evidently racist ("nativist") extremes and the presumed legitimacy of liberal immigration discourse, but rather to interrogate what may be the intrinsic continuities between the two. Such an approach then might enable a more far-reaching investigation of their complicities.

Native identity may be (and commonly is) grounded on "racial" or "cultural" particularities but need not be. Nativism can be plausibly disarticulated from overt racism or xenophobia altogether. If, as I am arguing, nativism is understood as a promotion of the priorities of natives, simply on the grounds of their being so, then the most vexing formulations of nativism will be found to come from the political left. A sure measure of the extent of nativism's impact on the political climate of the United States in the 1990s was revealed by the convergence of some liberal/left scholars with dominant anti-immigration discourse. There is perhaps no more explicit and unapologetic articulation of this nativism from the left, at least on the part of an academic intellectual, than the immigration restrictionist position advanced by Stephen Steinberg in *Turning Back: The Retreat from Racial Justice in American Thought and Policy* (1995). The book's argument illuminates many of the central contentions of liberal nativism. What is singularly distressing about Steinberg's call for a policy of immigration restriction is that it is awkwardly smuggled into the debate over "racial justice." Indeed, the forcefulness of my critique is in no small measure driven by my considerable agreement with Steinberg's more substantial and laudatory principal argument in *Turning Back* for the defense and expansion of affirmative action entitlements for African Americans.

Nativism from the left commonly takes as a starting point the facts of capitalist exploitation and racial oppression as entrenched features of the U.S. social order. One of Steinberg's fundamental postulates in *Turning Back* is that "in the United States the essence of racial oppression . . . is a racial division of labor, a system of occupational segregation that relegates most blacks to work in the least desirable job sectors or that excludes them from job markets altogether" (1995, 179–80). This system, which Steinberg calls "occupational apartheid," has its origins in African American slavery and is central to what he characterizes as the irreducible uniqueness of the oppression of Black people in the United States. Indeed, on this basis, Steinberg advances a comprehensive argument for the defense of affirmative action, and still more important, for a dramatic renewal and extension of such preferences for African Americans in particular. However, by largely treating racial oppression as an exclusively African American affair, Steinberg's case for racial justice, with respect to other racially subordinated groups, inadvertently becomes yet another configuration of the same racial backlash that he is otherwise critiquing.

Such avowedly antiracist liberal calls for severely restrictive immigration policies appear to be reasonable and justified when the deleterious effect of racism is accounted for, myopically, only with regard to African Americans. Steinberg introduces his case against "immigration" by asserting that "the economic fortunes of African Americans have *always* been linked to immigration" (1995, 185; emphasis added). Indeed, even slavery, he contends, owed its existence, if only indirectly, to immigration by way of its absence: had Europeans been "flocking to the New World in the seventeenth century . . . the nation would have been spared the ignominy of slavery" (185). More central to Steinberg's argument, predictably, is the *presence* of immigration as an alternative to African American labor in the decades following the end of slavery. He points to immigration as the decisive component, historically, in the maintenance of a racialized regional division of labor: "The exclusion of blacks from the industrial sector was possible only because the North had access to an inexhaustible supply of immigrant labor" (180). (Notably, in this account, the nineteenth- and early-twentieth-century experiences of Asian and Latin American migrations in the West are occluded altogether.) "The lesson of history," Steinberg claims, "is that blacks have overcome racist barriers in the occupational world only during periods when labor has been in tight supply. Given this well-established fact, the negative implications of such a massive volume of immigration would seem obvious" (186). Thus, Steinberg contends rather simplistically that, were it possible to close the borders of the "national" economy by means of an anti-immigration policy intervention, the subsequently "tight" labor supply could provide a more or less automatic solution to employers' racist exclusions of Black people from employment.[11]

Nativism from the left significantly relies upon the generic figures of immigration and immigrants as fundamentally undifferentiated and transhistorical. In spite of his own repeated invocation of the "lessons of history," by recourse to a notion of immigration that equates the nineteenth- and early-twentieth-century history of European migrations with overwhelmingly Latin American and Asian contemporary migrations, Steinberg essentializes the category "immigration" and evades any possible consideration of its historical specificities (see Balibar 1991d, 220–21; Lowe 1996, 177–78n6).[12] Thus, rather than frankly analyze what was, in fact, an extended consolidation of racist hegemony through the particular productions and reproductions of whiteness for the European-origin migrant working class of that earlier historical epoch (see Allen 1994; Brodkin 1998; Ignatiev 1995; Jacobson 1998; Roediger 1991 and 1994; Saxton 1990), Steinberg alleges merely that "immigration" in general is to be blamed. This "immigrant" essentialism, which tends in general to erase all substantive distinctions among historically specific migrations, here, selectively elides racialization for migrants in the past (i.e., for Europeans, who came to be racialized as white) and likewise sidesteps questions of racialization for migrants in the present (i.e., for the majority who are not Europeans and come to be racialized as nonwhite). Never adopting any overtly racist basis for immigrant exclusion, and relying upon structural rather than culturalist arguments, Steinberg's liberal call for immigration restriction as a means to racial justice must nevertheless be premised upon an *evasion* of the specificities of racialization for distinct migrations. Indeed, Steinberg can promote his anti-immigration prescription for "racial justice" only by ignoring the racist strictures, both overt and embedded, that have repeatedly guided the historic formulation of U.S. immigration policy itself (see chapter 6).

The liberal nativist argument must, in effect, deracialize the figure of immigration in a manner that abdicates any responsibility for analyzing the racial oppression of migrants of color, either historically or in the present. Steinberg does admit the empirical fact of the "racial" differences between early- and late-twentieth-century migrations, but only in order to negate its relevance. "Although immigration has produced a more racially diverse population," Steinberg muses, "paradoxically this new diversity has reinforced the preexisting structure of occupational apartheid" (195). However, even if the hegemonic polarity of whiteness and Blackness endures in a manner that routinely relegates African Americans to the most degraded position in the U.S. racial order, this hardly means that migrants of color automatically enjoy the racialized status of whiteness or even occupy positions within the political economy of the United States that are any less racially segregated. However, liberal nativism's "immigrant" essentialism must overlook the reality that racialization in the United States is simply not as bipolar as the reductive Black-and-white model of occupational apartheid implies. Notably, though in passing, Steinberg does indeed suggest an analogy between the plights of African American youth and many of the U.S.-born children of (non-white) migrants (e.g. 189). While Steinberg's case for racial justice can seemingly afford to accommodate the non-white racialized condition of these "second-generation" (U.S.-born) youth, however, it is simultaneously impervious to the nonwhite racialization of those same young people's migrant parents. In short, it is utterly crucial for Steinberg to insist that current U.S. "immigration policy amounts to a form of disinvestment in *native* workers" (193; emphasis added). Thus, Steinberg not only essentializes and deracializes immigrants but also inevitably collapses African Americans, as well as all other (U.S.-born) racial "minorities," into the dubious, similarly homogenized and racially unmarked class category of "native workers." Finally, then, what is decisive for Steinberg is the simple question of who is, and who is not, a "native."

Against an immigration policy that "amounts to a form of disinvestment in native workers," liberal nativism asserts that U.S. immigration policy should be subordinated to the rightful entitlements of natives. Steinberg argues: "Immigration policy must take into account the legitimate interests of *native* workers, especially those on the economic margin. After all, the meaning of citizenship is diminished if it does not include the right to a job at decent wages" (1995, 201; emphasis added). In the context of a presumed "scarcity" of jobs, Steinberg posits "decent" wage labor as the preeminent form of proper inclusion in the "nation," through substantive incorporation into a purportedly "national" economy, and upholds U.S. citizenship as a prerequisite. In effect, Steinberg's position is what Bosniak would characterize as a "cost argument." His argument against immigration can hardly be denounced as a mere proxy for any racist or xenophobic aversion to "foreigners"; indeed, it is explicitly formulated as a remedy to racial injustice. Yet, Steinberg's nativeism—his promotion of the priority of natives, on the mere basis of their being such—is robust and explicit. Relying not upon "race" or "culture" as the putative basis for national identity, however, Steinberg's nativism from the left invokes a politics of *citizenship*.

The narrow pragmatism that compels liberal nativism to take the side of racially oppressed "natives" against "immigrants," inevitably, is also positioned in a much wider, socially mediated zero-sum game that pits African Americans and other racially oppressed people ("immigrants") against one another and thus runs the risk of a tacit collusion with the effectively racist "divide-and-rule" logic of the anti-immigrant backlash. Steinberg never addresses the question of the resurgent right-wing nativism of the early 1990s or its abundant racism and thereby evades any examination of his own possible complicity with it.[13] Indeed, even Brimelow (1995, 10–11) can be found to defend his nativist position with recourse to the claim that immigration restriction could be presumed to automatically benefit poor African Americans. Steinberg insinuates the same uncomplicated, unmediated, one-to-one causal correspondence between migrant labor and African American "displacement," unemployment, and poverty. In Steinberg's account, jobs are treated as things —rather than as dynamic relations between social classes of employers and workers within a social order that systemically generates inequality, and naturalizes inequality as scarcity. Hence, for liberal nativists, jobs must be viewed as scarce resources. The claim that migrant labor displaces African Americans (or other racially subordinated, U.S.-citizen "minorities") from employment or indirectly displaces them from potential employment is highly debatable and indeed is commonly asserted on the basis of fallacious premises.[14] Without belaboring these economic arguments, what is indisputable, in any case, is the abundant evidence of racial discrimination against Black people in *all* aspects of the U.S. social order. Migrant workers, however, do not ever have the power to "displace" other workers from employment. The *displacement* thesis inverts the brute facts of unequal social power. The only tenable way to take this problem seriously would be to investigate the question of employers' tactical replacement of Black workers as a political solution to crises of labor subordination (see chapter 3). Such an approach would situate it in relation to racialized *class* conflicts, which could never be resolved simply by the restriction of immigration. Rather than reducing the matter to mere interracial, intraclass competition within the labor market, it would be necessary instead to examine the continuous racialized recomposition of the working class and the parameters of the labor market as a whole, in the context of relations of struggle *between* antagonistic social classes. Instead, the liberal nativist framework presupposes the immutability of an antagonistic social division between impoverished African Americans and migrant workers, who get automatically reduced to a generic, dehumanized mass of "cheap labor."[15] The dilemma of endemic racial inequality, moreover, is transposed into something else entirely, insofar as it can somehow be remedied by tackling "the immigration problem."

In spite of the fact that capitalism has been a thoroughly global affair since its inception and although there is effectively only one world economy, liberal nativist arguments consistently, stubbornly assess the case within a narrowly nationalist conceptual framework premised upon the coherence of a self-contained "national economy."[16] Steinberg's "national priority" thesis consequently treats transnational migrations to the United States as if they had no relation whatsoever, either historically or in the present, with U.S. imperialism and U.S. global hegemony. This assumption amounts to a familiar strain of "American" exceptionalism. "One of the central themes of American historiography," notes William Appleman Williams (1955, 379), "is that there is no American Empire." U.S. nationalism has long cultivated the view that the U.S. nation-state has always been committed to leaving the rest of the world alone, only intervenes in other countries for the sake of humanitarian goals and democratic ideals, and thus is fundamentally innocent of imperial power or ambitions. Such conceits are ubiquitous in hegemonic U.S. discourses of immigration when it is taken for granted that migrants from all over the globe have no other relation to the United States than their simple desire for "a better life." Yet the major countries of origin exporting transnational migrant labor to the United States have consistently tended to be the major recipients of direct capital investments from the United States (Sassen 1988 and 1989). In other words, there tends to be a more or less direct and consistently decisive link between U.S. imperialism and migration. Lisa Lowe (1996, ix, 3–7) traces linkages between U.S. imperial wars in Asia and "the genealogy of the legal exclusion, disenfranchise-ment, and restricted enfranchisement of Asian immigrants" within the United States. "The material legacy of America's imperial past is borne out in the 'return' of immigrants to the imperial center," Lowe contends (1998, 29–30), "immigrants are the survivors of empire, its witnesses, the inhabitants of its borders." Likewise, in his survey of Latino experiences in the United States, Juan González (2000) similarly characterizes migra-tions from Latin America as "the harvest of empire."

The refusal to recognize the history of colonization in U.S. nation-state formation has a rather direct relevance for any consideration of Mexican migration. What is now the southwestern United States, after all, was annexed from Mexico in 1848 for the westward expansion of the U.S. nation-state, as a consequence of an imperialist war of conquest (see chapters 3 and 6). Steinberg briefly acknowledges these distinctly Chicano claims, only to summarily call them into question: "Many immigrants— especially Mexicans who are immigrating to territory once possessed by Mexico—have historical and moral claim for access to American labor markets. . . . These factors, however, must be balanced against the deleteri-ous effects that the continuing volume of immigration has on groups on the economic margin—not only African Americans, but immigrants themselves and their children" (1995, 202).

Indeed, Steinberg disavows these specifically *Chicano* claims of histor-ical priority that might compete with the "national priority" of U.S. natives, by recasting them as merely claims "for access to American labor markets" on the part of "Mexicans," whom he figures universally as "immigrants." Furthermore, such claims, Steinberg concludes, must be subordinated to an assessment of their "deleterious effects"—on natives. In a strikingly paternalistic gesture, furthermore, Steinberg insinuates that restricting or halting their "access to American labor markets" would actually be in the best interests of the immigrants themselves. Indeed, on this particular point, it is instructive to note that Steinberg's nativism itself marks an astounding retreat from his own previous position. In an earlier book, Steinberg addresses the same issue and arrives at a strikingly different conclusion: "After annexing half of Mexico's territory, this nation spent the next 150 years patrolling 'our' borders and deporting 'illegal immigrants' from what one Chicano writer has dubbed 'occupied Mexico.' *If justice had its way*, Mexicans would be granted special rights of immigration to their former territories" ([1981] 1989, 299–300; emphasis added).

Clearly, Steinberg's notions of "justice" shifted dramatically from the 1980s to the 1990s, underscoring the fact that the nativism of the late twentieth century bore the indelible imprint of a distinct obsession with the subjugation of Mexican (especially undocumented) migration, in particular. In Steinberg's nativist scenario, where scarcity prevails and migrants' gains can signal only displacement and loss for African Americans, it appears that justice too is scarce. Finally, according to the contradictory impulses of Steinberg's liberal nativism, "racial justice" for Blacks can only be had at the expense of justice for Mexicans.

THE NATIVE'S POINT OF VIEW

A critical examination of nativism from the left demonstrates very forcefully that what is ultimately defining for nativism is precisely *not* a preoccupation with the foreignness of immigrants so much as with the nativeness of U.S. citizens, and the promotion of the priority of the latter—exclusively on the grounds of their being native. Nativism's identity politics poses a problem about the foreign, not necessarily because of any specific difference pertaining to the "race" or "culture" of the immigrant, but rather, more fundamentally, because the immigrant is simply *not* "native." Nativism's problem of the foreign, in other words, is never reducible simply to "cultural" differences marked as foreign, and furthermore never suffices to exhaust a deeper problem of the foreign for nationalism, more generally. Beyond the "foreign"-ness of immigrants (the foreignness of foreigners, that is), nationalism must also always contend with another kind of still more vexing foreignness—namely, the alterity of the nation-state's internal ("native") "minorities" (see Appadurai 1998a; Balibar 1991b; Chatterjee 1993; Fitzpatrick 1995; Lowe 1996). This, simply put, is why merely removing immigrants could never solve the problems of racism in the United States. Notably, a hybrid of both these quandaries arises from the particular ambiguities that attach to Mexicans, because they can be understood to originate simultaneously inside and outside the space of the U.S. nation-state, as both colonized Chicanos and transnational "illegal aliens." Due to this slippage (or excess) of racialized meanings, Mexican identity can always appear simultaneously to be both (native) "minority" and "foreign" (Kearney 1991, 54; see Appadurai 1998a, 226–27; see chapters 3 and 6).

In the liberal nativist case against immigration, it is precisely U.S. nationalism's problem of "internal minorities" that Steinberg seeks to redress: the racial injustices suffered by African Americans are a "national" disgrace. To stake his nativist claim for the primacy of African Americans on the basis of their U.S. citizenship, however, Steinberg first has to make the somewhat agonistic case for their more elementary "American"-ness. His nativism from the left, like all nativisms, must begin from a premise of (national) identity. Yet, due to white supremacy, an "American" identity has *not* historically been self-evident or secure for African Americans.[17] While affirming the nativeness of Black people and thus reinscribing them within the space of the U.S. nation-state, though, Steinberg also effectively consigns African Americans to the objectified status of an encumbrance of "the nation," on whose behalf it is called to act. Insofar as the legacies of slavery and racial oppression have blocked the integration of "the nation's minorities" into its "mainstream"—indeed, because *they* have been excluded from their birthright membership in a national *we* (within which Steinberg locates himself)—liberal nativism proposes that "the Black problem," *because* it is a native problem, commands priority (1995, 195). Steinberg thereby forecloses altogether any interest in questions concerning the possibility or impossibility of assimilation for immigrants, and demands immigration restriction exclusively on the grounds that immigrants are simply not natives. In this respect, an antiracist nativism from the left proves to be a more thorough and consistent nativism than even Buchanan's or Brimelow's.

Liberal nativism is preoccupied with precisely this problem of the unassimilated foreignness of "internal minorities" (such as African Americans) for U.S. nationalism: Steinberg proposes to resolve the problem of their marginalization, fundamentally, by eradicating it—such that the native/nonnative distinction could become properly identical with the inside/outside division delimited by the territorial borders of the nation-state. Right-wing nativists seek to remedy the same nationalist problem of internal foreignness, but given their general aversion to advancing the cause of racial justice, they can do so only by one of two routes. One option requires a retreat from the foundational pluralism of their own nativism—by recourse to the racialized proxy provided by discourses that purport to evaluate the greater or lesser prospects for various migrant groups' assimilation (as in Buchanan's Zulus versus Englishmen proposition). The second alternative involves explicitly rearticulating the national pluralism of their nativism as a "cultural" or "ethnic" or overtly racialized exclusivity, such that the national identity precludes the possibility of counting the nation's minorities among the legitimate natives (as in Brimelow's contention that the nation's genuine "ethnic core" has always been white). All of these nativist options (from both the left and the right), when challenged to confront U.S. nationalism's requirements for a national identity that can mediate not only the more conventional foreignness of immigrants but also the foreign within, eventually reveal that the particular "internal minorities," presumed to be essentially inimical to the "American nation," are systematically constituted in *racialized* terms. That is to say, the kind of "minorities" that pose a problem for "American" *national* definition are above all racial minorities. Thus, the equation of "American" national identity with racial whiteness inevitably surfaces as an operative premise of U.S. nationalism itself.

While nativism tends to be indifferent, if not hostile, to questions of assimilation because nativism's pluralist identity politics upholds the basic incompatibility of the difference between native and alien, the politics of immigration restriction nevertheless inescapably assumes the fact of migration and commonly tends to produce comparative appraisals of various migrant groups. These assessments almost invariably revolve around questions of "assimilation"—the degrees of its respective achievements and failures, its possibilities and impossibilities. Indeed, this eventual recourse to debating questions of assimilation—concerned with how well and to what extent "they" can or will adapt in "our" nation, and therefore what "we" will do about "them"—is precisely what brings the nativists into a shared community of discourse with the majority of those who *defend* immigrants and even support immigration. With regard to immigration, liberals and conservatives alike are all ultimately unified by a shared "native's point of view," in which an "American" native *we* is remarkably self-assured in its deliberations about an immigrant or "alien" *them*. With this native's point of view in mind, and having considered some of the decisive contours of the nativism that it enables, I turn now from these nativist discourses of immigration to consider the figure of the immigrant as it has been construed to be an object of knowledge for American studies and U.S. nationalism, more generally.

THE IMMIGRANT AS QUESTION AND PROBLEM: ASSIMILATION AND PATHOLOGY

The nativist rejection of the possibility of assimilation is almost always coupled with the allegation that immigrants refuse (or are simply unable) to assimilate (Michaels 1995, 136–37, 162n127). In other words, nativism projects its own repudiation of assimilation onto the migrants themselves as their own refusal to relinquish their foreignness. Nativism, therefore, tends to be articulated to the *fact* of migration. That fact inherently summons the subsequent question—a native's question, indeed—concerning what to do with the migrants. The nativist call for exclusion, however, is merely one plausible reply to that question and is accompanied commonly enough by the more pragmatic nativist stipulation for *inclusion*—the mandate to "nationalize before we naturalize" (Brimelow 1995, 12–13).

Ultimately, the range of plausible "answers" to the question of assimilation is not as meaningful, for my purposes here, as the conceptual apparatus that is required for the question itself to be asked. There is indeed a vast social science literature that has been devoted to the formulation of this question of "assimilation." It has thus been consecrated, effectively, as *the* singular and seemingly inevitable question to be posed of the immigrant. Sociologists at the University of Chicago in the early twentieth century, in particular, played a predictably founding role in effectively consecrating this question of assimilation as *the* decisive question in immigration studies (e.g., Park [1914] 1980 and 1950; Park and Miller 1921; Thomas and Znaniecki 1927; Wirth 1928 and 1964; Zorbaugh 1929). Thus, the figure of the immigrant was fashioned and fixed as part of the thematic repertoire that animated the Chicago School's programmatic agenda for all subsequent empirical research and theoretical inquiry in the sociology of the United States, as well as more broadly in American and ethnic studies (Park and Burgess 1924; Smith and White 1929; Short 1971; and see Bulmer 1984; Cappetti 1993; Lyman 1994; Persons 1987). The question of the immigrant thus became an effectively canonical and inevitable window onto the very meanings of "American"-ness in

American studies. Without rehearsing the fine points of the Chicago School's typologies of invasion and transplantation, symbiosis and culture contact, adjustment and adaptation, accommodation and acculturation, and assimilation and amalgamation, these and other well-worn distinctions in the hegemonic sociology of immigration were formulated and have continued to be elaborated in a tireless effort to produce a knowledge of the overall "assimilation cycle" by which immigrants supposedly "become Americans."

The assimilation process has often been posited as a modernizing and progressive evolution, the teleology of which is presumably inevitable and inexorable. Thus, the particular experiences of distinct migrants and the historical specificity of diverse migrations are subsumed into a more universal claim about a generic and essentialized immigrant experience. Real historically situated migrant men and women, therefore, substantively located in relation to a variety of historicities of racialization, religion, citizenship, nationality, and so forth, tend to be reduced to what is precisely nothing more than an abstraction—the ideological figure of the immigrant. In this hegemonic teleology of assimilation, then, to truly understand the experience of any immigrant group is sufficient to know what is essential to them all.

Whereas I have suggested that the concept of assimilation entails a *question* about the immigrant, however, the sociocultural evolutionism of the assimilation premise would seem to pose no question at all. From this perspective, the immigrant, after all, is merely "a marginal man" (Park [1914] 1980), a transitional type, and the supposedly progressive and irreversible force of assimilation will eventually, finally, tolerate no "hybrids." *E pluribus unum*. From U.S. nationalism's melting pot, there emerges a "new man"; from the immigrant, arises "the American." Although assimilation operates on the model of a singular, teleological, evolutionary scale that proceeds from "tradition" to "modernity" and from particular to universal, however, it retains a distinct residue of nativism's pluralism. Like the distinctly U.S. model of miscegenation, historically—whereby "race mixing" was reduced to an oxymoron, producing not a new category of persons of mixed race, but only more Blacks—assimilation, in its classic formulation, is not constituted as a fusion of two "races" or "cultures" that generates something new, but rather as the destruction of one by the other (Michaels 1995, 61; see F. J. Davis 1991). Thus, the threshold that the immigrant must cross is utterly precarious, and the crossing is profoundly ambivalent. Consequently, the assimilation process is also unpredictable.

Because the immigrant is figured as a transplant or hybrid and remains not fully a member of either the community of origin or the social order to which he or she has migrated, always oscillating between the two, so must assimilation stubbornly persist as a *question*, indeed, *the* question. Indeed, to be socially and politically inscribed as "immigrant" is, in effect, to be reduced to an indefinitely deferrable question about identity and difference, to assume the social status and occupy the social position of a question. "The stranger stays, but he is not settled," Robert Park suggests, following Georg Simmel (Park [1914] 1980, 242; see Simmel [1908] 1980, 235). "He is a potential wanderer. That means that he is not bound as others are by the local proprieties and conventions." Hence, it is the freedom of movement that makes the immigrant suspect. The question of assimilation, then, is the expression of that native's suspicion: Do they come to join us, or are they just passing through? Are they truly "settlers," or are they merely "sojourners"?

The analytic theme of assimilation ultimately involves an interrogation directed at particular migrants and their respective *specific* "differences." Whether such diversity comes to be signaled in terms of "cultural" differences (the sociohistorical specificities of particular migrants' beliefs and practices), or by the much more apparently palpable differences of "biology" (the heterogeneous materiality of their actual racialized and gendered bodies), assimilation problems tend to be depicted as arising as a consequence of *difference* itself. The various time scales of the assimilation process are ever uncertain, and its developmental rhythms always uneven. In order to encompass these complexities, the assimilation rubric necessarily relies upon a hierarchical conception of more or less commensurable differences that can be ranked on a single scale of assimilability. Still, it clearly retains a residue of nativism's pluralist claims of purely incompatible difference. Some groups are simply easier to assimilate than others; those more "similar" are intrinsically more assimilable, whereas others are plainly more "different." One is thus reminded of Buchanan's assessment of the greater assimilability of "Englishmen" in contradistinction to that of "Zulus." Indeed, the assimilationist and nativist positions collide and collude in the end, when the question of assimilation is put to work as a question of which differences (*whose* differences) are too different to subsume and finally eliminate.

The unrelenting reiteration of the question of assimilability is directed at fixing (sustaining) the difference of the immigrant for scrutiny, until such a point at which assimilation may be completed. Such a consummated assimilation means nothing less than the eradication of that difference, which is to say, the obliteration of the immigrant as such. But until that point at which the difference is conclusively "fixed" (remedied/eliminated), the figure of the immigrant is wholly subsumed by the question (assimilable? how different? too different?). And thus, the question of assimilation itself serves to fix (sustain) that difference as such—as immigrant (not native). The assimilation problematic is implicated in a broader hegemonic project aimed at differentiating, sorting, and ranking actual migrants even as it mandates their incorporation, subjection, and consent. That project potentially transforms "aliens" into "citizens," but only on the condition that their particular histories of racialized exploitation and disenfranchisement be disavowed in exchange for an orderly inclusion in the political sphere (see Basch, Glick Schiller, and Szanton Blanc, 1994, 41–42; Lowe 1996, 9–10, 205n4).

The hegemonic sociological theme of assimilation—because it is inherently a question and necessarily entails a degree of uncertainty—is also plagued by ambivalence. The same hybrid condition of the immigrant that renders assimilation a question, therefore, likewise interrupts it, and turns the question into a problem. Depicted as straddling "two worlds," effectively "displaced," and existentially homeless, the figure of the immigrant is often characterized by divided desires and a fragmented self. In short, it is always plausible that the immigrant may resist the social forces working to incorporate (and subordinate) his or her difference. And the immigrant who repudiates assimilation, by definition, becomes *pathological*. Thus, the theme of assimilation is always coupled with a parallel discourse of "pathology" (variously glossed as dysfunctionality, disorganization, or disorder, as well as their subsidiaries, deviance and delinquency). If, as a precondition for immigrant inclusion, the assimilation *question* sets into play a certain suspicion, then, the *problem* represented in terms of pathology serves to confirm it. However, if nativist calls for restriction and exclusion require the production of a generalized immigration problem, typically essentializing all migrations as effectively the same, the theme of pathology that accompanies the question of assimilation is one that makes distinctions *among* immigrant groups and differentiates between "good" migrants and "bad" ones. In this configuration of immigration discourse, there are those migrant groups who are assimilating relatively smoothly, and others who become a problem; there is not a generic "immigration problem," but rather only special cases for which the assimilation process has gone awry.

THE IMMIGRANT AS NON-QUESTION: "ETHNICITY" AND THE RECUPERATION OF ASSIMILATION

The conventional discourses of assimilation may appear woefully out-of-date, even irrelevant, in the wake of more recent academic interest in resilient "ethnicity" and "multiculturalism." Yet, most contemporary immigration discourse in the United States—in both public political debate and much scholarship—operates with a nationalist commonsense that perpetuates the assimilation problematic. Indeed, it is precisely the transposition of the figure of the immigrant into the figure of the "ethnic" that redeems the teleology of assimilation and finally renders the question of assimilation into a nonquestion. Whereas enduring "ethnicity" may appear to be contrary to assimilation, then, the unexamined assumptions that make this contrast plausible are themselves the effects of the larger assimilation problematic. Ultimately, these apparent complications secure the assimilation paradigm itself.

In hegemonic discourses of immigration, the consideration of migration—as *movement*—is hijacked by an epistemological obsession with stasis and social order. It is presumed that migration is an anomaly that must culminate in a *re*-establishment of "roots" and a normative sedentariness (see Malkki 1992). In other words, what might have been an inquiry into *migration* inevitably becomes an insistent affirmation of "immigration," foreclosing the possibility of continued movement. Inquiries related to contemporary migrations therefore tend to inevitably presume permanent settlement and thereby devolve into questions about the emergence of a "second generation." "Ethnicity" becomes the measure of their greater or lesser overall assimilation.

A scholarly preoccupation with the purported resilience of "ethnicity" already smuggles into the analysis a definite series of conceptual moves that deserve scrutiny. A decisive feature of this teleology is the conceptual move that first renders migrants as an immigrant *group*. Once produced as a group, it becomes possible to formulate the problem of migrants' reproduction *as a group*. Thus, migrants become simultaneously constituted as a "first generation," which itself can only be meaningful in relation to a "second generation," and so on. Yet one need only consider the simple question—first or second *in relation to what?*—and it becomes immediately manifest that these "generations" are constituted only in relation to their presence in the United States and their prospective assimilation into "American"-ness. Thus, the figure of the immigrant is transposed onto the multigenerational trajectory of an "ethnic group," and that trajectory is meaningful only because it is conceptually confined *within* the space of the U.S. nation-state. Furthermore, what was previously purported to be the inevitability of assimilation for the migrants themselves is thereby displaced from the immigrant to an indefinite "ethnic" posterity. The challenge of assimilation, finally, transcends individual immigrants and must be seen as the protracted problem of succeeding generations. This elision from the immigrant to "the second generation" thus constitutes assimilation now as a rather more virtual horizon, indeed the vanishing point, for all questions of the immigrant. To the extent that assimilation may have presented a problem, it is a problem that now gets handed down to posterity. The question of assimilation, then, is simultaneously deferred and bracketed. Precisely because assimilation is that horizon at which "the ethnic" ceases to be "ethnic," however, the inevitability of assimilation is secured by this indefinite deferral of the question. The question of assimilation, therefore, is dispelled by its own inevitability. As the question recedes from view, finally, there is really no question at all. The transposition of the immigrant into a multigenerational "ethnic group" defers the question of assimilation itself—indefinitely if necessary: the question becomes a nonquestion.[18]

The elision of the immigrant and the ethnic is always conceptually entangled with the theme of pathology. In the first place, abortive assimilation on the part of the immigrant is itself a precondition for the displacement of the assimilation question onto a second generation. That supposedly failed assimilation process is paradigmatically accomplished by a *repudiation* of assimilation as a desired end. The alleged act of repudiation, moreover, according to the progressivist terms of the assimilation teleology, is tantamount to a deliberate *retreat* into the immigrant (now "ethnic") community. Hence, questions about "settlement" and "the second generation" become virtually obligatory proxies for the assimilation *problem*. Especially when rendered in terms of intergenerational conflicts between migrants and their children, this problem—the presumed rejection of assimilation—appears to result from the challenges of "cultural" *duality*. The *retention* of "ethnicity" thus serves as the canonical hallmark of an assimilation process that has become pathological. The pathologized immigrant, furthermore, gets mutated into the pathologized ethnic. But with the deferral of the assimilation question from the immigrant to the second generation, this retention of ethnicity becomes an intrinsic part of the process itself, and thus, is refigured as a sign of its steady progress.

Finally, the systemic inequalities of class exploitation and racialized oppression in the divergent experiences of historically specific migrations assume the multiculturalist appearance of immutable, identitarian "cultural" or "ethnic" differences intrinsic to them as groups. The assimilationist ideal—perfect integration, equal representation, equal access, and equal opportunity—therefore seems to be perturbed only by the cacophony of fractious "diversity." It is the coupling of pathology and "ethnicity" that achieves the displacement and deferral of the assimilation problem from the immigrant to the ethnic—both the presumed "second" as well as subsequent generations. But this is precisely what secures the immigration teleology. Finally, then, assimilation seems to be truly inevitable—someday, it may even come to pass.

THE IMMIGRANT AS FETISH: "AMERICANIZATION"

Once I thought to write a history of the immigrants in America.
Then I discovered that the immigrants *were* American history.
—**Oscar Handlin,** *The Uprooted*

Once the question of assimilation is no longer a question, the figure of the immigrant can assume its genuine centrality and fullest significance for U.S. nationalism—as fetish. The promise of assimilation for U.S. nationalism, indeed, is the eventual obliteration of the immigrant through "Americanization." The assimilation problematic, after all, rationalizes a series of mutations through which the alien difference of the immigrant gets incorporated as the ethnic and eventually must become "American." Thus, the hegemonic immigration discourse that subordinates the immigrant to the assimilationist demands of "Americanization" is the ultimate route through which one or another "native's point of view" may contribute to the continuous production of an "American" national identity.

Because immigrants may be understood to affirm the desirability of "America" and validate its promises of "modernity" and "freedom," the figure of the immigrant performs a crucial ideological service for U.S.

nationalism. This service is finally only verified in the figure of the immigrant as a conventionally masculinized individual who has repudiated his homeland, emancipated himself from the grip of all "tradition," renounced the familiar comforts of his particular "ethnic" community, and vanquishes all traces of his previous foreignness. As Lisa Lowe clarifies (with regard to Asian American experiences): "Immigrants have been fundamental to the construction of the nation as a simulacrum of inclusiveness. Yet the project of imagining the nation as homogeneous requires . . . fundamentally 'foreign' origins antipathetic to the modern American society that 'discovers,' 'welcomes,' and 'domesticates' them" (1996, 5).

Indeed, U.S. nationalism requires the immigrant and needs for "the nation" to assimilate him. By domesticating and integrating the immigrant—by "Americanizing" him—the U.S. nation-state likewise subjugates his foreignness and triumphs over the foreignness of all nations beyond its borders. In this manner, the figure of the immigrant also provides a necessary mediation between U.S. nationalism's nativist moment and the global reach of its imperial power. Thus, the assimilationist melting-pot myth of the U.S. nation-state—as "a simulacrum of inclusiveness"—is coupled with the liberal-democratic myth of U.S. imperialism, as a simulacrum of universality, whereby the project of empire is equated with the defense of "democracy" everywhere and the limitless extension of "freedom."

This modernist theme of the immigrant who abandons "tradition" and foreignness in favor of masculinized individualism continues to be central to the perpetuation of the hegemonic mythology of "opportunity" and "success" in the United States. In her incisive analysis of immigration discourse in congressional testimony during the 1970s, Phyllis Chock (1991, 281) examines the repeated depiction of the immigrant as a (male) individual whose saga can be narrativized in a linear manner—"whose arrival in America, desire for betterment, striving in adversity, and putting down of roots make him a 'new man.' That is, he is the Promethean hero of his own story."[19] Chock identifies a recurring preoccupation with the individualized reasons and calculated motivations for migration, and an emphasis on personal transformations, such that the testimonials produce and reiterate a composite that bears a striking resemblance to what "Americans" tell as their common immigration heritage, recapitulating the hegemonic script of an "immigrant America" (290). These public immigration narratives cannibalize the kinds of more intimate efforts at collective memory staged in settings such as family, home, or community, but in the congressional immigration hearings they operate as exercises in ideological articulation for the purposes of the policy debates of the U.S. nation-state (290). "The contradictions between what might be said and what must be said emerge" (281), Chock notes, but she also clarifies that the opportunity myth nevertheless "presents immigrant experience as though it were outside history; in the myth's autochthonous terms no individual has a past that matters, only roots in American soil" (285). These individualized narratives are fashioned as "success sagas" and are conjoined to the ideological operations of the U.S. nation-state's more general "opportunity" myth; they "simultaneously compose the individual and the nation in the same terms" (281).

The hegemonic liberal nationalist mythologies of assimilation nonetheless continue to be recapitulated in contemporary anthropological representations of the immigrant. In his ethnographic monograph *Shadowed Lives: Undocumented Immigrants in American Society*, for instance, Leo Chávez (1992) affirms, "The important story to be told is that of the transition people undergo as they leave the migrant life and instead settle in the United States" (4; and see 1991). Chávez introduces a schema of transition, settlement, and incorporation for undocumented Mexicans (and other Latinos) in what he explicitly characterizes as their passage from sojourning "migrants" to (immigrant) "settlers": "For undocumented migrants, crossing the border is a territorial passage that marks the transition from one way of life to another. . . . A territorial passage, like more conventional rites of passage, can be divided into three important phases: *separation* from the known social group or society, *transition* (the 'liminal' phase), and *incorporation* into the new social group or society" (4–5; emphasis original).

Chávez embellishes the timeworn sociological model of "the assimilation process" by invoking an anthropological analogy—rites of passage in the life cycles of individuals—as the organizing theoretical metaphor through which he characterizes the process of settlement. This innovation, of course, only fortifies the teleology through which "liminal" migrants undergo a "transition from one way of life to another" and become "immigrants" who may be incorporated into "the new society." What finally seems to be of the utmost concern to Chávez is simply demonstrating that many undocumented Latino migrants in fact tend to settle in the United States and feel a sense of belonging in "the American community" (1994, 61).[20] In an effort to repudiate the timeworn nativist stereotype of Mexican migrants, in particular, as mere "sojourners" who may be disparaged as having no meaningful long-term stake in membership in the United States, therefore, Chávez (1991 and 1994) is centrally preoccupied with rehabilitating them as genuine "settlers" and thus legitimate immigrants who can rightfully imagine themselves into the imagined community of the "American" nation. Notably, in subsequent publications (e.g., 1997 and 2001), Chávez cautiously adopts an explicitly transnational perspective, but the symbolic significance of immigrants continues to be framed in terms of "who *we* are as a nation . . . as a people" (2001, xiv; emphasis added). Furthermore, asserting "immigrants are reminders of how Americans, as a people, came to be," Chávez upholds the myth of an "immigrant America" and explicitly concurs with Oscar Handlin that "immigration *is* the history of the nation" (Chávez 2001, 3; emphasis original).

If the teleology of assimilation is finally directed toward "Americanization," it also sustains the nationalist myth of a distinctly immigrant America. This ideological script universalizes "the immigrant experience" as the decisive confirmation that the U.S. nation-state is a global refuge, a veritable promised land of "liberty" and "opportunity," which nourishes itself upon the continuous infusion of immigrant energies. Bonnie Honig (1998; 2001, 73–106) provides a compelling interrogation of the ideological purchase of the myth of an "immigrant America." Indeed, it is precisely "the immigrant's *foreignness*," Honig contends, which "positions him or her to enhance or reinvigorate the national democracy" (2001, 76; emphasis original). Honig demonstrates that xenophobic calls for immigration restriction and exclusion simultaneously elicit a variety of what she calls "xenophilic" recuperations of the foreignness of the iconic immigrant. "The myth of an immigrant America," she argues, "depicts the foreigner as . . . an agent of national reenchantment that might rescue the regime from corruption and return it to its first principles" (74). Honig examines three key versions of the xenophilic myth, corresponding to three dominant constructions of the U.S. nation-state's "first principles": a capitalist version, celebrating immigrant entrepreneurialism and "ethnic" sagas in which hard work and dedication are fairly rewarded with upward socioeconomic mobility; a patriarchal version, celebrating the immigrant as a reinvigorating infusion of community values and institution-building, founded on the bedrock of "the family"; and a liberal version, celebrating the immigrant as the singular figure that can actually validate the state's foundation of democratic consent by performing the social contract (80–98). In each rendition of the xenophilic myth, the iconic figure of the immigrant provides a fetishized supplement of restorative foreignness that can be "Americanized," conscripted into the service of the relegitimation projects of U.S. nationalism. Notably, in the liberal version of the xenophilic impulse, Honig clarifies, the familiar spectacle of newly naturalized immigrant citizens taking the oath of citizenship, "reenact[s] liberalism's . . . fictive foundation in individual acts of uncoerced consent," and thereby "restores a disaffected citizenry's faith in the choice-worthiness of the regime," while likewise obscuring the regime's nonconsensual foundations in slavery, conquest, and colonialism, as well as present-day practices of racial oppression (75, 94–95).

Neatly eliding the histories of racial subjugation, dispossession, and genocide, the claim that *all* "Americans" are the descendants of presumably voluntary immigrants, yearning for freedom and seeking opportunity, supplies the predictable complement to the denial of imperialism, noted earlier, that has been a central theme of "American" exceptionalism. The celebration of an "immigrant America" and the myth that the United States is truly and fundamentally "a nation of immigrants," therefore, conclusively place the figure of the immigrant at the heart of U.S. nationalism itself.

"THE ALIEN" WHO IS NOT THE IMMIGRANT: "ILLEGALITY" AND THE RETURN OF THE NATIVE

The figure of the immigrant must be assimilable, and finally assimilated indeed, to properly serve as the "Americanized" fetish of U.S. nationalism. Even as xenophilic a nationalism as that of the United States, however, like all nationalisms, intrinsically requires that its nation be imagined with limits. Every nationalism must assert and uphold the integrity of its own putative national boundaries, and rely on nation-state borders to mediate between the circumscribed space of "the nation" and all manner of foreignness that comprises its outside. Thus, even U.S. nationalism at its most liberal and xenophilic could not possibly permit any and all foreignness to be transformed into the kinds of supplements that substantiate the conceits of "Americanization." Here, then, arises yet another instance of the interdependence and inseparability of nativism and assimilationism—namely, that some migrants simply cannot be figured as the iconic immigrant and must remain incorrigible "aliens."

The immigrant who naturalizes as a U.S. citizen, in Honig's account, provides a kind of solution to one of liberal democracy's constitutive problems of legitimacy by actively seeking and explicitly consenting to membership in its polity. However, the immigrant who consents always calls attention to another who, despite eligibility, chooses nonetheless *not* to naturalize. Further, and most importantly, this figure of the immigrant who consents similarly exposes yet another—"the illegal alien." Indeed, the liberal xenophilic impulse is epitomized for Honig by Peter Schuck and Rogers Smith's *Citizenship without Consent: Illegal Aliens in the American Polity* (1985), a work whose principal polemical aim and most palpable practical intent is to elaborate the putative constitutionality of rescinding the birthright U.S. citizenship of the children of undocumented migrants (see Delgado 1997). Thus, a premier example of xenophilic liberal nationalism is simultaneously a profound articulation of liberal nativism and, furthermore, a politically significant intervention on the side of "immigration control" and the restriction of citizenship. "The good, consenting immigrant, the model of proper, consensual American citizenship," Honig continues (2001, 96), "is shadowed by the bad immigrant, the illegal alien who undermines consent in two ways: he or she never consents to American laws and 'we' never consent to his presence on 'our' territory. Schuck and Smith's illegal alien takes things from us and has nothing to offer in return . . . a daily lawbreaker" (see Chock 1991, 281). Thus, the "illegal alien" not only fails to provide the magical supplement of political consent but also is figured as an affront to the rightful consent of the sovereign national polity itself (see Bosniak 1994 and 1996).

The figure of the immigrant as fetish—what Honig depicts as "the good immigrant"—underwrites the hegemonic script of "immigrant America" with a subtext of inexorable "Americanization" for which the question of assimilation has been effectively settled. The accompanying "bad immigrant," however, is more and more rendered, by the logic of assimilation itself, to be not an "immigrant" at all. Indeed, it is noteworthy that the strictly legal category for undocumented migrants within the regime of U.S. immigration and naturalization law is precisely not "immigrant," as this term is reserved only for those "legal" migrants who have been certified as such by the state. In contrast, the legal category that officially designates an undocumented migrant in the United States is simply *deportable alien*. The native's point of view that infuses the conceptual apparatus of assimilation finally requires a figure that is irreconcilably and irredeemably "alien" who is not recognizable as the immigrant at all—"the illegal alien" who must be expelled.

"THE ILLEGAL ALIEN" AS A QUESTION OF MEXICANS: SOJOURNERS AND SETTLERS

If undocumented migrants are figured as the iconic "bad immigrant," mere "illegal aliens" undermining the democratic sovereignty of "the nation" through their circumventions of "the rule of law," then nativism as well as the native's point of view that asks the assimilation question bear down with special force upon Mexican migrants in particular. Mexican migrants have been very commonly the implied if not overt focus of mass-mediated journalistic, political, and scholarly discussions of "illegal aliens" for much of the twentieth century (Chávez 2001; Johnson 1997). Indeed, for many years, the annual reports of the U.S. Immigration and Naturalization Service divided statistics for their apprehensions of "deportable aliens" into two discrete categories: Mexicans and All Others. A specific history of immigration lawmaking and selective border enforcement (which I examine in detail in chapter 6) was decisive in thus rendering *Mexican* as the distinctive national name for migrant "illegality." Predictably enough, upon being equated with a specific national-origin migrant group, the sociopolitical category "illegal alien"—inseparable from a distinct "problem" or "crisis" of governance and national sovereignty—has consistently come to be saturated with racialized difference. Indeed, the figure of "the illegal alien" has long been a pronounced feature of the racialization of "Mexicans," in general, in the United States.

Given this distinctive figuring of Mexican migrants as the iconic "illegal aliens" in the representational imagination of the U.S. immigration regime, the assimilation problematic has been elaborated in a somewhat unique way historically in the scholarship of Mexican migration. Mexican migration, like all migrations, is necessarily subjected to the intrinsic suspicion of the assimilation question, and may be predictably subsumed within the premises of the assimilation rubric in any case. However, the longstanding equation of Mexican migration with a presumably temporary, disposable (finally, deportable) labor migration predominated by men (who were predominantly single or left wives and children behind) also sometimes encouraged the suspension of the questions of assimilation that might have accompanied long-term settlement. Beginning with the very earliest efforts of social scientists to produce representations of Mexican (male) migrants in the United States, therefore, the scholarly literature has been distinguished by the singularly disproportionate, seemingly compulsive obsession with determining whether Mexican migrants were in fact "sojourners" or "settlers." As early as 1908, in a U.S. Department of Commerce and Labor Bulletin on "Mexican Labor," sociologist Victor Clark was principally interested in evaluating the prospects for a "transition . . . from an immigration of temporary laborers to one of settlers" ([1908] 1974, 520; see Bogardus [1934] 1970; Gamio 1930; Taylor 1932). More than eighty years later, as already seen above, Chávez (1988; 1991; 1992; 1994) uses virtually the same language in his effort to explore "the transition people undergo as they leave the migrant life and instead settle in the United States." Indeed, the themes that revolve around discerning whether or not Mexican migrants can or will "assimilate," and the variety of ways that this question is elaborated through the sojourner-settler binary have remained ubiquitous ever since (see, e.g., Cornelius 1992; Chávez, Flores, and López-Garza 1989; Durand and Massey 1992; Hondagneu-Sotelo 1994; Massey 1987; Massey et al. 1987; Portes and Bach 1985; R. C. Smith 1996; Suárez-Orozco 1998; Rouse 1992; Villar 1989 and 1990).

The preoccupation with what were, more often than not, rather dismal appraisals of the assimilation prospects of Mexican migrants has tended to be inseparable from the equation of the Mexican with his labor (Reisler 1976a, 127–50; Reisler 1976b). In 1911, the Dillingham U.S. Immigration Commission tellingly produced its own assessment, reaffirming the image of Mexicans as "sojourners": "Because of their [Mexicans'] strong attachment to their native land, low intelligence, illiteracy, migratory life, and the possibility of their residence here being discontinued, few become citizens of the United States" (quoted in Weber 1982, 24). And further, "while they are not easily assimilated, this is of no very great importance as long as most of them return to their native land. In the case of the Mexican, he is less desirable as a citizen than as a laborer" (quoted in Calavita 1992, 180). Clearly, if Mexicans' "migratory" lifestyle was not sufficient to prevent the "undesirable" prospect of their long-term but "not easily assimilated" settlement, then by implication, "the nation" could be comforted nonetheless by the state's capacity to ensure "the possibility of their residence here being discontinued"—their effective deportability. One way or the other, then, U.S. policy would ensure that "most of them" proved to be sojourners.

In a significant sense, the figure of the sojourner was always gendered as male, and the effectiveness of his exploitation relied upon the maintenance of relatively low "reproduction costs" due to the prearranged separation of (migrant) working men from the women (and children) who remained in Mexico (Chock 1991, 1995, and 1996; Coutin and Chock 1995; González and Fernández 1979; Hondagneu-Sotelo 1994; Kearney 1986; Rouse 1992; and see Burawoy 1976 and Kearney 1991, 1996, and 1998). The historical production of the racialized and gendered figure of "the Mexican" as (heterosexual) male sojourner came, moreover, to be increasingly rendered synonymous with the figure of the "illegal alien." Thus, with the persistent refinement of the U.S. nation-state's disproportionate illegalization of Mexican sojourners in particular, and with the increasing durability of their status as "deportable aliens" (see chapter 6), the assimilation rubric's preoccupations with "settlement" could long remain fairly well subdued, if not bracketed altogether. These linkages have become more readily visible, however, with the increasing equation of permanent (family) settlement with undocumented migrant *women* (Chock 1995 and 1996; Coutin and Chock 1995; Roberts 1997).[21] Chock (1995, 173) poignantly identifies the pervasive presumption that "a natural relationship between babies and mothers [blurs] lines of rights and responsibilities mapped by the state between two categories of people (citizen and alien)," such that undocumented women's fertility is understood to multiply "the risk to the nation." Thus, the incorrigibility of "illegal aliens" for the project of assimilation and "Americanization," finally, came by the 1990s to re-pose the settlement question with a palpable nativist vengeance (Roberts 1997). Notably, by the 1990s, Schuck and Smith's legal argument (1985) to disenfranchise the U.S.-born children of undocumented migrants of their birthright citizenship had been translated into concerted political campaigns, such as California's Proposition 187, which sought to deny rudimentary civil rights and public services not only to migrants but also to their citizen children. Such an increasingly hostile and intransigent atmosphere, of course, did not serve to restrict labor migration so much as it aimed to deter migration and settlement by *families*, in order to ensure that "most of them return to their native land." Thus, when Mexicans are subsumed by the canonical (assimilationist) narrative of the immigrant—and likewise, when they are excluded from it and relegated to demarcate its outer limits—they remain the object of the ideological maneuvers that underwrite and sustain that paradigm, leaving them accountable for its outcomes and on its terms (see Chock 1991).

REPUDIATING THE NATIVE'S POINT OF VIEW

In conclusion, then, research concerned with themes or topics related to migration to the United States is always already apprehensible from the "native's point of view," in terms of the ideological field of the immigrant. This chapter has engaged in a critical exercise that posits both the possibility and the necessity for such research to nonetheless refuse to be contained by the compulsive nationalist premises of a problematic of immigration. This critical demand gestures toward the possibility of a now no-longer-"American" studies scholarship that would consistently refuse to operate from the epistemological standpoint of the U.S. nation-state. In short, it would aspire to produce a knowledge concerned with migrant themes that would nonetheless foreclose upon the possibility of any "American" dreams or "Americanization" schemes. With these provisions in mind, I return in the next chapter to the challenge of conceptualizing Mexican Chicago as a transnational conjunctural space, in a manner that aspires to be inimical to the native's point of view of U.S. nationalism.

CHAPTER THREE

LOCATING A MEXICAN CHICAGO IN THE
SPACE OF THE U.S. NATION-STATE

A place on the map is also a place in history.
—**Adrienne Rich,** "Notes toward a Politics of Location"

How many maps . . . might be needed to deal exhaustively
with a given space, to code and decode all its meanings and
contents? . . . We are confronted not by one social space
but by many—indeed an unlimited multiplicity.
—**Henri Lefebvre,** *The Production of Space*

Transnational migration is constituted across spaces divided and regimented by nation-state borders. The social condition of transnational migrants, therefore, must be understood as a preeminently *spatialized* one, in which the spatial difference produced and sustained by nation-state boundaries is reproduced in the specific sociopolitical statuses ascribed to "natives" and "aliens," or "citizens" and "immigrants." In the previous chapter, I examined how dominant discourses of immigration in the United States correspond to the politics of nativism, and how their shared premises derive from U.S. nationalism itself. In this chapter, I shift the focus from the more generic discourses of natives and immigrants to the nation-state spaces of the United States and Mexico, and the production of the particular spatialized ("national") difference between them, through which the specific differences between "Americans" and "Mexicans" are constituted. This chapter deploys a critical transnational perspective in order to dislodge some of the dominant spatial ideologies that undergird a prevalent common sense about the naturalized difference between the United States and Mexico, as well as between the United States and Latin America more generally.

Through the lens of what I call "Mexican Chicago," I want to render an orthodox spatial knowledge about the relation of Mexican migrants to the U.S. nation-state more accountable to a regime of spatial power and inequality. A Chicago produced in relation to Mexican migration serves as a critical pivot that can orient the agonistic (ordinarily centrifugal) triangulation of Latin American studies, Chicano studies, and finally, that field concerned in one or another manner with the United States, known as American studies. Revisiting some of the crucial premises of Chicano studies, I suggest a critical reevaluation of the conceptual foundations of "Latin America" as it has been conventionally construed as an object of spatial knowledge for Latin American studies in the United States—which is really to say, from the epistemological standpoint of U.S. imperialism. In so doing, this transformed conceptualization of Latin America enables —and requires—a rethinking of the space of the U.S nation-state itself. As a result, this chapter also seeks to revise some of the principal concerns at stake in the project of Chicano studies.

Thus, this chapter considers the ways in which the spatial topography of the Americas historically has become intrinsically racialized and involves a continuous work of reracialization. Such reracialization is manifest in the unequal social relations through which global capital, nation-states, and transnational labor, together in the contradictions of struggle, unevenly produce the particular localities where "globalization" takes place. Mexican Chicago emerges as a distinct transnational conjunctural space where Mexican migrants engage meaningfully with their own reracialization and the reconstitution of their own "Mexican"-ness in relation to the racial order of the U.S. "Mexican"-ness, reracialized within the space of the U.S. nation-state, however, is never simply reducible to the beleaguered "assimilation" of an "Americanizing" ethnic group. Rather, implicated in an active ensemble of migrant social relations that defy the presumably hermetically sealed containments of nation-state spaces and border policing, this migrant "Mexican"-ness emerges as a racialized transnationality. From the standpoint of a *Mexican* Chicago—one that belongs, in some substantive sense, to Latin America—I therefore posit a critical transnational perspective that can reckon with U.S. nationalism and its imperial conceits by interrogating some of the constructions of race and space that intersect in the imagining and enforcement of the boundaries of the U.S. nation-state and its politics of citizenship. Toward this end, however, it is necessary first to defamiliarize the nation-state's artifice and artifacts, even as they continue to materially confine and practically constrict our efforts to subvert them.

The relationship between Mexico and the United States has its origins in a history of invasion and conquest, warfare and subjugation, exploitation and oppression. It is possible (indeed, productive) to comprehend this history as one of unstable frontiers and violable boundaries, as one where space is not merely contiguous but colonized, and hence, coterminous. Indeed, what is now the southwestern United States was annexed from Mexico in 1848 for the westward expansion of the U.S. nation-state, as the spoils of a war of conquest. After U.S. troops occupied Mexico City itself, Mexico ceded roughly half of its national territory (over 1 million square miles of land, roughly corresponding to the physical area of Germany and France combined). Approximately 80,000 Mexicans summarily became U.S. citizens. A new border was abruptly established along the Río Bravo/Rio Grande to separate territories (and a population) that had not previously been divided. A founding premise of Chicano studies has always been the recognition that "we didn't cross the border; the border crossed us" (Acuña 1996, 109; Rosaldo 1997, 31). "We do not recognize capricious frontiers on the Bronze Continent," declared the *Plan espiritual de Aztlán*, adopted on March 31, 1969, in Denver by the First National Chicano Youth Liberation Conference (Anaya and Lomelí 1989, 1). "We Are One People Without Borders [*Somos Un Pueblo Sin Fronteras*]," concurred the Center for Autonomous Social Action (CASA), a Chicano social welfare organization devoted to assisting and organizing undocumented Mexican/migrant workers, adding the affirmation that "We are One Because America is One" (D. Gutiérrez 1995, 190–91). In a similar gesture that overtly destabilized U.S. nationalism's presumptuous claim to "American"-ness, Rodolfo Acuña's classic synoptic account of Chicano history (1972) was aptly titled *Occupied America*.

The consideration of this history is a requisite protocol for any responsible account of Mexican migration to the United States. Scholarship concerned with Mexican migration that treats its subject without this necessary starting point, wittingly or unwittingly, reduces Mexican migration to just another "immigrant" story and tacitly participates in the erasure of both a distinct (racialized) historicity and the historical claims that the Chicano studies project alone has emphasized. From this vantage point, the westward extension of the U.S. nation-state—itself predicated upon relentless international conflict as well as a formidable accumulation of capital—laid the foundations for a distinctly transnational history that cannot be adequately represented, and should not be smugly sub-sumed, by the self-referential imperial-national chauvinism that has fre-quently been operative in American studies.[1] The United States—the current configuration of its national space—all too easily assumes the appearance of a pregiven, stable, and enduring "fact" in the present and becomes an unexamined, naturalized, and normative presupposition. Nevertheless, as Patricia Nelson Limerick (1987, 27) eloquently notes, "Conquest forms the historical bedrock of the whole nation." Not only a concern of the historical past, however, the present and future existence of the United States is likewise predicated and possible only on the basis of continuous and renewed imperial domination.[2] Rather than presume the fixity and integrity of the U.S. nation-state, I would like to emphasize its constitutive restlessness.

If the production and reproduction of the space of the U.S. nation-state has indeed entailed a relentless project—first of conquest and expan-sion, later of border policing and reinforcement—then surely these hege-monic spatial maneuvers can be properly understood only in relation to the insubordinate spatial practices of everyday life. In this respect, I want to introduce the agonistic proposition of a *Mexican* Chicago confined within the boundaries of the U.S. nation-state but also a site for their production. And here, by emphasizing the *production* of these bound-aries, which are always also limits, I want to suggest that Chicago likewise becomes a site of their contingency.

When I invoke a Mexican Chicago, what I am addressing is something more significant than the mere physical presence in Chicago of Mexican people—somehow considered to be "out of place"—in effect, outside of their supposedly natural habitat. This book, while rejecting the category "immigrants" because of its conventionally teleological underpinnings, is decidedly not interested in fashioning a postmodernist narrative of dis-placement, whereby transnational Mexican migrants are inadvertently reduced to "dis-placed persons," floating in some purported "postmod-ern hyper-space."[3] If, in the former configuration, it is presumed that there could be no other possible end for Mexican migrants than to settle permanently and "become Americans," in the latter, they never quite arrive or engage in social life in the United States in any substantive, meaningful sense. In one case, in the promised land at last, they might as well get down on their knees to kiss the ground; in the other, in a virtual world of their own, their feet never seem to touch the ground. Indeed, the conceptual framework of displacement provides an alternative to the assimilationist rubric, in effect, only by recapitulating the culturalist pluralism of the nativists' charge of incommensurable difference: on the premise that there is an "authentic" elsewhere in which people, culture, and place correspond perfectly, the migrants are figured as literally out of place but still contained within a coherently bounded "cultural" reality of their own. In accord with the dictates of the conventional immigration problematic, the thematic of continuity and disjuncture thus continues to be mapped onto the migrants themselves (see Malkki 1992, 33). As either assimilators or outcasts, migrants come to be represented by a condition of dis-placement that merely reinscribes the stability and security of separate places and the essentialized correspondence of particular people to those places as their respective "natives."

Instead, I want to emphasize the production of Mexican Chicago as a conjunctural space with transformative repercussions in all directions (Lefebvre [1974] 1991). In the spirit of Guillermo Gómez-Peña's appeal for "a new cartography . . . to interpret the world-in-crisis" (1993, 43), and Michael Kearney's (1991, 68) and Roger Bartra's concurrence that "Latin America does not end at the U.S. border" (in Gómez-Peña 1993, 11), I want to assert with the idea of Mexican Chicago that something about Chicago itself has become elusive, even irretrievable, for the U.S. nation-state. I want to insist, in other words, upon the admission of Chicago to its proper place within Latin America. This conceptual move, it bears emphasizing, ought not be misconstrued to operate within a nationalistic binary that would then purport to render Chicago somehow retrievable in turn for the Mexican nation-state; such a zero-sum proposition would be counterproductive and fanciful in the extreme.[4] Mexican nationalist intellectual and politician José Vasconcelos, for instance, seeing migrants in the United States during the 1920s as a potentially recuperable resource for the political projects of the postrevolutionary Mexican nation-state, characterized them as a *México de afuera*—a Mexico abroad, or a Mexico outside of itself (Skirius 1976). Decades later, Chicano folklorist and critic Américo Paredes adopted the explicitly culturalist formulation of "Greater Mexico" to refer to "all the areas inhabited by people of a Mexican culture—not only in the Republic of Mexico but in the United States as well—in a cultural rather than a political sense" (1976, xiv; quoted in Limón 1998, 215n1). Indeed, even as they otherwise seek to identify significant continuities and affinities, both of these earlier formulations construe the Mexican presence on both sides of the U.S.-Mexico divide in terms of an inside and outside of the originary Mexican space and thus tend to reinscribe precisely such a binary juxtaposition of nation-state spaces. In contrast, when I posit a Chicago that corresponds *sociospatially* to Latin America, the force of my intervention is directed specifically against the epistemological stability of the U.S. nation-state as a presupposition. The *Mexican* in Mexican Chicago, on the other hand, pertains not to the Mexican nation-state, nor to any presumed essential Mexicanness, but rather to the particular sociohistorical situation of transnational working-class migrants, originating in Mexico, for which *Mexican* (in my formulation) serves as shorthand, but through which the very meanings of *Mexican*—for these migrants themselves—come to be reconfigured. Rather than an outpost or extension of Mexico, therefore, the "Mexican"-ness of Mexican Chicago signifies a permanent disruption of the space of the U.S. nation-state and embodies the vital possibility of something truly new, a radically differential social formation.

I will begin by trying to situate the sociopolitical specificities of this Mexican Chicago within the wider relationship between the United States and Mexico, the consideration of which (within the U.S. academy) is conventionally subsumed under the rubric of Latin American studies. Latin American studies in the United States—like most institutionalized area-studies programs as such—owes its epistemological formulation and, most importantly, its original material endowments and legitimation, to a particular historical moment in the ascendant hegemony of U.S. imperialism as a global phenomenon following World War II (Berger 1995; Harootunian 2000, 25–58; McCaughey 1984; Nader 1997; Wallerstein 1997a).[5] There is no dearth of explicit commentary in the academic conference proceedings of the period bemoaning the lack of expertise and general ignorance prevailing in the United States with regard to geopolitical areas of "strategic importance" to "the national interest." Although some early antecedents to Latin American studies emerged during the prewar years of Franklin Roosevelt's Good Neighbor Policy, the real boom came only in the wake of the Cuban Revolution of 1959 (Berger 1995). Despite the critical political engagement and explicit anti-imperialism that has often distinguished scholars working within Latin American studies in the U.S. academy (see Chilcote 1997), it is necessary nonetheless to adopt this understanding of the imperialist epistemology that frames Latin American studies in order to enable certain preliminary considerations that may provide some operative premises.

The most elementary but also the most crucial of these considerations is to recognize the fact that something called Latin American studies (within the United States) was historically conceptualized and is inherently comprehensible as constituting knowledge about a geopolitical region that is *outside* of the physical space of the continental United States. The intellectual enterprise of Latin American studies was created as a way of knowing that is positioned from within the seemingly stable confines of the U.S. nation-state. Chicago could never have been conventionally conceived to belong to Latin America, plainly enough, because Chicago is located *inside* of "America"—that is, the United States of (non-Latin) America.

A second premise, therefore, is that the U.S. nation-state has enforced an "American" identity whose national community is imagined to be linguistically homogeneous: the United States has been manufactured historically to be English-speaking (Liebowitz 1984; Simpson 1986). Here, in the work of homogenizing the United States according to this Anglo hegemony, nearly everything south of the continental U.S. tends also to be homogenized—as "Latin," or Latino—despite the simple fact that many languages without Latin antecedents are represented among the populations included in the region called Latin America. What has therefore been definitive for the hegemonic construction of Latin America as such is precisely not any positive proposition (linguistic or otherwise) about that quite vast region of the globe, but rather, more simply, that the United States is *not* "Latin," and that Latin America is fundamentally *something else*. Indeed, as Gómez-Peña puts it, "For the North American . . . the [Mexican] border is where the Third World begins" (in Fusco 1995, 148–49). From the imperial epistemological standpoint of the U.S. nation-state that has historically fashioned Latin American studies, the "Latin" label is meaningful—fundamentally, and above all—as a marker of Latin America's essential otherness.

Hence, a third premise: the spatial difference between the United States and its imperial object, Latin America, is also a thoroughly *racialized* construction of difference. Historically, the hegemony in the United States of a ruling class descended from northwestern Europe (predominantly Anglo-Saxon) has involved the continuous task of *producing* a national "majority" racialized as "white," against other colonized, enslaved, or in any case disproportionately working-class or impoverished groups who were variously racialized as something else and subordinated specifically on those "racial" grounds (Allen 1994 and 1997; Almaguer 1994; Foley 1997; Hale 1998; Horsman 1981; Ignatiev 1995; Jacobson 2000; Montejano 1987; Roediger 1991; Saxton 1971 and 1990; Takaki 1979). Whiteness, therefore, has never been a fact of nature; it is a fact of white supremacy. It is the naturalized but eminently social fact, produced historically to uphold and sustain a racist sociopolitical order through the U.S. nation-state's laborious efforts to homogenize the pronounced class differences among its "majority." Thus, the racial formation of a "white" majority has likewise entailed an ideological manufacture of "American" national identity and citizenship, which were themselves inherently racialized as well (Haney López 1996; Nelson 1998; R. M. Smith 1997). These constructions, of course, are never separable from the actual heterogeneity and stark inequalities to which those efforts are directed. To the contrary, and still more important, they are precisely part of a contradictory and conflict-ridden process in which homogenization is inseparable from the continuous production of the differences that demarcate the boundaries of that hegemonic whiteness, as well as the regimentation and subordination of the racialized heterogeneity so produced. The boundaries of racial whiteness have predictably been produced and policed *within* the social order of the U.S. nation-state, but the pervasive equation of whiteness with "American" national identity itself has also required that such racialized boundaries overlap with "national" frontiers and nation-state borders. The historical consolidation of white supremacy in the United States is inseparable, therefore, from the entire history of the westward colonization of the North American continent in the making of the United States as a "nation" (Berkhofer 1978; Churchill 1992; Drinnon 1980; Horsman 1981; Jennings 1976 and 2000; Slotkin 1973, 1985, and 1992).

One centrally significant feature of that colonial history, moreover, was the imperialist war against Mexico that secured for the expanding United States the vast territory that would come to be called the Southwest, and which summarily colonized a preexisting Mexican population that would thereafter be subjected to multiple clearly racialized forms of displacement, disenfranchisement, exploitation, and oppression. Characteristic of the colonialist racism that embellished this Mexican episode in the history of U.S. expansion, one participant on the Texas–Santa Fe expedition proclaimed: "There are no people on the continent of America, whether civilized or uncivilized, with one or two exceptions, more miserable in condition or despicable in morals than the mongrel race inhabiting New Mexico" (quoted in Horsman 1981, 212). The "national" difference between the United States and Mexico has, in effect, been racialized from its inception. Given the profound devotion in U.S. racial ideology to the notion of "purity," and thus the fierce prohibitions against racial "mixing" and intermarriage at the symbolic core of white-Black segregation in the U.S. social order, the perception of Mexicans as a "mongrel race"—that is, a quintessentially miscegenated people—readily condemned them to white racist contempt and revulsion (see Perea 2001; De Genova and Ramos-Zayas 2003a, 11–22; De Genova and Ramos-Zayas 2003b). During the congressional debates concerning the war against Mexico, U.S. Senator John Calhoun of South Carolina effectively extended this anti-Mexican racism to all of Latin America when he declared: "Ours, sir, is the Government of a white race. The greatest misfortunes of Spanish America are to be traced to the fatal error of placing these colored races on an equality with the white race" (quoted in Perea 2001, 146). Furthermore, the intrinsic significance for all of Latin America implied by this racist imperialism toward Mexico is well exemplified by the following invective, published in the *Illinois State Register* in June 1846: "The Mexicans . . . are reptiles in the path of progressive democracy —who, with his bigboots on, is bound to travel from Portland to Patagonia—and they must either crawl or be crushed" (quoted in Horsman 1981, 236). Notably, U.S. imperialism and its racial project of white supremacy are equated here, tellingly, with "progressive democracy," in the face of which Latin Americans, like so many Mexican "reptiles," would all have to either willingly submit or be annihilated. Predictably, Mexico has been recurrently construed as the threshold between the U.S. nation-state and Latin America as a whole. Indeed, over the course of U.S. history, the racial denigration of Mexican people has always had repercussions both inward, with respect to the racial subjugation of both migrant and U.S.-born Mexicans, and outward, toward Mexico and beyond. Thus, the formations and transformations of "American" white supremacy, as a national as well as imperial project, have been mutually constitutive.

The insurgent critique that characterized the formation of Chicano studies exposed and interrogated the United States' "national" claims to Mexican territories that it had invaded and colonized, as a prelude to its subsequent career of empire building throughout the rest of Latin America. By recourse to the critical perspectives that Chicano studies enables, I have interrogated the production of "Latin America" in terms of its spatialized as well as racialized difference from the United States, in the hope of enabling a critical standpoint from which to further disrupt the commonsense of U.S. imperialism. The U.S. imperial view takes as its first predication the integrity of the U.S. nation-state itself and cherishes an otherwise naturalized notion of Latin America as somehow "out there," always necessarily elsewhere—a logic that dictates that Chicago could not possibly be considered to belong, in some meaningful way, to Mexico. Although there is an extensive and prestigious body of anti-imperialist scholarship in Latin American studies, it is nevertheless exceedingly uncommon to find the relationship between the United States and Mexican nation-states problematized according to the protocols of the kind of anti-imperialist historical sensibility that informs so much of the foundational work of Chicano studies. Instead, scholars conventionally tend to leave intact the stable juxtaposition of two territory-based nation-states, leaving national space entirely dehistoricized. In this regard, the imperialistic conceptual foundations of Latin American studies have so thoroughly fixed the parameters of knowledge that even the more responsible scholarship tends to reinscribe and naturalize the border between the United States and Mexico.

Yet there are also limitations intrinsic to the conventional ways in which space was conceptualized within the Chicano studies project itself. If a Mexican Chicago violates the constitutive premises of Latin American studies, so it likewise presents a dilemma for Chicano studies. The intellectual formulation and academic institutionalization of Chicano studies in the late 1960s and early 1970s were inseparable from the radical *political* project of Chicano nationalism and the avowed activism of the Chicano Movement across the Southwest (Muñoz 1989). One of the hallmarks of that movement was its bold confrontation with the racial oppression intrinsic to the Mexican experience in the United States. Rejecting the dominant mythology of the melting pot and its inherent assimilationism, the Chicano Movement asserted a new "Chicano" identity for Mexicans in the United States,[6] commonly cultivated a nationalist sensibility, and frequently articulated a separatism based on theories of the Chicano community as an internal colony (Barrera 1979; Barrera, Muñoz, and Ornelas 1972). Notably, for my purposes, such expressions of Chicano separatism involved a very pronounced politics of space: they generally culminated in a program of radical self-determination and national liberation that reclaimed the territory of the Southwest and renamed it Aztlán (see Anaya and Lomelí 1991).

There has long been much debate among scholars in the field about what may be legitimately considered Chicano studies. Vital controversies surrounding what is and is not appropriate for study persist, ultimately, as symptoms of conflict and crisis that are truly signs of health and renewal. For my purposes, what will serve as a basic working definition of what may be validly considered Chicano studies scholarship is not merely research concerned with Mexicans (or Chicanos), but rather scholarship that (a) takes as a fundamental premise that the U.S. colonization of Mexican territory and the subsequent legacy of racial oppression have an enduring relevance for the experiences of *all* Mexicans in the United States, and (b) self-consciously posits its intellectual enterprise as one that is politically committed to one or another project of radical social critique.

Given that the anticolonial spatial imagination of the Chicano nationalist paradigm commonly resulted in a rather narrow emphasis on the U.S. Southwest, Chicago never enjoyed an easy or secure place in the dreaming of the Chicano homeland Aztlán. The seeming incommensurability of Chicago with the mythic image of Aztlán resides precisely in the tension between Mexican Chicago's origins in twentieth-century labor migrations and the indigenist claims of a more conventional Chicano nationalism, distinguished by a territorial orientation to the occupied, colonized lands pillaged from Mexico during the nineteenth century. With great rhetorical emphasis on the historical priority and multigenerational longevity of Mexicans in that region, most of the explicitly Chicano-identified scholarship consciously explored themes related to Mexican experiences situated geographically in what was recast as "the American Southwest." Thus, Chicago has long been rather incidental—if not invisible—in most Chicano studies research (see Valdés 2000).[7] Consequently, conceptualizing the ways in which Chicago might be figured as a *theoretical* (and not merely empirical) question for Chicano studies has remained a complicated proposition.[8]

My critique is selectively focused on the specifically *spatial* presuppositions of Chicano studies, as originally formulated through the insurgent lens of a subaltern nationalism. On the one hand, that perspective has enabled an enduring anti-imperialist standpoint of critique that remains a vital conceptual resource for my own work. Yet, on the other hand, its specifically nationalist commitments characteristically fell short of a more far-reaching global articulation of its antagonism to U.S. imperial power, in favor of a more restricted claim to Chicano historical priority and prerogative within a particular territory.[9] The most rigorous and substantial critiques of Chicano nationalism have indisputably come from Chicana feminists, who have extensively problematized its masculinist and heteronormative assumptions.[10] These critiques, often following the theoretical appeals of lesbian feminist Gloria Anzaldúa (1983 and

1987), have likewise problematized characteristically nationalist obsessions with "authenticity" and "purity," as well as preoccupations with the conquest of territory, in favor of reconceptualizations of Chicana/o identity in terms of the inescapable hybridity (*mestizaje*) associated with the social conditions of life in cultural and political "borderlands."[11] Certainly, these various gestures toward a reconceptualization of the dominant spatial paradigm in Chicano studies have already anticipated some of the specific concerns of my critique, but there tends to be a rather persistent and vexing epistemological attachment between even the most fluid and metaphorical notions of "borderlands" and the more bluntly literal geographical reference point of the physical border between the United States and Mexico (see Alvarez 1995). Indeed, even in Anzaldúa's seminal and remarkably influential interpretation of the borderlands, there is an explicit and ultimately unresolved tension between "the actual physical borderland" of "the Texas-U.S. Southwest/Mexican border" and the purely metaphorical ("psychological," "sexual," "spiritual," "cultural," and "linguistic," as well as class- and race-inflected) borderlands that she posits as a shrinking space of intimate confrontation and encounter, effectively between any two individuals or social groups (1987). Anzaldúa's lyrical evocation of the U.S.-Mexico border as "an open wound" where "two worlds [merge] to form *a third country*" (1987, 2–3; emphasis added), however, like Rudolfo Anaya's proposition that "Aztlán can become *the nation* that mediates between Anglo-America and Latin America" (1991, 241; emphasis added), suggests still more metaphysical renovations of the fundamental territorial premises of Chicano nationalism. Yet, even in Cherríe Moraga's lesbian feminist reformulation of Chicano nationalism and her call for a distinctly Queer Aztlán (1993, 145–74), the Chicano homeland is still stubbornly equated with "that place—that 'sacred landscape' . . . of the North American Southwest" (150).[12] Conversely, taking a cue from Moraga's potentially deterritorializing analogy between the colonized land of the Chicano nation and the colonized bodies of women, lesbians, and gay men (150), whereby land is "more than . . . the territory of Aztlán" but also "that physical mass called our bodies" (173), and following Sergio Elizondo's plea for a more mobile understanding of the concept of Aztlán (1991, 217), it might nonetheless be possible to stretch the metaphor of Aztlán to wherever Mexican people migrate. In light of such intrinsic contradictions, however, it may be necessary to rethink the mythic narrative of Aztlán altogether, so that the critical impulse that has driven the Chicano studies project might be

retooled for the more complicated and bewildering sociospatial configuration that today more than ever has inextricably interwoven Mexico
and the United States and has transcended the traditional terrain of the
Chicano Southwest (see Saldívar 1991, xi). The tension between Mexican
Chicago and conventional understandings of what is a proper or authentic place for "Chicano" concerns, therefore, can provide an instructive
standpoint of critique from which to pose questions about the present
and future complications of Chicano studies.

One revealing exception to the general omission of Mexican Chicago
in the founding Chicano studies literature is Armando Rendón's *Chicano
Manifesto* (1971). Chicago's absence from most of the early writings of the
Chicano Movement is notably complemented by its striking prominence
in Rendón's discrepant account. On the one hand, Rendón predictably
characterizes the states of the Southwest as those that "generally describe
Aztlán" (1971, 17), but his simultaneous assertion that "we need not seek a
geographic center for Aztlán; it lies within ourselves, and it is boundless,
immeasurable" (16) established him as an early precursor of more deter-
ritorialized visions of the Chicano national project.[13] Indeed, Rendón's
chapter "The Chicano Nation" is distinguished above all by the effort to
figure the Chicano (or the Mexican American) as "a national person"
whose "strivings have taken him to every part of the land" rather than "a
regional problem to be solved on a regional basis" (17–18). Thus, the
Chicano "nation" is figured not in narrowly regional (Southwestern)
terms but rather as prospectively encompassing nothing less than the
space of the U.S. nation-state itself. In this light, Rendón poses the question of U.S. Mexican communities outside of the Southwest—the "norteño Chicanos"—as a decisive political problem for the Chicano Movement (21–22). Indeed, Rendón figures Chicago's Mexican community in
particular as the paradigmatic exemplar.

Notably, in the *Chicano Manifesto*, Mexicans in Chicago come to em-
body a depoliticizing "repatriation syndrome" attributed to *migrants*
who cannot relinquish the dream of an eventual "return to Mexico"—"a
limbo of expectation" that is manifested as an aversion to naturalizing as
U.S. citizens and equated with political complacency (Rendón 1971, 22–
27). Further, Rendón laments "the trap of a Chicago" for the "factionalism" and "irrational fissions" that divide Mexico-identified migrants,
insular Texas-identified Chicanos who have settled out of the migratory
stream, and "the native-born Mexican Americans, politically aware, conscious of the social problems surrounding them, seeking outlets for their

frustration" (27–28). The remedy that Rendón nonetheless proposes for such fragmentation among "norteño Chicanos" is, predictably, "realization and acceptance of a universal Chicanismo" (28). In "the trap of a Chicago," however, with its tensions between Mexican migrants and Chicano natives, Rendón discerns an "exciting . . . fluid microcosm of what is happening or has happened in many other Mexican American barrios" (33). Although Mexican Chicago is figured in the *Chicano Manifesto* as marginal—the epitome of "the norteño Chicano . . . at the fringe, not merely geographically, but philosophically and organizationally, of the Chicano revolt"—Rendón finally saw promise in the "Little Mexico" that Chicago could sustain: "The Chicano life style may be even stronger, since its roots are derived so directly yet are so severely isolated from the Mexican sources" (1971, 32–33). Thus, the disproportionate salience of contemporary migration and the evidences of migrant transnationalism, which inspired Rendón's account of Mexican Chicago's vexing "repatriation syndrome" and its marginal relation to the politics of Chicanismo, finally, were also equivocally figured as the prospective source of a renewed vitality.

Mexican migration has often been treated as a merely passive source of specifically "Chicano" renewal. As Moraga contends (1993, 155), for instance, "A new generation of future Chicanos arrives everyday with every Mexican immigrant." Yet much of the scholarship that is explicitly self-identified as Chicano studies has generally taken as its principal concern the experiences of U.S.-born, U.S.-raised "Chicanos," with a considerably more subdued and somewhat ambivalent interest in Mexican migration per se. This is not to say that research in Chicano studies has simply ignored migration, but rather that the specificity of Mexican/migrant experiences has often been rhetorically folded into a more prominent narrative about the civil rights struggles of "Chicanos" as a U.S.-citizen "minority" group. Historical scholarship in particular is the branch of Chicano studies that has most readily subsumed migrants from Mexico in depictions of a Chicano people, but this form of inclusion has tended to blur the substantive distinctions and potential conflicts between migrants from Mexico and Mexicans born or raised in the United States.[14] Certainly, the inclusive gesture that represents unitary Mexican/Chicano communities has not been entirely unwarranted. Indubitably, migrants and U.S.-born Mexicans have often lived and worked in close proximity, and commonly are neighbors if not members of the same families. Furthermore, their racialization, in particular, has very readily defined a common plight for both U.S.-born and migrant Mexicans—the shared condition prioritized, for example, through the use of *la Raza* as a preferred nomenclature for the Mexican/Chicano polity.[15] Nevertheless, the substantive sociopolitical distinctions between migrant and U.S.-born Mexicans persist, along with all the consequent incongruities and plausible antagonisms that result from those distinctions (Foley 1998; D. Gutiérrez 1995; Heyman 2002; Vila 2000). And these divisions—what Rendón decried as "factionalism" and "fissions"—beg the analytical question: Where does *lo mexicano* end and *lo chicano* begin? One representational strategy (that most favored by scholars who deploy the category "Chicano" to encompass *all* Mexicans in the United States) relies, at least by implication, upon the proposition that this transition occurs as soon as *mexicanos* cross the border, such that mere presence in the United States reconstitutes Mexicans as Chicanos. Another option (revealing a more conventionally sociological tendency) would focus instead upon the implicit and seemingly inevitable rupture between those same Mexican migrants and the "Chicano" (or, "Mexican American") children they raise in a "foreign" sociocultural environment. Still a third alternative would definitively ground Chicano identity in political struggle, and a feeling of belonging that is presumed to follow from the sense of entitlement authorized by actively making claims against the U.S. state. Moraga, for example, speaks explicitly of political radicalization in terms of a transition "when the Mexican ceases to be a Mexican and becomes a Chicano" (1993, 154); through her political militancy, "the Mexicana becomes a Chicana . . . that is, she becomes a citizen of this country, not by virtue of a green card, but by virtue of the collective voice she assumes in staking her claim to this land and its resources" (1993, 156).[16] Notably, the explicit problem of a divisive politics of citizenship, which systematically distinguishes and substantively separates most Mexican migrants from U.S.-born Mexicans, is resolved here only by an analytic evasion that treats "citizenship" in metaphorical terms. Finally, all three of these conceptions nevertheless rest upon a common premise—namely, they assume a radical and irreducible *spatial* discontinuity between the United States and Mexico. The first notion imputes a mysterious power to the border, such that the mere act of crossing it more or less automatically accomplishes a Mexican migrant's transformation into a Chicano. The second approach, relying upon conventional understandings of "the assimilation process," imagines Mexican migrants to be doubly condemned, both as more or less permanently displaced persons and as inescapably estranged from their own "Americanized" children. The third option implicitly recapitulates Rendón's notion of Mexican migrants' supposedly depoliticizing "repatriation syndrome," such that the political identity of "Chicano" signals a kind of de facto citizenship in the United States that follows from an acceptance of the United States as the primary, if not exclusive, sociopolitical frame of reference. In other words, no matter how one might define *Chicano*, and in spite of the founding transnational principle of *un pueblo sin fronteras* (one people without borders), the basic *spatial* premise of Chicano studies seems nonetheless to have consistently taken for granted the fixity (in the present) of an absolute separation between Mexico and the United States.[17] Still more important, that one-sided conceptual divide has persistently presupposed the U.S. nation-state as its defining and conclusive spatial and sociopolitical frame of reference.

Insofar as Chicano studies—as a mode of inquiry, an intellectual project, a standpoint of critique, and a position for political action—is founded upon an interrogation of the imperialist character of the westward expansion of the United States, it supplies a precious critical resource for disrupting and problematizing precisely such conventions. My aim therefore is to question and challenge the ways in which Chicano studies has nonetheless been confined within the boundaries of the U.S. nation-state. By foregrounding the systemic social and political inequality that has defined the predominant historical experience of Mexicans in the United States, Chicano studies' overtly antiracist, antiassimilationist intellectual premises have long provided a crucial alternative to the type of "ethnic saga" that might otherwise be construed as "Mexican American" in the hegemonic idiom of "Americanization." Furthermore, Chicano studies has embodied a bold effort at self-representation, not only against cultural invisibility, marginalization, and criminalization in the United States (see Blea 1988; Gómez-Quiñones 1977 and 1982; Madrid-Barela 1973b; Mirandé 1985; Montiel 1970; Rocco 1976; Romano-V 1968 and 1970; Vaca 1970a and 1970b), but also against the elitist class biases and Eurocentric cultural and racial chauvinism of earlier Mexican intellectuals' commonly disparaging accounts of Chicano "inauthenticity" (see Limón 1989; Madrid-Barela 1973a). Despite the vital necessity for the kinds of critical inquiry that has distinguished the field, however, Chicano studies' exclusive concern in the final analysis has largely resided *within* the United States, in a manner that is analogous to Latin American studies' defining and conclusive preoccupation with that which resides *outside* of it. The transnationalization of Mexican labor, which is at the heart of the production of a Mexican Chicago, requires us to reconsider the territorial confinements at stake in both of these perspectives.

Finally, it is necessary to examine one further conceptual framework that likewise impedes a genuine appreciation of the critical promise of this Mexican Chicago: the conventional inclination to treat the spaces of Mexican migrants in the United States as mere "immigrant" enclaves, predictably, either subjected to the inexorable assimilating forces of "Americanization" or stubbornly impervious to such influences in favor of pathological "ethnic" insularity. Mexican Chicago is no mere "immigrant" ghetto. The influential Chicago School of urban sociology promoted a purportedly "ecological" perspective that understood "the city" as a singular, universal, evolutionary, and natural fact, described as "a product of *nature*, and particularly of human nature," and as "the *natural* habitat of civilized man." This universalistic theoretical outlook was coupled, however, with ethnographic techniques, explicitly intended to emulate Boasian cultural anthropology's studies of "primitive peoples,"[18] such that the city could also be understood to be "a *natural* distribution of cultural isolation," "a complex of distinct social worlds which touch but never completely penetrate, each with its own scheme of life, separated by distances which are not geographical but social."[19] This conceptual framework served above all else to *naturalize* the spatial configurations of social inequality that are the hallmark of capitalist urbanism. The conflicting productions of urban space seemed to vanish, and what remained was "the city as a social laboratory" (Park 1929), where controlled experiments could be directed at controlling the "disorganization" and "pathologies" of migrants and others who appeared to be insufficiently assimilated.

To invoke a Mexican Chicago is not to invent a virtual island, or any other kind of discrete village-like space. Such would be the ethnographic never-never-land of distinctly sociological and anthropological fairy tales in American studies: a mythic place of essentialized and homogeneous "culture," in an inevitably naturalized and self-contained relationship to its bounded spatial location, merely situated in the context of the wider city, the broader U.S. social formation, and "modernity" in general. Urban anthropology has commonly involved something like a traditionally conceived "island" ethnography that simply happened to be conducted in an urban setting (see Hannerz 1980). Reproducing the presuppositions of the Chicago School's sociology, urban anthropology long relied upon the developmental paradigm of a "folk-urban continuum" that combined the functionalist illusion of discrete, synchronic, essential "cultures" with an evolutionist "civilizational" framework that sought to integrate these "folk traditions" into a larger narrative of "modernization."[20] Urban spaces were thus tautologically conflated with the ideological figures of modernity and progress and radically removed from their specific histories (Cohn 1987, 27). The conceptual stepchildren of these premises included such regrettable oxymoronic inventions as "urban villagers," "peasants in the city," and "men of two worlds." The city thereby tended to be reduced to an abstract container that accumulates naturalized sociocultural processes, indeed, a mere "context"—virtual background noise against which more familiar, holistic, "cultural" units could be put in their place and isolated for ethnographic objectification.

What my proposition of a Mexican Chicago is intended to suggest is precisely *not* the old-fashioned anthropological conceit about the essential durability and reproducibility of "culture" (in this case, that of Mexicans). Such culturalist constructions of Mexican communities in the United States can come dangerously close to the long-standing racist premise in U.S. immigration politics that Mexicans are "inassimilable" into the presumed "mainstream of American life" (as seen in chapter 2).[21] Inevitably related to such conventional notions of a monolithic and unchanging "Mexican culture" that encompasses Mexican people wherever they may go, furthermore, is the presumption that people and "culture" are likewise inseparable from the particular *place* they inhabit. Mexican migrants in Chicago would thus be positively enclosed by their own virtually impermeable space of "cultural" isolation, and the city would merely appear to be a negative field, where a discrete and essential "Mexican" social life happens to take place. Mexican Chicago is not so localized as to readily permit such fantasies; the physical coordinates of its innumerable localities are much more elusive. Indeed, Mexican Chicago is not reducible to any particular location as such. But even in the several neighborhoods that are inhabited almost exclusively by Mexicans, this would be a gross misrepresentation of the material and practical everyday life of Mexican Chicago.

Instead, Mexican Chicago is better understood as a spatial conjuncture of *social relations* that thus comprises innumerable places. It is a conjuncture, furthermore, constituted through the everyday social relations and meaningful practices that comprise the intersection of a transnational labor migration, capitalist enterprises, and the U.S. nation-state. There could not possibly exist within Chicago an idyllic Mexican "cultural" space, conceived to be somehow autonomous of the profound social inequality of Mexican migrants' subordination as racialized labor for the requirements of capital accumulation, or separable from the systemic violence of the U.S. nation-state's regulation and regimentation of their particular migrant condition. Mexican migration to Chicago thus partakes of an active reworking and (re)production of social space itself. As a result, Chicago and Mexico have come to be inextricably implicated into one another. As urban space, Chicago itself is continuously *produced* (and reconfigured) through the contradictions of struggles in which migrants are centrally implicated—where Mexican communities themselves can be constituted not in isolation but indeed only in the midst of social conflict. "Space's investment—the production of space—has nothing incidental about it," argues Henri Lefebvre, "it is a matter of life and death" ([1974] 1991, 417).

THE HISTORICAL PRODUCTIONS OF MEXICAN CHICAGO

As a privileged site in the historical development of North American capitalism, Chicago was always linked to the effectively transnational colonization of the North American continent by U.S. imperialism (Cronon 1991). Moreover, as a major industrial center, Chicago has been a premier destination for labor migrations throughout most of its history. As the United States' quintessential railroad metropolis during the nineteenth century and the early decades of the twentieth century (Cronon 1991, 55–93), Chicago quickly became an important (one might say inevitable) destination for Mexican migrant labor, the early patterns of which so thoroughly corresponded to the expansion of railroads (Año Nuevo Kerr 1976; Cardoso 1980; Reisler 1976a; Rosales 1978; and see Clark [1908] 1974; Jones [1928] 1971; Gamio [1930] 1971; Taylor 1932). By 1890, every railroad in Mexico was connected directly or indirectly to all forty-eight states of the continental United States (Cardoso 1980, 14–17), and Chicago was the breaking point throughout the nineteenth century for literally every rail network between the eastern and western United States (Cronon 1991, 83). At least as early as 1907, Mexican/migrant workers were employed by the railroads in Chicago (Clark [1908] 1974, 477).

The Mexican presence in Chicago first achieved a notable size in 1916 (Taylor 1932, 27). During World War I, Mexican migrants were originally enlisted into the service of U.S. industry as a reserve labor supply comprised of "temporary" or "replacement" workers who were needed to alleviate labor shortages caused by the exigencies of war-related production, and after the U.S. entry into active participation in combat, due to the mass transfer of male U.S. citizen workers into military service. Notably, during the strike wave of 1919, Mexicans were again enthusiastically recruited on deliberately racial grounds alongside African Americans from the southern United States to migrate, often initially as strikebreakers, as an alternate labor reserve for large industry, especially in steel, meatpacking, and the railroads (Taylor 1932, 117; see Año Nuevo Kerr 1976, 25–26; Calavita 1984, 135–37, 147–51; Necoechea Gracia 1998; Rosales 1978, 92–93). Despite the purportedly "temporary" status of Mexican labor, however, already as early as the 1920s, the largest single employer of Mexican migrants anywhere in the United States was Inland Steel's mill in East Chicago, Indiana, an industrial suburb southeast of Chicago. Inland had first hired Mexican/migrant workers during the national steel strike of 1919 and then summarily fired almost all of them after the strike was over; the company soon revised its hiring strategies, however, and by 1925, 35 percent of Inland's work force was Mexican (Rosales 1978, 145). By 1928, Mexican/migrant workers accounted for 43 percent of all railroad track labor and 11 percent of total employment in the most important steel and meatpacking plants. With two-thirds of the Mexican working-age population "unskilled" (the highest rate for any group in the city), the disproportionate majority worked in low-wage positions, and two-thirds of Mexican families were likewise relegated to living below the poverty level (Taylor 1932, 41, 77–79, 155, 157; see Año Nuevo Kerr 1976, 25–26; Arredondo 1999, 124).

From only 1,000 Mexicans in Chicago before 1916, the community had grown to over 25,000 in 1930, by which time there were established barrios on Chicago's South Side—near rail yards in the vicinity of Jane Addams's Hull House in the southern portion of the Near West Side, in the shadow of steel mills in the South Chicago neighborhood, and in the Back of the Yards area next to the Union stockyards and meatpacking houses (Jones 1928; Taylor 1932; and see Año Nuevo Kerr 1975; Arredondo 1999). By the mid-1920s, largely because they lived in close proximity with whites and were perceived to be competitors for whites' jobs, the arrest rates and levels of police violence against them were higher for Mexicans in Chicago than for Mexicans in the Southwest. Indeed, although arrested predominantly for rather minor offenses, Mexicans' arrest rates and the proportion of Mexicans killed by police surpassed those of virtually every other migrant group in Chicago (Rosales 1999, 28, 51–54, 79–80, 84; see Arredondo 1999,

171–75). In addition to mutual aid associations, community-based organizations emerged with the express purpose of defending Mexicans' legal rights (Rosales 1999, 28). However, in striking contrast to many "Mexican American" organizations in the Southwest, which often obliged members to be or to become U.S. citizens, Chicago's Mexican community organizing efforts in this period tended to repudiate assimilatory pressures toward naturalization and even restricted membership to Mexican citizens (J. García 1996, 162–63). As Gabriela Arredondo has demonstrated persuasively, already during this early period, there had arisen among Mexican migrants in Chicago "a tentative, transnational *Mexicanidad*" (1999, 12), which was inseparable from processes of racial formation whereby "Mexican"-ness had emerged as a subordinate racialized category situated uneasily between whiteness and Blackness (9, 156), and increasingly treated not only as "not-assimilable but also not-American and 'alien'" (18).

During the economic recession of 1921 and 1922, 65 percent of the Mexicans in Chicago lost their jobs, registering the highest unemployment levels for any group. While some opted to return to Mexico, others were forcibly repatriated (Taylor 1932, 39, 277–78; see Betancur, Cordova, and Torres 1993, 114). Notably, Mexicans' rate for naturalizing as U.S. citizens was the lowest among all migrant groups (Arredondo 1999, 115). With the advent of the Great Depression, by 1930, Mexican unemployment was second only to that of African Americans (124). Now, however, Mexicans were targeted nationally for mass expulsion. In 1930 alone, nearly 22,000 Mexicans (migrants as well as their U.S.-born children) were repatriated or forcibly deported from Illinois; although Mexicans in Illinois accounted for only 2 percent of the total U.S. Mexican population in 1930, the number expelled from Illinois comprised 5.3 percent of all Mexicans repatriated. Due to the forced removals of both Mexican migrants and their U.S. citizen children during the 1930s, Chicago's Mexican community was reduced by at least 36 percent to 16,000 by the end of the decade (Año Nuevo Kerr 1976, 69–77; Weber 1982, 213–69). With the advent of World War II and the commencement of the Bracero Program, however, Chicago's Mexican population began to rapidly grow again, especially with the added influx of more than 15,000 braceros contracted to work on the railroads (Año Nuevo Kerr 1976, 121; 1977).[22] Indeed, in the wake of severe labor shortages and the consequently competitive position of labor, a railroad industry study contended that the very low prevailing wage would suffice to attract U.S. citizen workers to fill only 5 percent of the necessary track maintenance labor (Año Nuevo Kerr 1977, 274). After a decade marred by mass deportations, so began anew the enthusiastic mass importation of Mexican migrant workers at state-regulated low wages to supply one of the most degraded forms of manual labor. Between mid-1943 and the autumn of 1945, the Chicago district (which included Wisconsin and Iowa, as well as northern Illinois) accounted for 11 percent of the total number of braceros contracted nationally (Año Nuevo Kerr 1976, 121). In the purported interest of "national security," however, defense-related industries seeking to exclude workers deemed to be potentially "subversive" sometimes made U.S. citizenship (or at least registration in a naturalization program) a requirement of employment during the war. As a consequence of this equation of "security" with U.S. citizenship, the great majority of Mexicans, including long-term Chicago-resident Mexicans who were undocumented, had only extremely limited access, if any, to the better wages that had come with wartime prosperity.[23] Thus, despite the renewed demand for their labor, little had changed for the overall situation of Mexicans in Chicago: a 1944 survey of employers during World War II established that Mexican workers continued to be predominantly concentrated in "unskilled" jobs in the same three industries where they or their predecessors had first been installed twenty-five years earlier during and immediately following World War I (Año Nuevo Kerr 1976, 143; 1977, 287).[24]

Although the provision of braceros to the railroad industry in Chicago was terminated with the end of World War II, the reenergized migration to Chicago continued unabated. By 1947, Inland Steel was once again recruiting and transporting Mexican workers from Texas as strikebreakers (Año Nuevo Kerr 1977, 295). Later that same year (notably, on Mexican Independence Day, September 16), the *Chicago Tribune* made what was probably its first report of the apprehension of "illegal Mexican aliens" in the city (Año Nuevo Kerr 1976, 131, 162; 1977, 281, 590).[25] Between 1940 and 1960, the Mexican population in the city more than tripled to 55,600. Newly arrived migrants rapidly outnumbered long-term Chicago-resident Mexican migrants and their U.S.-born children during this period (Año Nuevo Kerr 1977, 296). The most dramatic acceleration of Mexican migration to Chicago, however, would begin only in the late 1960s and early 1970s. Between 1960 and 1990, the Mexican population residing within the municipal boundaries of the city increased by more than six times—from 55,600 to 352,560—and by nearly ten times— to 550,000—in the Chicago metropolitan area. According to the U.S.

Census for the year 2000, Chicago is the second largest urban concentration of Mexican residence in the country (following Los Angeles), with numbers over 1.1 million in the metropolitan area, and as many as 625,000 in the city.[26] Mexicans alone comprise 18.3 percent of the population within the city limits. Notably, in 1980, the city's Mexican community was 48 percent "foreign-born" (Caruso and Camacho 1985, 9). By 2000, migrants constituted an even greater proportion of Chicago's Mexican population: 55 percent in the city, and 52 percent in the metropolitan area, were "foreign-born."[27] Thus, after more than eighty-five years of Mexican community formation in Chicago, the absolute majority continues to be comprised of those who have themselves migrated from Mexico, and a strikingly disproportionate majority are either migrants or the children of migrants.

Over the course of the twentieth century, the historic Mexican barrios of Chicago's South Side dramatically expanded into distinctively Mexican working-class and working-poor neighborhoods. Although the stockyards and major meatpacking companies shut down their Chicago operations and had almost completely relocated by the 1950s, and the railroads and steel became virtually moribund industries that no longer hire much newly arrived migrant labor in the city, these same historically Mexican neighborhoods have continued to sustain vibrant communities. The barrio on the far Southeast Side of the city, where Mexicans first settled due to employment at U.S. Steel's South Works, over time, came to encompass a significant portion of the community area known as South Chicago (see Kornblum 1974). Indeed, by 1980, due to the decline of the steel industry during the 1970s and the rapid and large-scale evacuation of the neighborhood by long-term white residents, known colloquially as "white flight," as well as continued and heightened migration from Mexico, South Chicago became predominantly African American (47.8 percent) and Latino (39.3 percent), with Mexicans making up 85.8 percent of Latinos. By 2000, despite the persistence of two majority-Mexican census tracts in the South Chicago neighborhood, much of the area's historical Mexican community had relocated to the adjacent East Side, South Deering, and Hegewisch community areas.[28] In the East Side neighborhood, notably, Mexicans have ascended to an absolute majority (60 percent).

The small Mexican community that originally was relegated to the most foul-smelling residential enclave immediately adjacent to the stockyards and meatpacking plants, in spite of the demise of Chicago's meatpacking industry in the 1950s and in the wake of accelerated migration during the 1970s, ultimately came to encompass most of the neighborhood that continues to be known as the Back of the Yards (within the community area officially designated New City by the Chicago Department of Planning).[29] Similar to the South Chicago experience, New City was distinguished during the 1970s by dramatic racial succession, as its overall composition was radically reconstituted from a predominantly white neighborhood to two starkly distinct neighborhoods, one predominantly Mexican and the other African American, severely partitioned by racial segregation.[30] According to the 2000 census, half of the area's population is Latino (of whom 90 percent are Mexican). A third of its total population, furthermore, live in six tracts that are 85–95 percent Latino, while another third reside in eight tracts that are more than 78 percent African American, including four that are 95–98 percent Black. Even as the New City community area's total population continued a long-term trend of slow but steady decline during the 1990s, furthermore, the Mexican population in the Back of the Yards neighborhood nonetheless registered a remarkable increase of roughly 25 percent.

Long considered to be the most important "port of entry" neighborhood for newly arrived Mexican migrants, the Near West Side (Hull House) neighborhood, where Mexican migrants first settled because of its proximity to railroad yards, was ultimately decimated by "urban renewal" projects associated with the construction of expressways and the University of Illinois's Chicago campus during the 1950s and 1960s (Rosen 1980). Much of its Mexican community, however, was merely displaced to the adjacent Lower West Side community area, immediately to the south and southwest, better known as Pilsen, or later, as *La Dieciocho* (the Eighteenth Street barrio). Whereas Pilsen had been only 0.5 percent Mexican in 1950, it had become 14 percent Mexican within ten years (Belenchia 1977, 21) and 55 percent Mexican by 1970. Pivotal in this rapid growth of Pilsen's Mexican community were the 22 percent who had migrated from Mexico only within the five-year period since 1965 (Año Nuevo Kerr 1976, 194). Not only the largest Mexican neighborhood and among the city's poorest in 1970, Pilsen was also the only Chicago neighborhood where Latinos had come to constitute an absolute majority. Likewise, the Pilsen community increasingly extended itself further westward and transformed the South Lawndale area into what has since come to be known as Little Village, or *La Villita*. Notably, even as early as 1970, South Lawndale was already 32 percent Mexican (Belenchia 1982, 126). By 1980, the Latino proportion of South Lawndale's population was more than 74 percent, having achieved virtual parity with Pilsen, where the Latino population had reached 77.6 percent. Between 1960 and 1980, the combined Mexican population of Pilsen and Little Village sky-rocketed from slightly under 7,000 to more than 83,000, with nearly one-fourth of all housing units officially overcrowded (Caruso and Camacho 1985, 8). By 1990, the number of Mexicans in Pilsen and Little Village had increased again to more than 101,000, and by the year 2000, had risen further to nearly 105,000, despite population densities among the highest in the city.[31] The disproportionate majority lived in twenty census tracts that were more than 90 percent Latino, and another ten that were at least 65 percent Latino. In both Pilsen and Little Village, moreover, Mexicans alone comprised 92 percent or more of the total Latino population.[32]

While Chicago's Southside Mexican communities generally continued to expand and surpass the delimited boundaries of their historically identifiable spaces during the latter decades of the twentieth century, continued migration also meant a burgeoning of Mexican communities on the city's North Side as well. Between 1970 and 1980, in the historically most significant neighborhoods of Puerto Rican concentration on Chicago's Near Northwest Side (Humboldt Park, West Town, and Logan Square), the Mexican population nearly quadrupled. By 1990, within these three contiguous neighborhoods, Mexicans had virtually reached parity with Puerto Ricans. As of U.S. Census 2000, Mexicans had become the majority among Latinos in *all* of the historically Puerto Rican neigh-borhoods on the North Side, as well as in the adjacent areas of more recent Puerto Rican resettlement (De Genova and Ramos-Zayas 2003a; Ramos-Zayas 2003). Thus, while Chicago's Southside Latino commu-nities have remained in fact overwhelmingly Mexican in contrast with the rather mixed Latino neighborhoods on the city's North Side, Mexicans have nonetheless become the preponderant group in virtually all areas of high Latino concentration.

Mexican Chicago similarly burgeoned in the city's suburbs. During the 1970s, either following the factory jobs out of the "inner city" or arriving directly from Mexico to satisfy the labor requirements of man-ufacturing plants that had been relocated outside of the city, the number of Mexicans in Chicago's suburbs more than quadrupled, from 25,555 to over 113,000 by 1980 (Squires et al. 1987, 111).[33] By 2000, that number had quadrupled again, perhaps to as much as 461,000 in the more proximate suburbs of Chicago's primary metropolitan statistical area, alone.[34] Thus, there has developed a quite significant Mexican presence throughout much of the metropolitan area that renders anachronistic, at best, any effort to circumscribe Chicago's Mexican communities within the original barrios on the city's South Side, or even to confine them, more generally, within historically Latino urban neighborhoods.[35] Instead, alongside a city where 500,000–600,000 Mexicans constitute slightly less than 20 percent of the total population, there are likewise another 500,000–600,000 Mexicans forming a constellation of suburban working-class Mexican communities, distributed in all directions across the greater (consolidated) metropolitan region (see map). Indeed, the Chicago metropolitan area includes at least twenty suburban towns and small satellite cities (with a combined Mexican population of 265,000) in each of which Mexicans constitute at least 20 percent of the population. In two of these suburbs, moreover, Mexicans are the absolute majority.[36]

All of these indices serve to underscore the fact that Chicago has been an increasingly prominent destination for Mexican/migrant labor in the United States, even as the total population of the city declined during the latter decades of the twentieth century in the wake of a dramatic loss of jobs in manufacturing (Betancur, Cordova, and Torres 1993; see Squires et al. 1987, 23–60). Finally, then, it is necessary to recognize the emergence and explore the significance of a Mexican Chicago that encompasses the full extent of the metropolitan region. In 1995, Edmundo, a migrant in his midtwenties who had been in the United States five years, living in East Chicago, Indiana, and working at the Caustic Scrub plant in Chicago saw things this way: "Almost all of Mexico is here in Chicago. Everywhere you go, almost, you see Mexicans and taquerías. Yes, there are Blacks [*morenos*] and whites [*güeros*] in some parts—some small areas— but almost everywhere, it's Mexican!"

A metropolitan Mexican *Chicago* emerges; it begins to be possible to discern its complex and convoluted outline. The everyday life practices of migrants produce a living space throughout metropolitan Chicago that conjoins it irreversibly to Mexico and renders it potentially irretrievable for the U.S. nation-state. In effect, Mexican Chicago's relationship to a more generic Chicago is analogous to Chicago's relationship to Latin America; both defy the segregationist's metaphysics of flat cartographic modes of knowing, so dear to the programmatic paradigms of anthropology and area studies alike (see Malkki 1992). A Chicago that belongs to Mexico, a Chicago that can be claimed for Latin America, does not cease to be confined within the domain of the United States, but it is likewise

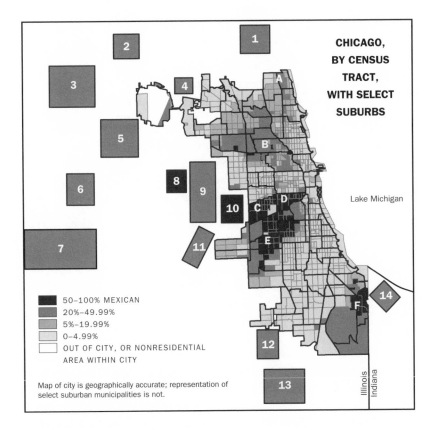

CHICAGO,
BY CENSUS
TRACT,
WITH SELECT
SUBURBS

Lake Michigan

50–100% MEXICAN
20%–49.99%
5%–19.99%
0–4.99%
OUT OF CITY, OR NONRESIDENTIAL
AREA WITHIN CITY

Map of city is geographically accurate; representation of
select suburban municipalities is not.

Illinois
Indiana

SELECT CHICAGO COMMUNITY AREAS

A   ROGER'S PARK

B   WEST TOWN, HUMBOLDT PARK, LOGAN SQUARE

C   SOUTH LAWNDALE (A.K.A. LITTLE VILLAGE)

D   LOWER WEST SIDE (A.K.A. PILSEN)

E   BRIGHTON PARK, NEW CITY, GAGE PARK

F   SOUTH CHICAGO, EAST SIDE

SELECT SUBURBAN MUNICIPALITIES

1	WAUKEGAN	7	AURORA
2	ROUND LAKE BEACH, ROUND LAKE PARK	8	STONE PARK
		9	MELROSE PARK, BERWYN
3	ELGIN	10	CICERO
4	ROSEMONT	11	HODGKINS, STICKNEY, SUMMIT
5	BENSENVILLE, ADDISON, NORTH LAKE, FRANKLIN PARK	12	BLUE ISLAND, POSEN
		13	CHICAGO HEIGHTS
6	WEST CHICAGO	14	EAST CHICAGO, IN

significant that the U.S. nation-state and U.S. imperialism are contradicted at the very core—in the heartland—in Chicago.

TRANSNATIONALISM GOES TO WORK:

MEXICAN LABOR AND "ILLEGALITY" IN CHICAGO

The need of a constantly expanding market for its products chases
the bourgeoisie over the whole surface of the globe. It must nestle
everywhere, settle everywhere, establish connections
everywhere. . . . National one-sidedness and narrowness become
more and more impossible.**—Karl Marx and Friedrich Engels,**
The Communist Manifesto

Capital by its nature drives beyond every spatial barrier. Thus,
the creation of the physical conditions of exchange—of the means
of communication and transport—the annihilation of space
by time—becomes an extraordinary necessity for it.
—Karl Marx, *Grundrisse*

National one-sidedness and narrowness are indeed impossible (although they surely continue to provide a last refuge for nationalists and nativists of all varieties). The perpetual annihilation of space, which Marx identified long ago, is ever more crucial for the ways that we must think—ever more necessary for the very ways that we can even begin to think critically —about social life. Whereas the master narratives of capital certainly supply the hegemonic form in which our world is continuously reinscribed, the global expansiveness of capital has never been anything but the alienated form of the productive power and creative dynamism of human labor itself, and so it is necessary to try to understand something of the heterogeneous human experiences that provide the subordinated stories which dialectically run both within and against the main currents of annihilation. Although Marx long ago delineated the intrinsically global character of capital, the term *globalization* has acquired a new distinction in the wake of the marked upsurge and dramatic diversification of foreign direct capital investments over the last few decades.[37] *Globalization* has plainly served as a euphemism for the accelerated and diversified mobility of capital on the world scale, an unmistakable and unprecedented transnationalization that marks the most recent reconfigurations of an imperialist global order. Thus, to speak of transnationalism requires a frank recognition of an imperialist world division of labor that perpetrates and perpetuates ever widening gulfs of inequality across the spaces constituted by nation-states—whose borders are rigorously enough enforced, and whose internal labor markets are quite commonly policed through strategically orchestrated coercion if not outright terror. Transnational labor migration, constituted across those borders, is the premier form of a more restless human side of the accelerated processes of global capital accumulation.

The incorporation of Mexican/migrant labor into low-wage jobs in both the downgraded manufacturing and expanded service sectors is one hallmark of Chicago's agonistic accession to the status of "global city" (see Sassen-Koob 1984 and Sassen 1991 and 1994). Of course, Chicago was already a relatively "global" city, though on a different order, corresponding to a different historical epoch; even during the nineteenth century, its manufacturing industries beckoned migrant workers from afar and supplied commodities across the world. More important, given radically shifting criteria, Chicago is perhaps less "global" now than it once was. Its newly globalized reconfiguration is agonistic in the sense that it is decidedly partial—still too much an industrial city in the convulsive throes of deindustrialization, not quite living up to the standards of glittering globalization that would ensure it a place on the capitalist world map of the twenty-first century. If Chicago is not exactly, as its boosters would have it, a "world-class" city, one distinctive feature of Chicago in the era of "globalization" is nonetheless that it has become a Mexican city, through the entrenchment of transnationalized labor and migrants' improvisational productions of space. This is not to pretend that other Chicagos have been somehow eclipsed altogether, but rather to emphasize a differential space that has been incubated in their midst. Thus, I am positing a pluralization of urban space that identifies transnational processes as simultaneously capable of violent disjunctures and creative ferments, both of which are disproportionately felt among the poorest people.

Transnationalism, as I employ the term, must exist in some *working* relation to imperialism. As capital has burrowed into every nook of the world and burst every apparent barrier in the making of an ever more unhindered global arena for profit-making and the continuous reconsolidation of an imperialist division of labor, one of the commodities that is exchanged, necessarily and inevitably, is labor-power . . . homogenized, abstract, highly mobile labor. But the migratory movement of homogenized, abstract labor is embodied in the restless life and death of concrete labor—which is to say, in this case, actual Mexican/migrant working men and women.

Mexicans in Chicago (including those raised in the United States) have continued to be concentrated in so-called low-skill occupations, and despite the disappearance of the city's most historically significant industries, roughly half hold jobs as industrial operatives, fabricators, and other types of manual laborers. As late as the 1980s, only 6.4 percent of the Mexican workforce in Chicago held managerial or professional positions of any kind (Caruso and Camacho 1985, 6), while 49.8 percent were employed in manufacturing (Betancur, Cordova, and Torres 1993, 131). Beginning in 1970 and continuing consistently through the 1990s, Latinos in Chicago (with Mexicans comprising roughly two-thirds, and thus revealing rather comparable trends) were more than twice as likely to be factory workers as whites or African Americans and were likewise employed for the lowest average wages in manufacturing (Betancur, Cordova, and Torres 1993, 125–32). These figures were even more pronounced for women. In 1980, for instance, Mexican women in Chicago had a labor force participation rate of 53.1 percent; of these, 38.1 percent were employed as operatives, fabricators, or other manual laborers, in contrast to only 14.7 percent of African American women and 9.5 percent of white women working outside of the home (Latino Institute 1987, 7, 17). Indeed, during the 1990s, the proportion of Latinos employed in factory work in Chicago (39.2 percent) was double the U.S. national rate for Latinos (19.6 percent), and also twice the percentage of Chicago residents in general.[38] Mexican migrants, and the undocumented in particular, have come to constitute an ever more important segment of the working class in general in metropolitan Chicago and occupy an especially central place at the deskilled core of industrial production.

The pervasive racialized equation of "Mexican"-ness with migrant "illegality" has long been a central and constitutive feature of the subordination of their transnational labor. Following the 1965 revisions in U.S. immigration law (see chapter 6), and especially in the aftermath of the explosive political militancy of the Civil Rights struggles of the late 1960s, undocumented Mexican/migrant labor rapidly became a racialized solution to an already racialized crisis. Although manufacturing employment in Chicago had peaked in 1947 and already registered a loss of nearly 160,000 jobs by 1963 as the city began to undergo a protracted period of economic restructuring (Betancur, Cordova, and Torres 1993, 124), much of Chicago's "deindustrialization" was in fact the effect of an aggressive wave of capital disinvestment by industries fleeing from the city, especially in reaction to the African American "riots" following Martin Luther King's assassination in 1968. Consequently, while large industry effectively evacuated the metropolitan region altogether, smaller manufacturing firms simply relocated to Chicago's suburbs. Indeed, during the immediate post-"riot" period between 1969 and 1974, the city of Chicago lost 212,000 manufacturing jobs (a decline of 12 percent), while overall employment in the suburbs increased by 18 percent, comprising 220,000 jobs (Preston 1982, 92; see Betancur, Cordova, and Torres 1993, 124–25). Thus, while both industrial capital as well as working-class whites repudiated physical proximity to African American urban communities and fled the city, Mexican migrants arriving in ever greater numbers simultaneously took up residence in the urban neighborhoods whites had abandoned, while also increasingly finding employment in factories in the suburbs.

The African American rebellion of the 1960s provides a crucial historical dimension that is very often neglected completely in official scholarly accounts of the relation between "globalization" and the deindustrialization of large urban centers in the United States. The transformations of the world (political) economy that became manifest in the early 1970s cannot be understood simply in narrowly "economic" terms, as they were immediately preceded by political upheavals, both at home and abroad, that acutely affected U.S. imperialism in particular. More important, the devastation of the industrial foundations of big cities in the United States needs to be recognized not as an unforeseen consequence of blind economic forces but rather as the cumulative effect of calculated decisions that had a disproportionate effect on Black America. It is precisely in this social climate that Mexican (largely undocumented) migration to Chicago came to serve the new labor requirements of small- and middle-scale employers who could not afford to simply pick up and leave the area altogether, but who would not tolerate the militancy of African American workers and needed a (legally) vulnerable and hence presumably more tractable alternative.[39] One of my fellow ESL instructors—a middle-aged white man who had been employed as a workplace literacy teacher in factories located in impoverished African American neighborhoods—disclosed to me in 1995 that white management personnel had admitted to him quite plainly in private conversations that they did not want to hire Black people, claiming "they'll just start trouble" and "cause problems." In the idiom of employers, these phrases ubiquitously serve as codes that are synonymous with refusing to be overworked, making demands for improved conditions, and wanting to organize a union. In light of this equation of Blackness with labor insubordination and militancy, these companies maintained virtually all-migrant workforces (Kirschenman and Neckerman 1991). Thus, the insertion of Mexican migrants into the bottom ranks of an already racially polarized working class served as a transnational fix for a political crisis of labor subordination within the U.S. nation-state, and beginning in the early 1970s, heralded the enforcement of an austerity regime for all workers in the United States that would begin to more closely correspond to the conditions of the global labor market (see Rodríguez 1995, 222).

The upsurge of Mexican migration after 1965 quickly became synonymous with "illegality." The number of INS apprehensions of undocumented migrants in Illinois, concentrated overwhelmingly in the Chicago metropolitan area, escalated dramatically during the late 1960s and early 1970s. The number of INS apprehensions increased to roughly 800 percent of its 1965 level by 1971, when a Chicago-based State of Illinois Legislative Investigating Commission, comprised of state senators and congressmen, published an alarmist report, *The Illegal Mexican Alien Problem* (1, 9).[40] The commission presumed that the statistics concerning who was *arrested* as an "illegal alien" transparently provided an accurate depiction of the broader phenomenon of undocumented migration. Among the 8,728 apprehended by the INS during the 1971 fiscal year, 85 percent were Mexican nationals. In light of these enforcement patterns, the commission was explicit, therefore, in its simplistic choice to seamlessly identify the particular national-origin category most commonly apprehended for undocumented immigration status as the group really culpable for "the illegal alien problem": "Since the illegal alien situation in Illinois primarily concerns Mexican nationals, this report will be restricted to that facet of the problem" (1).[41] Thus, the report effectively transposed migrant "illegality" into a specifically *Mexican* "problem." After twenty-five years, little had changed. Although the INS estimated in a 1992 study that Mexicans comprised only 44 percent of all undocumented migrants in Illinois, an analysis of INS apprehensions in the Chicago area during a period of heightened workplace raids, following the passage of the Immigration Reform of 1996, revealed that INS raids almost exclusively targeted Mexicans. Among all undocumented workers arrested in metropolitan Chicago between January 1996 and June 1997, a staggering 96 percent were Mexican.[42]

With the advent of severe economic recession in the early to mid-1970s, the INS dramatically intensified its campaign of mass apprehensions in Chicago. This period has become notorious not only for raids in factories but also for neighborhood roundups in public parks, Spanish-language movie theaters, and on the street in front of Mexican grocery stores (Mora n.d., 30).[43] Not only Mexican and other Latino noncitizen migrants, but also U.S.-born Mexicans as well as Puerto Ricans who were U.S. citizens, were inevitably persecuted as suspected "illegals" on racial grounds. This form of INS harassment provoked large protest demonstrations in 1974 and again in 1976, which mobilized to denounce this racial profiling of the Mexican community in particular, and Latinos in general. For the first time in its history, the INS was compelled to establish a community relations committee—in Chicago (Belenchia 1982, 123, 127). As an expression of the enduring repercussions of the Chicano civil rights movement, the Mexican communities of Pilsen and Little Village in particular witnessed the rise during the 1970s of a great variety of grassroots organizations (Año Nuevo Kerr 1976; see A. Baker 1995). The most prominent figure to emerge from this Mexican political awakening during the 1970s was Rudy Lozano, a U.S.-born Mexican who campaigned as an "independent Democrat" against Chicago's infamously corrupt Democratic Party machine and was eventually assassinated.[44] Notably, despite his career in electoral politics, Lozano's political credibility was fundamentally built through his efforts as a labor organizer, where his principal energies were devoted to undocumented Mexican/migrant workers who were themselves ineligible to vote (Piña n.d.; see Rosenfeld 1993). This example helps to make the point that it has never been viable for the political organization and "civil rights" struggles of Mexicans in Chicago to be narrowly confined only to the concerns of U.S.-citizen Mexicans (see Año Nuevo Kerr 1977). Seldom in the historical formation of Mexican Chicago has it ever been possible to extricate "Chicano" or "Mexican American" concerns from the persistent vitality of ongoing migration from Mexico, the ever more contradictory politics of citizenship in which the acute salience of undocumented migrants' "illegality" predominates, and the increasingly profound transnational commitments that render Chicago inseparable from Mexico.

The dynamic interconnections between the United States and Mexico created and cultivated by transnational migration have ensured the emergence of a Mexican Chicago that has been increasingly implicated in the ongoing affairs and imagined futures of Mexico itself. As early as 1928, José Vasconcelos, one of Mexico's preeminent public intellectuals and former Secretary of Education, carried his presidential campaign to Mexicans in Chicago (Skirius 1976, 487). Similarly, in 1988, as part of a landmark campaign challenging decades of one-party rule, Cuauhtémoc Cárdenas, in his first bid for the Mexican presidency as the candidate of the center-left opposition party, the Partido de la Revolución Democrática (PRD), resumed this transnational tradition of Mexican national politics in the United States and vigorously sought support among Mexican migrants in Chicago. During the 1990s, furthermore, Mexicans in Chicago played a singularly monumental role in political struggles over Mexican electoral reform, democratization, and the substance of "double nationality," by advancing the demand for the right of migrant Mexican citizens residing in the United States to vote in Mexican elections. In 1994, the Chicago-based Consejo Electoral Ciudadano (Citizens' Electoral Council) organized symbolic elections throughout the Chicago area, as well as in California and Texas, in which thousands of migrants enacted their rights as Mexican citizens to vote in the presidential elections in Mexico (Ross Pineda 1999). The Consejo's founder and the most prominent advocate for Mexican/migrant voting rights, Raúl Ross Pineda, who had originally come to Chicago as an undocumented migrant in 1987, went on to coordinate the movement called *Nuestro Voto en el 2000*—Our Vote in the Year 2000 Coalition of Mexicans Abroad (Gómez 1999, 248). During Mexico's national elections in 2000, with the support of the PRD for his Chicago-based campaign, Ross Pineda became the first Mexican residing outside of the country to run as a candidate for Mexico's congress, the Chamber of Deputies (Arias Jirasek and Tortolero 2001; see Ross Pineda 1999).

Today more than ever before, therefore, Mexicans in Chicago are frequently able, through numerous technologies and considerable human connections, to maintain active social relations across vast physical distances (see Boruchoff 1999; Guerra 1998; Zamudio 1999). In one very familiar and quite ubiquitous configuration, the U.S.-dollar wages of Mexican/migrant workers in Chicago are remitted to the agrarian villages of rural Mexico and provide crucial material sustenance to ways of life more apparently defined by subsistence farming and small-scale commerce (see Kearney 1996). Not only do these remittances provide deeply needed support to the immediate families of migrants in building homes, buying land or livestock, or capitalizing small businesses, migrant workers' wages also finance public works projects (often in conjunction with state funds and voluntary local labor): they build churches, sponsor festivals, and develop soccer stadiums, and sometimes they provide material aid for people who have been the victims of any variety of social calamities, not the least of which is the violence of local state apparatuses.

An instance of this latter occasion for transnational community formation was shared with me in lurid detail by Felipe, who had participated in an ESL course that I taught as part of a voluntary vocational training and job-placement program. Felipe was thirty-seven years old and had migrated from his small hometown in the Mexican state of Guerrero, ten years prior, first to northern California where he had worked in landscaping, and then to the Chicago suburb where he had been living for just over two years. He was working as a janitor in a machine shop. In the spring of 1995, I was tutoring Felipe in my home, but on this occasion he called me to cancel our planned meeting. When he contacted me, Felipe had just received a telephone call reporting news of a deadly shoot-out back home: cattle thieves, working in concert with the local police, had killed a man and had also wounded the deceased's brother. The wounded villager later reported having discovered the police driving over his brother's body to ensure that he was dead, and it was at that point that he had opened fire, as Felipe remarked, "just like in the movies." The wounded man's children (an eighteen-year-old woman and her sixteen-year-old brother) eventually arrived on the scene to discover the bullet-ridden corpses of three police officers, as well as their murdered uncle; their father had fled and was in hiding. The children were soon arrested when the police, hunting for their father, conducted a house-to-house search through the town. When Felipe first related the news to me, the children were still in jail and were being held incommunicado. Felipe was fairly sure, even then, that they were probably being tortured for some kind of revelation concerning their father's whereabouts. When I asked if the victims had been close friends of his, Felipe replied simply, "Both were friends of the whole town." Reflecting on the whole dreadful situation, Felipe assured me that the wounded man had always been very easygoing. "The town's people are very peaceful [*el pueblo es muy tran-*

quilo]," Felipe continued, "but they have a lot of guns to defend themselves."

From this small town of no more than a thousand families, there were some two hundred people in the Chicago metropolitan area. On Saturday evening, one man had telephoned home and was the first in Chicago to hear the news, and then immediately went visiting others' homes to explain what had happened. The following morning, in the space of an hour and fifteen minutes, Felipe accompanied that man and another to visit seven homes, where they managed to gather $290 to send to assist the family. By Sunday evening, through the efforts of an expanding circle of people, $1,600 had been collected, and the money was wired to Mexico on Monday morning. A wife and five children survived the man who had been murdered. The stolen cattle were already a very substantial loss, but the family were also being required to pay a fee to the police for the release of the body, and also had to post bail for the release of the two children who had been arrested. Felipe affirmed again that it was typical for the police in Guerrero to torture people—pulling out fingernails, hanging them, beating them, holding them under water, raping women. The following week, Felipe came to my apartment and reported the further news of these events. The children had been released from police custody after their mother had posted the bail—they had both been beaten, the young woman had been raped. "It's an incredible story," he acknowledged, "but yes, it happens in Mexico." Felipe also related that "all the heads of families [*jefes de familia*] who are here in Chicago from the town" sent a cosigned letter to protest the police crimes and to bring their pressure to bear upon various Mexican authorities. Felipe affirmed again, "They're not a people who look for trouble or like to go around fighting and killing people—but yes! they will defend themselves."

This narrative illustrates well the degree to which the preponderantly proletarian composition of Mexican Chicago is undeniably and irreducibly enmeshed, albeit to varying degrees, in the practical present and the imagined futures of countless agrarian communities across the Mexican countryside. And likewise, the innumerable "local" concerns of rural Mexico have a palpable presence in the everyday lives of migrant workers in Chicago. While the reciprocal ideological dichotomies between "the city" and "the country" and between wage labor and peasant subsistence may proliferate, the practical realities have become entangled in unprecedented ways.

Indeed, ironically, about one month before the violent events in his hometown, I had interviewed Felipe in my home in Pilsen, which was a notoriously "bad" neighborhood plagued with violence and crime. Felipe, who resided in a Mexican enclave in a relatively distant suburb, had admitted that he was afraid of Chicago, due to what everyone had told him about street gangs, shootings, car thefts, and so on. He fathomed that the young people growing up in such an environment must be "contaminated" by the violence and strains of urban life. Earlier in the same conversation, notably, when I had asked him to tell me about his town, he said:

> Well, it's a 100 percent rustic, peasant place [*un lugar campirano cien por ciento*], in that yes, the town is located between mountains, and there, well, what you can manage to grow is beans, corn, squash—it's farming and then cattle-raising too. . . . At times, water is very scarce, and that's when the work is more scarce too, because when there's no water, you can't plant anything, even including times when it's not possible to bathe either, because water just doesn't pass there. And you have to go to other towns too, right, larger ones, in order to go and stock up on so many vegetables, so much food such as meat, chicken, right, because sometimes, well, those same animals are scarce—for the same reason, that there's no water, so you can't raise animals either. [. . .] Normally, one had to get up early in the morning, around four or five o'clock, to go and work the fields, and then didn't come back home until about six or seven at night.

Following this frank account of stark rural poverty and arduous labor, Felipe added that his family had never owned their own land. With his wife and three children, like his parents with their eight children, he had always lived by sharecropping, working on someone else's land in exchange for half of the harvest.

Framed by his own experience, Felipe proceeded to make an explicit link between such bleak prospects for survival in rural towns and villages like his own with transnational migration to the United States:

> There is, in our country Mexico—the situation is a little difficult in that working in the fields earns approximately three or four dollars a day. It's an amount that we Mexicans cannot adjust to. And even more so, being the head of a family, it's a little difficult to live and, um, to be able to support all of the family—the kids in school. Then

that's one of the reasons I decided to emigrate here to the United States, the reason why I had to go away from the family, which always, well, was a little difficult and sad, too. . . .

Upon arriving at the border with the United States, well, the tension really takes on a life of its own from that same moment when you see the Immigration checkpoint from far away, [when you see] that they're trying to stop people from crossing. Nevertheless, I found a friend who did me the favor of bringing me across during the course of the night. We were waiting all night on the border line until, at eight in the morning, we were able to cross. They [the guides] immediately brought us to a motel—I went with various companions—and there, they locked us in a room. They went to bring us food—one of those McDonald's. They had us all day, and then at eight o'clock at night, they pulled us out and brought us walking along a beach, at night, and we had to climb hills and then descend again to the beach, and we walked approximately six or seven miles all through the night, until finally we arrived at . . . another checkpoint. At that second one, after all that . . . well, with such bad luck that at ten yards past it, they caught us. And they had us locked up all night in a room that was about five yards by five yards, *a room of five yards by five*—we were approximately sixty-four people, most of us standing, and all we had was a small corner to urinate, there were no facilities there. We were locked up there all night until eleven the next morning when they brought us all back to Mexico, all of us hungry because we hadn't had dinner or breakfast in all of that. So much as we got to Mexico, we went and had lunch, and immediately after, we took a taxi and again, went straight back to the border. And this time we ran with better luck, because we crossed in the daylight . . . and then they told us at five in the morning that they were taking us in a car, so we all got in squatting—there were five of us. We spent the whole ride crouched down like that, and well, we made it. . . . Now, well, always subsisting economically, well, it was good for the family, however much it may be that I'm not really earning much.

In contrast to well-worn racist stereotypes of Mexicans as a fatalistic or docile people always predisposed to accommodate themselves to their circumstances, Felipe began with an affirmation of the fundamental incapacity of Mexicans to adjust to the severe material deprivation that prevailed in many of his country's rural villages. The travails and sacrifices that accompanied undocumented migration, likewise, were figured in effect as simply so many more manifestations of the determination of Mexicans as a people to improve their lot in life.

Between Felipe's two narratives, it becomes more clear that the transnational production of a Mexican Chicago takes place nonetheless only across nation-state spaces, as mediated by the enforcement of borders and an immigration regime that is particularly disadvantageous for Mexicans. In one instance, the dynamic transnational connections between Chicago and a seemingly remote village in Mexico made the U.S.-Mexico border appear relatively inconsequential. In the other instance, it was clear that the border is not at all trivial. Felipe's story was striking in its resemblance to many other undocumented Mexican migrants' border-crossing narratives, in which an episode of great hardship is commonly followed by an account of relatively easy passage. This illustrates the fundamental character of the U.S.-Mexico border, to invoke James Cockcroft's (1986) incisive metaphor, as a "revolving door"—it always involves, simultaneously, the spectacle of apprehensions, detentions, and deportations, with the banality of a virtually permanent *im*portation of undocumented migrant labor, such that "illegality" may reinforce the specific working-class character of transnational Mexican migration (see chapter 6). Indeed, Felipe's narrative was also remarkably similar to many other undocumented Mexican migrants' accounts of their border-crossing experiences in that it concluded, tellingly, with a remark about low wages.[45]

Felipe's reflections on his experiences, furthermore, were notably gendered, in ways especially characteristic of the kinds of narratives related by Mexican/migrant *men*. His explanation of his own decision to migrate, as well as his depiction of the way that his specific migrant community mobilized to defend those victimized by police abuse in their hometown, were both meaningfully framed in terms of the responsibilities of the patriarchal male role as "head of a family." Although Felipe's portrayal of the sorrows that came with having to leave his family was quite sensitive, his melancholy was nonetheless framed by his deep emotional investment in his social role as husband and father. At another point in his interview, Felipe depicted the most desperate cases of poverty in Mexico as those in which several members of a family, "even the woman," all had to be employed for wages in order to more or less sustain the household. In this light, he also affirmed meaningfully that his own wife worked only in the home, caring for their three children. Felipe consistently wired part of his earnings to his family every month, and he noted that it was a comfort to know that they were content now and no longer went without the money required to provide for their needs. "As soon as I know the money has arrived," he explained, "well, I'm reminded that I concern myself with them and not myself." Felipe went on to explain that he hoped, within two years or a maximum of three, to be able to return to live permanently in Mexico with sufficient savings to buy a plot of land for farming and possibly a tractor. In spite of what he had already achieved and also what he still aspired to, however, Felipe denounced the exaggerations and outright lies [*puras maravillas, mentiras*] with which returning Mexican migrants had frequently represented their circumstances in the United States, fostering illusions that seduced others to follow their migrant trajectories. "You fall into a trap," Felipe contended, explaining further that in reality Mexican migrants inevitably have to suffer in the United States, working very hard for long hours, including Saturdays and sometimes Sundays, sometimes with a part-time job in addition to a full-time job, for miserably low wages. The humiliations of undocumented migration and the exploitation that were inseparable from the condition of "illegality," in Felipe's account, thus signaled a characteristic and distinctly masculine ambivalence about the Mexican/ migrant condition in the United States that often fortified enduringly transnational desires and investments.

It would be utterly false, on the other hand, to contend that Mexican/ migrant women did not share, both emotionally and practically, in deep transnational attachments to Mexico, and in many cases, one or another version of the dream of returning permanently as well. The life-history narrative of Luisa was illuminating in this respect. Luisa, a thirty-nine-year-old woman who like Felipe had originally migrated from a small village in Guerrero, was a worker at the DuraPress factory and participated in two of the ESL courses I taught there. Unlike Felipe, however, she had migrated from Mexico with her husband and a small baby. When I interviewed her in her home in 1995, Luisa had been in the Chicago area for eighteen years. Luisa's story was one replete with domestic violence, beginning from her earliest childhood memories. For twelve years or more, she had been trapped in an abusive marriage, ultimately with five children. Upon the family's arrival in 1977 in the United States, circumstances had almost immediately required Luisa to seek gainful employment and, for the first time in her married life, she began to work outside of the house. For years, however, the double demands of a full-time job in addition to the full burden of the household labor had left Luisa feeling anything but independent. Despite the tremendous hardships that she assumed in order to provide for her five young children as a single mother, Luisa had nevertheless managed to make a permanent break with her husband. After a period during which she received unemployment and then some form of public assistance, Luisa eventually sent her four younger children to live in Mexico with her mother. (By that time, however, Luisa's eldest daughter was in her teens, had already become a mother, and was living with her boyfriend.) Although Luisa felt certain that women had far more recourse in the United States to escape domestic violence and abusive situations, in no simple sense did she equate her migrant factory worker's life in a ghettoized Mexican enclave in a Chicago suburb with any unproblematic notion of "liberation." Neither had she relinquished the dream of returning to Mexico. She explained: "I've worked very hard and yes, yes, I was able to build a house in Mexico . . . not myself alone, with my siblings too, with their help, among the three of us, we built the house. And well, sometimes the plans are to leave and go to Mexico. [. . .] I want to be here and I want to be over there, and not be in the two places at the same time." Even after eighteen years in Chicago, Luisa's transnational migrant commitments remained quite substantial, and in very practical and material ways, she was sustaining a transnational family shared between a remote village in Mexico and an industrial suburb of Chicago.[46]

The experiences of exploitation and racial oppression in the United States likewise inspired migrant women with the sense that there was an integrity and dignity to be cherished about their former lives in Mexico. During the interview I conducted with Rosario and Carlos (discussed in chapter 1), there arose multiple examples of their experiences of discriminatory treatment in public places and even altercations between Carlos and belligerent white men who had randomly accosted him with racist insults. In addition to Rosario's distinctly racialized understanding of the ways in which migrants were persecuted for their Spanish language, Rosario reflected further:

> But there's one thing, which is that, in reality, in Mexico we have what we need to live. I don't know why we want to be here—here, where they really treat us so bad [*aquí donde nos tratan tan mal de veras*]. [. . .] There are people who have what they need to make a living in Mexico, and they come here to earn the minimum, less

than the minimum! [. . .] In reality, sometimes, what one comes for is nothing more than the discrimination one receives from people—it's really enough to make you sick. [. . .] Yes, they pay a little more here, but you also have to take the discrimination, and that is still stronger . . . than the economic [*eso es todavía más fuerte . . . que lo económico*], right? Knowing, from television, every so often, what's happening already, that they're against you [*que están en contra de uno*]—how many the police are killing, how many they're killing for nothing more than they see that they're Mexicans [*nomás porque ven que son mexicanos*]. [. . .] They've killed many young people who have done nothing, killed them only because they think, according to them, they confuse them with gang members, but it isn't true—it's because of nothing more than the rage they have toward you [as a Mexican].

Although he agreed with her grievances against racism, Rosario's husband Carlos responded nonetheless by objecting that he simply could not earn as much in Mexico as he did in Chicago. "Here, what I make in one hour is what they pay over there for a whole week! Where am I going to work over there if here I earn in an hour a whole week's wages?" Carlos demanded, adding, "It doesn't suit me to work there." Rosario acknowledged his complaint, but reaffirmed: "That's the thing that makes one hop over from Mexico, but without knowing that you're just coming from one problem to the other, to throw yourself here into the mouth of the wolf, as they say!"

MEXICAN CHICAGO AS A TRANSNATIONAL CONJUNCTURE OF RACE AND SPACE

If we question a pre-given world of separate and discrete "peoples and cultures," and see instead a difference-producing set of relations, we turn from a project of juxtaposing pre-existing differences to one of exploring the construction of differences in historical process.—**Akhil Gupta and James Ferguson**, "Beyond 'Culture': Space, Identity, and the Politics of Difference"

As Rosario affirmed, Mexicans of course do not go to Chicago *only* in order to make a living as migrant labor and thus, to produce economic value for capitalism; they also, to one extent or another, make their lives there. In the process, migrants also come to be embroiled in the social production of *racialized* difference—within the apparently "local" configurations specific to capitalist hegemony in Chicago, as well as transnationally, across a global capitalist topography of domination that corresponds to the larger inequality between the United States and Mexico. Rejecting conventional presuppositions of a "natural" segregation and autonomy of spaces and a perfect congruence of "people," "culture," and "place," and recognizing that social spaces have long been globally interconnected hierarchically, this production of racialized difference requires the production of a *space* for that difference, a space defined in and through difference.

Here, against the more commonplace, one-sided fascination with what transnationalism is doing to subvert, or at least unsettle, prior configurations of social order, I want to stress the inevitably dialectical character of the articulation that transpires between the forces of "globalization" and already established formations of social inequality. Global capital accumulation is not merely a juggernaut that sweeps through and blows over everything in its wake; rather, it articulates—in the course of its own localization—with prior, always localized configurations of social division and political conflict that have been elaborated historically. If, indeed, racialization has always been central in the history of labor struggles and class formation in the United States, a critical attention to the ongoing dynamics of racial formation in the present not only involves recognizing racism as a central problem of working-class consciousness and action *within* the United States, but also requires situating the laborious productions of racialized difference that regiment everyday life at the specific local intersections of an ever more transnational division of labor.

Mexican/migrant experiences in Chicago involve a multiplicity of difference-producing encounters and struggles that transpire, furthermore, around space itself. "The city and the urban sphere are . . . the setting of struggle," as Lefebvre points out; "they are also, however, the stakes of that struggle" ([1974] 1991, 386). Chicago's neighborhoods are often remarkably distinctive, identifiable, and historically enduring, but for a very durable reason—namely, that Chicago neighborhoods are commonly surrounded by quite material boundaries. The railroads and factories that played such a defining role in the historical genesis of Chicago entail enormous physical enactments of capital on the urban landscape. This is the capitalist built environment that hegemonic sociology has conventionally mystified as urban "ecology." Amid the industrial developments and the crisscrossing of elevated railroads that literally enclose whole sections of the city within concrete walls, working-class communities have historically been relegated to whatever space was left for residential use. These physical barriers have long provided a very effective material foundation for social distinctions and separations.[47] Indeed, Chicago is renowned to be a "city of neighborhoods" (e.g., Coniff 1991); by no mere coincidence, and by any measure, Chicago has likewise persistently ranked among the most notoriously racially segregated cities in the United States.[48] Ubiquitous distinctions in everyday discourse about neighborhoods, therefore, are virtually inseparable in Chicago from their overt or coded racial and also class-inflected meanings.

The incorporation of a burgeoning Mexican/migrant population into Chicago's segregated patchwork, historically, therefore meant that the social insertion of Mexicans (and Latinos, more generally) into the racial divide between white and Black was likewise an incredibly spatialized phenomenon in Chicago. The process of large-scale neighborhood-by-neighborhood evacuation of the city by whites to suburban areas, commonly known as white flight, dramatically accelerated in direct reaction to the African American rebellion of 1968. But it was precisely at that conjuncture that Mexican migration to Chicago began to really escalate. In 1970, "minorities" already constituted 43 percent of the total population in Chicago, but 90 percent of the city was either white or African American. As of the year 2000, "minorities" had come to comprise 68.7 percent of the city's total population, but 87 percent of all Chicagoans could still be sorted into the simple now-tripartite racial division of the city: Blacks (37.4 percent), whites (31.3 percent), and Mexicans (18.3 percent). Since 1968, therefore, *Mexican* has become an ever more pronounced "third term" in the racial order of Chicago.[49] Mexicans' degree of residential segregation from whites in Chicago in 2000 was ranked as "very high" (with a dissimilarity index of 62), and their segregation from Blacks measured "extreme" (with a dissimilarity index of 82).[50] Indeed, the degree of segregation even between Mexicans and Puerto Ricans was striking, with an official ranking of "high" (dissimilarity index of 51) (De Genova and Ramos-Zayas 2003a, 31–56). In the wake of white flight after 1968, Mexican migrants often found available to them exactly those panicked white working-class neighborhoods sharing boundaries with Black working-class neighborhoods that were inevitably poorer. The most numerically and historically significant Mexican and other Latino neighborhoods, therefore, have almost all shared starkly segregated boundary lines with virtually homogenous African American neighborhoods, coming to occupy veritable "buffer zones" between these Black communities and the receding neighborhoods of the white working class (Squires et al. 1987, 111; see Kornblum 1974, 30; Weber 1982). Thus, in spite of what has often, in fact, been a remarkably close physical proximity in Chicago between Mexicans (or other Latinos) and African Americans in terms of mere *geographical* distance, racial segregation has ensured rather extreme *social* distance between the two groups.[51]

One prominent case of this kind of spatialization of race between Blacks and Mexicans is the somewhat more fluid segregation effected by Douglas Park, a very large public park that divides the African American West Side (specifically, the North Lawndale community area) from Mexican Little Village. The park provides a recreational space in which both groups engage in any variety of activities, though in rather stark separation from one another. In an interview, my friend Olivia, a woman in her late twenties, related how, upon first migrating from Mexico City, she had moved into the Little Village apartment of her "aunt" (a cousin of her mother's, who had been in Chicago for many years). Olivia had been eager to enroll in ESL classes, and her interest in navigating the city independently inspired her aunt to supply her with a stern warning:

> Where are you going to take classes? In Douglas Park? Do you know what it's like over there? Uhck! You don't know that they sell drugs? Don't you know that there's a ton of Blacks there [*un montón de negros*]?!? Uhck! You're truly going to end up getting raped! You'll end up raped over there, you don't know what you're getting yourself into! You must think that I'm only saying these things because I want to keep you here in my house, but no—here, you're not in Mexico.

Remembering her aunt's reproves, Olivia complained:

> It was always the same song—[. . .] that the Blacks [*los negros*] are terrible—and all that was new for me. I had never had . . . for me, a Black [*un negrito*] was, um—in Mexico, it's not that I think that in Mexico there's no racism, but . . . I had never felt it in this way. And it made me ashamed that she was speaking of a human being like that, as "a Black" [*un negro*], you know. I was saying, "Ehck! No, no, no!" . . . and I felt bad as a human being, and I couldn't put my thoughts in order—it was, like . . . terrible.

Later in our conversation, Olivia continued:

> There was something different that I felt, not only about Blacks [*los negros*] but rather also I began to take note that Mexicans [*los mexicanos*] were seen in a different manner. It was, no, not that I took note but rather more that I heard, I heard this, because . . . I can tell you for the first year that I was here, basically I didn't leave this area [Little Village], you know. Although I went out to visit places, to see things, in order to know the sights—really, here was where I was working, here were the people that I knew, where I was studying, it was the place where I was moving.

Thus, Olivia made an explicit connection between her own sense of isolation within the profoundly segregated, virtually homogenous Mexican space of Little Village, on the one hand, and her dependence, as a recently arrived migrant, upon the pedagogical efforts of others to mediate for her the complexities of race in Chicago.[52] Even as she was consciously resistant at first to this U.S.-specific racial common sense, she was nevertheless subjected to its pervasive hegemony. Not only did this experience supply her with a newly rigid notion of racialized Blackness, it also began to shape a different sense of her own Mexicanness.

Olivia continued her narrative of racial reeducation in Chicago, and thereby shed important light upon her own resultant reracialization:

> What my aunt was telling me about Black people [*la gente negra*] [. . .] that stuff, not only was my aunt saying it but also I remember talking once with a friend of mine from work, and she was saying, "Yes, you know what [. . .] I always used to say that there are good and bad people in all races [*todas las razas*], but it happened that a Black [*un negro*] assaulted me and my daughter. It was a really bad experience, and now I cannot avoid it, you know I have a lot of reservations with Black people [*la gente negra*]." And later . . . I used to go running, and back then I ran all of this, all of the park, and I crossed over to the other side of the park which, you know, is the dividing line [*ya es la división*]—all Mexicans [*puros mexicanos*] on this side, and Black people [*gente negra*] on that side. So then people started telling me, "Don't you go crossing, running over there, because there's a ton of Blacks [*un montón de negros*]."

However, at this point in the interview, Olivia interrupted her story and added abruptly, "In some way, now—for example, when I am . . .

bathing, and I hear some noise that puts me like this [startled, scared], I imagine that it's the face of a Black man [*un hombre negro*] that's going to come out—you know, it could be a Mexican [*un mexicano*], it could be a white man [*un hombre blanco*], but, but that's how I imagine it. Aaahh! It's terrible." Despite Olivia's consciously antiracist impulses, her experiences of urban space in Chicago, and the pedagogical mediation of those experiences by others, had been so pronouncedly racialized that her most intimate fears had come to be phantasmatically embodied as a man who was specifically racialized as Black.

The transnational production of a Mexican Chicago is inextricable from the historically specific (re)racialized production of Mexicans themselves—*as "Mexicans"*—in the particular urban space of Chicago. Inserted into a preexisting polarity of white and Black in the racial order of Chicago, Mexican migrants' understandings of their own "cultural" or "national" identities themselves have become thoroughly saturated with ideologies of racial difference. While plainly conscious of and commonly outspoken about the racialized discrimination and injustice that confront them, Mexican migrants in Chicago nonetheless have come to frequently articulate their perspectives in the hegemonic idiom of U.S. racism against the African Americans who often appear to be their most palpable competitors for jobs and space (see De Genova and Ramos-Zayas 2003a). In this sense also, Mexicans in Chicago were very commonly moored ideologically to a contradictory intermediate space between whiteness and Blackness and produced collective understandings of themselves and their own "Mexican"-ness that were preeminently racialized (see chapter 5).

THE REINVENTION OF "MEXICAN"-NESS
IN MEXICAN CHICAGO

Racialization processes among Mexicans in Chicago, to a great extent, involve what is fundamentally a process of *re*-racialization. There is, after all, an important racialization that Mexicans universally undergo in Mexico before migration, which is obviously grounded in the specificities of a distinct social history of Spanish colonialism and Mexican nation-state formation. This process of reracialization in Chicago is itself transnational in its repercussions, however, and not merely confined to the U.S. side of Mexican/migrant experience. Transnational migration engenders an unrelenting circulation of not only money, commodities, and human beings, but also ideology. Or, as Jorge Bustamante puts it, along with undocumented migrants, undocumented capital, and undocumented contaminants polluting the transnational environment, there is also a movement of "undocumented values, ideas, and myths" (1992, 21). Especially salient among these myths are the ideologies of racial difference welded to the core of working-class experience and, indeed, all social life in the United States. While much of this racial ideology must be continually (re)elaborated in everyday life in places like Chicago, its consequences are increasingly evidenced throughout Mexico, even in seemingly remote villages, where the racialized encounters of transnational migrants have supplied a prominent angle of vision on the world. Thus, apparently local productions of difference, in the various corners of Chicago's poor neighborhoods and suburbs alike, in effect, also entail a transnational reinscription of the racialized difference between "Mexican"-ness and "American"-ness, and between Mexico and the United States, even as the two are conjoined more extensively than ever before. As migration experiences so thoroughly permeate the innumerable communities in Mexico in which migrants continue to participate, and as migrant knowledge comes to reshape even the worldviews of people who have never migrated, it becomes ever more agonistic to disentangle the presumably distinct social histories of Mexico and the United States. Thus, the production of a Mexican Chicago evokes not only the contingency of the space of the U.S. nation-state, but also a laborious process whereby what is at stake is, for better and for worse, nothing less than the reinvention of Mexico.

In an effort to disrupt the subsumption of the immigrant into the conventional narratives of U.S. nationalism, I have posited a Mexican Chicago as the locus for an interrogation of the space of the U.S. nation-state itself. I have sought to advance an explicitly anti-imperialist theorization of transnationalism that situates Mexican Chicago in Latin America—eluding any complete incorporation or conclusive subjection by the U.S. nation-state even as it is nuzzled dangerously close to its core. The boundaries between the United States and Mexico are ever more confounded and convulsed by transnational migration, yet these processes are continually embroiled in a relentless production (and regimentation) of racialized difference that enables the ultimate reimagining and enforcement of those same boundaries. The boundary lines have less to do with the border in and of itself, and more to do with the stark textures of everyday life and labor for Mexican migrants in the United States. Mexican migrants' racialization is plainly inseparable from their subordination as workers, and the social production of migrant "illegality" that is so essential to the exploitation of their labor is likewise deeply interwoven with the particularities of their racialization. Such productions of difference inevitably entail the production of a differential space—the production of a Mexican Chicago, a Chicago that corresponds to Mexico even as it is at work in the reinvention of "Mexican"-ness itself.

PART TWO

EVERYDAY LIFE: THE LOCATION

OF POLITICS

It is in everyday life and everyday life alone

that those interpretations which philosophers and

philosophy define in general and abstract terms

are concretely realized.**—Henri Lefebvre,**

Critique of Everyday Life

CHAPTER FOUR

THE POLITICS OF PRODUCTION

The secret of the everyday—dissatisfaction.—**Henri Lefebvre,**
Critique of Everyday Life

The establishment of a normal working day is . . . the product
of a protracted and more or less concealed civil war.
—Karl Marx, *Capital*

The history of subaltern social groups is necessarily
fragmented and episodic. There undoubtedly does exist a tendency
to (at least provisional stages of) unification in the historical activity
of these groups, but this tendency is continually interrupted. . . .
Subaltern groups are always subject to the activity of ruling groups,
even when they rebel and rise up.—**Antonio Gramsci,**
The Prison Notebooks

This chapter seeks to discern the traces of everyday dissatisfaction among
Mexican/migrant workers in Chicago that attest to what was, in effect, a
protracted and incessant but more or less concealed struggle over the
everyday norms of the labor process and capital accumulation. While in
the previous chapter I signaled the importance of Mexican labor migration for the transnational reconstitution of urban space in metropolitan
Chicago, this chapter is more directly concerned with the laboriousness
of everyday life for Mexican workers in Chicago. Furthermore, while this
book opened with a consideration of the contradictory frameworks of
labor subordination as enabling institutional conditions for my own
ethnographic practice, here I proceed to an ethnographic examination of
the politics of production and labor subordination in their own right.
Such ethnographic representations are necessarily fragmented and episodic. What follows, then, is an extended account of the various man-

ifestations of the everyday civil war over the terms of labor subordination, as these played out at one of the workplaces where I realized my research.

THE DIALECTICS OF LABOR SUBORDINATION
AND INSUBORDINATION

"Training" in workplace contexts has had to be situated within the unequal power relations of production, but such inequalities were never fixed once and for all time. There was a politics of production in each workplace that always hinged upon local conflicts over labor subordination. Given the constitutive and irreconcilable antagonism at the heart of the capital-labor relation, it is necessary to examine every question of labor subordination in terms of the restlessness and irresolution of struggles that always entail both subordination and insubordination simultaneously. These questions were thrown into stark relief at DuraPress, a metal-fabricating factory where workers organized and had a union certified in 1994, while I was teaching there.

By January of 1994, after I had already been teaching English as a Second Language at DuraPress for a few months, I was already quite aware of the seemingly effective way that a certain style of managerial paternalism had been cultivated by the "Human Resources" (or personnel) manager, a Puerto Rican woman in her forties named Rita. Rita took great comfort and confidence from what seemed to be a fair degree of success in managing the workers at DuraPress. This accomplishment owed partly to the fact that, as a Latina, Rita had been able to sustain an exceptionally warm and dynamic rapport with the overwhelmingly Spanish-speaking Mexican/migrant workforce. On one occasion, Rita delightfully boasted to me that the Mexican workers had even taken to calling her "Adelita," recalling the iconic image of a tough, courageous, pistol-packing woman during the Mexican Revolution. As Rita had been led to understand it, Adelita was "Pancho Villa's girlfriend." She felt encouraged that such a nickname was an indication that the workers had truly accepted her as one of their own: "You know," she said of the workers at DuraPress, "they're all from Durango—everybody carries a gun over there! They have feuds going back to their grandfathers!" And it was just such an allegedly gun-toting, vendetta-ridden lot whom I myself had also heard referring to her as "Mamá Rita" and "Tía Rita." It seemed undeniable that Rita, as a competent, assertive, vivacious Latina woman, gave management at DuraPress a "human face."

That Rita was relatively successful in her plight as personnel boss was not uncomplicated, however. The full extent of the contradictions of this paternalism and the latent irony in these seemingly congenial kinship appellations, in particular, became more evident to me in late March. On this occasion, members of the all-male ESL class I was teaching were discussing the news from Mexico of the assassination of Luis Donaldo Colosio, the ruling party candidate who had been the presumed presidential successor. This discussion among the rest of us provoked a frustrated response, however, from one course participant. Originally from Acapulco and later Mexico City, Miguel was thirty-nine and had been working in a long succession of factories since he had first come to Chicago eighteen years prior, after a short time working in Texas. "I don't care about any of that," Miguel challenged, "Why worry about what's happening over there? You're here—and here, you have to worry about Tía Rita!"

Over the next several weeks, the discussions in this ESL course were beginning to reveal what would eventually prove to be a deep undercurrent of discord among the workers. The course was held during the evening, and by early May, the group had become rather small. Some of the course participants had been switched from second shift to third, and this unanticipated requirement that they work midnights also meant that their participation in class was abruptly and summarily discontinued. "It's because the company doesn't care about the people, they only care about production," explained Adelberto, a twenty-three-year-old who had migrated a little more than six years prior from a rural village in the state of México. After an unsuccessful month in California, and then about fifteen months as a dishwasher and busboy in two local restaurants in the industrial suburb where the factory was located, Adelberto had spent five years at DuraPress. Compared to virtually all of his coworkers, Adelberto had been exceptionally successful in this factory: he had worked his way up from a machine operator position in production to an inspection job in the Quality Control department. But he harbored no illusions about the company's benevolence. Adelberto pointed out that the company had begun to create a climate of heightened insecurity among the workers, as there had been someone fired every week during the previous month. Workers in the plant were becoming increasingly disgruntled and many had begun to consider looking elsewhere for the prospect of more stable employment. Benito, a twenty-one-year-old migrant from a rural town in Jalisco who had been in Chicago three years after a couple of years in California, was himself going to be transferred to third shift and was thinking of quitting. As Benito saw it, "the only reason to stay is for the benefits." As this was a nonunionized factory with no contractual obligations to provide any benefits, Benito was referring to the fact that, once a worker had acquired some seniority, DuraPress granted a week (and then later, two weeks) of paid vacation leave, and the company often permitted people to take longer (unpaid) vacations as well. (For many of the workers, this meant having the freedom to spend a month in Mexico each year without losing their jobs). Among the other complaints, Ricardo, a thirty-five-year-old migrant from a small rural town in Durango who had been working in Chicago for sixteen years, sharply criticized Fidencio, one of the absent course participants. The company had recently designated Fidencio as acting supervisor for the new third shift. Whereas he had previously been employed in the relatively skilled position of die-setter, Fidencio was now functioning as boss over those who had hitherto been his coworkers. A migrant in his late forties, Fidencio had come to Chicago seventeen years earlier with his wife and two small daughters from the city of Monterrey, where he had worked as a long-distance bus driver. "He doesn't do the job," Ricardo complained, "He doesn't look after the workers because he doesn't care!" Adelberto defended Fidencio, however, suggesting, "Maybe he doesn't care because they don't pay him to do a supervisor's job, they just give him extra responsibilities." Indeed, when I spoke to Fidencio a week or so later, I learned that he was not being paid extra, but was doing the combined jobs of a supervisor, a die-setter, and a machine operator, as well as providing some machine maintenance—and he did not like it at all.

In general, it was loathsome to the workers that the company was abruptly and unexpectedly switching them to midnights—which normally required a rather lengthy physical adjustment process during which people were generally exhausted and less alert while operating the machines, and therefore more in danger of accidents on the job and potential mutilation. David, a migrant from Jalisco who had been working in the United States for ten years, related that Homero, another of the absent course participants, had also been switched to midnights and was worried that his new workstation was so isolated that "the machine could kill him and nobody would know for hours, because he's back there all by himself!" Miguel himself had recently had his finger seriously injured in one of the machines. Indeed, it was Miguel who pointed out that the company was being especially reckless with the workers' safety by having instituted a third shift only on a short-term basis to meet the momentary production demands of some special orders. "They're maybe going to end the third shift next week!" he said in disgust, highlighting how workers' personal schedules and well-being were so arbitrarily jeopardized whenever the company's production needs mandated it.

I asked a frank but genuine question: "Do you guys have a union?" While I knew that there was no certified union at the factory, my question was genuine because the mere presence of a bureaucratic union apparatus would not necessarily have guaranteed the absence of any of these managerial practices. Furthermore, the question seemed pertinent, and I intended it to provoke a critical dialogue about the workers' options. Indeed, my question clearly resonated with some of the workers' concerns, and a very engaged discussion ensued. Ricardo immediately asked my opinion and shared his own: "What do you think about unions, Nicolás? It's better, right? Look how the workers in the post office fuck up the job and still don't get fired! It's because they're protected by their union." Ricardo was referring to recurrent scandals in the local news about the alleged discovery of Chicago-area mail carriers burning undelivered mail, or dumping it in abandoned lots, or stockpiling it in their homes. We all laughed about this outrageous but endearing analogy. In reply to Ricardo's question, nonetheless, I suggested more seriously, "Well, it depends . . ." and began to discuss my sense of what workers can do for themselves when they are truly organized. I proposed that such mobilization and organization was what constitutes a "real union," regardless of the presence of an official, recognized, legally certified union, and I warned against the fallacy that merely having a bureaucratic apparatus authorized to function as their collective representative could ever serve to solve their problems. I added nonetheless that any legal protections that might be secured could be important for the workers' self-defense but again affirmed that it is always better to be more organized than less, and that even such presumed protections would be effective only to the extent that the workers themselves were prepared to enforce them through their own organized efforts.

Adelberto was encouraged then to share with me some of the prior history of the struggles between workers and management at DuraPress.

"We tried to get a union here a few years ago," he explained, "but we lost the vote—only by one!" I was curious how they accounted for having lost the vote, especially by such a close margin. Miguel explained, "The company said they would do many things for people—you know, as individuals—so many people changed their minds at the last minute." Because the company relied upon a divisive policy of paying workers unequal wages, due to favoritism by individual bosses and as a reward for loyalty to the company, there continued to be a great deal of invidious discussion among DuraPress workers of how much this or that person was being paid. "You see how it works," I remarked, "Divisions are created among the workers over tiny little differences—ten cents, fifty cents—next to nothing!" And Miguel affirmed what for him finally mattered most, that these rather petty distinctions were especially corrosive because they fostered divisions "between *compañeros!*" This particular word choice subtly suggested multiple shades of meaning, ranging from the more literal and prosaic "coworkers," to the more generic but affective "friends," to the more politicized "comrades." "Exactly!" I continued, "And it makes those with a little bit more start to think they actually have something to defend against everyone else—and for what? For fucking nothing! For pennies." By this point, Miguel seemed to be quite consciously supplying me with suggestive cues, perhaps strategically marshaling whatever moral authority and respect that I may have commanded among his coworkers in my capacity as their teacher, to promote the idea of labor organizing. Miguel provided another prompt: "They used to hire only families, too." "Another strategy, right?" I responded, "Someone arrives from Mexico, comes straight to work the next day, and has a big pressure to do a good job, to be a 'good worker,' not to make any trouble."

It had become quite manifest that this was a group of workers who had in fact been continuously engaged together in a struggle against the management at this company. Both sides had been "fighting" all along—though with radically uneven forces and unequal material, organizational, and political resources. But even if the management had sustained a rather steady offensive over many years and achieved a certain momentum, their campaign had not gone uninterrupted or unchallenged. After all, if the workers had lost the previous union certification drive by only one vote, then so also had management won by only one. Having reduced the workers to a defensive posture, management now had nonetheless to continue to calculate the terms of labor subordination rather more consciously than less and had always to be assessing the limits against which they ought not dare to transgress without incurring the risk of provoking some kind of mutiny. The particular delight that I had detected in Rita's self-congratulatory confidence about how much she had charmed the workers whom she managed, now, seemed both more well founded (given the fractiousness of recent labor-management relations at Dura-Press) and simultaneously more distinctly deluded into complacency by its own myth-making paternalism. The pungent, rancid smell of oil that saturated everything in the factory, the accumulated grime on the shop floor, the corrosive oil stains that seemed to pervade the place, and the ominous, unsteady, cacophonous but dull murmur of the booming punch press machines, as if they were hammering away the walls and foundation—all could seem now to portend the ways that a contentious past and a bitter present might bear upon the always uncertain future.

In the ensuing weeks, as we completed the ESL course, there was a persistent unpredictability about who would be able to come to class on any given occasion, as various workers had their shifts changed back and forth between second and third. David was openly contemplating quitting this job and had already begun looking for another job; his only reservation was that he was in the midst of taking on a mortgage (also known as "buying a house") and was more dependent upon a regular income than ever before. Benito was indeed eventually switched to third shift, which was interfering with his chances of ever spending time with his girlfriend; he expressed visceral contempt for working midnights and also contemplated quitting but hesitated because that would preclude the possibility of collecting unemployment compensation. The workers' situation at DuraPress seemed deeply demoralized when I concluded teaching there in the late spring.

By October, however, when I returned to teach a math course, again to an all-male group including some of the same workers who had previously participated in the springtime ESL course, the course of events was developing rapidly. One of the die-setters, Rolando (someone whom I did not know personally), had just had two of his fingers amputated after having nearly lost his entire hand and, having contracted the services of a lawyer, was apparently preparing to make some serious demands on the company. I happened to be in Rita's office one afternoon while she was on the phone with a nurse who was attending Rolando in the hospital. According to Rita, the nurse had apparently informed her that "although he seems like a nice man," Rolando had "some plans." Rita assured me that she was indeed already well apprised of Rolando's "plans" and had some vindictive plans of her own. In collaboration with Ted, the plant manager, Rita wanted to preempt any possible lawsuit and so was planning to find a full-time responsibility for Rolando in the factory, at a pay scale comparable to the rate he had been earning, rather than risk having to pay damages for keeping him for any extended period on "light duty" (at a lower pay scale). All of these preparations, however, were made with the explicit expectation that they would place Rolando in a job which he would inevitably be unable to perform competently, such as a position in quality control that would demand some relatively advanced mathematical skills. In my presence, Rita gloated with Ted that this was truly "a brilliant plan!" It seemed to ensure that, legally, management would be protected against any plausible claim that the company had failed to provide Rolando with the opportunity to remain employed at DuraPress at the same relatively high die-setter's pay scale. In the midst of this epiphany, Rita's gleeful face abruptly assumed a strikingly sober cast, as she suddenly turned to me, and said, "This is confidential, Nick!" She then proceeded to reassure me that they were pursuing this course of action only "because he screwed up, and it's his fault what happened—so we're sticking with that." "Uh-huh," I nodded. At that moment, I took note of a motivational poster displayed on Rita's office door, typical of the sort that often adorned the offices of personnel bosses in the various factories where I was employed; it proclaimed: "None of us is as strong as All of us."

During this period of intrigues, Rita was also fairly exuberant about having been able to bring about the termination of the former production manager. His replacement, apparently handpicked by Rita and Ted, meanwhile, was quickly earning the resentment of the workers. When I encountered Benito shortly thereafter, after having not seen him for several months, almost the first thing he had to say was, "We have *a lot* of problems now, Nico—because of the new boss." Rita had also informed me that she was hiring some new supervisors (as well as workers). She seemed to be imposing more severe and also more formal standards in an effort to reform the prevailing managerial regime. "The supervisors don't know how to discipline the people," she complained, "and then when they do it, they don't follow the right procedures." Such managerial irregularities tended to invite workers' disaffection and even legal disputes, whereas a more standardized but also more stringent enforcement of disciplinary norms promised more routine and less debatable penalties and firings and therefore more effective labor subordination overall.

Within the next week, however, DuraPress became still more unsettled. On one occasion when I arrived late in the afternoon and entered the factory through the office, I was greeted as usual by Guadalupe. A woman from a lower-middle-class background in Mexico, Guadalupe served as Rita's secretarial assistant in the office. Guadalupe's ordinarily cheerful demeanor now seemed strangely somber and gravely troubled, as she immediately indicated for me the official union notice on the company's bulletin board—"See what's happened! We have problems now with the union" [la unión, she said, transposing the word from English into Spanish, rather than using the Spanish term sindicato]. Feigning ignorance and also surprise, I said, "Oh, so right now there's not already a union?" I hoped to subtly convey that I would have expected for every workplace to have a union. "No! But they're collecting signatures already," Guadalupe replied. "How did all this happen?" I asked her, "How did it start?" Guadalupe explained her interpretation of the situation: "Somebody is angry. There are some people who are jealous and discontented. They're collecting signatures and they only have to get 30 percent—that's not many people—it's really bad! Unions are bad. It's just going to cause problems." I asked if she had some experience with unions. Guadalupe's reply seemed quite self-satisfied as she assured me, "I never worked for a union—but a few years ago they did this here. Some of them voted for it, but we didn't let them do it. Unions are bad, they just make trouble."

Guadalupe had gone to secretarial school in Mexico but had never worked there; she migrated to the United States, was soon married to a professional, and spent the next twenty years raising her children and not otherwise employed outside of her home. Seven years prior, she had taken a job as a machine operator at DuraPress but quickly came to be involved in other jobs, part of the time—first in quality control, and increasingly, in various clerical jobs. More recently, she had been promoted to a full-time position on the office staff as Rita's assistant. Guadalupe's devotion to Rita, and her loyalty to the company, testified to the fact that she had done exceptionally well at DuraPress. On this occasion, Guadalupe had prepared a multiplication table for me to distribute to the participants in the math course that I was teaching, and I joked that it was going to help me with my own calculations as well. "I don't think you need it! You're at a much higher level," she asserted, and then reflected further, "Education is good, isn't it? It makes your mind more open to different things—not just what I have and what I don't have, like these people around here!" The effort by workers in the factory to organize a union, she seemed convinced, was merely the vindictive manifestation of their envy and small-mindedness.

Before class began, as a few of the course participants and I were casually talking, I related that people in the office seemed quite unsettled. Now that the struggle was under way in earnest, and a completely public matter, we all could laugh a bit more lightheartedly about management's antagonism toward the unionization campaign and their hostility toward the workers. Knowing about my research interests, Miguel now asked meaningfully, "Hey, Nicolás, did you write your book yet?" Somewhat embarrassedly, I began to explain that it was going to take me a lot longer than the few months that had passed since I had first mentioned the subject to him. Miguel cut my reply short, however, to interject, "because right now, we have a lot of problems." He seemed intent to convey that this struggle between the workers and the company was the story that really needed to be told. In case I had any question about what it was that truly mattered, Miguel seemed to insist, this was it.

A few days later, on a Saturday afternoon, I called Benito at his home to discover that he had just worked an eight-hour shift of mandatory overtime. He also informed me that David had just quit his job because Rita had gotten angry and accused him of being involved in the union-organizing efforts. Benito marveled at this allegation, remarking, "He never even thought about that stuff! [¡*Nunca pensó en eso!*]" Luckily, David had already found a new job at another factory that was much closer to his home and, disgusted with the whole situation, Benito was considering going to work there too. Benito also told me that the company had just fired a supervisor, because he too was suspected of being behind the union organizing. The management seemed determined to isolate and eliminate anyone associated with the threat of unionization.

The following week, Rita's compulsion to root out the infectious source of the workers' organizing had inspired her to resort to new tactics. "How's the class going?" she asked. I began to praise the students, assuring her of their sincere devotion to learning math. She interrupted and cut to the point: "Tell them why we're doing this, tell them how much we care about them! You know, there's a union-organizing drive now and on December 1, we have to hold an election to see if there's going to be a union. We're going to be campaigning very hard; we've already fired some people. Lots of these people are really good, but we have some nasty people too—so we're getting rid of them! They did mean things—I can't go into it, for legal reasons, you know—but we had some sabotage, so we're firing people, and others might be quitting." Rita now intoned meaningfully, "And I'd be *very interested*, if you hear anything about it—you know, whatever they're saying." As she said this, Rita locked her gaze intensely upon me. For a moment, I caught a glimpse of what seemed to me like managerial terror, and also a more personal and bitter sense of betrayal in the face of the workers' insubordination. Confronted with Rita's very direct demand for surveillance, moreover, I felt with remarkable acuteness the contradictions that constituted the very conditions of possibility of my own pedagogical and ethnographic practice. It would not be the last time.

A week later, having not heard any reports from me, Rita purposefully sought me out, and asked "How's class goin'?" I started to supply an answer that was related to the workers' mathematical education, but she was not at all interested in the particular details of my teaching. Again, she cut directly to the point: "Did you hear anything about the union? Are they saying anything about it?" Rita's apparent presumption that I would naturally be complicit with her drive to defeat the union was striking. Of course, Rita may have been suspicious of me and could have been operating on the assumption that the only way to verify whether or not I would serve her ends was to demand that I do so and thus see whether or not I complied. Still, the unreserved expectation that I would abide by her mandate for surveillance was impressively forthright. In reply to her inquiry, I simply said, "No—nothing. They don't talk about it—just math." Struggling to make sense of the unfolding situation, Rita then declared, as if to reassure herself, "Well . . . that's good, it's better that way. That's really good . . . so, they like the class?" "Yeah," I said, reassuring her of their exemplary spirit and positive attitudes about learning—"but I haven't heard anything. To tell ya the truth," I continued, "if Guadalupe hadn't told me already, I wouldn't even know about it." Rita seemed quite pleased.

"Vote No" posters campaigning against the Machinists' Union had by now been visibly posted in several heavily trafficked areas of the factory. The bilingual poster, which had been supplied to the company by a Chicago-area manufacturers' association, detailed what it alleged to be the high number of strikes called by the union, the number of workers affected, the number of workdays lost, the number of dollars lost (at a rate of $8 an hour, it notably was more than most DuraPress workers were paid). In English, it concluded with the question "Sound Like Fun?"

In Spanish, it challenged, "Are you ready to go through this experience?" Meanwhile, the experience the workers at DuraPress were in fact living had become decidedly punitive. In the company's last-minute drive for pre-union profits, DuraPress was wringing inordinate hours of mandatory overtime from people—so much so that there was no longer any need for a third shift, as two shifts effectively worked around the clock. Indeed, with the union certification vote approaching on December 1, the company announced that both shifts would be required to work a "full day" (which was to say, with obligatory overtime hours) on the Saturday following the Thanksgiving holiday. This was hardly a congenial way to persuade workers that the company cared about them, but in fact it revealed that the company had little hope that their antiunion propaganda campaign would succeed. The mandatory overtime was really intended to simultaneously squeeze the most production possible out of the workforce and to drive ever-greater numbers of the workers to the point of quitting. DuraPress was apparently hoping to win the vote through a war of attrition. When I bumped into Fidencio, whom I had not seen much during this time period, he said with an air of exhaustion and disgust: "How are you, Nico? . . . Me, I'm no good, I'm very tired." The previous week, he had worked ten-and-a-half-hour shifts, four days in a row, then a nine-hour shift, and then another mandatory five hours on Saturday; and there was no indication that any of this would change anytime soon. I gestured toward the antiunion posters, and said simply, "The bosses are afraid." Fidencio replied with a wide grin, "They're *very* afraid!" A few days later, I noticed that the management's "Vote No" poster had been vandalized with a "Yes."

After the truncated Thanksgiving holiday weekend, in the last days before the union certification vote, management installed a company Christmas tree on the plant floor. The tree was decorated with the contemptible metal stampings that DuraPress manufactured as its unique ornaments! In the November–December issue of a recently initiated company newsletter, an article explained that the Christmas Decorating Committee was organized under the direction of the plant's Total Quality Management coordinator. In addition to the rather ugly gray metal plates and baskets, there were also handmade ornaments prominently featuring family photographs of some employees' children—and their pet dogs. Predictably, these more personal ornaments had principally been supplied by the predominantly white office staff or management personnel, presumably intended to encourage the disproportionately Mexican production workers to hang their kids on the company tree, too. A garland read: "We are all family, working together for our children."

The union, of course, had no such propaganda rights. The labor organizing drive was entitled to merely a nondescript government-issued notice, confirming the workers' legal right to unionize. Meanwhile, the company had posted several new large, brightly colored, antiunion posters, declaring "The Union Strikes Out"/"Se 'Poncha' La Union." This title was followed by the injunction: "Workers at DuraPress are winners, not losers—Don't strike out with the union" ("Guard your future," in Spanish). The posters included bar graphs purporting to demonstrate the union's bad track record: the alleged numbers of decertifications, dismissals before certification, plants that were closed (by implication, as a result of the union's obstruction), and so on. All of the posters, however, had been quickly graffitied with a simple "Yes" in place of the "Vote No" appeals.

The company's potentially most effective way of undermining the organizing drive and subverting the unity of the workers at DuraPress, however, soon became more apparent. Fidencio asked me in class, "Hey Nicolás, can you teach Spanish too? Maybe one day soon, they'll have you teaching Spanish to the little Black ones [*prietitos*]—because they don't speak Spanish, and lately, they're the only ones coming in here." Fidencio was articulating what many at DuraPress were feeling—a sense of suspicion and dismay at the prospect that the company had decided to simply replace the increasingly organized and intractable Mexican/migrant workers with African Americans. With little patience for Fidencio's irony and in a manner not very conducive to dialogue, I responded abruptly: "I doubt it, because the fucking bosses say they want everyone to speak English, and they're the ones who are giving the orders, so it seems to me that the so-called *prietitos* are the same as all the rest of you—you ought to see them as your *compañeros,* and you'd better start organizing them, too." The racialized hiring strategy of the employers, of course, also served very effectively to practically divide these predominantly Spanish-speaking workers from their new English-speaking coworkers on the basis of language as well as race. In response to Fidencio's frustration, however, my irritable reply revealed that I unfortunately had very little to offer other than my own frustration with the increasingly difficult situation at DuraPress.

Later that week, a solid absolute majority of the workforce certified the union. As Juanito, one of the participants in the math class I was teaching, described the results, it had been one-third "for the company," and two-thirds "for the union." German, another of the class members, said confidently, "We're on the path now—straight ahead!" Meanwhile, despite the workers' jubilation about the vote, the entire plant would be working regular ten-and-a-half-hour shifts, with mandatory Saturdays, "until further notice." With respect to the company's upcoming holiday party, workers on the second shift were graciously being extended the option to work a double shift that day, because, in Rita's words, "We want everyone to attend the Christmas party." Having lost the battle over union certification, the company was winning the everyday struggle over labor-time.

Despite their victory, the workers in the math class were seething nevertheless about being overworked. "When I started here, they told me 'five days, eight hours, that's all.' Five days, eight hours, that's perfect! But not *this!*" complained Benito, who had not ended up quitting after all. The workers in the class seemed visibly unable to really concentrate on math, because as German stated plainly, "We're too tired, physically and mentally." Benito added, "I don't care if they fire me. Remember, Nicolás, you saw me that time in the office and I told you we had a lot of problems —they wanted to fire me then, but they couldn't. I wasn't born here, in this factory—there are other ones [*yo no nací aquí, en esta fábrica—hay otras*]. Look at David, he went to another factory—he started at $10 an hour, on first shift!" Now with more reserve, but also a quiet indignation, Benito went on to recall how his cousins had been killed in Mexico earlier in the year, but the company had refused to grant him a leave of absence to attend the funeral. "Now they're working overtime every day," German continued. "Other times, they don't have work and they send people home, without paying them. It's against the law, but they don't care about the law around here. All this overtime should be illegal, too. We've had enough overtime already—they're working us like slaves." "Like dogs!" Benito responded. "They say they want the company to grow," Pablo added, "but they don't want to let the worker's pocket grow."

During this period, I repeatedly complained to Rita about how half of my class was regularly absent because they were being held back for production priorities. Rita would shrug her shoulders, saying that there was nothing she could do because there were orders that had to be filled, but that the workload would eventually return to normal. Then, more plaintively and perhaps with a hint of vengefulness, Rita added:

The union knew they had a prime target in this company . . . because the people want more money and we've had lots of problems, because the people are working hard and they think the company is making lots of money. But they don't understand that it's all backed up, it's not productive! The productivity is the lowest ever, so we're working a lot but it's just to keep up with the backlog. But these people don't understand—and really, I pity them, because the union can't give them something the company doesn't have. So now we're negotiating, and they think they're just gonna get a contract with everything they want, but it could take six months or a year, and they'll end up with the same thing that we gave them before, but they'll be paying union dues for it. No other company would be as nice to them as we've been, but they don't know any better, because this is the only company they've worked for.

Clearly, the DuraPress management seemed intent to stall for as long as possible any kind of resolution to contract negotiations and persist in working people mercilessly in the meanwhile, firing as many as possible along the way. If they were really crafty, they might even succeed to get the union decertified before a contract was ever settled. Indeed, Evelyn, another instructor in the workplace literacy program, who had a more personal rapport with Rita and whose outlook was decidedly more managerial than mine, admitted to me that she also felt that DuraPress was trying to penalize the workers for having unionized. Evelyn confessed with regret that the DuraPress management "would be happier if they could just get rid of everyone working there now, close the place down, and then reopen it and hire a fresh bunch of people." This, of course, is a timeworn strategy for breaking unions, and it seemed plain that this is what the company was aiming to do, but it now appeared as if Rita had confided as much to Evelyn.

When she declared that the workforce at DuraPress "don't know any better, because this is the only company they've worked for," Rita casually articulated a smug managerial condescension toward the largely Mexican/migrant workers. Rita's remark alluded to the fact that DuraPress had previously relied on a deliberate policy of recruiting much of the workforce directly from Mexico (indeed, mostly from one or two small towns in Durango), through the personal contacts of workers who were already employed in the factory. By implication, she now reinscribed the workers' transnationalism as the naive parochialism of people from rural backgrounds who had no experience in the United States beyond their employment under her own paternalistic supervision in this factory. This effectively transnational strategy of familial-network internal hiring had long seemed to work to the company's advantage. More recently, however, the extensive intimate connections among the workers may have backfired on management and facilitated the organizing drive.

DuraPress was located in a heavily industrial zone in a Chicago suburb that I will call "Marshall Park." Indeed, on one occasion in conversation with Elaine, my direct supervisor in the workplace literacy program, when I referred in passing to the fact that most of the DuraPress workers lived in the same town where the company was located, she exclaimed, only half-ironically, "You mean people *live* in Marshall Park?!? I didn't think anybody lived there; I thought it was all factories!" Of course, people had always lived there; it was an industrial suburb whose inhabitants historically had been white working-class people.[1] For many of the Mexican/migrant workers whom the local factories recruited, this meant that many of them not only had been employed together but also lived together in a ghettoized Mexican enclave of neglected two-story apartment buildings nearby that was surrounded by factories on three sides and was accessible only by two small, unpaved, and pockmarked side streets. Originally, the local whites had unofficially baptized this Mexican/migrant factory workers' quarter with the racist label "The Jungle." Through their inevitable contacts with the town's white police, the Mexican residents had been rudely informed of the name of their neighborhood, and so it likewise came to be known among themselves as *La Selva* (The Jungle), despite the efforts of some to recuperate a more dignified identity for their community by renaming it *Los Jardines de Guadalupe* (Guadalupe Gardens). This kind of racialized spatial segregation constituted a de facto company town for several nearby factories. Insofar as this notorious Mexican ghetto was routinely subjected to extraordinary policing, furthermore, such spatial confinement also tended to serve the ends of labor discipline, both inside and outside of the factories. Nevertheless, such a densely populated community of coworkers, in the recent turn of events, may likewise have revealed its own contradictory character for the DuraPress management as a space of intensive organizing possibilities.

A few days before the Christmas holiday, the workers in class informed me, "We're one short again. We're missing another one this time, and we don't know when he's coming back—Benito is on a forced vacation." They explained that Benito had been put on probation for "a bad set-up." The company had alleged that Benito had been careless in setting a die in the press, but his coworkers reported that the die had broken only after the press had already run for some three hours and had produced some 1,500 pieces without a problem. In short, the workers felt that the situation was rather suspicious, especially since the problem had arisen only during the following shift, after Benito had already left and the job had been running without any problem. "You make just one mistake around here," Ignacio remarked, "and they get rid of you." Shortly thereafter, German asked, "Were you talking with my friend Rita?" Ignacio and German were eager to share the latest news. It seemed likely that someone in the upper echelons of the plant management would now have to be held accountable for the success of the union certification. "She's not smiling anymore, because they're also sending Ted on a forced vacation, but he's not coming back—they're firing him," the workers related with satisfaction. "And since Rita and Ted are so close and united in everything they do, maybe she's next! And maybe after her, they'll get rid of Ralph [the production manager] too! There are a lot of problems around here, and *they* have some *big* problems!" The workers' sage grins revealed a bitter satisfaction at this modest measure of justice. Indeed, this kind of reprisal at the top was merely the logical consequence of the same managerial ideology that had rationalized the company's unreasonable and unrelenting demands on the workers. This ideology was well encapsulated in a poster on the wall of the quality control inspection office, which presented the image of a bumblebee and a honeycomb, and declared: "If Nature can produce without defects, so can we." Evidently, if the workers had succeeded to mobilize and organized a union, management had failed at its own job, its own central mission, which was to ensure the subordination of labor for the smooth and uninterrupted profitability of the company's production facilities. Meanwhile, the company's vigilant efforts to extract the maximum surplus value from the workers' labor, and their simultaneous drive for perfectly efficient and faultless production, had manifested itself in a new form of surveillance. One of the workers marched me through the plant to show me the latest DuraPress innovation. He insisted that I simply had to see this: a video camera that had been installed by the company president behind Juanito (whose attendance in my math class had been permanently discontinued), to record his movements while he was working the press. Presumably, this documentation would make it possible to "scientifically" detect every unnecessary motion in order that a model might be devised to ensure only the most efficient possible labor.[2]

During the Christmas and New Year's holidays, which both had fallen on weekends, the plant had worked four-day weeks with ten-hour shifts —allowing the company to pay the workers for only forty hours, with no overtime pay, and no holiday pay. By January, upon resuming classes after my own holiday break, they were once again working ten- and eleven-hour days, and also eight-hour Saturdays, and the company was talking about instituting twelve-hour shifts on a quasi-permanent basis. Likewise, Benito had been fired, in connection with his recent probation. Again, there was little hope for mathematics, and much more seriously, an ever higher risk of accidents on the job. "We're too tired," the workers declared, "and you can't do the job well when the mind gets tired." Only half-jokingly, expressing a combination of despair and angry desperation, German proclaimed, "We need to follow the examples of Chiapas and Guatemala." Ignacio concurred, "Yes, that's right, isn't it? They're doing good over there!" German continued, "We came here to work, but not to slave." I pointed out that workers had fought for the eight-hour-day more than one hundred years earlier, but that if workers were not mobilized and organized, and whenever workers stopped fighting, the employers found ways to take back those gains, little by little. It was evident, however, that a growing demoralization among the DuraPress workers was steadily eroding the prospect of continued and more militant struggle.

Later, when we heard Rita's voice emanating from the quality control office nearby, German joked bitterly, "Who's running around over there —the Cockroach?" At least for now, as long as DuraPress did not close its doors, and as long as these workers held out against the company's attrition-driven strategy of accumulation, the days of "Adelita" and "Mamá" and "Tía" Rita seemed long gone. The company's paternalism had soured. As upper management's foremost representative to the production personnel (over whom she had once fancied herself a protector), Rita had come to view the workers now as childish, impudent, and ungrateful. Likewise, the resentment that these male workers felt toward the company could be fixed most easily and directly upon its human face, the Latina woman who managed the factory's so-called human resources. Now, however, that face was recast as inhuman, and reprehensible, like vermin—like a cockroach.

164   CHAPTER FOUR

During the following month, there was probably never a class session when German did not say that they were now working "like slaves [*como esclavos*]." Ignacio and German eventually revealed that they had started to look for work elsewhere. I told them, "It's exactly what the company wants." They nodded, and said simply, "We know." Everyone recognized that the workers' physical exhaustion was taking its toll. "Another thing is this noise," German added, recalling into the foreground the pounding of the machines that was incessantly present in the background, "After eight hours, it makes your head pound!" Indeed, as the rate of production had been accelerated, the ever-present pounding of the machines had become distinctly more brutal; the machines had been literally sped up for higher productivity. Similarly, the exhaust fumes that clotted the air in the plant seemed thicker as the frenetic pace of various machines and forklifts had been intensified. "They want us to work so much," Ignacio demanded, "when can we ever be with our families?" And now in resentful exasperation, German reiterated the growing sense of insecurity that Fidencio had voiced previously: "And then they hire Blacks [*morenos*] who don't know how to work!"

As the Latino workers were now increasingly inclined to articulate their distrust of the newly hired African American workers in terms of contentious claims about which group "knew how to work"—a defensive argument about who was more hard-working, in racialized opposition to who was "lazy"—the fragility of the workers' unity was coming to be exposed for its own contradictions and tenuousness. In effect, recourse to this defensive posture posed the problem in terms of which group's labor-power would be the more prized commodity for the company to consume in its relentless quest to realize surplus value. "The workers say they're worried," Evelyn, the daytime ESL instructor, similarly reported, "because the company has hired some new workers, who are African Americans." The DuraPress management was now increasingly and effectively implementing the timeworn strategy of racialized divide-and-rule in a renewed effort to shatter the frail unity that the workers had ultimately succeeded to consolidate.

THE SPACE OF MY ethnographic research in workplaces like DuraPress was constituted within the contradictory space of workplace literacy education, and that space, as seen in Rita's repeated overtures, was presumed to be one of surveillance and discipline in the service of labor subordination. The ethnographic space, therefore, was always one whose contours were already defined, above all, by the politics of production, and more generally, by social relations of unequal wealth and power—"the secret of the everyday," "a concealed civil war." The "fragmented and episodic" efforts of many of the Mexican/migrant workers whom I knew to organize and defend themselves as workers, however, repeatedly came up against the limiting horizon of their racialization *as Mexicans*, as well as the spatial specificity of their status as migrant workers. It is precisely with these questions, then, that the remaining chapters of this book will be concerned.

CHAPTER FIVE

RERACIALIZATION: BETWEEN

"AMERICANS" AND BLACKS

A momentous critique of ethnographic authority in anthropological writing erupted in the 1980s (Clifford 1988; Marcus and Fischer 1986). One of the important contributions of that critique was that it enabled an enduring recognition of irony as a distinctive characteristic of anthropology. Notably, in James Clifford's characterization of this ironic stance, it is particularly embedded in the ambivalence of anthropology as a white man's enterprise. "Ethnographic liberals," he writes, "have tended to be ironic participants. They have sought ways to stand out or apart from the imperial roles reserved for them as whites" (1988, 79). Whiteness—as the racialized status of the anthropologist—emerges remarkably as a problem of anthropology's inextricability from the colonial nexus; irony—as a reflex of ethnographic liberalism—emerges likewise as a technique for the mediation of that problem.

The array of ironic positions that constitute this kind of anthropological liberalism, ultimately, have historically served nonetheless to underwrite the ethnographer's authority to operate cross-culturally in the enunciation of a totalizing humanism. Committed to the project of rendering difference familiar and comprehensible, such an anthropological humanism comes, however, to require what Clifford identifies as a "surrealist" sensibility. In other words, it strategically assaults the familiar and provokes the startling eruption of various manifestations of "otherness" that at first appear irreducible (1988, 145–46). "The surrealist moment in ethnography," Clifford argues (146), "is that moment in which the possibility of comparison exists in unmediated tension with sheer incongruity. This moment is repeatedly produced and smoothed over in the process of comprehension." Ethnography, then, in Clifford's appraisal, is a "science of cultural jeopardy" that presupposes an openness to being shocked and a willingness to be surprised (147). Yet, the textual critique of ethnography has largely reserved the ironic posture as one to which crafty anthropologists seem to have virtually exclusive recourse, first "in the field," and then in the representation of such research practices through the production of ethnographic texts. Irony, defamiliarization, and surrealism—as rhetorical devices and representational strategies—appear in Clifford's and others' accounts to be principally available to the (typically white) ethnographic author, but not generally to the (conventionally nonwhite) people represented in anthropological texts. In this sense, the textual critique never truly destabilizes the basic assumptions that authorize ethnographic practice as the signature methodology by which the discipline of sociocultural anthropology aims to render "otherness" knowable and "difference" manageable. In short, the textual critique of ethnography could posit defamiliarization as a rhetorical strategy and surrealism as a mode of esoteric experimentation on the part of the anthropological writer but could hardly entertain the notion that surrealism might be a discursive strategy of everyday life on the part of those about whom anthropological "knowledge" is crafted.[1] Nevertheless, when "the absurdly impossible is not only possible but commonplace," as Smadar Lavie has suggested with respect to conditions of military occupation (1990, 317), the absurdities of the real require mediation on the parts of all involved. Surrealism thus becomes a facet of everyday life itself.

In a discussion of the creative expressions and artistic production of Mexicans in the United States, Ramón García (1997, 172) notably makes a startling declaration: "Identity is no longer knowable or recognizable, it is a ghost, an enigmatic sign of fear and desire. It is surrealism, the other face of Chicano identity." When García treats the racialized subject of Mexican/Chicano identity in the United States by conjuring ghosts and enigmas, one is reminded of the ways that "race" itself is inherently unstable, phantasmic, and, frankly, surreal. "Attempts . . . to define the appropriate meaning of race in institutional life and to establish coherent racial identities based on that meaning . . . continue to be unattainable," suggests Howard Winant (1994, 58–59), explaining, "This is because race, a preeminently social construct, is inherently subject to contestation; its meaning is intrinsically unstable." Indeed, Theodore Allen (1994, 28) has characterized the intrinsic contradictions that arise in attempts to sociologize "race"as such, in a telling turn of phrase, as "howling absurdities."

This chapter is concerned primarily with clarifying and rearticulating a standpoint of critique that was incipient in Mexican migrants' engagements with the contradictions of their own reracialization in Chicago and thus operates in the face of the absurdities of "race." Immersed in the systemic mediation of everyday life in the United States by the hegemony of racial oppression, and thus, confronted always with the real social power of the absurd fictions and intrinsic incoherence of race itself, Mexican migrants in Chicago sometimes negotiated their own racialization through instances of surrealistic defamiliarization and ironic humor. In this chapter, I consider what can be characterized to be some of the tactics of everyday surrealism through which Mexican migrants in Chicago grappled with the contradictory tangle of terribly familiar and apparently mundane racialized distinctions and meanings that circumscribed their everyday experiences. Despite their playful irony and humorous defamiliarizations, however, what was at stake in these migrants' reracialization finally entailed a profound reconfiguration of what it meant to be "Mexican" in relation to the dominant U.S. racial order and its hegemonic polarity of whiteness and Blackness. Therefore, these Mexican/migrant experiences and perspectives provide a crucial standpoint of critique from which to interrogate the racial economy of the U.S. nation-state. Notably, such a serious matter commonly assumed a humble and elusive form and appeared to be mere *relajo*.

TACTICS OF EVERYDAY SURREALISM:
RELAJO AND THE LIMITS OF ETHNOGRAPHIC KNOWLEDGE

Relajo is not a term that can be easily fixed or conclusively defined. It has been variously rendered as "carrying on, banter, play" (Limón 1989, 477–79; 1994, 132–36), as "fun," supplemented with "a dimension of mockery (as in 'making fun') and transgression" (Monsiváis 1997, xiii), as "dissipation, laxity, disorder, mess" (Bartra 1992, 142n8), or as "chaotic disorganization," supplemented with a sense of creativity and disruptive intentionality, "a kind of antistructural pasttime that could be characterized in terms of subordinating one's time to one's on-the-spot ideas and desires" (Lomnitz-Adler 1992, 259, 182). "*Relajo*," Roger Bartra contends further (1992, 140), "is that gelatinous slackening of norms which permits a limited insubordination, a measured relaxation of the rules of social behavior." Bartra continues, "the notion of *relajo* doubtless originates in an attitude of popular self-defense, which tries to tangle up and throw into disorder the mechanisms of domination and exploitation" (141).

The classic statement and clearly most extended commentary on the concept of relajo—to which Bartra is in part responding—is that of Jorge

Portilla in his sober treatise on Mexican "national character," entitled *Fenomenología del relajo* (1966).[2] Relajo, Portilla admits, "presents itself, in the generality of things, accompanied by hilarity" (42), but its more profound and essential significance or sense "is to suspend seriousness," which is to say, "to annihilate the subject's adherence to a value proposed to his freedom" (18). Relajo, Portilla clarifies, may manifest itself in diverse acts that "can vary from the most imperceptible facial expression to the formulation of perfectly coherent and rational positions, ranging from bodily postures, words, cries, noises, etc." (21); whatever its specific form, however, relajo serves as an infectious "invocation to others" (23), reiterated "until the vertigo of complicity in the negation takes possession of the group" (24). Thus, relajo, he declares more bluntly, is "nihilism disguised as good humor" (41), "an action directed toward disorder, toward tangling and confusing the channels of action" (83). In a resounding summation of his dismal assessment, Portilla conclusively proclaims: "*Relajo* seeks irresponsibility . . . literally, a freedom for nothing. Freedom to not choose anything. It promotes disorder so as to not have to do anything" (84).[3] "After *relajo*," Portilla passes his final judgment, "things proceed exactly the same as they were before" (85).[4] In this sense, as Slavoj Žižek contends (1994, 311), "laughter, irony, are, so to speak, part of the game."

In *The Labyrinth of Solitude*, an analogous but more renowned meditation on Mexican "national character," Octavio Paz ([1950] 1985) likewise addresses the nexus of humor, absurdity, and nihilism, but only to pathologize them as the destructive and vindictive excesses of "the *macho*." He writes:

> The *macho* . . . is a humorist. His jokes are huge and individual, and they always end in absurdity. The anecdote about the man who "cured" the headache of his drinking companion by emptying his pistol into his head is well known. True or not, the incident reveals the inexorable rigor with which the absurd is introduced into life. The *macho* commits *chingaderas*, that is, unforeseen acts that produce confusion, horror, and destruction. He opens the world; in doing so, he rips and tears it, and this violence provokes a great, sinister laugh. And in its own way, it is just: it re-establishes the equilibrium and puts things in their places, by reducing them to dust, to misery, to nothingness. The humor of the *macho* is an act of revenge. ([1950] 1985, 81)

Paz's remarks are situated in relation to a more extended discussion of what he deems to be the specific maladies of Mexican masculinity.[5] For present purposes, however, it suffices to note that for Paz, as for Portilla, humor and laughter—when they are entangled with absurdity and nihilism—are apprehensible only as sheer negativity, and must be judged in only the gloomiest of terms. Paz offers a comparably bleak discussion of dissimulation as a putative characteristic of "the Mexican" (40–46), and explicitly links this with irony: "Suspicion, dissimulation, irony . . . are traits of a subjected people who tremble and disguise themselves in the presence of the master" (70).

Indirectly, Renato Rosaldo supplies a poignant reply to Paz's disparagingly elitist presumptions: "Precisely because of their oppression, subordinate people often avoid unambiguous literal speech. They take up more oblique modes of address laced with double meanings, metaphor, irony, and humor. . . . The subversive potential and the sheer fun of speech play go hand in hand. Wit and figurative language enable not only the articulation of grievances and aspirations under repressive conditions but also the analysis of conflicts and ironies produced by differences of class, race, gender, and sexual orientation" (1989, 190; see Lomnitz-Adler 1992, 312). Moreover, speaking of "distinctively Chicano forms of irony," Rosaldo maintains: "When the protagonists speak in self-deprecating voices, their humor can be so understated that its wit, not to mention its barbed edges, often escapes straight-faced readers and listeners. Culturally distinctive jokes and banter play a significant role in constituting Chicano culture, both as a form of resistance and as a source of positive identity" (149–50).[6] Indeed, despite its availability for cooptation and institutionalization, the nihilistic but subversive laughter of relajo that Portilla so disdains, and which Paz so casually dismisses as belligerent and futile, seems always to retain its resilient and unpredictable power. "Play is not a trivial thing," Roger Lancaster likewise observes, "and the simultaneously destructive and creative power of laughter should never be underestimated" (1997, 11).

It is especially revealing to consider when relajo's tactics of defamiliarizing humor and subversive laughter enter the ethnographic frame. José Limón, for instance, contends that relajo produces a sense of solidarity, trust, familiarity, and respect (1989, 478; 1994, 133) and creates "a temporary forum of nonalienation" (1989, 479; 1994, 135).[7] More important for interpretive considerations of the ethnographic encounter, however, Limón specifies that relajo initiates "a play world in which open aggression can appear *only by mistake*. Such a mistake can occur when a novice or an unacculturated person fails to recognize the scene, or when he is less than competent in the requisite artistic skills" (1989, 477; 1994, 133; emphasis original).[8] Here, Limón gestures provocatively toward a critical fault line, a site of contingency where the possibility of ethnographic knowledge itself may approach a limiting horizon imposed by the researcher's own dogmatic seriousness.

In this respect, Limón takes his cue from Américo Paredes's classic essay "On Ethnographic Work among Minority Groups" (1977, 73–110; see Rosaldo 1985 and 1986a). Paredes revisits some of the classic Chicano critiques of anthropology and their indictment of its culturalist apologism for Mexican poverty in the United States (especially Romano 1968 and 1970). By rereading the infamous ethnographic monographs that inspired outrage among earlier Chicano critics, Paredes is able to skillfully reveal the ironic workings of formulaic tropes and performative genres that went unrecognized by white anthropologists and then were mistakenly transposed as straight ethnographic "data." In so doing, Paredes produces a memorable critique of ethnographic literalism, especially as it manifests itself as a bald insensitivity to irony and humor:

> Ethnographers may find it useful to keep in mind that Chicanos and Mexicans do have a sense of humor, and they love to put strangers on. . . . Ethnographers working with Chicanos sometimes fail to make this distinction between factual report and the possibility of joking or some other types of performance. . . . [and tend] to proceed as if language had only one level of meaning, or as if informants were incapable of any kind of language use but that of minimum communication. . . . The informant is seldom seen as a competent artist in language use, who may in fact be taking the anthropologist's measure. (81–82)

Paredes situates this kind of "intercultural jest" as an ironic (and artistic) mediation of the racialized disparities of wealth and power that constitute conditions of possibility for the ethnographic encounter itself. He discusses how the crude stereotype of the "dumb Mexican peon" comes to be conjured up as parody through performative role playing, and then recapitulated by the ethnographer whose literalism and gullibility expose latent racist preconceptions (86–91). "The informant not only has his stereotypes about the Anglo fieldworker," Paredes confirms, "he also has some definite ideas as to what stereotypes the Anglo holds about him" (110).[9]

Relajo, then, calls attention to the playful, sometimes anarchic irony that presents a challenge to the very possibility of ethnographic comprehension and "knowledge" across the embattled divides of racialized class inequalities. Adopting Paredes's technique of rereading the ethnographic archive, Miguel Díaz-Barriga (1997) executes a careful, critical, ultimately devastating critique of Oscar Lewis's ethnography and creatively problematizes Lewis's infamous "culture of poverty" thesis in terms of relajo—specifically, that of Lewis's informant Guillermo Gutiérrez. Díaz-Barriga identifies how Gutiérrez's relajo could be understood to convey a distinctly situated critical knowledge, however humorously.[10] He also repeatedly identifies Gutiérrez's sophistication and ironic creativity, as well as Lewis's literal-minded incognizance and will to collapse relajo into pathology. Díaz-Barriga is even more ambitious in his analysis, however: "Gutiérrez's *relajo* is an attempt to engage Lewis in dialogue," he argues. "The irony is so evident that it begs Lewis to recognize it" (55). If, as Portilla insists, the true sense of relajo is to subvert seriousness, then, Díaz-Barriga's insight into the fundamentally dialogical character of the ethnographic encounter serves as a reminder of James Carse's important insight (1986, 19): "Seriousness is a dread of the unpredictable outcome of open possibility. To be serious is to press for a specified conclusion. To be playful is to allow for possibility whatever the cost to oneself."

Rather than the pure negation that Portilla ascribes to relajo, Díaz-Barriga discerns an effort at engagement and genuine communication that, like the practice of ethnographic research itself, entails a great risk. "*Relajo* poses interpretive problems," Díaz-Barriga continues, "both in its deployment in everyday life and its implosion, when misunderstood, into dominant stereotypes" (60). In this regard, Laura Nader is credited with having advanced the important caution: "Don't study the poor and powerless because everything you say about them will be used against them." Indeed, Díaz-Barriga demonstrates decisively that Gutiérrez's ironic invitation to dialogue is met with a dogmatic seriousness on Lewis's part that resolves itself in a one-sided, monotonous ethnographic caricature. "*Relajo*," Díaz-Barriga therefore concludes, "highlights and challenges the relations of power through which ethnographic truth is produced" (60). Here, it may be advisable to recall the racialized status and colonial inheritance of the discipline of anthropology itself and to revisit the sage suspicion of Othman Sullivan, reported in John Gwaltney's ethnography *Drylongso* (1980, xix), when he declares: "I think this

anthropology is just another way to call me a nigger." On this precaution-
ary note, then, taking a cue from Clifford, this chapter will have to
presuppose a willingness to be surprised and an openness to being
shocked. What is fundamentally at stake here, however, is not a "science
of cultural jeopardy" through which the mutual "otherness" of discrete
and essential "cultures" are rendered commensurable, but rather a critical determination to throw into jeopardy the very coherence and presumed integrity of the racial categories that meaningfully engulf all of us
and confine us hierarchically within a sociopolitical order of white
supremacy.

RACIALIZED IRONY AND THE POLITICS OF LAUGHTER

On the first day of an ESL course at Die-Hard Tool and Die that I would be
teaching during the spring of 1995, just before class was to begin, Gonzalo
was cheerful as he teased a U.S.-born white coworker: "School is only for
white people, no *negritos*—you can't go." No Blacks allowed, Gonzalo
declared to the white worker—*you*'re not welcome, because this is only
for us white people. Gonzalo's bubbly laughter was as infectious for his
Latino classmates as it was a kind of mischievous provocation to the
white guy who had unsuspectingly become the object of Gonzalo's ironic
tactic of defamiliarization. Indeed, in its affront to racialized "common
sense," Gonzalo's relajo enacted precisely what Richard Rorty (1989, 73)
discerns as the definitive feature of irony—radical and persistent doubts
about the "final" vocabulary currently in use. "The opposite of irony is
common sense," Rorty continues, "for that is the watchword of those
who unselfconsciously describe everything important in terms of the
final vocabulary to which they and those around them are habituated"
(74). Startling from the very start, Gonzalo's devotion to disrupting the
habitual vocabulary of racial knowledge quickly established that he
would be teaching me a great deal about what Rosaldo has called "the
politics of laughter" (1986b), and likewise, what Roger Lancaster has
called "the politics of play" (1997, 27). Beside the counterintuitive (indeed, surrealist) racial discourse that Gonzalo articulated, this instance
was also remarkable as an unusual reversal: the typically racialized stigma
of a workplace ESL course (whereby Latino migrant workers' Spanish
language is produced as an absence of English language, and hence, as
"lack" or "need") was ironically reconstituted as a privilege or even a
luxury, and thereby reracialized accordingly.

Two days later, before the beginning of class, I proposed that some of the people who had already arrived help me move the tables in the "training" room, so that we could reorganize the learning space to suit our purposes. I was surely under the influence of some kind of critical pedagogic impulse. After all, Paulo Freire (1996, 123) has written: "It does not seem to me that care for what we do can coexist with indifference or disregard for the space in which we operate." So on this occasion, I was inspired to motivate a reorganization of the tables in the classroom. Gonzalo was already present, but he was unwilling to be troubled with moving furniture. "You guys do it," he chuckled, "because I am white!" (*Ustedes, ¡porque yo soy blanco!*).

It had also already become abundantly evident that Gonzalo was in the habit of using a peculiar nickname to refer to his closest friend in the class, Osvaldo—Gonzalo regularly called him *Negro*. It is not at all uncommon for Mexican people to nominate as *negro* someone (for example, a family member) whose complexion is relatively dark; indeed, this kind of situational and relatively flexible deployment of skin-color categories is a distinctive feature of what may be appropriately called "racial" discourse in Mexico. Still, Osvaldo was not generally dark-complexioned by the standards of the Latinos who worked in this particular factory, nor would he be considered particularly dark among most Mexicans. Perhaps most importantly, Osvaldo was lighter than Gonzalo himself. Nevertheless, the nickname was clearly an affectionate one. Indeed, two weeks into the course, Gonzalo wistfully explained to me, "We've been together [*juntos*] for seventeen years—like a marriage [*matrimonio*], me and my *negro* Osvaldo."

Gonzalo was in his early forties. He had originally migrated from a very small agrarian village in rural Zacatecas. Twenty-one years before I came to know him in 1995, he had first migrated to Texas where he was a farm laborer, went back to Mexico, then returned to the United States, this time to an Illinois town two hundred miles south of Chicago, where he joined a friend working at a tree nursery. When he lost that job, Gonzalo continued, alone, to Chicago. For the first two years, he worked for a Hilton hotel; then, because he knew someone who was working there, he applied for a job at Die-Hard Tool and Die. Over time, I learned from some of the women workers' barbed teasing, as well as his own good-humored replies, that Gonzalo had remarried in Chicago without ever having ended his relationship with his first wife in Mexico, with whom he still stayed during his visits to Zacatecas. Although he had other children in Mexico, when asked about his plans for the future, Gonzalo said that he planned to stay in the United States because his children had been born and raised in Chicago. Indeed, Gonzalo seemed to be exceptionally involved in the upbringing of his young daughters, with whom he took daily walks or bicycle rides in the park after work. It was not at all a surprise, therefore, when Gonzalo called me two years later for advice about how to enroll in classes that would prepare him to apply for U.S. citizenship.

Osvaldo was sixty-three years old and had grown up in a small rural town in the state of San Luis Potosí. After finishing the sixth grade, he had migrated to Mexico City, where he proceeded to spend more than twenty-five years working as a local and long-distance truck and bus driver. The worldliness attributed to Osvaldo's previous work was often projected in a predictably masculinist idiom, with abundant jokes about the unnumbered women with whom he had left children scattered all across Mexico. Osvaldo had first migrated to the United States in 1956 and spent six months working in Texas before being apprehended by the INS and deported. Then, again in 1966, he migrated for a relatively brief time after his union had gone on strike and the bus company retaliated with a lockout, firing all of the workers who had been involved in the union. When I came to know him in 1995, Osvaldo had already been in the United States continuously for twenty-five years and had naturalized as a U.S. citizen the year before. He was remarried in Chicago to a Guate-malan woman and had two stepdaughters, as well as grandchildren whom he looked after and cooked for every afternoon. Nevertheless, Osvaldo also still maintained regular contact with the seven children he had with his first wife, all of whom had remained in Mexico, and made annual visits to Mexico every September. Indeed, Osvaldo owned a house in his hometown in San Luis Potosí and was planning to also buy a home in a border town in Texas where his brother lived, so as to more easily spend his retirement shuttling back and forth across the border. After Osvaldo had spent his first years in Chicago working as a cook in various fast-food restaurants, a Mexican friend named Cuco, who still worked at Die-Hard and was also a participant in the ESL class, had encouraged Osvaldo to apply for a job in the factory.

All told, Gonzalo had been working at Die-Hard Tool and Die for roughly seventeen years, and Osvaldo had been employed in the factory for even longer. As Gonzalo recounted sweetly, he and Osvaldo (who was many years his senior) had been there "together—like a marriage," Gon-zalo and his *negro*, his "black" Osvaldo.

A couple of weeks later, Osvaldo—for no apparent reason on this particular occasion—opted to momentarily contest Gonzalo's habit of calling him *Negro*. "I'm not Black—I'm white, right?" There was no immediate reply forthcoming—not from Gonzalo, nor from myself, nor from anyone else in the room. I seized the opportunity to ask Osvaldo, "Why does he call you *Negro*?" To this, in a matter-of-fact manner (although I would like to imagine that there was also, possibly, a fleeting hint of regret), Osvaldo replied, "Because I work too much." Gonzalo laughed, "Yeah, he's *mi negro!*" And Osvaldo continued, "*Como esclavo.*" Like a slave.[11]

I came to understand that Osvaldo's nickname had been elaborated from his job on the shop floor as the day shift's material handler. Indeed, Osvaldo was now the only material handler, whereas there had previously been three people performing these tasks—servicing all of the operators like Gonzalo at the machines to which each was respectively attached. Not only had the company compressed three men's jobs into one, management had eliminated the position altogether on the second shift, requiring Osvaldo to help the next shift get started and leaving the responsibilities of material handler for the remainder of the second shift to another participant in the ESL course, Venustiano. Venustiano was required to divide his energies among three jobs, combining the material handler tasks with those of machine operator as well as die-setter. Some of the other workers, machine operators who depended upon the quick and efficient services of the material handler in order to perform their own jobs according to the company's demands for high productivity, tended to overlook Venustiano's excessive workload and unsympathetically disparaged him as "lazy," whereas Osvaldo managed to avoid such criticisms only by working, as he had once remarked, "like a *burro*," a donkey or a pack-mule, whose thankless fate is to always haul a heavy load. Osvaldo's job as material handler required him to run to and fro among the machines, at the beck and call of the operators, supplying them with metal coils and other raw materials, and hauling off the parts that they produced at the presses. Operators like Gonzalo were stuck tending the huge punch-press machines, but Osvaldo's job required that he come running whenever the operators needed his services—in his own words, "like a slave" . . . and in Gonzalo's pronouncedly racialized idiom, like a Black, indeed, his very own *Negro*.

In these instances of Gonzalo's racialized irony, he implicitly posited an equation of whiteness with privilege, and specifically, with the kind of luxury that is constituted through either a freedom from labor, or a power to control or at least command the labor of someone else. And although he was the most vocal in articulating these perspectives, Gonzalo was not at all alone. On one occasion, when two of the other workers in the class had a question about whether they would be paid for coming in before their shift started, in order to register for the company's new health insurance plan, it was Osvaldo himself who advised them on what to say (in English) to their bosses: "Tell them, I'm not Black, I'm white— you gotta pay me!"

This perspective on the privileged status of whiteness, obviously, and inevitably, could in no way be disentangled from a concomitant denigration of Blackness. Two days later, for instance, when workers in the class were chatting about one another's vacation plans to return to Mexico, Osvaldo joked, "Me, I'm going to Africa this year!" Indeed, there were ultimately several occasions during the course when Osvaldo repeatedly made jokes about visiting Africa and seemed to presume that the mere mention of Africa was sufficiently preposterous as to be automatically funny. On this occasion, in an attempt to not treat his claim as something outlandish in and of itself, I feigned seriousness and asked Osvaldo why he was planning to go to Africa. Seizing the opportunity for a bit of relajo, Gonzalo immediately demanded of Osvaldo, "Yeah, why? Do you have your family over there?" Osvaldo then deftly deflected Gonzalo's insinuation that he was Black and turned the joke on his longtime friend and classmate Cuco. "No," Osvaldo answered Gonzalo, "but Cuco's got his sister over there." Then, as if to further punctuate the racially charged irony of his remark, Osvaldo changed the terms of his innuendo-laden humor. "I'm going to see friends," he declared, "There are a lot of monkeys in Africa, and I have a lot of monkeys as friends." With the perfect performative finesse that manifests itself in well modulated understatement during such contests of one-upmanship, Osvaldo dryly insinuated, since Gonzalo and Cuco were both his good friends, that *they* were a couple of monkeys. By implication, furthermore, the racialized double meaning of Osvaldo's playful insult was that his friends were also Black.[12]

Gonzalo was also accustomed to using a secondary nickname to refer to Osvaldo. In addition to calling him *Negro*, Gonzalo was also in the habit of referring to him as *Indio*. As is common usage throughout Mexico (and much of Latin America), *indio*—far from being a neutral term for "Indian," or referring plainly to someone from an indigenous community—is a derogatory racial epithet that Gonzalo and others would casually volunteer to be otherwise synonymous with "rude," "uncouth," and generally "backward."[13] Here, of course, it is instructive to recall that Mexicanness (or *mexicanidad*) itself emerged historically only as the contradictory and conflicted product of a variety of nationalist projects and struggles in Mexico, which were substantially racialized in their own right (Lomnitz-Adler 1992 and 1996; see Bartra 1992; Schmidt 1978). Interestingly, although he would never have identified himself as *indígena*, Osvaldo was, in fact, acquainted with some vocabulary and expressions in Nauhuatl and Huazteco, the indigenous languages of groups that had gathered routinely for the weekly market day in the small rural town in San Luis-Potosí where he had spent his childhood. Although Osvaldo seemed quite proud of this knowledge and occasionally made comments that conveyed a certain reverence for the accomplishments of Mexico's indigenous peoples, he nonetheless would also readily pronounce words and phrases from an indigenous language upon Gonzalo's command, with much comedic affect. Gonzalo commonly responded with amused laughter and questions, such as, "What are you saying, crazy man?" Indeed, the performance of such "knowledge" of indigenous peoples' languages and customs was a characteristic way of establishing precisely a non-Indian identity and distancing oneself from "real" "Indian"-ness. "Ostentatiously using one or two Indian words in a manner that is simultaneously jocular and derogatory," notes Lomnitz-Adler (1992, 30) in his discussion of anti-Indian racism in the Huasteca Potosina, frequently went hand-in-hand with projecting idleness, laziness, and shiftlessness onto Indians so as to justify their exploitation (31). Likewise, knowledge of Indian languages, he suggests further, "was valued on the count that it allowed communication and control over the Indians, and not in the sense that it was knowledge to be assimilated to one's own personal customs" (171). Thus, there was a remarkable conversance, if not collusion, in Gonzalo's and Osvaldo's racialized vocabularies between the respective conventions of the kind of anti-Indian racism that is pervasive in Mexico and the preeminently anti-Black racism that is hegemonic in the United States.

During the second week of class, when Gonzalo learned that I lived in Chicago near Eighteenth Street, his immediate reaction was somewhat enigmatic. "You live on the South Side!?!" Gonzalo responded, "I don't like the South Side, because there's a lot of niggers on the South Side."[14] It was not particularly surprising to hear a Mexican migrant articulate what seemed plainly to be an expression of the hegemonic racism against

African Americans, but it seemed inconceivable that anyone from Mexico, who like Gonzalo had spent many years in Chicago, would not already know that "Eighteenth Street" (*La Dieciocho*) referred to the almost homogeneously Mexican Pilsen neighborhood. Taking Gonzalo's racialized language too literally, my response conveyed my disbelief—I replied that where I was living was "all Mexican, completely Mexican!" Indeed, my reaction was not without a certain defensiveness about how my street address was supposed to serve as a kind of credential with respect to my ethnographic location. Others in the class made the same rebuff, laughing at the preposterous notion that he would not know about the Eighteenth Street barrio. Of course, this was simply another gesture of Gonzalo's ironic sense of humor, his unpredictable and anarchic relajo. Indeed, Gonzalo revealed to me the following week that he was perfectly acquainted with Pilsen, mentioning a place on Eighteenth Street where he frequently went to buy *carnitas*. Did the previous remark merely confirm what seemed to be Gonzalo's plainly "racist" attitudes against African Americans? Perhaps the remark had been Gonzalo's way of testing my reaction and evaluating me just as I was trying to evaluate him; he would have had no other means to judge decisively whether or not I might be a racist, whether or not I could be trusted—after all, I am racialized as white. Furthermore, Osvaldo might willingly and artfully perform his designated role as the straight man for Gonzalo's humor. More important for the subversiveness of his relajo, however, was that I (as the white English teacher) be unwittingly enlisted as the unsuspecting straight man whose seriousness could be frustrated by Gonzalo's unpredictable tactics of defamiliarization (see Lancaster 1997, 12). But then again, as Gonzalo clearly did know that Eighteenth Street, although it was on the South Side, was a Mexican and not African American neighborhood, this may have been still another of Gonzalo's surrealistic gestures, whereby all those Mexicans (whose poverty required them to live in as rough and notorious a place as Pilsen) could be disparaged and dismissed as so many "niggers." Or, if Gonzalo perhaps did not intend to disparage *all* Southside Mexicans as "niggers," at least those whom Gonzalo could consider to be the ones culpable for Pilsen's notoriety, such as the members of street gangs (so often the children of migrants not unlike himself) —perhaps *they* were the reason that he did not like the Eighteenth Street barrio and could thereby be disdained as "a lot of niggers on the [Mexican] South Side." Furthermore, in this murky light of reracialization where nothing was quite as it seemed, perhaps Gonzalo required me (in my whiteness) to acknowledge his own agonistic claims to whiteness, just as he required other Mexicans (such as Osvaldo) to stand in, in various ways, as his "niggers."

Although Gonzalo's frequent and casual use of the term *nigger* clearly referred to a far wider social framework than any of the particularities of this one workplace, it is nonetheless important to note that when Gonzalo spoke of the so-called "niggers" at Die-Hard Tool and Die, he was never referring to any actual Black people in the factory itself. The company's workforce was comprised entirely of (non-black) Latinos and whites. (Among the Latinos, although the great majority were originally from Mexico, this was an exceptionally diverse workplace, including migrants from Puerto Rico, Guatemala, El Salvador, Panama, Bolivia; among the white workers, many were of Appalachian origin.) There were no African Americans working there. Hence, Gonzalo's habit of referring to his Latino and U.S.-born white coworkers as "niggers" always had its surrealist edge. Gonzalo's performances of his own "whiteness" came to evince an even greater irony, however, as he began to destabilize the very same racialized ground where previously he had tried to secure a footing for himself. As Gonzalo trudged into the classroom on one occasion, he announced: "I'm tired! Because I work too hard, all day long." As we had been discussing the problem of "speed-up" in our class discussions, I suggested, "Maybe you need to work slower." Gonzalo explained further, "I can't, because my boss pushes me hard all day long—because I'm a darker color, because I'm a nigger!" Since he was using the word with reference to himself, which seemed in itself to be a remarkable turn of events, I felt encouraged that I could challenge him more directly than usual. In a rather didactic tone, I admonished, "You know, Gonzalo, that *nigger* is a racist word." Gonzalo summarily deflected my criticism, while also now displacing the racial epithet from himself to his good friend: "I'm not a racist, I just use that word with my nigger Osvaldo!" Again, it was Osvaldo who intervened to explain, apologetically: "He means *esclavo* [slave]."

Indeed, Gonzalo had been generally deploying the word *nigger* to refer to his white and Latino coworkers in the factory, and now, at least at this moment, he was actually using it to refer to himself. Furthermore, at least in this framework of the factory, he seemed to use the word fairly consistently (or in any case, most regularly) to name anyone who was, at any given moment, most subordinated to a certain laborious condition. Yet later that same day, in a discussion about the politics of learning English as a Second

Language, Gonzalo declared with his usual jocularity, but also with an authoritatively conclusive (not quite ironic) tone: "You learn English by speaking with the white people, but not the niggers, because they talk pure blah-blah-blah." Despite whatever surreal collage of defamiliarized uses he could improvise for the category *nigger*, here was an instance where, in Gonzalo's estimation, migrant Latinos (confronted with the challenge of learning English) had to orient themselves to those who were native speakers of the language, represented reductively as U.S.-born whites and Blacks. In such instances, it was evident that Gonzalo ultimately had recourse to a rather fixed and objectified social framework where the word *nigger* was still reserved to do a very specific linguistic work—the generically derogatory racialization of African American Blackness.

Gonzalo's sporadic and divergent deployments of the category "nigger" continued to proliferate, nonetheless. One day, at the end of class (which ordinarily was quitting time for most of the course participants), almost all had to go back into work, as the management had mandated a new schedule of ten-and-a-half-hour days. Gonzalo didn't have to return to work, however. "My color is different," he explained, "Only the niggers have to go back." Perhaps with a bit of envy toward Gonzalo, who could go home early, and certainly disgruntled at his own impending return to the factory, Osvaldo interjected, "Gonzalo is half white and half black." Osvaldo was now directing some irony of his own at what had become increasingly more obvious to me—that Gonzalo's "color"—which is to say, his own self-styled if ambivalent accounts of his status in racialized terms—seemed to be always oscillating back and forth between white and Black, largely depending on the company's production schedules. The surrealistic "estrangement effects" of Gonzalo's ironic racial discourse seemed to operate in tandem with the estrangement of his labor. Indeed, Gonzalo exuded a particularly strong sensitivity to the onerousness of his exploitation. At the end of virtually every class meeting, specifically notifying me that the allotted time for class was finished, Gonzalo habitually announced, "*Frijolillo* time!" "Time to go home and eat beans!" he routinely declared at the anointed hour. As if to reaffirm that the workers' time in the ESL course was really labor-time after all, Gonzalo regularly underscored the crucial difference between the company's time and the workers' free time, and notably did so in terms that were implicitly but irreducibly identified with the specificity of being Mexican.

Gonzalo's critical relation to the alienation of his labor was memorably revealed on another occasion when I had initiated a discussion framed by the questions, "Do you like to work? Why or why not?" Osvaldo had been the first to respond, explaining in earnest, "Yes, of course I like to work because it means I have more money for my family. I can pay my car insurance, pay the rent, fix up my home in Mexico . . ." Taso, one of the Puerto Rican workers in the class, injected a bit of humor, however, answering ironically, "Yeah, I like work—I make some money, and I get some exercise, too!" More seriously, and with recourse to a rather vivid metaphor, Catarino, a Guatemalan course participant, added his perspective: "Sometimes it's fun, sometimes it's hard—but the essence of money is work [*la esencia del dinero es el trabajo*], work is the essence of money. When you're working, you're drawing out money [*sacando el dinero*], just like when you milk a cow, you draw out milk [*sacas la leche*]." At this point, however, Gonzalo's patience had been tried, and he predictably resorted to a quite revealing bit of relajo. "When I work hard, I get real tired, and then I go home and sleep better! Everybody says they like money, but I say no . . . I like to work because I like to leave here good and tired!" After we all shared a good laugh, the discussion resumed in earnest. Inocensio, a Mexican migrant from an agrarian village in Michoacán, explained that when he had started at Die-Hard six years earlier, he was assigned to the welding machine, which was infamous among the workers because anyone operating it inevitably was engulfed in the acrid smoke that it emitted. Now, working on an automatic punch press, Inocensio affirmed that he was content because his job was "not hard, and it's good pay." Gonzalo, who also worked on an automatic press, interrupted: "OK, go ahead, tell him another lie! I'm not gonna lie—I don't like to work! Because it makes me tired. When I stay home, I'm relaxed, I can go walking in the park, or just take it easy in the house." In response, a Salvadoran coworker, Beatriz, declared, "It's Gonzalo who's lying, because he needs money like all the rest of us." Now assuming an uncharacteristically serious posture and answering Beatriz's criticism sincerely, Gonzalo corrected her: "I *have to* work because I need money . . . but I don't *like* it!" Beatriz nevertheless seized upon the opportunity to give Gonzalo a taste of his own relajo, proclaiming still more confidently, "If they didn't pay us, nobody would come to work—only Gonzalo would come, because he doesn't like money!" Beatriz mercilessly challenged the seriousness of Gonzalo's critical stance toward his thankless wage labor. Unlike the rest of his coworkers, Gonzalo alone would willingly volunteer his labor without pay, Beatriz suggested, insinuating that he was not only a "slave," but worse, merely a *servile* fool.

On another occasion in April of 1995, Gonzalo happened to mention the infamous name of California's Governor Pete Wilson, the politician most prominently identified with California's anti-immigrant Proposition 187, who had been flirting with the prospect of presenting himself as a Republican presidential candidate. Another course participant, Meche, who had been living in the Chicago area for only two years after having previously lived in California for fifteen years, and who still had family living and working there, had strong opinions on the matter. A woman in her early thirties from the border city of Ciudad Juárez, Chihuahua, Meche had first migrated to the United States when she was pregnant, at the age of fifteen, and immediately assumed the laborious life of an undocumented migrant worker. Upon the loathsome mention of Pete Wilson's name, Meche instantly reacted with bitter resentment: "California is dying! Lots of people are leaving and coming here already. Pete Wilson wants to be president—maybe somebody will kill him!" In his characteristically ironic manner, Gonzalo abruptly seemed to negate the seriousness of Meche's righteous anger altogether. "We shouldn't be talking about politics," he declared mischievously, "Politics is for whites [*los güeros*], not for us Mexicans. If Wilson becomes president, I'll just go back to my country." In a political climate of exaggerated nativism and anti-immigrant racism, Gonzalo assumed what appeared to be a cynical and even fatalistic posture toward the fact of white supremacy and his own racialized subordination as a Mexican, leading him to frankly repudiate any illusion of having the right to even discuss politics. Bluntly thwarting the momentum of Meche's critique, Gonzalo seemed to affirm that the U.S. nation-state really belonged to the whites after all.

Gonzalo made an analogous remark when the company held a small graduation ceremony after the ESL course had finished. The event took place in the factory, coordinated with the workers' lunch break, in conjunction with a report from the vice president about productivity and quality control statistics, with the entire workforce in attendance. Chairs had been arranged to stage the requisite audience for the boss's presentation, as well as the graduation proceedings that would follow. As people gathered, many of the seats were left empty; most of the workers stayed back and remained standing. Some of the graduating course participants, however, felt entitled to be seated. Gonzalo was standing along the side of the assembly, in the furthest corner from the management personnel who would be speaking. I encouraged him, as one of the graduates, to move forward and take a seat. Grinning playfully, but laughing somewhat more tentatively than usual, Gonzalo said, "No, that's for the white people, not me." At the end of the course—and at the proverbial end of the day—Gonzalo's surrealistic racial discourse seemed to be inevitably tempered by the starker realism incumbent upon a racialized condition that was hardly as idiosyncratic as his own imagination, nor as playful as his ironic sense of humor. Just as in the beginning of the course, when he had refused to help move tables in the classroom, Gonzalo identified the luxury of sitting with the status of whiteness; plainly (but not so simply), the striking difference was that he had felt entitled then to remain seated, and now he seemed insistent in his decision to remain standing. "No," he said, "that's for the white people, not me." Among other things, at least by implication, Gonzalo was reminding me—as the white English teacher—that it had never even occurred to me to question whether or not I myself was entitled to sit in the front of the assembly.

The occasion of the graduation ceremony at Die-Hard provided other revealing moments that helped to trace the broader outlines of the racialized condition of the Latino workers in the factory. Afterward, for instance, when Raúl (a Puerto Rican worker who was fluent in English) was talking with me, a white male coworker teased that next time Raúl also would need to go to class to learn English. Raúl turned abruptly and, pointing demonstratively at the flesh of his forearm, replied forcefully, "I don't go to classes—I'm white!" Reconfirmed was the way that the stigma of having to attend ESL classes, itself, operated within the larger process of racialization for Latino migrant workers whose Spanish language was rendered as a "lack" of English, a "need" for remediation, and a general failure to have already learned English by their own devices of ingenuity and intelligence. In this instance, a Latino who did indeed speak English relied upon his language proficiency as a resource with which to produce his own surrealist claim to a whiteness that could (as if magically) be conferred upon his skin through the tenacious insistence of his index finger, as well as the fluency of his mouth. Shortly thereafter, I was also approached by Jeannette, a white worker, who asked, "Are there gonna be some classes for *us*? Or is it just gonna be another class for the Spanish people to learn English? Ya know, because the rest of us are out here workin' and we'd like a chance to go to school, too—that's why I'm askin' is there gonna be somethin' for *us*?" Here again, one encounters from the opposite standpoint—that of one of the excluded U.S.-born, English-speaking white workers—Gonzalo's initial appreciation that participation in the workplace literacy program, if nothing else, could be counted as a privilege, based upon the simple luxury of being exempted from the labor process. Whereas Gonzalo had ironically characterized that privilege through a racialized lens by which it became the accoutrement of a surreal whiteness, Jeannette seemed distinctly bitter to have discovered her "real" whiteness to be strangely disadvantaged ("because the rest of us are out here workin' and we'd like a chance"), positing her own "us" in sharp juxtaposition to "the Spanish people."

Given the wider racialized context of the factory, Gonzalo's surrealistic appropriations of whiteness had now to confront the greater irony and more bitter absurdity of his white coworkers' less-than-ironic assertions of their own whiteness. Keeping back, choosing to remain standing, Gonzalo identified the privilege of sitting to be "for the white people, not me." Nevertheless, Gonzalo's explicit disavowal of whiteness—as it were, in the last instance—was tantamount to an implicit and ironic reclamation of whiteness in practice. Gonzalo's refusal to sit with his Latino classmates during the graduation, under the gazes of both the white management and the white workers, can also be understood as a desire to evade the racializing limelight that would have foregrounded his own place among Jeannette's implicit "them," the Spanish-speakers whose "need" of access to English language was always merely one sign among many of the impossibility of their ever really accessing whiteness.

Gonzalo's ironic tactics of defamiliarization and his oscillation between his own surrealistic claims to whiteness, on the one hand, and his portrayals of himself as a "nigger," on the other, gestured toward what was ultimately his own captivity as a Mexican at an intermediate racialized location somewhere between white and Black. At Die-Hard Tool and Die, there were obviously quite pronounced class differences between the white bosses and the white workers—inequalities that tended to be refracted, but marked nonetheless, in terms of differences of education and regional origin, among others. This heterogeneity of whiteness and its intrinsic social contradictions notwithstanding, the white management personnel and the white factory workers were never impeded from recognizing one another as racially white, in direct contradistinction with the Latino workers in the factory. And this is the rocky racial terrain upon which Gonzalo's tactics of everyday surrealism had to maneuver and were ultimately constrained. Nevertheless, everyone involved was already ensconced in a much wider social framework that transcended the particularities of this workplace. In this broader setting, notably, neither whites nor Latinos were impeded from considering themselves to be not-Black. Now, however, to more fully examine the broader issues at stake in the reracialization of Mexican migrants, it is necessary to transcend the peculiar idiosyncrasies of an individual such as Gonzalo and the particularities of the factory where he worked.

The racialized intermediacy of Mexican migrants has been constituted historically through the hegemonic polarity of white and Black in the United States. The racialized Blackness of enslaved Africans and their descendants was produced as the absolute bottom of a rigidly hierarchical social order of "American" white supremacy, whereas that same racist society as a whole (the U.S. nation-state) was simultaneously produced in opposition to indigenous peoples whose societies were conceived to be always beyond its frontiers and thus irreducibly "outside," irreconcilably separate, and doomed to extinction as such (De Genova in press).[15] Whiteness, as it has been produced in the United States, can consequently never be extricated from its historicity as a social category that operates in categorical opposition to Blackness. Thus, those racialized as neither white nor Black, to the extent that they come to be incorporated *within* the space between these two poles, are inevitably relegated to racial locations that become socially meaningful only with reference to both.

The intermediacy of Latinos' racial location(s) between whiteness and Blackness is registered on a mass scale in U.S. Census data on "race," although there it assumes the appearance of a peculiarly equivocal racial indeterminacy (see De Genova and Ramos-Zayas 2003b; C. Rodríguez et al. 1991). The U.S. Census did not provide, either in 1990 or 2000, a "racial" category that would correspond to most Mexicans' experience of their racialization, specifically *as Mexicans,* or generically, as Latinos (or Hispanics). Instead, in 1990, Mexicans and other Latinos responding to the Census Bureau's question about "race" found themselves presented with the options of (1) White, (2) Black, (3) American Indian/Eskimo/Aleut, (4) Asian/Pacific Islander, or (5) Other Race. In 2000, this list was slightly adjusted. "Asian" was disaggregated from "Pacific Islander," and the latter was augmented to explicitly include "Native Hawaiian." Likewise, "American Indian" was now coupled with "Alaska Native" (which replaced "Eskimo" and "Aleut"). In both censuses, however, a distinct racial category for Latinos was strictly avoided in favor of treating "Latino" or "Hispanic" as a specifically "ethnic" and thus, officially nonracial category. Latinos were presumed to be whites, or Blacks, or perhaps American Indians, or some conceivable mixture of those supposedly pure and essential racial categories. Given these options for identifying themselves racially, in the city of Chicago, roughly 40 percent of Latinos in 1990 and again, 40.8 percent in 2000 apparently aspired to the privileged racialized status of whiteness by electing to identify themselves as white. Moreover, virtually none chose to call themselves Black or Indian. In light of the strikingly visible racial oppression of African Americans and the abundant racist denigration of Blackness, to which all migrant newcomers to the United States become acutely aware, it ought not be terribly surprising that less than half of one percent of Chicago's Latinos opted to embrace a notion of themselves as "Black." Likewise, given the legacies of racialization throughout Latin America, why the number of Latinos who identify themselves as "Indian" was even lower is not difficult to fathom. What is most remarkable, therefore, and truly the greatest racialized irony of all, is the response of nearly all of the rest. Indeed, in both censuses, the absolute majority of Latinos in Chicago—in 1990, approximately 60 percent, and in 2000, 51.5 percent—opted for the nondescript, none-of-the-above category, identifying themselves as "some other race."

Confronted with the hegemonic racial categories of the U.S. state, Latinos in Chicago (much as in the rest of the country), in a kind of mass act of surrealist relajo, identified themselves racially as "something else." This mass phenomenon, of course, establishes *not* that the majority of Latinos do not know what their "race" is, but rather that it is precisely *neither* white nor Black. What appears in the Census data to be racial indeterminacy, therefore, really serves as an index of racialized social intermediacy. However, Latinos' seemingly surreal responses to the Census questionnaire revealed their condition of being confined to a racial location between whiteness and Blackness, only as an *effect* of the very categories by which the U.S. state orders its racial hierarchy. Indeed, the Census itself plays a vital part in the (re)production of these reified social categories of racialized difference (Goldberg 1997, 27–58; 2002, 188–95; and see B. Anderson [1983] 1991, 163–70; Appadurai 1996, 114–35; Cohn 1987, 224–54; Dirks 2001, 198–228). Furthermore, for the first time, in the 2000 Census respondents were given the choice to select multiple racial categories if they considered themselves to be a mixture of the available categories. While some Latinos did designate various combinations, that number was fairly small.[16] Notably, the 51.5 percent of Chicago's Latinos who identified as "some other race" did so *singularly;* they declared themselves as having *only one* race, but whatever it was, it was "none of the above."

Entangled with its own profoundly problematic and ultimately debilitating racialized contradictions, much of Gonzalo's and Osvaldo's aversion for finding themselves in the condition of "niggers" implied nevertheless a certain class consciousness about the excesses of their own exploited predicament. By desiring the opposite of Blackness, in this particular sense, they also aspired for some measure of relief from their own laborious plight as Mexican/migrant workers. Notably, the same equation of Blackness and slavery that Gonzalo and Osvaldo had invoked was also commonly articulated among Mexican/migrant workers in other factories. A year earlier, I had called Ramiro from Imperial Enterprises on the phone one Saturday afternoon. "My wife just came back from work," he informed me, and then added with a self-satisfied, slightly defiant laugh, "but not me—I'm a lazy-ass [*huevón*]." I was lucky to have caught him at home, Ramiro went on to explain, because most of his coworkers at Imperial were all working six and even seven days a week, in addition to mandatory overtime every day during the week. His wife Rosa, who worked at the same factory, was working Saturdays as well. "That's fucked up!" I replied in response to the general predicament, "You [plural] are really working *a lot!*" With both regret and disdain in his voice, Ramiro simply concurred, "Yeah, like slaves . . . like Blacks [*sí, como esclavos . . . como negros*]."

In this equation of Blackness with slavery, what was particularly significant was Ramiro's explicit juxtaposition of the laborious condition of his coworkers in the factory (including his wife) with his ironic characterization of himself as lazy. Ramiro, of course, was celebrating his own refusal to work on that particular Saturday, and probably intended to imply that he had resisted the company's pressure for overtime where many others had capitulated. Ramiro was not explicitly presenting his rejection of the overtime as an extraordinary or heroic feat—to call himself lazy might even seem to have been a self-effacing gesture—but he was indeed boasting, nevertheless. Rather than working overtime for the company, Ramiro had opted in favor of work he was doing at home for himself and his family—a long-term construction project remodeling his attic. Notably, he did *not* mention that his choice to stay home, while Rosa was out earning overtime wages in the factory, also involved babysitting his three daughters. Instead, Ramiro overtly underscored the contrast between himself with his wife, who had just returned from work, in a distinctly masculinist idiom. After all, *huevos* (literally, "eggs") connotes "balls" (testicles). Having *huevos* is a metonym for masculinity, and related masculinist constructions of courage, willfulness, or aggressiveness; its superlative form is to have *muchos huevos* ("a lot of balls"). The term *huevón*, however, which literally means "someone with big balls," connotes having testicles so big and so heavy as to be unable to move; to be *huevón* connotes being lazy, and is usually said as a reproach.[17]

Most conventionally, those who felt resentful of their own laborious condition tended to deploy the term *huevón* disparagingly (but also ambivalently) toward others, such as bosses (see Lugo 1995, 75). There were several incidents, for example, at Imperial Enterprises when Carlos would stroll past the office of Howard, the white personnel manager, loudly and cheerfully greeting his boss, only then to turn to me, laughing even more gleefully as he mischievously snorted, "¡Huevón!" Likewise, on another occasion, Carlos interacted in a manner that was superficially friendly with Jimmy, an African American coworker, only to then turn to me and mutter derisively, "Fucking lazy-ass [*Pinche huevón*]." Similarly, at Caustic Scrub, many workers frequently devoted considerable energy to denouncing other workers as well as their white supervisors as lazy. However, like Ramiro, workers at Caustic also deployed the notion of laziness in jest almost as a badge of honor, as a kind of masculinist recognition and valorization for workers who successfully resisted the mandates of their exploitation. Javier and Hipólito, for instance, were both men in their midforties from small agrarian towns in Guanajuato and Zacatecas, respectively, and had each been in the United States only five or six years. The two had a very congenial rapport, which seemed to be regularly punctuated, upon my prompting of the course participants to interview one another in our ESL conversations, when Javier repeatedly asked Hipólito, "Are you very lazy? [¿*Eres muy huevón*?]." Always asked in the playful and teasing spirit of relajo that inspired good-humored grins and laughter, Javier's question seemed nonetheless to also be intended as an expression of admiration.

On one occasion, when Javier had just returned from a trip to Mexico, Epifanio, a man already in his sixties who had migrated from the same place, was eager to hear the news of their hometown. Our conversation primarily revolved around the construction of a new house that Javier was financing from his wages at Caustic Scrub. As it turned out, Javier had spent a considerable portion of his visit assisting the builders, mainly members of his own family, with the work of laying the bricks. Upon hearing Javier's report, Edmundo, a migrant in his midtwenties, asked simply, "Were you happy in Mexico?" Javier gave an immediate and robust reply: "Yeah, man! Because I wasn't working! I was being lazy!" Just as Javier, who had partly spent his vacation engaged in manual labor on his new house, could celebrate the work that he had done for himself as "not working" and "being lazy," so also Ramiro, spending his day off from the factory's grinding overtime working on the renovation of his home, was inspired to proclaim his own "laziness" with satisfaction.

By referring to himself as *huevón*, Ramiro could lay claim to laziness as a kind of masculinist self-determination. If not the freedom from work altogether (and, by implication, the power to live off of the labor of someone else), manliness was hereby constituted at least in terms of the liberty to work for oneself without being subjected to the authority and prerogatives of a boss.[18] The resonances here between Ramiro's constructions of a kind of privileged, luxuriating, masculinist laziness, on the one hand, and Gonzalo's constructions of whiteness, on the other, are striking. Ramiro figured a servile Blackness in sharp contrast with the kind of masculinized laziness that he was celebrating. Ramiro's phrase "like slaves" evoked a condition among his coworkers that was excessively onerous, in a double sense: it was both oppressively exploitative and also feminized, because it was work that was coerced, and by implication prostrate to someone else's will. Here, it may be instructive to revisit Gonzalo's characterization of his relationship with Osvaldo (*Negro*)— indeed, *his* Black, *his* nigger—as a marriage. Not merely a suggestion of the intimacy and longevity of the two men's friendship, this "marriage," like any other, implied a patriarchal hierarchy. In short, it signified Gonzalo's assertion of his own dominant masculinity and Osvaldo's subordination. That subordination was emphatically racialized, but it also implicitly reinscribed Osvaldo's position through the feminized figure of Gonzalo's subservient "wife."[19] Such gendered insinuations on Gonzalo's part, however, as with the overtly racialized gestures of calling Osvaldo his "nigger," served to regularly reaffirm the strength of the friendship and deep affection that the two men shared—precisely by the ease with which otherwise abusive expressions could be used without insult (see Wade 1993, 260).

Gonzalo's ironic proclivity to nominate as "niggers" any and all workers (regardless of race) who were excessively subordinated by the conditions of their labor—glossed by his steadfast companion Osvaldo to be simple equations of Blackness with "slavery"—commands further interpretation. As we have already seen, this more playful and fluid notion of the laborious condition ascribed to Blackness was never fully separable from more rigid social conventions that held Blackness to be the singular and contemptible racial condition of African Americans in particular. Moreover, the operative equation of Blackness with "slavery" (as an excessively drudging condition of exploitation or servitude, as well as a feminized status of subjection), seemed, in effect, to insinuate an *opposition* between Blackness and "laziness." In what follows, however, it will become abundantly clear that the metaphorical or analogical constructions of Blackness that came to be equated with subjection and servitude, operated in largely unmediated tension with a rampant, explicit denigration of African Americans as "lazy" in the racial discourses of many Mexican migrants.[20]

THE CURSE OF "LAZINESS" AND
THE SEDUCTIONS OF "HARD WORK"

When I met Patricio in an ESL course in a Pilsen community organization in October of 1994, he had only been in the United States for about three weeks, and was only planning to stay for six months before returning to Zacatecas. Patricio invited me to visit him where he was staying in the home of an elderly aunt—Juana—who had been living in the United States for twenty-two years. She had come to the United States with four of her children, "legally," following her husband who had originally been contracted as a bracero and had spent many years working in various parts of the United States. Two of her children had remained in Mexico when the rest migrated, however, and so Juana returned to Mexico for long visits at least twice a year. Living off the social security pension that her deceased husband had earned over so many years working in the United States, Juana was quite proud to ·declare that she had never worked a day in the United States (outside of her own home, of course).

Although Juana herself had never been employed for wages in the United States, she spoke at length and with considerable authority about the laborious condition of Mexican/migrant workers. Indeed, she was exceptionally conversant with the range of ways that the U.S. state and private employers collude in the exploitation of undocumented labor. She knew many things and was confident in her knowledge. Juana's extended monologue began with how "the poor Mexicans [*los pobres mexicanos*] want to work and are ready to work very hard [*duro*], for very little." Juana produced many examples of how Mexican/migrant workers (and especially the undocumented) are taken advantage of, but increasingly came to punctuate her succession of narratives with a singular refrain: "All the Mexicans who work in factories tell of how very lazy the Blacks are [*que son muy flojos los morenos*]."

"They tell of how the Mexicans do the Blacks' [*prietos*] work," continued Juana, and she went on to relate:

They're so lazy—they just stand around watching while the Mexican does everything . . . and then if they hear anything about it, they'd sooner go on welfare because they're able to collect from the government . . . and they don't live in luxury, true, but they can pay for their needs, because the government here won't let them die of hunger. The government in Mexico *will* leave you to die of hunger, which is why we Mexicans are all over here! But then the Mexicans do all the work because they have to be in fear all the time about getting sent back. . . . And you see it in the stores, too—the Blacks have their carts stacked with meat and all kinds of food, and at the bottom is a pile of food stamps. Meanwhile, the Mexicans are eating beans and tortillas! And the Blacks all have very nice cars— although many don't even go to work!—while the Mexicans may not even have a car. The post office on Ashland [in Pilsen] is full of Blacks—all Blacks! [*puros morenos*]—I don't even think there are any whites [*güeros*] there—no whites, no Mexicans . . . And on the buses, too [as drivers], the Blacks have all the jobs.

In the midst of Juana's extensive account, I sought politely and strategically to suggest facts and perspectives that might have complicated the picture and possibly disrupted her discourse, but Juana was not persuaded. Repeatedly, stubbornly, she would return to the foil against which all of her central themes were organized: "Yes, they're very lazy [*flojos*], the Blacks—all the Mexicans will tell you this."

If it is not entirely accurate that "all the Mexicans will tell you this," as Juana asserted, such articulations of the hegemonic racism against Black people in the United States were nevertheless quite ubiquitous in Mexican Chicago.[21] To introduce this particular genre of Mexican/migrant discourse about the purported "laziness" of African Americans, although many other examples could have sufficed, this instance is especially instructive because Juana, who claimed to have never worked outside of her own home, felt so certain and confident about her knowledge of the relations between Mexican migrants and African Americans in the work-place. Likewise, Juana had never lived in any neighborhood where she would have had extensive everyday contact with African Americans. Not-withstanding these limitations of Juana's specific experiences, the firm-ness of her convictions simply serves to verify and underscore precisely how pervasive these racialized discourses truly were among Mexicans in Chicago. Juana's account of the "laziness" of Black people was largely informed and mediated by what other Mexican migrants recounted, and although it was supplemented by her own observations, its authority relied upon the collective common sense.

It is revealing to consider Juana's contradictory vacillation between an emphasis on what appeared to her to be African Americans' privileged access to employment (and government jobs, at that)—"the Blacks have all the jobs"—and, on the other hand, her insistence upon their laziness and purported predilection for welfare. "Welfare" was typically equated in both Mexican/migrant as well as hegemonic public discourse with "dependency" and was routinely invoked by Mexican migrants as a sup-posedly self-evident manifestation of laziness. Furthermore, as Juana emphasized, the "laziness" of Black people was, in effect, rewarded—while Mexicans must eat only beans, Blacks buy meat with food stamps. Notably, the figure of the U.S. state apparatus lurked in the background on all counts—producing the vulnerability of undocumented Mexican/migrant workers who had to live in permanent fear of deportation, re-serving government jobs for African Americans, and cultivating the de-pendency of Black people who would "sooner go on welfare . . . because the government here won't let them die of hunger." In short, beneath the pronouncedly racialized antagonisms that Juana articulated were the abundant substantive differences generated materially and practically by the divisive politics of citizenship that enforced juridical inequalities between migrant workers (especially the undocumented) and even the most impoverished U.S. citizens (see De Genova and Ramos-Zayas 2003a, 57–82).

The discursive production of the racialized difference between Mexi-cans and African Americans, therefore, relied profoundly upon such renderings of the extraordinarily laborious and exploited condition of Mexican/migrant workers in opposition to the "laziness" equated with Blackness. In Juana's testimony, the allegation of Black laziness was fol-lowed almost seamlessly with the assertion that "the Blacks" were indeed so *lazy* that "the Mexicans" were inescapably saddled with the egregious double burden of performing not only their own work but also that which their African American coworkers stubbornly neglected. The issue of welfare, predictably, then followed—as a willingness to collect public aid that was directly correlated with the presumed unwillingness to work. Thus, "the poor Mexicans," in Juana's account, were effectively plagued by their own distinctive virtue—the noble willingness to work and a resilient readiness for toil.

In this equation of Black people with "laziness," furthermore, it is crucial to examine how the language has shifted: *huevón* (lazy, as having big balls) tended *not* to be the preferred term for depicting Black people; instead, they are *flojos* (lazy, as literally flaccid, or loose, or weak).[22] Plainly, there seemed to be an operative distinction between this flaccid laziness and the labor of Mexican migrants, characteristically described as "hard" work. By way of this juxtaposition, the Mexicans' industrious and productive work was thereby recuperated as a masculinist kind of virility.

The "manly" hard work that Mexican/migrant working men and women alike so commonly identified with their own labor and heroized in racialized opposition to specifically Black laziness, however, was always left to confront the recalcitrant injustices of a system whose racism against them, as Mexicans, so perniciously secures its profits at the expense of their well-being. Capitalism not only threatened their very lives and bodies, as seen in chapter 4, with the mutilation and death that were the more or less banal "facts of life" that accompanied the often brutal subordination of their labor in the United States, it also routinely menaced the security of their livelihoods with unrelenting exploitation and persistent poverty. Thus, their particularly laborious condition also jeopardized the stability of Mexican/migrant men's patriarchal authority over their families. Recognizing how the standard of living for all working people in the United States had been steadily eroded, Juana felt that "nobody can make a decent living now in this country." The direness of the situation was most starkly demonstrated for her by the sense that "in order to survive now, both husband and wife must go to work in this country." Juana's pride about never having worked a day in the United States can now be better situated in relation to what this depiction of her own life's domesticity was intended to testify about her husband—as a working man and dependable provider.

Juana did certainly exude a modestly defiant attitude about her own entitlement to the pension earned by her husband's lifetime of migrant labor, and she confidently fortified this stance with a more general critique. Indeed, over the course of our long discussion, she frequently reaffirmed her perspective that "all the wealth of the U.S. was built up and created by the wetbacks" (*los mojados;* literally, "the wet ones"), by which she referred specifically to undocumented *Mexicans*. But Juana's critical perspective operated within a gendered and racialized regime of "truth." The laboriousness of Mexican/migrant everyday life and the racialized subordination of Mexican migrants' labor (which, as we have seen, was not uncommonly likened to slavery) enabled a critical standpoint on the U.S. nation-state and capitalism but seemed to be always trapped in the idiom of a hegemonic racism against African Americans and recurrently reconfigured against the foil of a flaccid Black "laziness."

THE SURREAL INCOHERENCE OF RACIAL REALITIES:
MIGRATIONS OF MEANING

As is already evident, there are several ostensibly neutral racial categories in Mexican Spanish for identifying dark-skinned persons—such as *negros, morenos, prietos*—that were variously deployed in Chicago to refer to African Americans. These terms existed alongside others, predictably, that were decidedly derogatory, such as *changos* (monkeys),[23] or *xicotes* or *mayates* (dung beetles).[24] The term that was by far the most pervasive, however, was *los morenos*. The genesis of this usage may largely originate in a more or less collective strategy of concealing racial discourse. In an effort to circumvent any possibility of the relatively easy and predictable confusion of the Spanish term *negros* with the inflammatory English epithet *niggers*, many Mexicans may have opted for a term that more effectively disguises discourse about Blacks from the purview of African Americans.[25] (Indeed, Gonzalo may have used the Spanish word *negro* so freely at Die-Hard Tool and Die for the same reason that he could so uninhibitedly use the English word *nigger*—precisely because there were no African Americans in his workplace who more probably would have confronted him about it.) What is most remarkable in the ubiquitous usage of *moreno* in place of *negro*, however, is that many Mexicans (perhaps the majority) would have been most commonly inclined to describe *themselves* in Mexico (before migrating) as *morenos*, and—excluding diminutive uses that are always relative and highly contextual—would have tended to reserve the category *negro* for Mexicans considered to be of recognizable African ancestry. In the course of reracialization in the United States, however, the two were conflated as markers of Blackness, and the term *moreno* was displaced onto African Americans as a generic and collective (racial) category.

As Juana's nephew Patricio had only very recently arrived in the United States, his reracialization was undoubtedly already under way, but as yet remained somewhat incomplete and unresolved. Thus, Juana's account of the racialized differences between Mexicans and African Americans seemed to also have a pedagogical tenor, even a didactic insistence, about it.[26] Notably, whereas Juana repeatedly and most consistently referred to African Americans (collectively) as *los morenos*, Patricio still persisted in employing the same category *moreno* to refer to other (individual) Latinos. Resembling what Clifford has characterized as ethnography's "surrealist" moment, the possibility of comparison existed in unmediated tension with sheer incongruity and epitomized the kind of "cultural jeopardy" that Clifford posits. In this instance, that moment of surrealist jeopardy erupted between distinct migrant generations around the incoherence and incommensurability of incongruous racial meanings.

The reelaborations of Mexican migrants' racialized lexicon reveal something crucial, not really about Mexicans per se, so much as about the racialized social order of white supremacy in the United States. Mexican migrants' displacement of the category *moreno* from themselves onto African Americans is especially remarkable because there are, in fact, other terms—such as *prieto*, for instance—that could conceivably have provided the euphemistic equivalent for *negro* presumably required to disguise references to Black people in the United States. Thus, the fairly ambiguous, highly contextual, sweeping middle term *moreno*—the color category that brushes the broad mass of "brown" Mexicans within Mexico's distinct and relatively fluid racial order—is deflected altogether from Mexicans *as a group* in the United States and tends to be fixed unequivocally upon African Americans as a rigid generic racial category.

Even as Mexican migrants juxtaposed their own laborious condition to "the Blacks" (*los morenos*) whom they commonly alleged to be lazy, however, the excessively exploitative subordination of their labor seemed always to threaten them with the indignity of prostration, degrading them "like slaves . . . like blacks [*como negros*]." Here, too, there was a significant shift in vocabulary revealing the contradictory disjunctures of reracialization: the equation of Blackness with laziness consistently tended to involve the Blackness of *morenos* (which is to say, African

Americans), whereas the equation of Blackness with slavery regularly tended to refer to the blackness of *negros* (that is, most likely, Afro-Mexicans). In other words, Mexican migrants' acknowledgment of slavery, and its inseparability from racial blackness, seemed to express a historical consciousness of slavery *in Mexico* but seemed tantamount to a simultaneous dissociation (or even disavowal) of the historical fact of slavery from the past experience or enduring condition of African Americans and *their* Blackness.

In contrast to the pronounced fixity with which the term *moreno* comes to be attached unequivocally to African Americans, the category that serves in Mexico to refer to "white" or light-skinned Mexicans—*güero*—acquired an enhanced degree of ambiguity in the United States. This term was generally retained as a way of referring to lighter-complexioned Mexicans in Chicago, but it simultaneously operated as the more or less ubiquitous category for U.S. whites. As in Gonzalo's characteristically more polarized racial idiom, there was certainly an occasional usage among Mexican migrants in Chicago of the literal term *blanco* (a category largely absent from popular discourse in Mexico) to refer to "native" U.S. ("American") whites. However, rather than establishing a categorical distinction between U.S. and Mexican versions of "white"-ness—by adopting one term, such as *los blancos*, to refer to U.S. whites, and a separate category to name light-skinned Mexicans, for instance—Mexican migrants tended to refer to U.S. whites as *los güeros*. This heightened racial ambiguity is undoubtedly revealing in much the same way that Latino responses to the U.S. Census expose a definite inclination among some to tenuously embrace the elusive promise of whiteness. Notably, the division between Mexicans and African Americans commonly assumed the apparent form of a conclusive rupture, a definitive separation. Whiteness, on the other hand, assumed the treacherous and equivocal form of an alluring prospect of privilege and power. If only for that fleeting moment when presented by the U.S. Census Bureau with some semblance of a choice in the matter, one need only recall that roughly two of every five Latinos in Chicago aspired to be "Hispanic whites."

In everyday life in Chicago, certainly, even very light-skinned Mexican migrants tended to be not at all deluded into imagining that their racialized status could in any way approximate that of whites. Indeed, as the category *los morenos* was deflected onto Blacks, and as *los güeros* increasingly referred to whites, Mexican migrants (and U.S.-born Mexicans as well) tended to be racialized *as a group* in the United States simply as "Mexicans." Thus, the rather contextual "color" distinctions among themselves—say, the difference between who is *moreno* and who is *güero*, according to conventional Mexican standards—certainly did not vanish but seemed nonetheless to become less pronounced. In other instances, Mexicans likewise found themselves included in a more inclusive but homogenizing racialized category—as "Latinos" (or "Hispanics"). Most importantly, though, their own sense of what it meant to be *mexicanos* itself had been significantly transformed; it had become thoroughly (re)racialized.

RACIALIZED TRANSNATIONALITY: "MEXICAN"-NESS IN THE SPACE OF THE U.S. NATION-STATE

While attending a baptism party in the spring of 1997, a recent migrant in his early twenties told me a joke that was circulating in Mexican Chicago. Pared down to its basic elements, the joke can be summarized as follows. It is the time of the Mexican Revolution, and Pancho Villa's army has just captured an invading U.S. regiment. Addressing his lieutenants, Pancho Villa gives the order: "Take all the Americans [*americanos*]—shoot them, kill them; the Blacks [*morenos*] and Puerto Ricans—just let them go." The lieutenants are confused and dismayed: "What? What are you saying? But why?" Coolly, Pancho Villa replies: "Don't waste the bullets—they'll all just die of hunger—because *here*, there's no welfare."

This joke clearly reiterates the hegemonic racial script concerning "laziness" and welfare "dependency" that informed many Mexican migrants' production of their difference from African Americans. Here, notably, analogous antagonisms between Mexicans and Puerto Ricans are likewise signified.[27] In the joke's imagined space of reterritorialized confrontation, transnational migrants contend with the U.S. racial economy as Pancho Villa's soldiers (which is to say, as Mexicans), battling the arrayed forces of the United States. These forces, however, are in no simple sense comprised only of "Americans," but rather include "Blacks" and "Puerto Ricans" as well. Thus, the joke posits a fundamental opposition between "Mexicans" (as migrants) and an array of variously racialized U.S. citizens. Three of the four operative categories might be mistaken for nationality, but the key to the puzzle is precisely the remaining term— *Blacks*. Although the lines of conflict are drawn around the critical axis of citizenship, therefore, the antagonism becomes overtly apprehensible only when it is further fractured in racialized terms. However, both African Americans and Puerto Ricans, like Mexicans, are perceived to be separate, distinct, and indeed excluded from the category "Americans"— exposing the fact that "American" comes to specifically connote racial whiteness.[28] As such, neither for African Americans nor for Puerto Ricans does birthright U.S. citizenship secure the status of "American"-ness. From the Mexican/migrant standpoint of the joke, then, "American"-ness is unavailable to both Blacks *and* Latinos, because it is understood, in itself, to be a national identity that is intrinsically racialized—as white.

Despite their shared exclusion from "American"-ness, the Mexican protagonists of the Pancho Villa joke, as "aliens," are nonetheless pitted against both African Americans and Puerto Ricans whose specific association with "welfare" signals a substantive entitlement of their U.S. citizenship. Such invidious acts of racialized competition, of course, were also very commonly directed *against* Mexicans. Figured as the U.S. nation-state's iconic "illegal aliens," undocumented Mexican migrants were widely denounced during the 1990s as opportunistic freeloaders abusing public services. Thus, Mexican migrants, undocumented or not, inevitably had to contend with pervasive allegations of undeservingness, especially on the parts of "legal" migrants from other countries who found themselves increasingly at pains to justify their own increasingly beleaguered "alien" status.

In the spring of 1994, I was teaching an ESL course at Czarnina and Sons. In this factory, the workforce was comprised predominantly of Polish migrants, with a substantial minority of Vietnamese and other Southeast Asian migrants, and then only a relatively small minority of Mexicans. The various groups' incapacity to effectively communicate with one another only exacerbated what seemed to be an ever-present atmosphere of distrust and resentment. During one particularly fractious class session, a Vietnamese worker who called himself Michael seemed intent to instigate a controversy when he provocatively declared, "Only the Mexican people come [to the United States] illegally." Having been in the United States longer than the other Mexican participants in the course, and with three U.S.-born children, Evangelina, a woman in her midthirties, was the Mexican in the group who spoke English somewhat more effectively and with greater confidence. Scandalized, Evangelina immediately cursed Michael in Spanish under her breath and then rose to the defense of her people, initially trying to express herself in English and then resorting to Spanish. Visibly angry, literally rising from her seat and gesticulating demonstratively, she asserted: "The Polish and others come illegally too, with tourist visas—they're wetbacks! [¡son mojados!] Only Americans and Blacks [los americanos y los negros] are from here. Even if they [immigrants] have papers, they all come as wetbacks—because they're not from here [aunque tengan papeles, todos vienen mojados—porque no son de aquí] . . . And then, it's true even for their children or grandchildren—they're Chicanos, but not Americans!"[29]

Evangelina's rhetorical tactics were striking for their unorthodox and defamiliarizing estrangement effects. In a flourish of everyday surrealism, she dispensed with any conventional distinction that would designate one migrant's status as "legal" and another's as "illegal"—"even if they have papers, they all come as wetbacks"; indeed, she contended, even if they are documented, they are undocumented; even if they are legal, they are illegal. In this instance, sheer incongruity was compelled into un-mediated tension with the possibility of comparison. All migrants are mere "wetbacks"—"illegals" all—Evangelina insisted, "because they are not from here." They are neither "Americans" nor "Blacks," but rather come to be caught, somehow, somewhere between.

While four of Evangelina's five categories (Americans, Polish, Mexicans, Chicanos) were not overtly racialized, much as in the Pancho Villa joke, what is decisive is precisely the remaining, seemingly incongruous term—Blacks, where the salience of race is stark and decisive. Likewise, insofar as Evangelina bluntly characterized the presumably real U.S. "natives" as belonging exclusively to one or the other category—either "Americans" or "Blacks"—it is again transparent that American served to narrowly connote racial whiteness.[30] In effect, Evangelina was grappling with what she seemed to perceive to be the impossibility of her own and other migrants' access to a bona fide "American"-ness—the impossibility of "assimilation." Notably, this impossibility of "becoming American" was initially expressed in terms of not being "from here." In other words, it was first articulated in terms of migration as such, and hence, might be mistakenly glossed as pertaining to "nationality" or "culture." However, not only did she posit the impossibility of "assimilation" for migrants, Evangelina contended further that this condition would endure through the generations. Without regard to birthright citizenship, and regardless in fact of simply being "from here," the migrants' children and grand-children will not be "Americans" either, but merely "Chicanos." Rather than presuming that Chicanos are merely "Americanized" Mexicans, therefore, the apparently "cultural" differences between Mexicans from

Mexico and those born or raised in the United States simply do not suffice to account for the decidedly racialized meaning introduced by Evangelina's concluding remark.[31] Rather, she seemed to insist, Chicanos —like Blacks—despite their birthright U.S. citizenship, will never secure a legitimate "American"-ness.

Because the U.S.-born generations were presumed to become, specifically, Chicanos, this was of course the articulation of a distinctly *Mexican*/migrant position. Furthermore, this was a Mexican migrant's response to a Vietnamese migrant's contention that only Mexicans migrate to the United States "illegally." Evangelina's intervention, therefore, was situated within a discourse about questions of "American"-ness and "assimilation" as such a debate could be conducted specifically between two differently racialized migrants, neither of whom was racialized as white. The Latino-Asian particularity of this exchange radically complicates the simplistic and misleading fiction of the U.S. racial order as a binary of white and Black, but the content of Evangelina's reply requires an examination of how that fiction nonetheless remains hegemonic and continues to supply the polarized framework for migrants' reracializations (De Genova in press). Hence, within the unequal parameters of the politics of citizenship in the United States, non-Mexican migrants such as Michael might have felt compelled to marshal their own juridical advantages to relegate Mexicans to the more degraded immigration status of "illegality" that, in effect, approached the undeservingness or even criminality otherwise attributed to Blackness. Conversely, Mexican migrants such as Evangelina could find themselves taking recourse to a reply that drew its force from a blunt acknowledgment of the unequal politics of race. Whereas both Latinos and Asians may have been equally invested in maintaining that they were *not* Black, Evangelina seemed intent to remind her Vietnamese coworkers, neither were they, nor could they ever be, "Americans." Thus, the best that a Vietnamese migrant could expect in the United States, Evangelina retorted, was to have his children become a bunch of "Chicanos."

Insofar as the production of "illegality" introduces ranks of social differentiation among all migrants, it was hardly surprising that a Vietnamese migrant rehearsed the hegemonic ideological script wherein *Mexican* becomes synonymous with *illegal alien*. In this sense, it is intriguing to consider how Evangelina staked her position by attempting to rhetorically obliterate such distinctions altogether—not in the humanistic idiom of the common immigrants' rights slogan that protests, "No Human Being Is Illegal!" but rather, by asserting that *all* migrants are effectively "illegal," indeed, that they are all "wetbacks." One year later, at Die-Hard Tool and Die, Gonzalo could be heard to articulate a position that was somewhat analogous to Evangelina's. Gonzalo boldly declared that the term *wetback* is not derogatory, and went on to explain with an ironic pride, "I am a wetback; when someone calls me 'Hey, wetback!' I tell him, 'Thank you for remembering my country.'" Gonzalo was certainly not asserting that *all* migrants are "wetbacks," as Evangelina had argued; in fact, Gonzalo seemed to be reserving migrant "illegality" for Mexicans in particular. If he may have appeared to recapitulate the dominant discourse, however, Gonzalo was also appropriating it for his own ironic ends—by reclaiming the category and revalorizing it. However, both Gonzalo and Evangelina adopted strategies of defamiliarization as deliberate interventions. Furthermore, both staked their distinctly Mexican/migrant politics of location on a refusal to disavow the racializing "illegality" that had circumscribed their specific migrant status as "Mexicans," and a frank recognition of the blunt fact of having been racialized as something other than white, which combined to exclude them from any viable access to "American"-ness.

Initially, Evangelina's argument relied upon the assertion of a fact, something that she knew to be true and verifiable—namely, that not all undocumented migrants are Mexican, that there are indeed Polish migrants who overstay their tourist visas and are likewise "illegal." Notably, Evangelina's recourse to the category of "Polish" served to identify a European-origin migrant group who, in her account, remained disqualified from "American"-ness. Thus, she apparently counted among the mass of "wetbacks" excluded from "American"-ness a group of migrants who might be presumed to be "white," and might seem to confound my argument about the racialized underpinnings of "American" national identity. However, it seems plausible that Evangelina's remarks would be better understood to contend that these migrants from Poland were still not quite white—that they had not yet come to be fully racialized as white. In other words, and notwithstanding the Polish workers' very probable investment in their own reracialization as "American" whites, Evangelina was identifying what David Roediger (1994, 184) has characterized as that moment of irresolution during which European migrants in the United States remain "not-yet-white ethnics." Indeed, on this occasion, the Polish people in the class abstained from participating in the argument between Evangelina and Michael altogether, preferring to talk among themselves in Polish.

Interestingly, on another occasion during the ESL class at Czarnina and Sons, Ludmila, a Polish woman in her late forties, related how she had gotten a flat tire one night on her way to work. As if to underscore her sense of peril at having found herself alone and in distress on the street, Ludmila performatively assumed an expression of fright and made her eyes bulge. "Maybe nigger help me!" she exclaimed (in English) with thoroughly racialized irony, laughing heartily at the presumably outlandish prospect, "Maybe nigger help me!" The Polish migrant's ongoing reracialization in the United States almost inexorably ensured that she had become invested in embracing and affirming her whiteness. Later, during the same class session, Ludmila's reracialization as white was meaningfully revealed to be deeply entangled with an incipient "immigrant Americanism." When the ESL discussion turned to the approaching Thanksgiving holiday, I learned that all of the Polish workers would be celebrating the very peculiarly "American" occasion with turkey dinners, complete with all of the conventions of the traditional holiday meal. Evangelina, however, was not planning a Thanksgiving feast and would be observing the welcome occasion of a long holiday weekend only by preparing tamales. As Ludmila explained: "Pilgrim holiday is very special holiday for immigrants. Poland is my first country, but America is second country, just like pilgrims . . . You pilgrim, too, Nick, your grandfather and grandmother come from Italy." Before I had the chance to reply, however, Evangelina immediately responded from a rather more distinctly transnational perspective: "Me, I'm 100 percent Mexican. Even my kids, they're not Chicanos, they're not Americans—they're also 100 percent Mexican. My oldest son doesn't even like to speak English!" The contrast between these two divergent migrant perspectives could not have been more stark.

Despite a laborious childhood in Mexico, followed by already many years of travail as a migrant working woman in the United States, Evangelina's transnational commitments remained substantial. Evangelina had migrated to the United States when she was fifteen years old, from a small rural town in Guanajuato where she had only finished the fifth grade. Although she had been the second youngest of eight children in her family, Evangelina had been designated from an early age as the daughter who would be charged with much of the housework. From the age of eight, she had been responsible daily for washing the entire family's laundry, in addition to working in the field. Later, her parents decided to send Evangelina to work in the United States in order to remit money so that her siblings would be able to go further in school. Thanks in large part to the remittances of her migrant wages, two of the children had become engineers, and another two had become schoolteachers. Once Evangelina had married in Chicago, she soon had three children in rapid succession. When her kids were very small, she had supplemented her husband's income by watching other Mexican/migrant women's children for eight hours a day, five days a week, for which she had earned a meager $25 a week per child. Later, she returned to factory work. When I came to know her, Evangelina had already been working in the Czarnina and Sons factory for nearly eleven years. "This is an easy job," she once declared, "In other companies, the work is too heavy, there's too little break time, the bosses are always telling you something, and you make shitty money. I'm going to stay here until I retire. Then I'll retire to Mexico. Right now, I go back every two years." Although she very consciously planned to remain in the United States for many years to come, however, Evangelina was seriously considering the possibility of sending her children back to Mexico. She was increasingly frustrated with her family's predicament in the deteriorating working-class suburb of Cicero, which was already a majority-Mexican community, and she wanted to move to a less densely populated place "with fewer gangs and drugs." If she and her husband could not find the means to relocate, Evangelina explained, she would send her kids to live with her family in Guanajuato. She noted, however, that her oldest child (a boy who was already thirteen) was not enthusiastic about being made to go live on a farm in Mexico. Although she had indicated that her son was more comfortable speaking Spanish than English, Evangelina remarked nonetheless, laughing, "He doesn't even like to eat beans!"

Evangelina had previously posited that the children and grandchildren of "wetback" migrants became not "Americans" but rather only "Chicanos," but it became more evident in the exchange surrounding the Thanksgiving holiday that she, like most of the Mexican migrants I knew in Chicago, was profoundly invested in the prospect that her children were not, and should never become, "Chicanos." Indeed, because Evangelina intuited that "American"-ness was plainly not available to U.S.-born Mexicans, she now seemed to be positing the subordinate racial status of "Chicanos" to be a kind of abject and degraded derivative of "American"-ness.

The other alternative for Mexican migrants and their children, of course, was not any less conclusively racialized, but it was definitively transnational in its orientation: Evangelina aspired for her U.S.-born children to be "100 percent Mexican." In effect, reracialized within the space of the U.S. nation-state, between Americans and Blacks, this reconfigured Mexicanness came to be formulated as a racialized transnationality.

THE BITTER IRONY OF PLAYING BY THE RULES

The fierce nativism of the 1990s, as already suggested in chapter 2, was distinguished by a pronounced anti-immigrant racism that was disproportionately directed against Mexicans in particular, due to the hegemonic conflation of "Mexicans" with "illegal aliens." It is useful, by way of conclusion, to recall the clear correlation between the passage of the so-called Immigration Reform and Welfare Reform legislations of 1996. Indeed, the Illegal Immigration Reform and Immigrant Responsibility Act of 1996 was passed within five weeks of the so-called Welfare Reform, which itself included extensive anti-immigrant stipulations and bore a title that was equally self-righteous and still more hypocritical: the Personal Responsibility and Work Opportunity Reconciliation Act. Both were extraordinarily punitive laws, and together represented the two-pronged material and practical culmination of a more generalized ideological onslaught against "immigration" and "welfare" that had raged in the United States throughout the early and mid-1990s. These legislations especially targeted Mexican/migrant women (and their children), who had come to be equated with Mexican long-term settlement, families, reproduction, and thus, the dramatic growth of a "minority group." Migrant families, and especially those of the undocumented, were relentlessly charged in the public debate over immigration with being significantly motivated by a desire to avail themselves of social services in the United States. "Immigration," in effect, was denounced as yet another flagrant abuse of the presumed beneficence of the public welfare infrastructure. Rather than highly exploited workers, undocumented migrants were thereby prominently refigured as a fiscal "burden" and an overall "drain" on state resources (Calavita 1996). This exacerbated anti-immigrant racism operated in tandem with what was, in effect, the inherent racism and sexism of the assault against welfare—because it was disproportionately identified with African Americans, and especially women (and their children).

The anti-immigrant politics of the 1990s was therefore profoundly connected, both in discourse and its implementation, with the furious ideological condemnation and practical dismantling of the social welfare safety net for impoverished U.S. citizens. Whether these campaigns were directed against more or less permanently unemployed and underemployed U.S. citizens, on the one hand, or the consistently overemployed migrant working poor, on the other, both targeted social categories that are disproportionately represented by groups not racialized as white. Both legal assaults can be seen as disciplinary measures intended to intensify the subordination of labor in general in the United States. By rendering precisely the poorest of working-class people more vulnerable, and thus, more tractable and flexible, such legislative interventions served to aggravate the desperation that would prevail throughout the entire U.S. labor market. However, these hegemonic projects relied in part on the extent to which the frustration of impoverished U.S. citizens could be effectively articulated as a nativist resentment for the "cheap labor" of migrants who were purportedly displacing "American" workers from "American" jobs. On the other hand, migrant (and especially undocumented) workers' legal vulnerability ensured that their hold on their own employment always remained relatively tenuous. Such a climate of insecurity could thus quite readily inspire migrant workers to disparage (as unproductive, or "lazy") the labor-power that was the commodity for sale on the part of their most proximate competitors in the labor market —namely, impoverished U.S. citizens. Other racially subordinated "minorities," including Puerto Ricans and even U.S.-born Mexicans, but above all, African Americans—who often could variously marshal other potential labor-market advantages, such as U.S. citizenship, English-language fluency, and higher levels of formal schooling—thus became prime targets for Mexican migrants' accusations of laziness. As seen in chapter 4, these parallel processes served as a kind of double disciplining. Employers, and indirectly the state, used both the U.S.-born poor and the migrant working poor as disciplinary mechanisms, one against the other. Furthermore, because migrant workers were always at pains to demonstrate to their overseers that they were "hardworking" and not "lazy," the momentum of their efforts at self-defense served to subvert the possibilities for resistance, and they effectively participated in their own intensified exploitation (Kearney 1996, 156; 1998, 29).

In this chapter, I have sought to delineate the tensions between Mexican migrants' efforts to grapple with the racialized subordination of their labor and their entrapment in a racialized intermediacy between white and Black in the U.S. social order. Such intermediate racial locations consistently seemed to be already ensnared in a hegemonic denigration of the Blackness of African Americans, even as those who occupied such positions were themselves subjected to distinct forms of racial oppression. This dialectic of racist hegemony commonly involved an apparent equation of "American"-ness with racial whiteness, and came to be represented in Mexican/migrant racial discourse as a disqualification (or exclusion) of African Americans from the category "American" altogether. Toni Morrison has poignantly addressed the racist script in the United States, which demands that migrants partake of a dominant racial discourse that has "no meaning other than pressing African Americans to the lowest level of the racial hierarchy," rendering "blacks as noncitizens, already discredited outlaws . . . the real aliens" (1994, 97, 98). Indeed, Morrison argues, this is "the organizing principle of becoming an American" (100). Morrison belongs to a prestigious lineage of African American intellectuals—including W. E. B. Du Bois, Ralph Ellison, and James Baldwin among many more—who have made similar critiques of the hegemonic erasure of Black people's central role in the historical constitution of the United States and all things "American" (see Morrison 1992). Nevertheless, these commentators have always had nonetheless to posit their claims to "American"-ness in terms of a critique of the racialized and subordinate citizenship of African Americans. Predictably, these intellectuals' eloquent perspectives have emerged from racially oppressed people's everyday traditions of scrutinizing white people, and formulating and disseminating critical knowledge about the workings of white power.[32] For communities of color, such critical resources have proven, as often as not, to be a matter of life and death.

There is, indeed, a pernicious conjuncture between "American"-ness and white supremacy in the United States. "Whatever the ethnicity or nationality of the immigrant," Morrison asserts (1994, 98), "his nemesis is understood to be African American," so that "the public is asked to accept American blacks as the common denominator in each conflict between an immigrant and a job" (99). But if there is indeed this insidious conjuncture, then we know something more surely about the whiteness that lurks just behind "the American," and likewise, we know something more certainly about the racialized condition of African Americans, than we can so readily ascertain with respect to that of "the immigrant." The racialization of the particular migrants in question, is, finally, *the* question. The example that Morrison requires to make her case as definitively as she does is one in which "it is the act of racial contempt [toward an African American] that transforms [a] charming Greek [migrant] into an entitled white. Without it, [his] future as an American is not at all assured" (97). However, as David Roediger suggests, "If the legal and social history of Jim Crow often turned on the question 'Who was Black?,' the legal and social history of immigration often turned on the question 'Who was white?'" (1994, 181–82; and see Haney López 1996). Roediger has argued, moreover, that "the central political implication arising from the insight that race is socially constructed is the specific need to attack *whiteness* as a destructive ideology rather than to attack the concept of race abstractly" (3; emphasis original). One of my critical purposes here has been to identify the effective inseparability in the United States of whiteness and "*American*"-ness, and thereby to underscore the specific antiracist necessity of repudiating "American"-ness as well.

In the ethnographic research that I conducted in Mexican Chicago, it was exceedingly seldom that Mexican migrants whom I knew would entertain the slightest illusion that they had any future of becoming "Americans"—even in those cases where legal residency and ultimately U.S. citizenship were tenable—precisely because "American" was more or less transparently a category for racialized whiteness, and such was not their lot. If Mexican migrants in Chicago did in fact very commonly understand their nemesis to be African Americans and were actively complicit with larger social forces pressing Blacks to the lowest level of the racial hierarchy, this was not sufficient for Mexican migrants to secure any kind of future as "Americans," nor was it a conclusive indication that any kind of "assimilation" was under way or even plausible. In short, if the migrants in question were Mexican, there was no act of racial contempt that would accomplish their transformation into entitled whites. They remained the captives of that space between "Americans" and Blacks.

PART THREE

HISTORICITY: THE POLITICS OF LOCATION

History begins . . . with the here-and-now, with
each passing minute. Historical becoming is immediately
upon us, and immediately it becomes history, known and
recognized historicity, historical consciousness, chained
to a vaguely distant past according to which the present
vainly attempts to situate itself.**—Henri Lefebvre,**

Introduction to Modernity

CHAPTER SIX

THE LEGAL PRODUCTION OF MEXICAN/

MIGRANT "ILLEGALITY"

History, as Lefebvre suggests, is made in the present, and this is so in a double sense. On the one hand, we are historical actors inescapably engaged in the everyday work of producing our own sociopolitical circumstances and potentially making history by transforming the social relations that constitute our world. On the other hand, this historicity is inextricable from our distinct location within the tangled historical trajectories that we have inherited, which implicate us in either reproducing or rectifying the enduring consequences of the past. Throughout this book, I have repeatedly emphasized the historical specificity of the sociopolitical climate that prevailed in the United States during the precise period of my research, my ethnographic "present." That moment was distinguished by a fiercely anti-immigrant politics of racist nativism, targeting undocumented Mexican migrants in particular, that manifested itself in legal campaigns and was ossified in the law. Likewise, I have located the living and open-ended historicity of my ethnographic interlocutors at the decisive conjuncture formed by ongoing histories—most prominently, the racialization of Mexicans and the spatialization of their transnational condition as labor migrants in relation to U.S. nationalism and "American" national identity. In all of this, the U.S. nation-state has played a predictably powerful and inordinately important role. Having devoted so much of this study to the task of producing an archive of the ever-fleeting "present," that contemporary moment at the end of the twentieth century when I realized my ethnographic research, now, from the vantage point of the present and with the urgency of present purposes as my guide, I turn to the task of reconstructing the history that only in retrospect may be most clearly seen to have framed some of the defining parameters of race, space, and "illegality" in Mexican Chicago. And such a history of Mexican labor migration to the United States, as will be seen here, is inseparable from a history of Mexican migrants' sociopolitical relation to the U.S. state, its immigration policies, and the law.

Mexican migration to the United States is distinguished by a seeming paradox that is seldom examined: while no other country has supplied nearly as many migrants to the United States as has Mexico since 1965, most major changes in U.S. immigration law during this period have created ever more severe restrictions on the possibilities for "legal" migration from Mexico. Indeed, this apparent paradox presents itself in a double sense: on the one hand, apparently liberalizing immigration laws have in fact concealed significantly restrictive features, especially for Mexicans; on the other hand, ostensibly restrictive immigration laws purportedly intended to deter migration have nonetheless been instrumental in sustaining Mexican migration, but only by significantly restructuring its legal status—as undocumented. Beginning precisely when Mexican migration escalated dramatically in the 1960s—and ever since—persistent revisions in the law have effectively foreclosed the viable prospects for the great majority who would migrate from Mexico to do so in accord with the law and thus played an instrumental role in the production of a legally vulnerable undocumented workforce of "illegal aliens."

The argument of this chapter is not simply that the category "illegal alien" is a profoundly useful and profitable one that effectively serves to create and sustain a legally vulnerable—hence relatively tractable and thus "cheap"—reserve of labor. That proposition is already so well established as to be irrefutable. This is undeniably an important critical insight into the *effects* of migrant "illegality." But by itself, this crucial insight is insufficient, precisely insofar as it may leave unexamined, and thus naturalized, the fundamental *origin* of this juridical status in the law itself—what I am calling the legal production of migrant "illegality."

This chapter, therefore, discerns the historical specificity of contemporary Mexican migration to the United States as it has come to be located in the legal (political) economy of the U.S. nation-state, and thereby constituted as an object of the law, especially since 1965. More precisely, this chapter interrogates the history of changes in U.S. immigration law through the specific lens of how these revisions have had a distinct impact upon Mexicans in particular. Only in light of this socio-legal history does it become possible to elaborate a critical perspective that is not complicit in the naturalization of Mexican migrants' "illegality" as a mere fact of life, the presumably transparent consequence of unauthorized border crossing or some other violation of immigration law.

In addition to simply designating a juridical status in relation to the U.S. nation-state and its laws of citizenship, immigration, and naturalization, furthermore, migrant "illegality" signals a specifically *spatialized* sociopolitical condition. "Illegality" is lived through a palpable sense of deportability —which is to say, the possibility of deportation, the possibility of being removed from the space of the U.S. nation-state. Deportability is decisive in the legal production of Mexican/migrant "illegality" and the militarized policing of the U.S.-Mexico border, however, only insofar as some are deported in order that most may ultimately remain (undeported)—as workers, whose particular migrant status has been rendered "illegal." Thus, the legal production of "illegality" provides an apparatus for sustaining Mexican migrants' vulnerability and tractability—as workers—whose labor-power, because it is deportable, becomes an eminently disposable commodity. In the everyday life of Mexican migrants in innumerable places throughout the United States, "illegality" reproduces the practical repercussions of the physical border between the United States and Mexico across which undocumented migration is constituted. In this important sense, migrant "illegality" is a spatialized social condition inseparable from the particular ways that Mexican migrants are likewise racialized as "illegal aliens"—invasive violators of the law, incorrigible "foreigners," subverting the integrity of "the nation" and its sovereignty from *within* the space of the U.S. nation-state. As a simultaneously spatialized and racialized social condition, migrant "illegality" is also a central feature of the ways that the "Mexican"-ness of Mexicans is thereby reconfigured in *racialized* relation to the hegemonic "national" identity of "American"-ness. Before examining these more contemporary dimensions of the historicity of Mexican migration to the United States, however, it is crucial to locate these conjunctures of race, space, and "illegality" in terms of an earlier history of the intersections of race and citizenship in the United States.

CITIZENSHIP, RACE, AND THE RACIALIZATION OF NATION-STATE SPACE

> Each new form of state . . . introduces . . . its own particular administrative classification of discourses about space . . . and people in space.—**Henri Lefebvre,** *The Production of Space*

Citizenship appears to be a universal, distinctive, and central feature of modern political life. Literally every modern state deploys the institution of citizenship as the political means by which it publicly identifies its official members, assigns them an enduring legal status as "individuals," and disburses to them specific rights, entitlements, and obligations. In this way, a state attaches a specific population to its particular politically enclosed space, usually equated with a bounded territory. Citizens are thus defined as a state's insiders. Indeed, most modern states largely derive their legitimacy from a claim that their power over people actually rests precisely upon the sovereignty of those same people, taken together to comprise a particular, bounded collective body—usually called a "nation"—presumed to be not some random collection of individuals but rather imagined to be a coherent community of "citizens" (B. Anderson [1983] 1991; see Agamben 1998). In short, modern states need citizens: a state must constitute people as its citizens in order to justify its power over them.

If the institution of citizenship defines a kind of membership to the state and so appears within purportedly democratic states such as the United States to be broadly directed toward inclusion, it is likewise always also a definition by default of those who are *not* citizens, and thus outsiders, "foreigners," or "aliens." Despite the liberal and egalitarian conceits of universalistic inclusiveness, then, citizenship—in the guise of sovereign self-government by the insiders—justifies the coercive rule of the state over the excluded, purportedly on behalf of its proper citizens. National identities—whether they be hegemonic or subjugated—can therefore be understood to be "national" only because they have been produced *politically*, in relation to processes of state formation and the inclusions and exclusions of citizenship (see Balibar 1991c; Wallerstein 1991). Thus, a brief examination of the history of the institution of U.S. citizenship—a consideration of how exactly it has been defined and refined in law, historically—reveals much about what have been the real inclusions and exclusions shaping a U.S. national identity of "American"-ness.

The first United States Congress mandated in 1790 that a person who was to become a naturalized citizen of the United States must be "white."[1] Before this Naturalization Act of 1790, there had been no official formulation of who would be considered the citizens of the new nation. The original U.S. Constitution (1787) had nowhere defined who were citizens or what specific entitlements, privileges, or immunities they would enjoy, leaving it a prerogative of the individual states. Thus, this was the first legislative determination of access to U.S. citizenship, and in effect, the first official definition of U.S. nationality. Revealingly, it passed with no debate or dissension whatsoever. Much as whiteness was never a transparent, stable, or natural category and has been the object of a history of relentless ideological production and reelaboration, there was nonetheless an intrinsic link between whiteness and access to citizenship within the U.S. nation-state since its inception. What is perhaps most remarkable about this whites-only policy for migrant access to U.S. citizenship, however, is that it remained in effect until 1952, with the passage of the McCarran-Walter Immigration and Nationality Act, and its practical effects largely persisted until the landmark overhaul of U.S. immigration law in 1965, which then did not go into effect until 1968. In other words, the substantive decoupling of racial whiteness from migrants' access to U.S. citizenship has been in effect for only a few decades. For roughly three-fourths of U.S. history, despite the eventual extension of an ostensible (but palpably inferior) citizenship to racially subordinated "minorities" within the United States, the law declared that migrants representing the great majority of the world's people would continue to be strictly ineligible for U.S. citizenship simply and solely because of their presumed "race." From the very outset, a nation that fashioned itself as an asylum for liberty would be, at best, a promised land only for *white* liberty.

If the newborn republic was already steeped in a distinctly white nationalism (Takaki 1979, 15; see Lubiano 1997, 235), so also was it constituted by an imperial confidence about its explicit and unquestioned mission of expansion and colonization (W. Williams 1980; see Nobles 1997). These imperial ambitions anticipated what would, by the 1840s, come to be widely celebrated as self-evident and inevitable—indeed, Manifest Destiny (Hietala 1985; Horsman 1981; Jacobson 2000). The settler-state discourses of Manifest Destiny that dominated much of the nineteenth century were invariably pronouncements of an unequivocal white supremacism, but they typically celebrated the "progress"—"ordained by Divine Providence"—inherent in an extension of "American civilization," identified with the moral superiority of its liberal ideals, egalitarian laws, and republican institutions.

LEGISLATING MEXICAN "WHITENESS," ENACTING MEXICAN DISENFRANCHISEMENT

One of the decisive junctures in the westward expansion of the U.S. nation-state was the imperialist war against Mexico that culminated in the annexation in 1848 of what has come to be called the American Southwest. This particular interlude of imperialist warfare was pivotal in the historical consolidation of U.S. national space. There was negligible substantive dispute in the United States that ever questioned the desirability or putative necessity of territorial expansion as a general objective. Indeed, in the wake of a military invasion and reign of terror by U.S. troops that ultimately extended as far as Mexico City, there was considerable debate around the question of annexing the *entirety* of Mexico (Fuller 1936). Notably, concerned with the prospect that U.S. troops would become quickly embroiled in a protracted guerrilla war, the debate largely centered on whether it would be manageable to maintain a colonial administration over the more densely populated Mexican territories. Some promoted the idea that Mexicans could simply be removed to reservations, as had been done with Indians. The position that finally prevailed, however, was that articulated by Senator Lewis Cass of Michigan, who declared: "We do not want the people of Mexico, either as citizens or subjects. All we want is a portion of territory, which they nominally hold, generally uninhabited, or, where inhabited at all, sparsely so, and with a population, which would soon recede [i.e., Indians], or identify itself with ours [i.e., whites]" (quoted in D. Gutiérrez 1995, 16). Hence, as Neil Foley (1997, 22) characterizes it, the color line was drawn at the Rio Grande and the new border between the United States and Mexico "was drawn in such a way as to take as much land and as few Mexicans as possible." Nevertheless, the war did indeed occasion a major intervention on the part of the U.S. state in the historical formulation of both citizenship and "whiteness," specifically as they pertained to Mexicans.

The Treaty of Guadalupe Hidalgo of 1848, which concluded the war and finalized the terms of the conquest, entailed critical provisions concerning citizenship. Due to the deliberate and insistent pressure of the Mexican delegation during the treaty negotiations in favor of explicit protections for the civil rights of Mexican nationals (Griswold del Castillo 1990, 40), the nationalization of the conquered territory, in effect, came to have significant implications for the naturalization (as U.S. citizens) of the Mexicans who already inhabited the land. Article VIII of the treaty stipulated that Mexicans in the newly annexed territories would have the option of "removing" themselves from the now-U.S. territories to south of the newly created border; or they could retain their Mexican citizenship (by official public declaration) and remain in their own lands, now as something like "permanent resident aliens"; or they could do nothing and automatically, after one year, "be considered to have elected to become citizens of the United States." Article IX, however, specified further that those who did not retain their Mexican citizenship "shall . . . be admitted, *at the proper time (to be judged of by the Congress* of the United States) to the enjoyment of all the rights of citizens of the United States according to the principles of the Constitution" (189–90; emphasis added). It is noteworthy that this was a significant revision of the treaty language negotiated in Mexico, which was unilaterally imposed by the U.S. Senate. The original unmodified text had said that these newly incorporated persons would be "admitted *as soon as possible*, according to the principles of the *Federal* Constitution, to the enjoyment of all the rights of citizens of the United States" (179; emphasis added). Furthermore, an Article X, concerning the sanctity of Mexican property and land grants, was stricken altogether. Despite the Protocol of Querétaro, which assured the Mexican delegation that these changes would introduce no substantive difference (180–82), the modifications opened up the gamut of equivocations that would subsequently undermine virtually all the ostensible guarantees of the treaty.

With regard to citizenship, the revised Article IX's overt deferral— from "as soon as possible" to "at the proper time"—was indicative of the still more fundamental change of language that implicitly relegated Mexican citizenship to the jurisdiction of the state constitutions (rather than the federal). It was the state constitutions, in their petitions for admission to statehood, which would eventually be "judged of by the Congress" (Griswold del Castillo 1990, 66–72). In California, for example, when a state constitution was established in 1849, the Treaty of Guadalupe Hidalgo did indeed serve to obstruct white supremacist efforts to exclude Mexicans from suffrage, but significantly, only by extending the vote to "White male citizens of the United States and every White male citizen of Mexico, who shall have elected to become a citizen of the United States" (Almaguer 1994, 56; Menchaca 2001, 220–23). Likewise in New Mexico (which included Arizona until 1862), a convention in 1849, attended by a majority of delegates who represented the Hispano elite, restricted citizenship within the U.S. territory to "free white males" (Griswold del Castillo 1990, 70; Menchaca 2001, 223–28). Texas, on the other hand, having already achieved statehood in 1845, claimed to be exempt from the terms of the treaty altogether. Although the debate over suffrage in Texas had also revolved around an explicit distinction between "white" Mexicans (or "Spaniards") and "Mexican Indians," the disenfranchisement of

Texas Mexicans was primarily left to informal methods of intimidation and violence (Menchaca 2001, 228–33; Montejano 1987, 38–40). While Mexican "whiteness" was generally associated with notions of "Spanish descent," the practical legal determination of which Mexicans were "white" was seldom defined authoritatively, and was widely left to the "common sense" of Anglo whites who exercised power at the local level (Menchaca 2001, 215–76). Thus, the men of the Mexican ranchero elite secured their citizenship status, predictably at the expense of women, but also only on the basis of Indian and Black disenfranchisement, including Indians who had been granted Mexican citizenship in 1824 and thus were supposed to have been entitled by the treaty (Griswold del Castillo 1990, 69). Moreover, they were able to do so only by having their own legal status racialized as white, thereby destabilizing the prospects of citizenship status for any and all Mexican men who could be racialized as Indians or mestizos (sometimes including many of the elite themselves).

The great majority of former Mexican citizens who might have been entitled under the treaty's apparent protections saw their putative citizenship systematically circumvented and subverted. Most were despoiled of their land and their civil rights were routinely violated, often through outright racist terror (Acuña 1981; De León 1983; Menchaca 2001, 215–76; Montejano 1987; Pitt 1966). The real accomplishment of the treaty, therefore, was that perhaps as many as 100,000 Mexican nationals were summarily disenfranchised of their Mexican citizenship and became colonized U.S. subjects. As scholars in Chicano studies have frequently affirmed, the treacherous triangulation of whiteness, citizenship, and empire already prefigures any viable account of subsequent Mexican migrations to the United States and situates the production of the national difference between the United States and Mexico on a resolutely racialized terrain.

While the everyday life experience of most Mexicans within the space of the U.S. nation-state has always been constrained by their racialization as not-white, the very limited extent to which the treaty genuinely enabled citizenship status for Mexicans, however unstable and insecure, came only with the compulsory requirement that it be racialized as the preserve of "white men." This was put to the test in a racial prerequisite case for the Naturalization Act of 1790—*In re Rodriguez* (1897). In that case, a federal court in Texas considered the application for citizenship of a "pure-blooded Mexican" who, "if the strict scientific classification of the anthropologist should be adopted . . . would probably not be classed as white." Positing the absurd legal fiction that Ricardo Rodríguez was "white" according to the treaty's provisions of citizenship for Mexicans, the court concluded that the applicant was indeed eligible for naturalization (Haney López 1996, 61; G. Martínez 1997, 210–13; Menchaca 2001, 215–76, 282–85). In 1933, however, the U.S. Supreme Court revisited the issue of Mexicans' putative whiteness by treaty, calling this precedent decision into question (Haney López 1996, 242n37). Indeed, by 1930, in the wake of mass migration from Mexico during the first decades of the twentieth century, the U.S. Census Bureau had already officially designated "Mexican" to be a separate and distinct racial category (Goldberg 1997, 42).

THE REVOLVING DOOR AND THE MAKING OF A TRANSNATIONAL HISTORY

Originating in this shared, albeit unequal, history of invasion and war by which roughly half of Mexico's territory came to be conquered and colonized by the U.S. nation-state, the newly established border between the United States and Mexico long remained virtually unregulated, and movement across it went largely unhindered. During the late nineteenth century, as a regional political economy took shape in what was now the U.S. Southwest, mining, railroads, ranching, and agriculture relied extensively upon the active recruitment of Mexican labor (Acuña 1981; Barrera 1979; Gómez-Quiñones 1994). There was a commonplace recognition of the fact that Mexicans were encouraged to move freely across the border to come to work without official documents or authorization (Calavita 1992; J. García 1980; Samora 1971).[2]

If the Naturalization Act of 1790 had restricted migrants' access to U.S. citizenship on the basis of racial whiteness, it had very definitely *not* prohibited labor migration by groups deemed to be not-white. Beginning in the late nineteenth century, however, there also began a campaign for increasing restriction and prohibition against "immigration" in general. Not only was citizenship barred on the basis of race, now began an era of immigration regulation that sought to exclude whole groups even from entry into the country, solely on the basis of race or nationality. Eventually, following the prohibition of labor migration from China in 1882 and from Japan and Korea in 1907, the passage of the Immigration Act in 1917 (Act of Feb. 5, 1917; 39 Stat. 874) instituted an All-Asia Barred Zone.[3] In the wake of repeated restrictions against "Asiatics," Mexican migrant labor became an indispensable necessity for capital accumulation in the region. During and after the years of the Mexican Revolution and World War I, from 1910 to 1930, approximately one-tenth of Mexico's total population relocated north of the border, partly owing to social disruptions and dislocations within Mexico during this period of political upheaval, but principally driven and often directly orchestrated by labor demand in new industries and agriculture in the United States (see Cardoso 1980).

During this same era, a dramatically restrictive system of national-origins immigration quotas was formulated for European migration and put in place through the passage of the Quota Law of 1921 (Act of May 19, 1921; 42 Stat. 5), and then further amplified by the Johnson-Reed Immigration Act of 1924 (Act of May 26, 1924; 43 Stat. 153). The 1924 law's national-origins system limited migration on a country-by-country basis, with unequal numerical allotments for immigrant visas. The national-origins system was devised according to a convoluted formula that permitted for a maximum annual quota of migrants from European countries that, in each instance, would equal only 2 percent of the total of each national-origin population as it had been tabulated in the U.S. Census of 1890. In addition, the 1924 law reaffirmed the virtually complete prohibition against migration from Asian countries and upheld the extant Asiatic Barred Zone. In effect, this regulatory apparatus confined migration from the entire Eastern Hemisphere to approximately 150,000 annually; within that ceiling, it guaranteed that roughly 85 percent of the allotments were reserved for migrants from northwestern European countries of origin and secured the exclusion of most of those who might have come from Southern and Eastern Europe (Higham [1955] 1988; Reimers [1985] 1992). Drawing upon forty-two volumes (published in 1910 and 1911 by U.S. Immigration Commissions) that compiled "findings" concerning the "racial" composition and "quality" of the U.S. population, the 1924 Immigration Act codified and rationalized a whole terrain of popular prejudices about the greater and lesser inherent degrees of "assimilability" among variously racialized and nationally stigmatized migrant groups. Furthermore, it legitimated racialized classificatory schemes as the most pertinent and valid means for knowing and ordering the world's people and likewise produced new schemes of hierarchically differentiated fixity for a bewildering array of conflated categories of race and nationality (Higham [1955] 1988). The Congressional Record of legislative debate surrounding these measures bears ample testimony to the avowed preoccupation with maintaining the white/

"Caucasian" racial purity of "American" national identity. It was, as Edward Hutchinson notes (1981, 167), "an unmistakable declaration of white immigration policy." Remarkably, in spite of the vociferous objections of some of the most vitriolic nativists and, more important, as a testament to the utter dependency of employers upon Mexican/migrant labor, particularly in the Southwest, migration from the countries of the Western Hemisphere—Mexico, foremost among them—was left absolutely unrestricted by any numerical quotas.

It is revealing that the U.S. Border Patrol, from 1924—when it was first created—until 1940, operated under the auspices of the Department of Labor. By the late 1920s, the Border Patrol had assumed its distinctive role as a special police force for the repression of Mexican workers in the United States (Mirandé 1987; Ngai 2004). Selective enforcement of the law—coordinated with seasonal labor demand by U.S. employers (as well as the occasional exigencies of electoral politics)—instituted a revolving-door policy, whereby mass deportations would be concurrent with an overall, large-scale importation of Mexican migrant labor (Cockcroft 1986). Although there were no *quantitative* restrictions (numerical quotas) on "legal" Mexican migration until 1965, Mexican migrants could nonetheless be conveniently denied entry into the United States, or deported from it, on the basis of a selective enforcement of *qualitative* features of immigration law, beginning at least as early as the 1920s.

During this era, the regulatory and disciplinary role of deportation operated against Mexican migrants on the basis of qualitative rules and regulations governing *who* would be allowed to migrate, with *what* characteristics, *how* they did so, as well as *how* they conducted themselves once they had already entered the country. Thus, attempted entry could be refused on the grounds of a variety of infractions: a failure upon entry to pay a required $8 immigrant head tax and a $10 fee for the visa itself, or perceived illiteracy, or a presumed liability to become a "public charge" (due to having no prearranged employment), or conversely violation of prohibitions against contract labor (due to having prearranged employment through labor recruitment). Likewise, Mexican workers could be subsequently deported if they could not verify that they held valid work visas or could otherwise be found to have evaded inspection, or to have become "public charges" (retroactively enabling the judgment of a prior condition of "liability"), or to have violated U.S. laws, or to have engaged in acts that could be construed as "anarchist" or "seditionist." All of these violations of the qualitative features of the law rendered deportation a

crucial mechanism of labor discipline and subjugation, not only coordinated with the vicissitudes of the labor market but also for the purposes
of counteracting union organizing among Mexican/migrant workers
(see Acuña 1981; Dinwoodie 1977; Gómez-Quiñones 1994).

With the advent of the Great Depression of the 1930s, however, the
more plainly racist character of Mexican illegalization and deportability
became abundantly manifest. Mexican migrants and U.S.-born (U.S.-
citizen) Mexicans alike were systematically excluded from employment
and economic relief, which were declared the exclusive preserve of "Americans," presumed to be more deserving. These abuses culminated in the
forcible mass deportation of at least 415,000 Mexican migrants as well as
many of their U.S. citizen children, and the "voluntary" repatriation of
85,000 more (Balderrama and Rodríguez 1995; Guerin-Gonzáles 1994;
Hoffman 1974). Notably, Mexicans were expelled with no regard to "legal"
residence or U.S. citizenship or even birth in the United States—simply
for being "Mexicans."

In the face of the renewed labor shortages caused by U.S. involvement
in World War II, however, the U.S. federal government, in a dramatic
reversal of the mass deportations of the 1930s, initiated a mass *im*portation
through what came to be known as the Bracero Program, an administrative measure to institutionalize and regiment the supply of Mexican migrant labor for U.S. capitalists (principally for agriculture in the Southwest, but also for the railroads). The Bracero accords were effected
unceremoniously by a Special Committee on Importation of Mexican
Labor (formed by the U.S. Immigration Service, the War Manpower
Commission, and the Departments of State, Labor, and Agriculture)
through a bilateral agreement with Mexico. The U.S. Department of
Agriculture was granted primary authority to coordinate the program.
Ostensibly an emergency wartime measure at its inception in 1942 (Public
Law 45), the program was repeatedly renewed and dramatically expanded
until its termination in 1964. This legalized importation essentially reduced Mexican/migrant contract laborers to a captive workforce under
the jurisdiction of the U.S. government and promised U.S. employers a
federal guarantee of unlimited "cheap" labor. Employers quickly came to
prefer undocumented workers, however, because they could evade the
bond and contracting fees, minimum employment periods, fixed wages,
and other safeguards required in employing braceros (Galarza 1964).
Through the development of a migration infrastructure combined with
employers' encouragement of braceros to overstay the limited tenure of

their contracts, the Bracero Program thus facilitated undocumented migration at levels that far surpassed the numbers of "legal" braceros. Some have estimated that four undocumented migrants entered the United States from Mexico for every documented bracero.[4] Indeed, as early as 1949, U.S. employers and labor recruiters were assisted with instantaneous legalization procedures for undocumented workers—which came to be known as "drying out wetbacks" (Calavita 1992). Early in 1954, in an affront to the Mexican government's negotiators' pleas for a fixed minimum wage for braceros, the U.S. Congress authorized the Department of Labor to unilaterally recruit Mexican workers, and the Border Patrol itself opened the border and actively recruited undocumented migrants (Cockcroft 1986; Galarza 1964). This period of official "open border" soon culminated, predictably in accord with the revolving-door strategy, in the 1954–55 expulsion of at least 2.9 million "illegal" Mexican/migrant workers under the militarized dragnet and nativist hysteria of Operation Wetback (J. García 1980; see Cockcroft 1986). Thus, the Bracero years were distinguished not only by expanded "legal" contract-labor migration, but also the federal facilitation of undocumented migration and the provision of ample opportunities for legalization, simultaneously coupled with considerable repression and mass deportations. Long-term or permanent Mexican/migrant settlement, as well as the subsequent history of continuous and accelerated migration, moreover, have finally exposed the defining myth of the Bracero era that the state could orchestrate Mexican migration as a strictly "temporary" labor flow, regulated by contract, available or disposable on command (Massey and Liang 1989).

The Mexican government's complicity in the excessively exploitative arrangements of the Bracero Program was merely the most blatant and transparent occasion when mass migration to the United States was deemed an appropriate safety valve for the mitigation of potentially explosive social crises within Mexico. During my ethnographic research in Chicago, there frequently emerged expressions of an acute political critique of the Partido Revolucionario Institucional, Mexico's long-entrenched ruling party. Likewise, these critiques occasionally revealed a certain historical sensibility about the Mexican state's compromises with the United States, particularly at the expense of migrant workers. On one memorable occasion in an ESL class at Caustic Scrub, when all of the participants were overtaken with laughter due to someone's difficulties with English pronunciation, I happened to call out, "Oh, you guys! [¡*Ay, chavos!*]" Taking his cue, Edmundo followed by exclaiming, "¡*Ay, mexicanos!*" Laughing all along in robust good humor, Edmundo mimicked my expression, but notably transposed my words into a reformulation that specifically identified the workers' racialized Mexican/migrant transnationality and also underscored the difference between them and myself. Javier then responded exuberantly, crying out, "¡Ay, mexicano! Why did you ever leave your small town? [¿Por qué saliste de tu pueblo?]." In this moment of levity, however, Javier suddenly gathered himself and turned to Hipólito, now putting the question to him half-seriously, "Tell us, Polo, why did you leave your small town?" I encouraged him, asking simply, "Yeah, why?" Hipólito, in his characteristically laconic manner, replied with a sigh, "I can't even remember anymore." Javier, however, intervened to supply the answer to his own question, "Because they sold us! It was a deal cut by the government—they sold us because there were too many people in Mexico."[5]

On many other occasions, furthermore, Javier was fond of appealing to another historical memory in similar terms. Recalling the white slaveholders' rebellion in Texas in 1836 and the subsequent U.S.-Mexican War, Javier specifically invoked the name of the Mexican general, Antonio López de Santa Anna, who had initially triumphed against the Texan secessionists' insurrection in the Battle of the Alamo but then was defeated, captured, and required to personally preside over the grant of Texas's independence in exchange for his life before returning to Mexico in disgrace, only to later have his troops infamously defeated at Churubusco outside of Mexico City by the U.S. invasion in 1848. Especially when confronted with the difficulties of learning English, and playfully framing this dilemma in terms of the more general indignity of his Mexican/migrant condition— as if to ask, "By what misfortune did we ever end up here?"—Javier would simply cry out, "¡Ay, Santa Anna! Come back and bring your people home! [¡Recoge a tu gente!]."

THE VISIBILITY OF "ILLEGAL IMMIGRANTS" AND
THE INVISIBILITY OF THE LAW

Due to the critical function of deportation in the maintenance of the revolving-door policy, the tenuous distinction between "legal" and "illegal" migration was deployed to stigmatize and regulate Mexican/migrant workers for much of the twentieth century. As we have seen, originally by means of *qualitative* regulations, "illegality" has long served as a constitutive dimension of the specific racialized inscription of "Mexicans," in general, in the United States (see Ngai 2004). In these respects, Mexican/migrant "illegality," per se, is not new. Indeed, this reflects something of what James Cockcroft (1986) has characterized as the special character of Mexican migration to the United States: Mexico has provided U.S. capitalism with the only "foreign" migrant labor reserve so sufficiently flexible that it can neither be fully replaced nor be completely excluded under any circumstances. What is crucial, however, is to critically examine how the U.S. nation-state has historically deployed a variety of different tactics to systematically create and sustain "illegality," and furthermore, has refined those tactics to generate ever more severe constraints for undocumented Mexican migrants living and working in the United States. After all, the history of legal debate and action concerning immigration is, precisely, a *history*.

This chapter is centrally concerned with the task of denaturalizing Mexican/migrant "illegality," and locating its historical specificity as an irreducibly social fact, *produced* as an effect of the practical materiality of the law. By emphasizing the law's productivity, I aim to trace the historical specificity of migrant "illegality" within the contemporary U.S. Immigration and Naturalization regime. Furthermore, as this book has been emphatically concerned with Mexican migration in particular (in contradistinction to some presumably generic immigrant experience), I also underscore the history of a distinct "illegality" that predominates specifically for Mexicans. Mexican/migrant experiences certainly have meaningful analogies with the sociopolitical conditions of other undocumented migrations, but such comparisons will be intellectually compelling and politically cogent only if they derive their force from precise accounts of the particular intersections of historically specific migrations and complex webs of "legality" and "illegality."

Legislation, of course, is in fact only one feature of "the law" (see Lee 1999), but my discussion will principally focus on the more narrowly legislative history affecting "illegality" for Mexican migration, because this subject itself has been sorely neglected, if not misrepresented altogether. The history of immigration law is nothing if not a contradictory succession of rather intricate and calculated interventions. Indeed, the complex history of lawmaking is distinguished above all by its constitutive restlessness and the relative incoherence of various conflicting strategies, tactics, and compromises that the U.S. nation-state has implemented at particular historical moments, precisely to mediate the contradictions immanent in crises and struggles around the subordination of labor. Thus, rather than a master plan, U.S. immigration laws have served more as a kind of permanent crisis management, tactically supplying and refining the parameters of labor discipline and coercion. As such, immigration laws are part of the effort to make particular migrations into disciplined and manageable objects, but the ongoing fact of class conflict ensures that such tactical interventions can never be assured of success. In other words, immigration laws, in their effort to manage the migratory mobility of labor, are ensnared in a struggle to subordinate the intractability intrinsic to labor's constitutive role within capital as well as the capitalist state—the sort of "protracted and more or less concealed civil war" depicted in chapter 4. As John Holloway suggests, "Once the categories of thought are understood as expressions not of objectified social relations but of the struggle to objectify them, then a whole storm of unpredictability blows through them. Once it is understood that money, capital, the state . . ." (and here I would add, emphatically, the law) "are nothing but the struggle to form, to discipline, to structure what Hegel calls 'the sheer unrest of life,' then it is clear that their development can be understood only as practice, as undetermined struggle" (1995, 176; see Bonefeld 1995; Pashukanis [1929] 1989). And it is this appreciation of the law—as undetermined struggle— that best illuminates the history of the U.S. immigration law, especially as it has devised for its target that characteristically mobile labor force comprised of Mexican migrants.

Migrant "illegality" is ultimately sustained not merely as an effect of such deliberate legal interventions, however, but also as the ideological effect of a discursive formation encompassing broader public debate and political struggle. Social science scholarship concerning undocumented Mexican migration is itself often ensnared in this same discursive formation of "illegality" (De Genova 2002). The material force of law, its instrumentality, its productivity of some of the most meaningful and salient parameters of sociopolitical life, and also its historicity—all of this tends to be strangely absent. Yet, with respect to the "illegality" of undocumented migrants, by not examining the actual operations of immigration law in generating the categories of differentiation among migrants' legal statuses, scholars largely take the law for granted. By not examining those operations over the course of their enactment, enforcement, and revision, furthermore, scholars effectively treat the law as transhistorical and thus falsely presume it to be fundamentally unchanging—thereby naturalizing a notion of what it means to transgress that law. The treatment of "illegality" as an undifferentiated, transhistorical thing-in-itself colludes with state power in creating a remarkable visibility of "illegal immigrants" swirling enigmatically around the stunning invisibility of the law.

LEGISLATING MEXICAN "ILLEGALITY"

Before 1965, as already suggested, there were absolutely no numerical quotas legislated to limit "legal" migration from Mexico, and no such quantitative restrictions had ever existed.[6] The statutory imposition of previously unknown restrictions that reformulated "illegality" for Mexican migration in 1965 and thereafter, furthermore, transpired in the midst of an enthusiastic and virtually unrelenting *im*portation of Mexican/migrant labor. The end of the Bracero Program in 1964 was an immediate and decisive prelude to the landmark reconfiguration of U.S. immigration law in 1965.[7] Thus, a deeply entrenched, well organized, increasingly diversified, and continuously rising stream of Mexican migration to the United States had already been accelerating before 1965. As a consequence of the successive changes in U.S. immigration law since 1965, therefore, the apparently uniform application of numerical quotas to historically distinct and substantially incommensurable migrations has become central to an unprecedented, expanded, and protracted production of a more rigid, categorical "illegality" for Mexican/migrant workers in particular than had ever existed previously.

An ever-growing, already significant and effectively indispensable segment of the working class within the space of the U.S. nation-state, Mexican/migrant labor is ubiquitously stigmatized as "illegal," subjected to excessive and extraordinary forms of policing, denied fundamental human rights, and thus consigned to an always uncertain social predicament, often with little or no recourse to any semblance of protection from the law. Since the 1960s, Mexico has furnished from 7.5 to 8.4 million ("legal" as well as undocumented) migrants who currently reside in the United States (in addition to unnumbered seasonal and short-term migrants).[8] By 2000, approximately 4.7 million of them were undocumented, of whom as many as 85 percent had arrived in the United States only during the 1990s (Passel 2002). No other country has supplied even comparable numbers; indeed, by 2000, Mexican migrants alone constituted nearly 28 percent of the total foreign-born population. It may seem paradoxical, then, that most major changes in the quantitative features of U.S. immigration law during this period have created ever more severe restrictions on the conditions of possibility for "legal" migration from Mexico. Indeed, precisely because of Mexico's unique standing during this time period, all of the repercussions of the uniform numerical restrictions introduced by these legislative revisions have weighed disproportionately upon Mexican migration in particular. This legal history, therefore, is a defining aspect of the historical specificity— indeed, the effective singularity—of contemporary Mexican migration to the United States. With elaborate migration networks and extensive historical ties already well established, Mexicans have continued to migrate, but ever-greater numbers have been relegated to an indefinite condition of "illegality."

The seeming enigma largely derives from the fact that the very character of migrant "illegality" for Mexicans was reconfigured by what was, in many respects, genuinely a watershed liberalization in 1965 that dismantled the U.S. nation-state's openly discriminatory policy of immigration control. The Hart-Celler Act of 1965 (Public Law 89-236; 79 Stat. 911, which amended the Immigration and Nationalities Act of 1952, Public Law 82-414; 66 Stat. 163) comprised a monumental and ostensibly egalitarian overhaul of U.S. immigration law. The 1965 reforms dramatically reversed the explicitly racist exclusion against Asian migrations, which had been in effect and only minimally mitigated since 1917 (or, in the case of the Chinese, since 1882). Likewise, the 1965 amendments abolished the draconian system of national-origins quotas for the countries of Europe, first enacted in 1921 and amplified in 1924. Predictably, then, the 1965 amendments have been typically celebrated as a liberal reform.

U.S. immigration policy suddenly appeared to be chiefly distinguished by a broad inclusiveness, but with respect to Mexico, the outcome was distinctly and unequivocally restrictive. This same "liberal" reform (taking effect in 1968) established for the first time in U.S. history an annual numerical quota to restrict "legal" migration from the Western Hemisphere. Indeed, this new cap came about as a concession to "traditional restrictionists" who fought to maintain the national-origins quota system, and as Aristide Zolberg puts it (1990, 321), "sought to deter immigration of blacks from the West Indies and 'browns' from south of the border more generally." Although hundreds of thousands already migrated from Mexico annually, and the number of apprehensions by the INS of "deportable alien" Mexicans was itself already 151,000 during the year before the enactment of the new quota, now no more than 120,000 "legal" migrants (excluding quota exemptions) would be permitted from all of the Western Hemisphere. Notably, the Eastern Hemisphere quota—170,000—was higher than the 120,000 cap set for the Western Hemisphere, but the individual countries of the Eastern Hemisphere were each limited to a maximum of 20,000, whereas the quota for the Western Hemisphere was available to any of the countries of the Americas on a first-come, first-served basis, subject to certification by the Department of Labor. Nevertheless, although no other country in the world was sending numbers of migrants at all comparable to the level of Mexican migration—and this has remained true, consistently, ever since—the numerical quota for "legal" migrants within the entire Western Hemisphere (i.e., the maximum quota within which Mexicans would have to operate) was now restricted to a level far below actual and already known numbers for migration from Mexico.

Following more than twenty years of enthusiastic "legal" contract-labor importation, orchestrated by the U.S. state, a well-established influx of Mexican migrants to the United States was already accelerating before 1965. The severe restrictions legislated in 1965 necessarily meant that ever-greater numbers of Mexicans who were already migrating increasingly had no alternative other than to come as undocumented workers. Beginning in 1968 (when the new law took effect), the numbers of INS apprehensions of "deportable" Mexican nationals skyrocketed annually, leaping 40 percent in the first year. Although apprehension statistics are never reliable indicators of actual numbers of undocumented migrants, they clearly reveal a pattern of policing that was critical for the perpetuation of the revolving-door policy: the disproportionate majority of INS apprehensions were directed at surreptitious entries along the Mexican border, and this was increasingly so. In 1973, for instance, the INS reported that Mexicans literally comprised 99 percent of all "deportable aliens" who had entered surreptitiously and were apprehended (see Cárdenas 1975, 86). While apprehension totals for all other nationalities from the rest of the world (combined) remained consistently below 100,000 annually, the apprehensions of Mexicans rose steadily from 151,000 in 1968 to 781,000 in 1976, when migration was, once again, still more dramatically restricted. These persistent enforcement practices, and the statistics they produce, have made an extraordinary contribution to the common fallacy that Mexicans account for virtually all "illegal aliens." This effective equation of "illegal immigration" with unauthorized border-crossing, in particular, has served furthermore to continuously restage the U.S.-Mexico border as the theater of an enforcement "crisis" that constantly rerenders *Mexican* as the distinctive national name for migrant "illegality."

The 1965 Amendments have also been characterized as expansively liberal in their provisions for migrant family reunification. For both hemispheres, some family members would be considered "exempt" from the quota restrictions, and thus could migrate without being counted against the quotas, but the exemptions were different for the two hemispheres. For the Western Hemisphere, these quota exemptions for family reunification included the spouses, children, and parents of U.S. citizens or permanent residents. Within the annual quota for migrants from the Western Hemisphere, but not the Eastern Hemisphere, therefore, there was a provision for "legal" migration by the parents of U.S.-citizen *minors*. Thus, a kind of legalization procedure became available to undocumented Western Hemisphere migrants who had children in the United States. Notably, these undocumented migrants had to apply to legalize their status by registering at the U.S. consulate nearest their hometown in their country of origin. In practice, this provision ensured that such an option was considerably easier for migrants from Mexico than virtually any other country. In effect, a baby born in the United States to an undocumented Mexican migrant served as a virtual apprenticeship for eventual legal residency. Thus, in a manner analogous to earlier "drying-out" procedures, many Mexican migrants were required to serve a term as undocumented workers but then could eventually have their immigration status adjusted.[9]

Immigration law, of course, was not the only thing that was changing in 1965. It has been widely recognized that the sweeping 1965 revisions of immigration policy emitted from a generalized crisis of cold war–era liberalism, in which U.S. imperialism's own most cherished "democratic" conceits were perpetually challenged. Taking shape in a context of the international relations imperatives that arose in the face of decolonization and national liberation movements abroad, this crisis was further exacerbated within the United States by the increasingly combative mass movement of African Americans in particular, and "minorities" generally, to denounce racial oppression and demand civil rights, which is to say, their rights of *citizenship*. Thus, U.S. immigration policy was redesigned in 1965 explicitly to rescind the most glaringly discriminatory features of existing law. Furthermore, the end of the Bracero Program had been principally accomplished through the restrictionist efforts of organized labor, especially on the part of the predominantly Chicano and Filipino farmworkers' movement. The specific historical conjuncture from which the 1965 amendments emerged was therefore profoundly characterized by political crises that manifested themselves as both domestic and international insurgencies of racialized and colonized working peoples. So began a new production of an altogether new kind of "illegality" for migrations within the Western Hemisphere, with disproportionately severe consequences for transnationalized Mexican labor migrants in particular—a kind of transnational fix for political crises of labor subordination.

Tellingly, the explicit topic of "illegal immigration" had been almost entirely absent from the legislative debate leading to the 1965 law. David Reimers ([1985] 1992, 207–8) notes the irony that the U.S. Congress "paid little attention to undocumented immigrants while reforming immigration policy in 1965," but "as early as 1969 [i.e., the first year after the 1965 law had taken effect] Congress began to investigate the increase in illegal immigration along the Mexican border." By 1976, however, legislative debate and further revisions in the law had succeeded to produce "illegal immigration" as a whole new object within the economy of legal meanings in the U.S. Immigration regime—the explicit "problem" toward which most of the major subsequent changes in immigration policy have been at least partly directed.

In 1976, within days of the national elections, a new immigration law was enacted (Public Law 94-571; 90 Stat. 2703).[10] The 1976 amendments subjected the quota for nonexempt Western Hemisphere migration for the first time to a system of ranked qualitative preferences for family reunification that was already in place for the Eastern Hemisphere. This meant that the possibilities for migration within the quota was now considerably more regulated, and moreover that quota exemptions for family reunification were now further restricted to the spouses, unmarried minor children, and parents of adult U.S. *citizens* only (usually migrants who had already been naturalized). By thus privileging the kin of U.S.-citizen migrants, notably, these exemptions in fact disadvantaged Mexico because of the pronounced disinclination of most Mexican migrants, historically, to naturalize as U.S. citizens (González Baker et al. 1998). Likewise, the 1976 revisions thus summarily eliminated the legalization provision, described above, that had been available primarily to undocumented Mexican/migrant parents of U.S.-born children. Far more importantly, however, the 1976 statutes established a maximum number (excluding quota exemptions) of 20,000 "legal" migrants a year for every country in the world, now imposing a fixed national quota to Western Hemisphere nations for the first time. Mexico was immediately backlogged, with 60,000 applicants for 20,000 slots, and the backlog became consistently more severe thereafter (Joppke 1999, 30). Once again, and explicitly in the name of "equity," the revision of immigration law had a singularly and incomparably disproportionate restrictive impact on Mexico in particular. Then, after legislation in 1978 (Public Law 95-412; 92 Stat. 907) abolished the separate hemispheric quotas and established a unified worldwide maximum annual immigration cap of 290,000, the Refugee Act of 1980 (Public Law 96-212; 94 Stat. 107) further reduced that maximum global quota to 270,000, thereby diminishing the national quotas to an even smaller annual maximum of 18,200 "legal" migrants (excluding quota exemptions). In the space of less than twelve years, therefore, from July 1, 1968 (when the 1965 amendments went into effect), until the 1980 amendments became operative, U.S. immigration law had been radically reconfigured for Mexicans.

Beginning with almost unlimited possibilities for "legal" migration from Mexico (literally no numerical restrictions, tempered only by qualitative preconditions that, in practice, had often been overlooked altogether), the law had now severely restricted Mexico to an annual quota of 18,200 nonexempt "legal" migrants (as well as a strict system of qualitative preferences among quota exemptions, with weighted allocations for each preference). At a time when there were (conservatively) well over a million Mexican migrants coming to work in the United States each year, the overwhelming majority would have no option but to do so "illegally."

There is nothing matter-of-fact, therefore, about the "illegality" of undocumented migrants. "Illegality" (in its contemporary configuration) is the product of U.S. immigration law—not merely in the generic sense that immigration law constructs, differentiates, and ranks various categories of "aliens," but in the more profound sense that the history of deliberate interventions beginning in 1965 has entailed an active process of inclusion through illegalization (Calavita 1982, 13; see Calavita 1998, 531–32, 557; Hagan 1994, 82; Massey, Durand, and Malone 2002, 41–47; Portes 1978, 475).[11] Indeed, the legal production of "illegality" has made an object of Mexican migration in particular, in ways both historically unprecedented and disproportionately deleterious.

As the culmination of years of recommendations, a new kind of landmark in the history of U.S. immigration law was achieved in 1986 with the passage of the Immigration Reform and Control Act, or IRCA (Public Law 99-603; 100 Stat. 3359), because its principal explicit preoccupation was undocumented migration. Once again, the law instituted a legalization procedure for those undocumented workers who had reliably (and without evident interruption) served their apprenticeships in "illegality," while intensifying the legal vulnerability of others. Indeed, IRCA provided for a selective "amnesty" and adjustment of the immigration status of some undocumented migrants, while it foreclosed almost all options of legalization for those who did not qualify, and for all who would arrive thereafter.[12] Furthermore, the INS seemed intent to reserve the amnesty for those whose undocumented status derived from having "entered without inspection" (surreptitious border-crossers), rather than those who had overstayed their visas. In other words, the INS persistently battled in the courts to exclude from the amnesty those applicants who did not match the profile of "illegality" most typical of undocumented Mexican migrants (González Baker 1997, 11–12). As a predictable result, although Mexicans were estimated to be roughly half of the total number of undocumented migrants, Mexican migrants accounted for 70 percent of the total pool of amnesty applicants, and even higher proportions in California, Illinois, and Texas, the areas of highest Mexican/migrant concentration (13). In Illinois, Mexicans (predominantly concentrated in the Chicago metropolitan area) comprised 84 percent of the undocumented migrants who applied for the amnesty (Gordon 1997). Thus, INS decisions concerning the implementation of IRCA legalization procedures contributed to the pervasive equation of *illegal alien* with *Mexican*.

The Immigration Reform and Control Act of 1986 also established for the first time federal sanctions against employers who knowingly hired undocumented workers. Nevertheless, the law established an "affirmative defense" for all employers who could demonstrate that they had complied with a routine verification procedure. Simply by keeping a form on file attesting to the document check, without any requirement that they determine the legitimacy of documents presented, employers would be immune from any penalty. In practice, this meant that the employer sanctions provisions generated a flourishing industry in fraudulent documents, which merely imposed further expenses and greater legal liabilities upon the migrant workers themselves, while supplying an almost universal protection for employers (Chávez 1992, 169–71; Cintrón 1997, 51–60; Coutin 2000, 49–77; Mahler 1995, 159–87; see U.S. Department of Labor 1991, 124).[13] Likewise, given that the employer sanctions would require heightened raids on workplaces, inspectors were required to give employers a three-day warning before inspections of their hiring records, in order to make it "pragmatically easy" for employers to comply with the letter of the law (Calavita 1992, 169). In order to avoid fines associated with these sanctions, therefore, employers would typically fire or temporarily discharge workers known to be undocumented before a raid. In light of the immensely profitable character of exploiting the legally vulnerable (hence, "cheap") labor of undocumented workers, moreover, the schedule of financial penalties imposed by IRCA simply amounted to a rather negligible operating cost for an employer found to be in violation of the law. Thus, IRCA's provisions primarily served to introduce greater instability into the labor-market experiences of undocumented migrants and thereby instituted an internal revolving door. What are putatively employer sanctions, then, have actually aggravated the migrants' conditions of vulnerability and imposed new penalties upon the undocumented workers themselves.

The Immigration Act of 1990 (Public Law 101-649; 104 Stat. 4978) was not primarily directed at undocumented migration, but it did nonetheless introduce new regulations that increased the stakes of "illegality." Specifically, this law imposed a new global cap on the numbers of family-reunification migrants who were exempt from the official quotas. Thus, the quota-exempt migration by immediate relatives of citizens was now subject to an indirect numerical restriction. Their numbers were no longer unlimited and would now be subtracted from the quotas available for migrants entering under the numerically restricted categories. The 1990 legislation also created a special visa program which sought, in the name of "diversity," to encourage more "legal" migration from countries that had been sending relatively low numbers of migrants (clearly not Mexico!). This law also strengthened the Border Patrol, expanded the grounds for the deportation of undocumented migrants, introduced new punitive sanctions, and curtailed due-process rights in deportation proceedings. In addition, the 1990 legislation restricted jurisdiction over the naturalization of migrants petitioning to become U.S. citizens, rescinding a practice that had been in place since 1795 permitting the courts to award citizenship. This authority was now confined exclusively to the federal office of the attorney general.

When undocumented migrants are criminalized under the sign of the "illegal alien," theirs is an "illegality" that does not involve a crime against anyone; rather, migrant "illegality" stands only for a transgression against the sovereign authority of the nation-state. With respect to the politics of immigration and naturalization, notably, sovereignty (as instantiated in the unbridled authoritarianism of border policing, detention, deportation, and so forth) assumes a pronouncedly absolutist character (Simon 1998). Such an absolutist exercise of state power, of course, relies decisively upon a notion of "democratic" consent, whereby the state enshrouds itself with the political fiction of the social contract in order to authorize itself to act on behalf its sovereign citizens, or at least "the majority." This circular logic of sovereignty conveniently evades the racialized history of the law of citizenship, just as it sidesteps altogether the laborious history in the United States that has produced a "majority" racialized as "white." The racialized figure of Mexican/migrant "illegality," therefore, can be instructively juxtaposed to what is, in effect, the racialized character of the law and the "democratic" state, itself. Because the political culture of liberalism in the United States already posits and requires "the rule of law" as a figure for "the nation," the instrumental role of law in the work of racialization reveals its vital stake in the whiteness at the heart of what comes to be glorified as "American" sovereignty and "national culture."

In the dominant discourses of "immigration control," state sovereignty and "national culture" are invariably conjoined. Anti-immigration stalwart Alan Simpson (former U.S. senator from Wyoming), for example, supplies a classic articulation: "Uncontrolled immigration is one of the greatest threats to the future of this nation, to American values, traditions, institutions, to our public culture, and to our way of life . . . we intend to clearly exercise the first and primary responsibility of a sovereign nation which is to control our borders" (quoted in Harris 1995, 85). The standard cant of right-wing nativists in the United States of the late twentieth century incessantly invoked the menace of a stark and immanent immigrant peril facing this "American" national "culture"— its values and institutions. One such foreboding image was that of an inassimilable and inevitably separatist Mexican "Quebec" rapidly arising in the southwestern United States (Barrera 1979, 2; N. Rodríguez 1997).

Former CIA director William Colby raised the specter of this "Spanish-speaking Quebec" in 1978, insisting that Mexican migration posed a greater threat to the United States than did the Soviet Union (Cockcroft 1986, 39). During the nativist convulsions of the mid-1990s, in an article prominently featured in the *Atlantic Monthly*, immigration historian David Kennedy of Stanford University invoked the same metaphor:

> Mexican-Americans . . . will have sufficient coherence and critical mass in a defined region so that, if they choose, they can preserve their distinctive culture indefinitely. They could also eventually undertake to do what no previous immigrant group could have dreamed of doing: challenge the existing cultural, political, legal, commercial, and educational systems to change fundamentally not only the language but also the very institutions in which they do business. . . . In the process, Americans could be pitched into a soul-searching redefinition of fundamental ideas such as the meaning of citizenship and national identity. . . . There is no precedent in American history for these possibilities. . . . The possibility looms that in the next generation or so we will see a kind of Chicano Quebec take shape in the American Southwest. (1996, 52–68)

Notably, Kennedy titled his essay's penultimate subsection with a question: "What Does the Future Hold?" On the opposite page, that question was juxtaposed to a color photograph depicting a mass protest mobilization, budding with brown faces and bristling with Mexican flags. (The caption identified Los Angeles—a march against California's anti-immigrant ballot initiative Proposition 187, which specifically targeted undocumented migrants and their children.) The concluding subsection from which the quote is extracted, furthermore, was ominously (and revealingly) called "The Reconquista." Clearly, for Kennedy, the immigration question had become a decidedly *Mexican* problem, in which what was at stake was nothing less than the prospect that the U.S. nation-state might see its own history of conquest subverted through a reversal of its imperial fortunes. Baldly echoing the "Save Our State" rhetoric of Proposition 187's campaign against "illegal immigration," Kennedy closed his essay with an appeal to "save our country." Who was, and who was not, included in that national *we* appears to have been long settled by conquest and colonization.

"Illegality" has thus been rendered to be so effectively inseparable from the Mexican/migrant experience, historically, that it should hardly come as a surprise that during the mid-1990s in Mexican Chicago, one could find for sale bumper stickers simulating an Illinois license plate that proudly announced, "100% Mojado" ("100% Wetback"), or caps and T-shirts that declared defiantly: "Ilegal—¿Y Qué?" ("Illegal—So What?") Despite such audacious Mexican/migrant expressions of their "illegal" identity, however, the considerable legalization provisions of the 1986 Amnesty had afforded Mexican migrants a rare opportunity to "straighten out" or "fix" [*arreglar*] their status that few who were eligible opted to disregard. The immigration status of "legal permanent resident" vastly facilitated many of the transnational migrant aspirations that had been hampered or curtailed by the onerous risks and cumbersome inconveniences of undocumented border crossing. By 1990, however, 75.6 percent of all "legal" Mexican migrants in the state of Illinois notably remained noncitizens (Paral 1997, 8). In other words, the rush to become "legal" migrants did not translate into an eagerness to naturalize as U.S. citizens. By the mid-1990s, nonetheless, amid the political climate of heightened nativism and anti-immigrant racism that was widely associated with the passage of California's vindictive Proposition 187, Mexican migrants began to seriously consider the prospect of naturalizing as U.S. citizens in much greater proportions than had ever been true historically. Whereas in 1995 only 19 percent of Mexican migrants eligible to become U.S. citizens opted to do so, by 2001 the naturalization rate among eligible Mexicans had risen remarkably to 34 percent (Margon 2004).

During the spring of 1995, Meche, the worker at Die-Hard Tool and Die who had relocated from California only two years earlier (when the anti-immigration campaign had been gathering steam), was quite unequivocally determined to become a U.S. citizen. She had already submitted her application to the INS and was regularly attending citizenship classes on Saturdays. "Who discovered America?" Meche laughed sarcastically as she mimicked the inane substance of the citizenship exam for which she was studying—"Christopher Columbus." Meche had no romantic illusions about "becoming an American"; rather, she was very clear about the pragmatic reasons for naturalizing. Meche had a sister who was still undocumented, and she hoped to be able help her sister to get her papers "straightened out." Notably, her sister was still living in California, now notorious for the odious Proposition 187, but was considering a move to Chicago. "Lots of people are coming from California now," Meche affirmed. Even as a "legal" migrant, Meche was also quite reasonably concerned about her own prospects in the United States.

"Maybe the laws are changing," she hypothesized, "and if I get laid off, maybe they won't give me any unemployment money if I'm not a citizen." Furthermore, living in the two-thirds-majority Mexican suburb of Cicero, Meche was painfully aware of the extent to which noncitizenship meant political disenfranchisement. "I want to vote," she declared, "because my kids asked me why I can't vote, and why the only ones who can vote in Cicero are the old people, the citizens." Referring to recent electoral struggles in the town where she lived, which were quite baldly racialized, she explained further, "So a white person won the election with ten thousand votes, and the Mexican lost because he only had three thousand. The white people don't want to pay taxes for the schools, and we [Mexicans] can't do anything about it."

Later that year, when I was teaching English at the Pilsen community organization Casa del Pueblo, Faustino, a migrant in his fifties originally from a small town in San Luis Potosí who had been in Chicago for twenty-six years, initiated a conversation about citizenship that expressed strikingly similar concerns.

A lot of people are coming here for citizenship classes. Many say that the government is cutting out our rights and wants to try to deprive us and rob us of many of our rights and benefits, and so they're becoming citizens now to protect themselves. And it makes sense. All you have to do is look at the news. There are rumors that later they'll even deny us our social security pensions, that all this is happening little by little. There's a lot of racism against us, and they'll take anything they can from us. I've been here twenty-six years—I'm already entitled to something, I have my rights [ya tengo mis derechos]. Many of us have been here a long time working, but they want to take away the rights we've earned. So you start to worry. At the factory where I am now, I've been working five years with no health insurance for me or my family. We don't have anything. And when I retire I have my right to a pension, but maybe they'll try to take it from me.

Faustino went on to contrast hardworking migrants such as himself to "those who want welfare but don't have any right to it [quieren pero no tienen el derecho]," citing the example of young women whom he knew— "mostly they're Tejanas [Texas Mexicans], and they're always in the cantinas." These U.S.-born Mexican women had "three, four, and five children." He contended, "They have them just to get the money. That money is supposed to be for your food and rent . . . And because of them, the government wants to take away our rights that we've worked for. It's not right. But that's why I'm thinking about becoming a citizen." Resembling many Mexican migrants' discourses about Blacks and Puerto Ricans (as seen in chapter 5), Faustino insinuated that it was the laziness, debauchery, and welfare "abuse" of impoverished U.S.-citizen Mexicans that was to blame for the persecution of migrant Mexicans, whose rightful entitlements were now in jeopardy (see De Genova and Ramos-Zayas 2003a). Meaningfully coupled with his allegations of others' undeservingness, Faustino nonetheless also asserted, though agonistically, a positive politics of citizenship that affirmed that Mexican migrants had earned their "rights" through their labor and thus ought to be entitled to various social welfare benefits. His considerations of naturalization, notably, had been instigated only by the greater injustice of a system that sought to deny Mexican migrants what was already rightfully theirs.

As the veritable culmination of precisely the anti-immigrant campaigns that Meche and Faustino were confronting, the Illegal Immigration Reform and Immigrant Responsibility Act of 1996 (Public Law 104-208; 110 Stat. 3009) was quite simply the most punitive legislation to date concerning undocumented migration in particular (see Fragomen 1997, 438). It included extensive provisions for criminalizing, apprehending, detaining, fining, deporting, and also imprisoning a wide array of "infractions" that significantly broadened and elaborated the qualitative scope of the law's production of "illegality" for undocumented migrants and others associated with them. It also barred undocumented migrants from receiving a variety of social security benefits and federal student financial aid. In fact, this so-called Immigration Reform (signed September 30, 1996) was heralded by extensive anti-immigrant stipulations in the Anti-terrorism and Effective Death Penalty Act, AEDPA (Public Law 104-132, 110 Stat. 1214, signed into law on April 24, 1996), as well as in the so-called Welfare Reform, passed as the Personal Responsibility and Work Opportunity Reconciliation Act (Public Law 104-193, 110 Stat. 2105; signed August 22, 1996). The AEDPA entailed an "unprecedented restriction of the constitutional rights and judicial resources traditionally afforded to legal resident aliens" (Solbakken 1997, 1382). The Welfare Reform enacted dramatically more stringent and prolonged restrictions on the eligibility of the great majority of "legal" migrants for virtually all benefits, defined as broadly as possible, available under federal law, and also authorized states to similarly restrict benefits programs. Without belaboring the extensive details of these acts, which did not otherwise introduce new quantitative restrictions, it suffices to say that their expansive provisions (concerned primarily with enforcement and penalties for undocumented presence) were truly unprecedented in the severity with which they broadened the qualitative purview and intensified the ramifications of migrant "illegality." Given the already well-entrenched practices that focused enforcement against undocumented migration disproportionately upon Mexican migrants, there can be little doubt that this act, at least before September 11, 2001, likewise weighed inordinately upon Mexicans. Indeed, the language of this legislation, with regard to enforcement, was replete with references to "the" border, a telltale sign that could only portend a further disciplining of Mexican migration.[14]

THE BORDER SPECTACLE

Mexican migration in particular has been rendered synonymous with the U.S. nation-state's purported "loss of control" of its borders and has supplied the preeminent pretext for what has in fact been a continuous intensification of increasingly militarized control (Andreas 1998 and 2000; Dunn 1996; Nevins 2002; see Chávez 2001; Durand and Massey 2003; Heyman 1999; Kearney 1991). And it is precisely the border that provides the exemplary theater for staging the spectacle of "the illegal alien" that the law produces. Indeed, throughout the twentieth century, U.S. immigration enforcement efforts consistently and disproportionately targeted the U.S.-Mexico border, sustaining a zone of relatively high tolerance within the interior. "Illegality" looks most like a positive transgression—and can thereby be equated with the behavior of Mexican migrants rather than the instrumental action of immigration law—precisely when it is subjected to policing at the border. The elusiveness of the law, and its relative invisibility in producing "illegality," requires this spectacle of enforcement at the border, which renders a racialized Mexican/migrant "illegality" visible, and lends it the commonsensical air of a natural fact.

The operation of the revolving door at the border that is necessary to sustain the "illegality" effect always combines an increasingly militarized spectacle of apprehensions, detentions, and deportations with the banality of a virtually permanent importation of undocumented migrant labor.[15] This was remarkably illustrated in the narrative that emerged when I interviewed Carlos (whom I knew from Imperial Enterprises) with his wife Rosario in their home. I asked about their experiences in coming to the United States. Carlos joked that he had come on vacation, but decided not to go back. "But you had your adventures, when you crossed," Rosario prompted him. Carlos simply asked her, "Adventures?" Rosario continued (now addressing me), "Because they locked him up in jail—he was in jail!" Carlos clarified that he had been apprehended in 1976 when he sought to reenter the United States after a workplace raid that had led to his deportation, but noted simply that when he had first crossed, ten years earlier, it had been "really easy." Now, however, Carlos began to relate the story in earnest:

I went three months in that adventure because Immigration had pushed me back all the way to Mazatlán, Sinaloa—and then I turned back again for Tijuana. [. . .] I didn't want to go home, because I didn't have even a nickel, and I was wearing my work clothes, and I was really filthy. So from there, I just turned back around and it took me like five weeks to get to Tijuana, hitching rides. And then I crossed, and they grabbed me, and they had me two months in jail, in Chula Vista . . . Chula Vista, California, right there stuck on the line [at the border]. They were saying that I was the *coyote* [the migrant guide, or "smuggler"]. Because they caught us, some thirty people, and I told them, "Save yourselves, whoever can!" And everyone ran, and many saved themselves—they slipped right out from under the feet of the Immigration! But me, they succeeded to grab! And they said that I was the one who was bringing them across, and no, no, I wasn't. I was set back two months there, locked up. [. . .] The first days, like the first eight days, it was hard . . . They had me in a cell by myself, in a tiny little room, just me, I stayed in there alone. And no, no, I couldn't even lie down because it was tiny. It was like a punishment cell. [. . .] It was so that I would say that I was the one who was bringing the people across. They had me like a month there in that cell. I slept sitting up because I couldn't lie down. And daily they pulled me out for a confession, three times a day, every day. And they were asking me the same questions . . . but I couldn't say anything else because I didn't have anything else. Then when they pulled me out of there from that cell, they threw me in the one they called "the farm" [*la granja*]—and it is a farm, and they have it full of the people they go catching! And there they had me another month. [. . .]

And when I got out, they dumped me in Tijuana, and from there,

I was already headed home. Because I didn't want to come here any more, not any more! I didn't have any thoughts of going back because of what had happened to me, and . . . Well, it turns out that I was on the international bridge when a few people arrived—a van passed, and they knew me. I didn't know them. [. . .] I said, "You know what? I was just three months here, and now I'm a wreck, and I'm going home now." And he says, "No, wait right here for me, right at this same place, wait for me. I'm going back to Los Angeles and I'll be back in a little while." And from there he went and took one of his brothers across, and then he came back and said, "Let's go!" and "Here, use my brother's green card." And the brother didn't look anything like me, nothing! He was dark [*moreno*] and I'm a little more, more white [*más blanco*]. [. . .] No, well, so there we went, and crossing the bridge, I told the Immigration, "Here you go, I have it here. It's just the two of us, him and me," and he [the Border guard] just said, "I caught it," and he said, "It's not necessary, go ahead." And so we followed the road up to San Clemente, and there's another guard station, another checkpoint, and just as we were arriving—like some ninety feet before arriving, they left, and we passed freely. I arrived easily in Los Angeles with someone else's green card. And then from there, I decided to come here [to Chicago] because [. . .] because there were more jobs here that paid better, and there, in the ten years I spent, I almost always was earning the minimum wage, or two bits more than the minimum.

Carlos's narrative bears a distinct resemblance to those of many other Mexican migrants (especially men, as already seen, for example, in Felipe's narrative in chapter 3), in which stories of great hardship commonly alternate with accounts of quite easy passage (see Chávez 1992; Kearney 1991). It was not at all uncommon, furthermore, for Mexican migrants to tellingly conclude their border-crossing narratives—again, as Felipe also did—with remarks about low wages. The fact that Carlos was being originally deported in his filthy work clothes, of course, was yet another decisive detail. These narratives of the adventures, mishaps, as well as genuine calamities of border crossing seem to be almost inevitably punctuated with accounts of life in the United States that are singularly distinguished by arduous travail and abundant exploitation.

If Mexican/migrant "illegality" is truly produced by the law and *not* through "crime and punishment" at the border, this legal production of "illegality" nevertheless requires the spectacle of enforcement at the U.S.-Mexico border. The border spectacle is necessary precisely in order for the spatial difference between the United States and Mexico to be socially inscribed upon Mexican migrants themselves, as their distinctive spatialized (and racialized) status as "illegal aliens," as Mexicans "out of place." The production of their difference in terms of both race and space is crucial, therefore, in the constitution of the class specificity of Mexican labor migration.

The "illegality" effect of protracted vulnerability in everyday life has to be recreated more often than simply on the occasion of crossing the border, however. Indeed, as noted above, the 1986 legislation that instituted employer sanctions was tantamount to an extension of the revolving door to the internal labor market of each workplace where undocumented migrant workers were employed. This became quite manifest on one occasion at the Czarnina and Sons factory. Karina, a Mexican raised in the United States, was in her midtwenties and worked as the secretarial assistant to the personnel boss. On one occasion, she casually mentioned: "I'm calling Immigration to check on whether some of these people are legal residents." I was surprised, and said plainly, "I thought you hire illegal people here." Karina replied, now more theatrically, in a half-heartedly clandestine tone: "We *do*! But we're not supposed to, and we could get fined if we ever got caught, and I could get in a lot of trouble for not checking them when they look so fake. Look at some of these! They're really bad! You can tell they're fakes." "You're checking for Mexican people?" I asked, hoping to make some appeal to any residual sense of loyalty she might have had to people who, like her own parents, had migrated from Mexico. "Everybody! This one's Polish, this one's Mexican," Karina replied, "You don't think I should do it?" Now, careful to protect myself, just as Karina was simply hoping to safeguard her own intermediary position in the larger structure, I rephrased my own implicit argument: "I'm not sayin' what you should or shouldn't do, *pero*. . ." Now, switching to Spanish to perform my own semitheatrical clandestinity, I added, "But people have to work, they need the jobs." Karina admitted, "I know, but . . . at least they should give me something that *looks* good—not this stuff where you can see the jagged edge around the picture, and you can see where they just stuck it on there! Because I can get in trouble for accepting it—at least make it look good, not this phony-looking stuff."

Much like their employers' policing of the jagged edges of their fraudulent "papers," the policing of public spaces outside of the workplace likewise served to discipline Mexican/migrant workers by exacerbating their sense of ever-present vulnerability (Chávez 1992; Heyman 1998; Rouse 1992; and see Coutin 2000; Mahler 1995). The lack of a driver's license, for instance, was typically presumed by police in Chicago to automatically indicate a Latino's more generally un-documented condition (Mahler 1995).[16] In the Pilsen neighborhood, it was a commonplace to hear the menacing voices of police amplified over the loudspeakers of their patrol cars. On one occasion, outside the window of my apartment, I heard the police detaining a car. I peered out to see a tall, burly white cop bellowing to the Latino driver of the detained vehicle: "Do you have a license? Then why are you driving? Park this car or I'll take you to jail!" And it was precisely such forms of everyday "illegality" that confronted many Mexican migrants with quite everyday forms of surveillance and repression. During the spring of 1995, I was teaching an ESL course for a vocational training program intended to prepare people for work in hotel kitchens. Blanca, a migrant in her thirties from the city of Guadalajara who had been in the United States eight years, arrived late and reported that she had just been pulled over by the police. As she had no driver's license, nor any insurance card, the cop had written her a $200 ticket. Blanca had not been asked for a cash bribe to "settle" the fine for the infractions, but this incident inspired Estela to relate how, on multiple occasions, police had demanded payments of $100 in cash from her, as well as others she knew who were undocumented migrants without driver's licenses. Indeed, among undocumented migrants, similar stories were ubiquitous. Notably, although she had only spent five years in the United States, Estela was a U.S. citizen, born to Mexican/migrant parents in Texas before the family returned to the small town in Durango where she had grown up. Estela told us that she had personally had to pay several hundred dollars in bribes of this sort. While her U.S. citizenship had hardly shielded her from this pervasive sort of casual police corruption and abuse, it was precisely Estela's status as a Mexican/migrant woman who spoke virtually no English that facilitated the police's cynical presumption that she was legally vulnerable and therefore easily exploitable.

The illegalities of everyday life were often, literally, instantiated by the lack of various forms of state-issued documentation that sanction one's place within or outside of the strictures of the law (Cintrón 1997; Coutin 2000; Hagan 1994; Mahler 1995). But, as was already evident in Estela's case, there are also those illegalities that more generally pertain to the heightened policing directed at the bodies, movements, and spaces of the poor, and especially those racialized as not-white. On one occasion, my friend Salvador and his two brothers, migrants in their early twenties from a small town in Puebla, were waiting for their sister in the parking lot of a museum. A white man whose car was parked nearby decided that their mere presence was threatening and reported to the police that they were "gang members" and wanted to rob him. They were arrested for "loitering," and their protestations were met with the convenient additional charge of "resisting arrest." Many Mexican migrants' subjection to such quotidian forms of intimidation and harassment was ultimately intensified by their undocumented condition. In effect, there was virtually no way for undocumented migrants to not be always already culpable of some kind of legal infraction. Because any confrontation with the scrutiny of legal authorities was already tempered by the discipline imposed by their susceptibility for deportation, these mundane forms of harassment likewise served to relentlessly reinforce Mexican migrants' distinctive vulnerability as a highly exploitable workforce.

Yet the disciplinary operation of an apparatus for the everyday production of migrant "illegality" is never simply reducible to a quest to achieve the putative goal of deportation. There of course has never been sufficient funding for the INS to evacuate the country of undocumented migrants. Indeed, the Border Patrol has never been equipped even to "hold the line" and actually keep the undocumented out. Rather, it is *deportability*, and not deportation per se, that has historically rendered Mexican labor to be a distinctly disposable commodity. Douglas Massey and his research associates (2002, 41, 45) have understandably characterized the effective operation of U.S. immigration policy toward Mexico since 1965—"the era of undocumented migration"—as "a de facto guest-worker program." This is an inevitable and indisputable conclusion for any sober analysis of the facts. Here, however, one must also underscore what have been the real *effects* of a history of instrumental revisions in U.S. immigration law. Presumptively characterizing the law's consequences as "unintended" or "unanticipated" amounts to an unwitting apologetics for the state that is even more reckless than conspiratorial guessing games about the good or bad "intentions" of lawmakers. In contrast, the challenge of critical inquiry and meaningful social analysis commands that one ask: What indeed do these policies *produce*?

At least until the events of September 11, 2001, the very existence of the enforcement branches of the now-defunct INS were always premised upon the persistence of undocumented migration and a continued presence of migrants whose undocumented legal status has long been equated with the disposable (deportable), ultimately "temporary" character of the commodity that is their labor-power. These contradictions were memorably illustrated when my friend María's grandmother, an elderly migrant visiting Chicago from California for the first time, related the story of how her husband had once come as an undocumented migrant to work in Chicago. When he decided that he had had enough, and that he wanted to return home to Mexico, he proceeded to turn himself in to the INS. He announced that he was none other than an "illegal alien," and requested that they deport him. His hopes that they would pay for his trip home, however, proved to be unfounded; the INS refused his repeated requests. Much as he tried to denounce himself as "illegal," the INS refused him the right to be deported. In its real effects, then, and regardless of competing political agendas or stated aims, the true social role of much of U.S. immigration law enforcement (and the Border Patrol, in particular) has historically been to maintain and superintend the operation of the border as a revolving door, simultaneously implicated in importation as much as (in fact, far more than) deportation. Sustaining the border's viability as a filter for the unequal transfer of value (Kearney 1998; see Andreas 2000, 29–50), such enforcement rituals also perform the spectacle that fetishizes migrant "illegality" as a seemingly objective "thing in itself."

With the advent of the antiterrorism state and a deadly eruption of genuinely global imperialist ambition, the politics of immigration and border enforcement in the United States has been profoundly reconfigured under the aegis of a remarkably parochial U.S. nationalism and an unbridled nativism, above all manifest in the complete absorption of the INS into the new Department of Homeland Security on March 1, 2003. Nevertheless, given U.S. employers' intractable dependency on the abundant availability of legally vulnerable migrant labor, the Bush administration proposed on January 7, 2004, a new scheme for the expressly temporary regularization of undocumented migrant workers' "illegal" status and for the expansion of a Bracero-style migrant labor contracting system orchestrated directly by the U.S. state. Such a legalization plan aspires only toward a more congenial formula by which to sustain the permanent availability of disposable (and still deportable) migrant labor, but under conditions of dramatically enhanced ("legal") regimentation and control. Like all previous forms of migrant legalization, and indeed, in accord with the larger history of the law's productions and revisions of "illegality" itself, such an immigration "reform" can be forged only through an array of political struggles that are truly transnational in scale and ultimately have as their stakes the subordination—and insubordination—of labor.

CONCLUSION

"They should call it 'The Jungle,' in place of the United States—The Jungle, right?" proclaimed Juanita, a migrant in her midtwenties from the small city of Cuernavaca. "Here you meet every kind of people—I'd call it, 'The Jungle of All the Animals.'"

I met Juanita during a group interview conducted in the home of a twenty-one-year-old machine operator named Gloria, whom I had taught in an English class at the DuraPress factory. Gloria was the mother of a seven-year-old daughter and had migrated to Chicago seven years earlier with her husband and newborn infant. However, Gloria's older sister Juanita had been in the United States the longest, more than eight years, and was the most outspoken among the gathering of several siblings, among whom was their seventeen-year-old brother who had only arrived from Mexico fifteen days prior and was eagerly looking for work. It seemed as if Gloria and Juanita's parents—who themselves had migrated from a rural village in Guerrero to the city where they had had to send their children to sell bread and peanuts on the streets—must have already witnessed the departure of every one of their children in the mass migratory movement northward of Mexico's youth, seeking to exchange the vitality of their bodies and minds for the U.S.-dollar wages paid by jobs in factories and restaurant kitchens.

Earlier in the interview, when I asked what they had heard in Mexico about life in the United States, before migrating, Juanita had replied quite frankly: "What we had heard were just stories. But really, it was that those who were returning were bringing back lots of stuff—they were bringing back clothes, money, and they had . . . things. And one has the dream of having them too, and the idea that you have to take advantage of the opportunities that you're given by coming here. But there's something else you discover—the United States has *nothing* to offer you, only discrimination." While her siblings laughed, somewhat nervously, at the audacity of her scathing indictment, Juanita simply replied, "It's the truth! This is the truth, and I'm not going to tell lies, because this is the truth."

Juanita's poignant critique of the oppressive racial order of the United States and the severely exploited condition of Mexican migrants resonated with countless comparably acute insights that had so frequently been shared with me by others. From the vantage point of their immanent locations as transnational migrant workers—simultaneously within the global order of capitalism, U.S. imperialism, and white supremacy, and likewise within the particular nation-state space of the United States and its distinctly racialized social order—the working men and women of Mexican Chicago produced a critical knowledge of everyday life. This book's critique has been made possible only in dialogue with them. As is true of all contributions to any dialogue, and likewise as is true of all perspectives immanently formulated *from within* the irresolution and inherent incompleteness of social relations of struggle and incipient becoming, my critical contribution in this book, like each of theirs, inevitably remains only partial.

Both because of the intrinsic limitations of its particular location and historicity within a larger system of social relations, and moreover because of the partisanship of its own political stakes, my own analysis—like the various perspectives of my ethnographic interlocutors—is partial, and perhaps even exposes outright omissions and blind spots as well. It could not be otherwise, as this is ultimately the case with *all* social theory and analysis, precisely because none of us can ever be magically removed from his or her own substantive sociopolitical location within the dynamism of the relations and conflicts that constitute "society" itself. There simply is no omniscient, comprehensive, and perfectly objective view from the outside. Furthermore, posited as part of a collaborative dialogue, this study and its "conclusions" must remain, and ought to be, tentative at best, subject to critique, and a provocation for further dispute and debate. As such, I offer this book as a contribution to the history that we are all collectively implicated in making, here and now, in the present.

When she casually repudiated the appropriateness of the name of the United States, and declared that it would be better called the Jungle, Juanita incited us to laughter, but her ironic humor conveyed a precious critical insight that invites us to reflect upon her proposition. It is, of course, one of the most cherished conceits of liberal U.S. nationalism to celebrate the United States as a haven of "diversity," a promised land whose apparent cosmopolitanism purportedly reveals that it has been and continues to be a refuge of "liberty" and "opportunity" for people from virtually everywhere in the world. Conventionally figured in this way, U.S. nationalism fashions its particular brand of "nation" as one distinguished for its egalitarianism and inclusiveness, and in effect, as the anticipation and best approximation of a truly global society. Formulated from her distinctly Mexican/migrant vantage point, Juanita's proposition that the United States is really more like a jungle, however, suggests a compelling critique of the proverbial law of the jungle, by which "freedom" is presented as little more than the definitively capitalistic opportunity of the powerful to mercilessly exploit and subjugate the weak. Likewise, in a manner reminiscent of Frantz Fanon's ([1952] 1967, 109–40) juxtaposition of racialization with *humanization*, Juanita's formulation of "diversity" in the United States conjures not so much a festival of the world's peoples as a frightful wilderness in which everyone is reduced by racism to the loathsome status and brute condition of animals.

Precisely this critical sensibility concerning the dehumanization of Mexican/migrant encounters with racism in the United States, and its specific analogy between racialization and the experience of being reduced to the despicable status of an animal, was eloquently expressed in an interview with Alfredo from Imperial Enterprises, a man in his fifties who had been working in the United States for eighteen years. Alfredo spoke with visible feeling: "We arrive and we do jobs that the white [*el güero*] doesn't do, Blacks [*morenos*] don't do it . . . and nevertheless, how one feels in his own flesh as if he were a type of beast . . . as if he's screwed over so that he can just be screwed over some more. Aah, Nico, how lacking is a little humanity [*humanismo*] for each person!"[1]

In explicit racialized juxtaposition to whiteness and Blackness, and likewise in the specific context of migrant labor, Alfredo identified his bestialization as a Mexican/migrant worker and appealed melancholically to the elusive ideal of a shared humanity that seemed inescapably negated in his account of life in the United States.

The critical knowledge of everyday life in the United States that migrants articulated in Mexican Chicago commands an unrelenting interrogation of the fatuous conceits and complacencies of the hegemonic "common sense" of U.S. nationalism. This book has taken its cue from the seemingly mundane experiences and perspectives of working men and women like Alfredo and Juanita, transnational Mexican migrants, in an effort to deploy ethnographic techniques toward the ends of a radically counternationalist critique of U.S. nationalism, its sociopolitical order of white supremacy, and their inseparability from the U.S. nation-state's imperial relation to global capitalism. "It is in everyday life and everyday life alone," asserts Lefebvre, "that those interpretations which philosophers and philosophy define in general and abstract terms are concretely realized" ([1947] 1991, 95). If this book has boldly aspired to some modest approximation of what Marx had in mind when he called for "a ruthless criticism of everything existing" ([1843] 1972, 13), it is likewise and nevertheless in everyday life alone that my critique must be made real and concrete.

NOTES

1   For reasons of racial politics, I capitalize *Black* and *Blackness* as they refer to the social condition and historical specificity of African Americans, whereas I deliberately do not capitalize *white* or *whiteness*. Ralph Ellison, for instance, referred to the capitalization of the term *Negro* as "one of the important early victories of my own people in their fight for self-definition" (1953 [1964], 253). In contrast, as David Roediger explains (1994, 13), "It is not merely that whiteness is oppressive and false, it is that whiteness is *nothing but* oppressive and false. . . . Whiteness describes not a culture but precisely . . . the empty and therefore terrifying attempt to build an identity based on what one isn't and on whom one can hold back."

2   I deploy quotes wherever the term "illegality" appears, and wherever the terms "legal" or "illegal" modify *migration* or *migrants*, in order to emphatically denaturalize the reification of this distinction. The appearance of quotes around these terms should be understood to indicate not the precise historical terminology that pertains in any particular instance so much as a general analytic practice on my part. For further discussion, see chapter 6.

3   During this period, I generally was employed in three or four factories concurrently, in each of which I was teaching courses that ordinarily met twice a week over periods of three months and included fifteen workers each, regularly affording abundant occasions for discussion and debate. Allowing for redundancies among workers who participated in two or even three courses, I came to know two to three hundred Mexican migrants over more or less extended periods of time in my capacity as the instructor of these courses. As a complement to the dialogues that ensued in these workplace classrooms, my position also required me to conduct informal, thirty-minute, one-on-one interviews with what eventually amounted to approximately four hundred Mexican/migrant workers, as part of the overall assessment of spoken English capabilities in these respective workplaces. Likewise, due to the requirements of my job, periodic consultations with management personnel provided ample opportunities to engage in participant observation and conduct informal interviews with these workers' bosses.

4   These two periods of research were augmented, furthermore, by continued communication during an interim sixteen-month period (April 1996–August 1997).

5   Almost all of the more extended ethnographic interviews were initiated with

individuals whom I had come to know, usually over several months, through my work as a literacy teacher and generally were conducted with either those individuals alone or, as often as not, with their spouses. Three interviews involved larger gatherings as a result of the initiative of the persons originally contacted.

6   I consistently deploy quotes around the terms *America* and *American* whenever they modify the United States in order to emphatically problematize the appropriation of American-ness by U.S. nationalism, which of course has always been an affront to the rest of the Americas (see Saldívar 1991). For further discussion with regard to the academic field of American studies, see note 2 in chapter 2.

7   I use the term *Latino* rather than *Hispanic* when referring to people of varied Latin American origins or ancestry, wherever they may have been born or raised. The sociopolitical processes by which Latin American groups have come to be homogenized in the U.S. as "Hispanics" cannot be divorced from the ways in which that label was first formulated by the U.S. federal government, especially as an operative device of the U.S. Census Bureau, a deliberate strategy of erasure of the more particular histories of Chicanos and Puerto Ricans, precisely at that historical moment characterized by the racial militancy of the 1960s and 1970s (Oboler 1995; see Omi and Winant 1986). The term *latinoamericano* is the far more frequently used term within Latin America. Hence, *Latino* has been the widely preferred category among those who embrace a pan–Latin American identification but reject the "Hispanic" label. For further discussion, see De Genova and Ramos-Zayas 2003b.

1. DECOLONIZING ETHNOGRAPHY

1   Some of the people who have been my interlocutors in this research are vulnerable to the punitive legal recriminations that could be brought to bear upon their undocumented immigration status, and thus in the interests of protecting their anonymity, all personal names that appear in the text are fictive.

2   During the mid-1990s, there were approximately four hundred amateur soccer teams, organized in several leagues to compete in public parks throughout the Chicago metropolitan area, comprised almost exclusively of Mexican/migrant men who usually hailed from the same home towns or states of origin, which commonly supplied the teams with their names as well as their constituencies of regular spectators. Soccer teams served primarily as focal points for weekend socializing, especially for young unmarried migrant men, but in many ways were analogous to hometown organizations in their capacity to facilitate the exchange of news from the participants' communities, both in Chicago and Mexico, and information about employment opportunities, used cars and other goods for sale, various services for hire, as well as other social events, such as parties or dances. For an interpretation of Mexican migrants' weekend soccer festivities, see Rouse 1992.

3 For an analogous discussion of the politics of research among Mexican/Chicana/o factory workers, but from the standpoint of a Chicana anthropologist, see Zavella 1987, 20–29.

4 One need only consider, for example, the still widely celebrated anthropological classic *The Nuer*, by E. E. Evans-Pritchard (1940). Not only did Evans-Pritchard have only a rudimentary competence in the language of the Nuer, but far more important, the British colonial administration was actively engaged in military expeditions against the Nuer, and the villagers candidly expressed their hostility and disgust toward the anthropologist whom they viewed plainly "not only as a stranger but as an enemy" ([1940] 1969, 10–11). Consequently, Evans-Pritchard's ethnography involves no dialogue with "regular informants" whatsoever and instead relies entirely on his own "direct observation" (9). Rhetorically turning this grim predicament into a methodological virtue, however, Evans-Pritchard claims unequivocally that he "knew [the Nuer] more intimately" as a result of the lack of their trust, which compelled him to live at close quarters and observe their daily practices "from the door of [his] tent" (15). For an extended critique, see Rosaldo 1986c.

5 For emphasis and clarity, I have adjusted the translation here, replacing "research" for "investigation," and "researcher" for "investigator."

6 Within the field of education, there are well-established ethnographic traditions of "participatory" and "action" research, more or less explicitly influenced by the Freirean project (e.g., Lankshear and McLaren 1993). The academic discipline of anthropology, however, has largely ignored scholarship primarily identified with pedagogical (and thus, "applied") concerns.

7 Devon Peña's ethnography of maquiladora labor and women workers' struggles in Ciudad Juárez, *The Terror of the Machine* (1997), provides a remarkable case in point. Peña acknowledges his debt to Guillermina Valdés de Villalva, the director of the community organization through which he conducted his research, for insisting on his political responsibility to develop his study in continuous dialogue with the workers who were his "subjects," such that they might participate in redefining the research agenda (1997, ix). However, one eventually learns—but only in passing, as if incidentally—that Freire's dialogical pedagogy was a central component of the organization's praxis (139–40) and that Valdés had done postgraduate work on Freire's pedagogy (355n7, 356n20). Thus, while Peña admirably valorizes intersubjective dialogical research practice, his text regrettably never accounts for it methodologically and never examines the centrality of the Freirean genealogy.

8 Freire has been criticized in fruitful ways from a wide range of perspectives. His patriarchal assumptions and the masculinism of his language have been roundly problematized. Likewise for Freire's ontological humanism, and the related problems of his universalism and his homogenizing treatment of "the oppressed" as an internally undifferentiated analytic category, as well as his uncritical erasure of his own relative privilege and its entailments (Aronowitz 1993; Weiler 1994).

9   For an extended ethnography of adult literacy and orality in a transnational Mexican community in Chicago, see Guerra 1998; for a study of rhetorical practices among Mexicans in a satellite city within the greater Chicago metropolitan area, see Cintrón (1997).

10 Ethnographic dialogue—as research practice—ought not be confused with the fetishization of dialogue as a "fashionable metaphor" for the arrangement of the anthropological text (Page 1988, 164), nor as an alibi whereby merely recapitulating whatever the ethnographer's interlocutors happen to say during the research becomes a representational surrogate for critical analysis. While the textual transcription of dialogue does indeed "show that the heart of ethnographic analysis must be in the negotiation between the ethnographer and subject of shared realities" (Marcus and Cushman 1982, 43), Stephen Tyler is surely correct in arguing that "dialogue rendered as text . . . is no longer dialogue, but a text masquerading as dialogue, a mere monologue about a dialogue . . . mediated through the ethnographer's authorial role" (quoted in Marcus and Cushman 1982, 44).

11 Freire transposes a Marxian conception of praxis, such that dialogue itself can be apprehensible, variously, as "practical consciousness," as purposeful social activity, as work, and as production. See Vološinov ([1929] 1986) on "language."

12 Ira Shor has identified this "anthropological" protocol in Freire's pedagogy, but he does not consider the explicit imperative for dialogue in Freire's adaptation of ethnographic methods and the anthropological conception of "culture"; indeed, Shor (1993, 31) erroneously represents Freire's ethnographic plea as a one-sided procedure of observation.

13 An interest in "the dialogical" within anthropology owes much to Bakhtin's very provocative critical theories of language and literature (e.g., Clifford 1983 and 1986; Rabinow 1986; Stewart 1996). For Bakhtin, "dialogism" is part of "a methodology for the study of the novel," premised upon an always prior and permanent *social* condition characterized by a heterogeneous proliferation of competing voices, sounds, inflections, and meanings ("multivocality," "polyphony," "speech diversity," and "heteroglossia") in all deployments of language and the production of any discursive text, regardless of its representational modalities or paradigms (Bakhtin 1981, 326–30, 426; see Fabian 1990, 163–66; Mannheim and Tedlock 1995; Page 1988, 163–64). V. N. Vološinov, widely presumed to be Bakhtin's alter ego, effectively refers to this same condition when he posits "the social multiaccentuality of the ideological sign" ([1929] 1986, 23). The often textually suppressed but nonetheless ever-present fact of heteroglot speech diversity in social life is an inescapable dimension of ethnographic research.

14 In this regard, even silences may be productively understood as dialogical, and—much like the hostile silence of the Nuer in Evans-Pritchard's ethnography discussed in note 4—potentially, a tactic of resistance in the presence of oppression, especially as oppression may be embodied in the educator or ethnographer.

Characterizing "the oppressed" as those "whose words have been stolen from them" ([1968] 1990, 129), Freire decries "the culture of silence" (1985, 83) that he deems to be inextricably entangled with oppression and dehumanization. "Human existence cannot be silent," Freire contends, "To exist, humanly, is to *name* the world, to change it. . . . Men [*sic*] are not built in silence, but in word, in work, in action-reflection [praxis]" ([1968] 1990, 76; emphasis original). Freire's presumption that the occasion of silence is unequivocal and unambiguously synonymous with subjection to oppression, however, is one-sided and ultimately paternalistic. Bakhtin provides a necessary complement to this compulsive refusal to abide by any silences, by clarifying that even silences are a modality of the dialogics of the ethnographic situation (see note 13). Indeed, the elusiveness of silences reveals that anthropological "knowledge" is always provisional, fragmentary, and incomplete (see Stewart 1996, 6).

15 Here, Freire's critique implicitly underscores the affinities between such objectification in social science research and Marx's analysis of the fetishism of the commodity form and reification in the capital-labor relation ([1867] 1976, 125–77).

16 Freire transposes the categories of sadism and necrophilia from the later writings of Erich Fromm (see 1994, 40), who originally borrowed the concept of necrophilia from Miguel de Unamuno.

17 As with personal names, this company name and all others that appear in the ensuing text are fictive. Not only in the interest of protecting the anonymity of people depicted here, but also of protecting myself legally against any possible charges of breach of contract or confidentiality on the part of the companies where I was employed, I have opted to exclude or alter any extraneous descriptive details that I deem to be inconsequential for my analysis, but that could potentially serve nonetheless to identify particular companies or workplaces. Thus, the space of research ("fieldwork") is indeed shown to be inextricable from the politics of the researcher's social locations.

18 For research among workers, especially when conducted within the physical confines of such always-politicized (and usually, privately owned) spaces as factories or other workplaces, a critical reflexivity about these institutionally mediated conditions of possibility for research would seem to be obviously necessary; yet, these questions often go inadequately problematized, or not addressed at all.

19 "The amnesty" in Howard's remarks refers to provisions of the Immigration Reform and Control Act of 1986, which allowed for an adjustment of status for undocumented migrants (see chapter 6).

20 Throughout the extracts of tape-recorded interviews, the inclusion of ellipses in brackets indicates an omission from the original transcript, whereas non-bracketed ellipses indicate a pause in speech. For a further examination of related excerpts from Alfredo's interview transcript, see De Genova and Ramos-Zayas (2003a, 187, 194–95).

21 Freire notes the impossibility of literacy campaigns in languages that are "not part of the social practice of the people"; see Freire and Macedo (1987, 108–19), and Freire's "Letter to Mario Cabral, 15 July 1977" (in Freire and Macedo 1987, 160–69; also in Freire and Faundez 1989, 110–16; see also 107–21). In the best spirit of Freire's intellectual project, I have sought less to apply his actual methods than to reinvent them. As Freire declares, "It is impossible to import pedagogical practices without re-inventing them. Please, tell . . . American educators not to import me. Ask them to recreate and rewrite my ideas" (quoted in Macedo 1994, xiv).

22 Indeed, the "immersion" method of ESL instruction perfectly replicates what Freire describes as the "banking concept" of education ([1968] 1990, 58–63).

23 Any confusion with the grocery store by this name is purely coincidental and strictly not intended.

2. "THE NATIVE'S POINT OF VIEW"

1 There are tremendous historical and political differences that I do not wish to trivialize between the respective locations of American studies and ethnic studies within the institutionalized hierarchies of legitimacy within the U.S. academy. Nonetheless, I underscore the shared assumptions by which the ethnic field is consistently treated as already somehow the more narrow and delimited of the two, and in effect, a mere subset of the purportedly more universal and inclusive "American" national-cultural formation. At its best, ethnic studies scholarship is surely no mere derivative, and indeed provides a genuinely counter–American studies framework, which inspires my own critique of "American"-ness as a racialized national identity and U.S. nationalism itself as a racial formation.

2 Despite the academic enterprise of American studies' "failure . . . to reconceptualize a field that is clearly no longer mappable by any of the traditional coordinates" (Porter 1994, 471), Radway's address typifies the intellectual effervescence among a wide array of scholars in American studies who have now spent several years trying to break out of the epistemological confinements of the field's most foundational nationalist presuppositions (see Buell 1998; Desmond and Domínguez 1996; Kaplan 1993 and 2002; Kaplan and Pease 1993; Lowe 1998; Mackenthun 1996; Pease 1990; Pease and Wiegman 2002; Rowe 1998, 2000a, and 2000b; Saldívar 1991 and 1997; Singh 1998).

3 It is noteworthy here that Higham's definition, although it is primarily concerned with hostility toward the foreignness of immigrants, does nonetheless open up the question of foreignness to a consideration of nonmigrant "internal minorities." The "distinctively American" term *nativism*, according to Higham, was coined in the United States around 1840 ([1955] 1988, 3–4). Notably, at least until recently, "nativism" has not been well distinguished as an analytic category. For important discussions of nativism in non-U.S. contexts, which notably examine

the nationalist politics of nativeness and foreignness with little or no reference to contemporary migrations, see Goswami 2004, Harootunian 1988, and Mamdani 2001.

4   I avoid the more phenomenological and psychologistic term *xenophobia* because it lends itself to transhistorical and potentially primordialist notions of nativism.

5   This is precisely the type of identity politics most appropriate for a politically responsible critique of identitarian claims, because its preoccupations with native (or "American") identity—much like white, male, or heterosexual identities—presume the privileged normativity that comes with being *hegemonic* identities. For an analogous argument, see Lipsitz 1998.

6   A pluralist conception of "culture" is itself one of the hallmarks of modernist anthropology (Stocking 1968, 195–233; see Michaels 1995, 35–36, 173n199). Notably, cultural pluralism preserves the primacy of "identity" without the inconsistencies or incoherence of biology (or "blood"), where the mere requirements of reproduction, of course, ensure that notions of purity are always untenable. It was in this manner, historically, that the "culture" concept could be proclaimed in opposition to "race" (see L. Baker 1998; di Leonardo 1998; Michaelsen 1999; Smedley 1993). The idea of a plurality of separate and distinct "cultures" (or "nations"), however, could be marshaled for the assertion of defining and enduring differences among groups, but only because their identities as groups were already presupposed. Without ever considering the sociopolitical and historical production of them *as* groups, the apparently comprehensive, bounded, and effectively closed character of "a culture" could be once again naturalized as synonymous with the presumably substantial identity of a group constituted by the shared kinship and common ancestry of its members as the ultimate basis for community. Thus, the elasticity of the concept of "culture," when substituted for "race," not only preserves but also intensifies it (Fanon 1956, 29–44; and see Balibar 1991a and 1991b; Gilroy 1990; Goldberg 1993; Michaels 1995, 13–15, 64–65).

7   While the hegemonic discourse of antiterrorism has reenergized conventional nativist obsessions with enforcement against undocumented migration along the U.S.-Mexico border, it is noteworthy that a heightened policing of the U.S. border with Canada in the aftermath of September 11, 2001, merely underscores the remarkable extent to which the northern border previously had gone virtually without any policing whatsoever and the prospect of undocumented migration from Canada (predominantly racialized as white) has historically been deemed effectively undeserving of enforcement.

8   The principal argument of Peter Brimelow's book was anticipated in his editorial essay that appeared in the *National Review*, "Time to Rethink Immigration?" (1992).

9   It is noteworthy that having meticulously sought to justify his explicitly *racial* reasoning, at the moment of his most resolute vindication of racial whiteness as the core essence of "American" national identity, Brimelow resorts to characteriz-

ing it as "*ethnic*," a category Raymond Smith has persuasively derided as one that "distracts attention from the continuing power of racism, and trivializes more complex processes of nationalism" (1996, 187).

10   Here, the unstated object of Brimelow's critique is the Fourteenth Amendment, that "institutional accident" which conferred U.S. citizenship upon formerly enslaved African Americans. For a related argument effectively challenging the extension of birthright citizenship to the U.S.-born children of undocumented migrants, see Schuck and Smith 1985.

11   In counterpoising immigration with a tight labor supply, Steinberg presupposes a self-contained "national" labor market that is isomorphic with a bounded "national economy," and abides by a free market mechanism that arrives at an equilibrium between labor supply and employer demand. Migrants are presumed to simply undersell African American workers in a scramble for "scarce" jobs. Although he certainly does not have illusions about the market's capacity to automatically correct the occupational segregation that he discerns as the engine behind African Americans' oppression, Steinberg's corrective policy proposals for restricting labor supply retain a simplistic market model for remedying Black poverty. While Steinberg does rightly identify employer self-interest as a motive behind immigration policies that facilitate the influx of presumably "cheap" labor, he nonetheless dramatically oversimplifies how employment discrimination operates against Black workers, as if it were merely a luxury of labor surplus.

12   Indeed, in significant ways, this is a striking departure from the central concerns of Steinberg's earlier work ([1981] 1989).

13   Jack Miles (1992, 51), whom Steinberg cites favorably, is notably much more candid about the racialized underpinnings of this kind of liberal nativism, when he proposes "a new paradigm: Blacks vs. Latinos." For valuable discussions of African American nativism, see Fuchs 1990, Hellwig 1982, and Shankman 1977.

14   The "displacement" thesis obeys a quasi-Malthusian logic whereby increased population ensures expanding misery. It presumes that the supply of capital as well as the number of available jobs are both fixed, and that productivity and therefore output are likewise constant. Unemployment, then, comes to be explained purely in terms of population, or more precisely, labor market supply. Unemployment, however, is not a function of increased supply, but rather of declining employer demand, which is not a function of supply. Despite mass deportations of Mexicans during the Great Depression of the 1930s, for instance, unemployment was not at all mitigated, and likewise, but still more dramatically, the post–World War II baby boom in the United States expanded the labor supply in numbers drastically outstripping migration (minimally by a multiplier of four) without generating mass unemployment. "It is solely because immigrants are foreigners," Nigel Harris concludes forcefully (1995, 198), "that they are made the target of resentments concerning the business cycle."

The "displacement" thesis also operates with a model that tends to treat labor (or at least, "unskilled" labor) as perfectly homogeneous and disregards or underestimates the extent to which the labor market might be complexly differentiated, hierarchically stratified, or horizontally segmented, especially in terms of various configurations of the politics of race and citizenship inequalities. Although Steinberg's argument, in fact, relies upon the "dual-economy" distinction between a protected (or insulated) sector composed predominantly of white workers, and a competitive sector where "native minorities" and immigrants (especially the undocumented) compete, his nativism is nonetheless driven by the illusion that such bifurcated inequalities in the labor market could be resolved simply by eliminating migration.

15   By conflating liberal defenders of migrant workers with "free-market economists and business interests [who] have championed the cause of expanded immigration," Steinberg (1995, 187, 260n41) charges that proimmigration social scientists serve as apologists for the maintenance of a sub-minimum-wage tier in the U.S. labor force. In doing so, however, Steinberg thereby reveals that he operates with the fixed presupposition that *immigration* and *immigrants* are inevitably and irreversibly synonymous with *cheap labor*. These pervasive presuppositions, as Michael Burawoy clarifies (1976, 1057), are profoundly tautological; they assume "that migrant labor exists because it is cheap and it is cheap because it exists," and seldom engage the question of any particular migration's historical specificity by means of the crucial consideration, "Cheap for whom with respect to what and under what conditions?" (see also Kearney 1998).

16   The inclination to treat economic matters in terms of "the wealth of nations" was not firmly established until the late eighteenth century and is largely a residue of classical (European, bourgeois) political economy, which articulated the historically specific appearance of "economy" as a distinct category and relatively autonomous sphere of social activity, in relation to the initial rise of nation-states. Capitalist society, then, came to be conventionally represented on the model of self-contained "national" economic units. Historically, the emergence of a "national economy" is always preconditioned by the violence of the accumulation process. Once outright coercion and violence come to be separated and abstracted from the immediate process of exploitation, however, the effective particularization of the political from the economic assumes the form of the organized violence of a territorially defined national state (Marx [1867] 1976, 899–900; Pashukanis [1929] 1989, 143; see Holloway 1994, 31). Notably, Karl Marx depicts capitalist accumulation as global from its very inception ([1867] 1976, 915–16). Thus, before the great majority of the world's nation-states came into being, and furthermore, before the global capitalist economy ever came to be organized as a system of separate and discrete "national economies," the work of producing the spaces for capitalist accumulation was carried out, principally, by *imperialist* states.

17   Indeed, W. E. B. Du Bois is merely the most prominent of African American

intellectuals who have famously explored the equivocal "American"-ness of African Americans ([1903] 1982, 43–44). For related discussions of the theme of African American disqualification from "American"-ness, see Hellwig 1982 and Morrison 1994. For an important consideration of the history of the legal disenfranchisement of African Americans and Native Americans through recourse to figures of the alien and the foreign, see Wald 1993 and R. M. Smith 1997, 197–285. For a repudiation of the conventional assumption that Black experiences of racial oppression and Black-identified cultural formations should ever be construed in narrowly national terms, see Gilroy 1993.

18   A brief survey of the immigration theory in contemporary U.S. sociology readily confirms an increasing emphasis on "the contiguity of ethnic resilience and assimilation" and the enduring dominance of the theme of assimilation, generally (Morawska 1990). For prominent examples, see Portes 1995; Portes and Rumbaut 1990 and 2001; and Rumbaut and Portes 2001. For characteristic conflations of the immigrant and the ethnic, see Portes and Bach 1985, 200–68, and Waldinger 1996.

19   The individual (male) immigrant, in Chock's account (1991, 286), becomes a "new man," significantly, by "putting down roots and having a family" in the United States (see Coutin 2003). "The opportunity myth is what connects family histories with America," Chock explains (290), but "these family sagas, with regard to women, are almost always fragmentary and incomplete" (292n11; and see Chock 1996).

20   Chávez (1992, 5) acknowledges the fact that some undocumented Latinos "remain 'liminals,' outsiders," but immediately forecloses upon any consideration of the question of those whose "full incorporation" is "blocked," suggesting that they merely become "sojourners."

21   Pierrette Hondagneu-Sotelo's ethnography *Gendered Transitions: Mexican Experiences of Immigration* (1994) provides an important extended emphasis on the centrality of gender for these processes, but like Chávez, she regrettably makes settlement the definitive, organizing theme of her analysis (xiii–xiv, xxiii) and insinuates that an accumulation of social "ties" and "connections" in the United States eventually and inevitably prevails over migrants' "dream to return" (xxiii). Ultimately, Hondagneu-Sotelo's argument relies upon a divergence of interests between migrant husbands and wives, whereby "a general trend toward the establishment of more gender-egalitarian familial relations . . . motivate[s] immigrant women to prolong . . . [and] consolidate family settlement" (xxiv).

3. LOCATING A MEXICAN CHICAGO

1   For critical perspectives on the profession of American studies from various standpoints within it, see note 2 to chapter 2.

2   An explicit consideration of empire, imperialism, and colonialism in the field of

American studies long remained the domain of a relatively small number of revisionist historians, such as William Appleman Williams (1955, 1959, and 1980). A more robust scholarship of U.S. imperialism has emerged only very slowly (Cabranes 1979; Drinnon 1980; Jennings 1976 and 2000) and, in large part, rather recently (Burnett and Marshall 2001; Cabán 1999; di Leonardo 1998; Go and Foster 2003; J. González 2000; Jacobson 2000; Joseph, LeGrand, and Salvatore 1998; Kaplan 2002; Kaplan and Pease 1993; Lindsay-Poland 2003; Rafael 2000; Renda 2001; Rowe 2000a; Saldívar 1991; San Juan 2000).

3 The phrase is Fredric Jameson's, as adopted by Roger Rouse (1991, 8).

4 This is not to imply that the Mexican state has no material or practical stake in the political and also economic mobilization of migrant communities; on the contrary, the direct involvement of the Mexican national government, especially through its consulates, as well as Mexican opposition political movements, have become increasingly crucial to migrant political organizing, and even organized Mexican/migrant participation in U.S. politics (see Cano n.d.).

5 My personal understanding of this history was greatly enriched by many conversations with Barney Cohn (see 1980 , 18–49; 1996, 3–15; Cohn and Chatterjee n.d.).

6 See Madrid-Barela (1976) for an attempt to produce a genealogy for the term *Chicano*, which reveals that, despite contemporary connotations, the term originally referred (with derision) to migrants. Rendón (1971, 325), however, rejects such etymological impulses: "Chicano is the one unique word of the Mexican American people. Its derivation is strictly internal; it owes nothing to the Anglo penchant for categorizing ethnic groups. In a way, Chicano is indefinable, more a word to be understood and felt and lived than placed in a dictionary or analyzed by Anglo anthropologists, sociologists, and apologists."

7 In the wake of the Chicano Movement, a few Chicano scholars did indeed resume valuable historical research on Mexican community formation in Chicago after more than forty years of scholarly neglect. Regrettably, most of this research was principally conducted for what ultimately remained unpublished doctoral dissertations; see, for example, Año Nuevo Kerr 1976; Rosales 1978; Sepúlveda 1976; Weber 1982. In this regard, I am not including the work of latter-day Chicago School sociologists, such as Gerald Suttles (1968) and Ruth Horowitz (1983), who produced ethnographies concerned with the "delinquency" of youth gangs in Mexican communities in Chicago. Neither am I including the rather more felicitous but much more recent resurgence of research on Mexican communities in the Chicago area, much of which remains as yet unpublished (Arredondo 1999; A. Baker 1995; Boruchoff 1999; Cintrón 1997; Davalos 1993; Guerra 1998; Villar 1989, 1990, and 1999; Zamudio 1999), and which, in general, has notably *not* situated itself in explicit relation to the Chicano studies project as such. Mexican Chicago does, however, figure significantly in the literary work of two of the most prominent Chicana authors, both of whom happen to have grown up in Chicago: Ana Castillo (1994) and Sandra Cisneros (1986 and 2002).

8 The conceptual limitations of the Southwestern regional paradigm, notably, were recognized and addressed in the Chicano studies journal *Aztlán*, in a "Special Thematic Issue on Chicanos in the Midwest" (Summer 1976); see the issue's introduction by Gilbert Cárdenas (1976); and see J. García 1996; Valdés 1991 and 2000; Vargas 1993. However, the specific recognition of Chicago (or the Midwest) as a *theoretical* (and not merely empirical) question for Chicano studies has come about much more slowly. Though in only a rather preliminary fashion, Sergio Elizondo (1991) poses precisely this question. Likewise, in a review essay, Dennis Valdés (2000) provides an instructive outline of the theoretical dissonances between research on Mexican communities in the Midwest and the predominant frameworks derived from Chicano historical scholarship on the Southwest.

9 In an analogous argument, Walter Mignolo formulates his conception of "border thinking" on the model of Chicana/o experience (2000, 6) but similarly contends that the decolonizing/emancipatory possibilities of his "subaltern" approach can never be fulfilled on the basis of a *territorial* perspective (45).

10 For an instructive overview of the feminist critique of Chicano nationalism, see Ruiz 1998, 99–126.

11 For an insightful Chicana feminist critique of Anzaldúa's deployment of the category of *mestizaje*, see Saldaña-Portillo 2001.

12 Notably, although she explicitly characterizes the Chicano movement as a nationalist struggle that extended "from Chicago to the borders of Chihuahua," Moraga (1993, 151) depicts Aztlán, as the concept that inspired the struggle, to be decisively "located in the U.S. Southwest."

13 Notably, though in a characteristically masculinist idiom, Rendón (1971, 13) likewise affirms the defining "mestizo character" of Chicanos and thus was also an early precursor of the distinctly Chicano recuperation of the Mexican nationalist notion, famously articulated by José Vasconcelos ([1925] 1983), of Mexicans as a "cosmic race," which has come to be associated with Gloria Anzaldúa's (1987) and others' Chicana feminist celebrations of *mestizaje* and "mestiza consciousness."

14 Indeed, David Gutiérrez's landmark 1995 historical study of the antagonisms and divisions between "Mexican Americans" and "Mexican immigrants" is described by Ramón Gutiérrez (2000, 105), in a review essay on paradigm shifts in Chicano historiography, as "particularly innovative" for having "shattered the unity" that had formerly prevailed in Chicano studies concerning migration, precisely, in its refusal of the more characteristic "backward projection of 1960s Chicano identity." Also see Vila 2000.

15 The term *raza*, which may be roughly translated as "race," in colloquial Mexican Spanish tends to conflate a loose notion of collective shared identity or peoplehood with a more plainly racialized understanding of common ancestry. Ramón Gutiérrez (1991, 202) confirms that the first edition of the Dictionary of the Spanish Academy, published in 1737, defined *raza* as "caste or racial status of origin" but added that it connoted illegitimacy and "stain or dishonor of the

lineage" associated with miscegenation in the colonial American context, in contradistinction to the honorable social status associated with "purity" of Spanish blood.

16 This formulation resonates significantly with Renato Rosaldo (1994 and 1997) and his research associates' conception of "Latino cultural citizenship," a vernacular understanding of citizenship as rightful membership which is characterized as offering subordinated Latino communities "the possibility of legitimating demands made in the struggle to enfranchise themselves," and thereby "claim[ing] rights to belong to America" (Rosaldo and Flores 1997, 57–58; see Flores and Benmayor 1997).

17 David Maciel provides one admirable exception in a Mexican publication where a Chicano anti-imperialist perspective frames the narration of Chicano and Mexican/migrant labor struggles in the United States, not as U.S. history, but rather as part of a larger Mexican history—namely, the history of the Mexican working class (1981, 10).

18 Robert Park, for instance, in his introduction to Harvey Zorbaugh's ethnography of Chicago's Near North Side, characterizes the study as exemplary of "a kind of investigation of urban life which is at least comparable with the studies that anthropologists have made of the cultures of primitive peoples" (Zorbaugh 1929, xx).

19 These formulations (and their derivatives) recur with remarkable regularity throughout the work of the Chicago School's sociology. For references to several of their representative publications, see the related discussion in chapter 2.

20 The "folk-urban continuum" concept was advanced by Robert Redfield (1956), an anthropologist at the University of Chicago with significant professional as well as personal connections to the Chicago School of sociology. His conception of "the village" as the spatialized metonym of a "folk culture" was consciously developed in contrast to the Chicago School's notion of "the city." Notably, Redfield formulated his theoretical position primarily on the basis of research in Mexico (1930 and 1956) and also collaborated with Manuel Gamio in his research on Mexican migrants in Chicago (Redfield 1929; 1931; see Arredondo 1999; Necoechea Gracia 1998).

21 Overly sanguine accounts of the transnationalism of Mexican migration too easily run this same risk of inadvertently appearing to recapitulate these time-worn, intrinsically racist representations of Mexican migrants as mere sojourning "homing pigeons." On this score, Chávez 1994 critiques Rouse 1991. This problem especially pertains to specifically culturalist accounts of transnationalism.

22 In the face of the renewed labor shortages caused by U.S. involvement in World War II, the U.S. federal government initiated what came to be known as the Bracero Program as an administrative system of legal contracting, to institutionalize and regiment the supply of Mexican migrant labor for U.S. agriculture in the Southwest, and also for the railroads. For further discussion, see chapter 6.

23 Mexicans who had migrated to the United States before 1924 (when registration was first required of Mexican migrants for "legal" entry, retroactively rendering them "illegal aliens"), as well as those who were simply unable or unsure of their ability to prove "legal" entry, or many others who had, deliberately or not, evaded this registration procedure after 1924 at the time of crossing the border, were all effectively undocumented and subject to deportation (Año Nuevo Kerr 1976, 145–46; 1977, 287–89).

24 These entrenched patterns of racialized occupational stratification and segmentation, as well as the relegation of Mexican workers, alternately, to the status of a "buffer group" or an expendable industrial labor reserve, are all remarkably consonant with what scholars in Chicano studies have described as a colonial labor system (Barrera 1979).

25 The symbolic significance of arresting Mexican migrants on Mexican Independence Day may very likely not have been coincidental. Just a few years earlier, in 1943, an activist in the Mexican community in Chicago had called for a nationwide public celebration of Mexican Independence Day by all Mexicans in the United States as a protest against the anti-Mexican "zoot suit" riots in Los Angeles, and "in honor of the ideal of democracy and of human rights" (Año Nuevo Kerr 1977, 278).

26 The U.S. Census 2000 counted 530,462 Mexicans in the city of Chicago, and 1,121,089 Mexicans in the Chicago Consolidated Metropolitan Statistical Area (CMSA), which extends from Kenosha, Wisconsin, to Gary, Indiana. According to estimates by researchers at the Lewis Mumford Center (State University of New York, Albany), intended to correct undercounting by the U.S. Census Bureau, the number of Mexicans in the city itself was estimated at 624,533, with 1,117,025 for the more restricted Chicago Primary Metropolitan Statistical Area (PMSA).

27 Mexico has been the most prominent source of migration to Chicago since the 1960s. In 2000, Mexican migrants comprised 46.5 percent of the total "foreign-born" population in the city of Chicago, and 41 percent in the greater metropolitan area. Based on 1997 estimates from Census Bureau's Current Population Survey, Polish migrants were the next largest migrant group, representing less than 9 percent of the total (Paral n.d., 9).

28 According to U.S. Census 2000, the South Chicago community area is 70 percent African American, 23.5 percent Mexican, 3.5 percent other Latino, and 3 percent white. While 35.5 percent of South Chicago's Latino population resided in only two of South Chicago's ten census tracts, each of which was nearly two-thirds Latino, there were also three tracts in which the proportions of Latinos and Blacks were roughly comparable, as well as three other predominantly African American tracts in which Latinos comprised 21–24 percent. South Chicago's overall Latino population had dropped from more than 18,000 in 1980 to 10,565 by the year 2000. Meanwhile, the Mexican populations of community areas further south experienced substantial gains: South Deering 27.2 percent, East

Side 60 percent, and Hegewisch 24.4 percent. Although South Deering and Hegewisch each have relatively small total populations, the Mexican population of East Side is more than 14,000.

29 The Back of the Yards (or Packingtown) neighborhood, historically, encompassed all of the New City community area (Jablonsky 1993, Slayton 1986). Since the demise of the meatpacking industry, however, the predominantly Mexican northern and western portions of the New City community area have continued to be identified as the Back of the Yards, whereas the almost homogeneously African American southern and eastern sections have come to be largely dissociated from their historical relation to the stockyards and packing houses.

30 As late as 1970, the entire New City community area's population was tabulated by the U.S. Census as 95.6 percent white (Jablonsky 1993, 150). This figure is somewhat exaggerated by the fact that those "racially" identified by the census as white included a significant minority of the Mexican population, who when responding to the census have consistently indicated their "race" as "white." Nevertheless, the (non-Latino) white population of New City in 1970 can be reasonably estimated to have been more than 90 percent. Within ten years, as a result of "white flight," that figure had plummeted to only 42.4 percent, whereas the Latino and Black proportions of the total population in 1980 had increased dramatically, to 35.7 percent and 21.9 percent respectively. As of the 2000 Census, the New City community area is 45.4 percent Mexican, 4.8 percent other Latino, 36.3 percent African American, and 13.5 percent white.

31 All 1990 figures for Chicago Community Areas are based on U.S. Census data, compiled by the Latino Institute, June 1991.

32 Pilsen's total population was 44,031, of whom 89 percent were Latino (with 8.1 percent of those remaining being white). Notably, the largest concentrations of whites in Pilsen were confined to three census tracts in the eastern section of the neighborhood, which had undergone significant gentrification; however, even these tracts nonetheless remained 65–70 percent Latino. The total official population of the South Lawndale community area (predominantly comprised of Little Village) was 91,071, of which 83 percent was Latino (with 13 percent of those remaining being African American). These figures, however, are misleading in the extreme, due to the distortion that results from inclusion of the Cook County Jail within the "community area" designated as South Lawndale. If data are adjusted to not include the jail census tract (#3013), with a population of more than 10,000, then South Lawndale is 91.9 percent Latino (with African Americans 4.8 percent, and whites 2.7 percent). Excluding the incarcerated population, all of the largest concentrations of African Americans were confined to four census tracts, located along the northern edge of the officially designated South Lawndale community area, next to the virtually homogeneously Black Westside neighborhood of North Lawndale.

33 As early as the late 1940s, there was evidence of migrants recruited directly from

both Mexico and Texas for factory labor in Chicago's suburbs (Año Nuevo Kerr 1977, 282).

34 This figure has been estimated by researchers at the Lewis Mumford Center, intended to correct undercounting by the U.S. Census for 2000. The comparable U.S. Census 2000 figure is nearly 438,000.

35 On this score, Mike Davis's characterization of Chicago's Latino urban spaces as "polycentric barrios" is insufficient; in fact, there is a more viable analogy to be drawn between Latino Chicago (or more precisely, Mexican Chicago) and Davis's model of Latino Los Angeles as a "city within a city" (2000, 39–49).

36 As of 2000, two working-class suburbs have populations that are more than two-thirds Mexican: Cicero (68.4 percent) and Stone Park (66.7 percent). Another eighteen suburbs have Mexican populations of at least 20 percent: Addison (24.3 percent), Aurora (27.5 percent), Bensenville (31.5 percent), Berwyn (31 percent), Blue Island (34 percent), Chicago Heights (20.9 percent), East Chicago, Indiana (37.8 percent), Elgin (29 percent), Franklin Park (31.4 percent), Hodgkins (41.9 percent), Melrose Park (45.3 percent), Northlake (27 percent), Rosemont (30.9 percent), Round Lake Beach (26.6 percent), Round Lake Park (22.7 percent), Summit (44.3 percent), Waukegan (34.9 percent), and West Chicago (45 percent). (In all instances, the proportion of each town's total population that is Latino is modestly higher than the figures for Mexicans alone.) Notably, during the 1990s, three of these municipalities—Addison, Cicero, and Waukegan—were among five suburbs nationally sued by the U.S. Department of Justice for housing discrimination against their Latino communities. The class-action suit against the town of Addison became a federal case that received national attention. See Pam Belluck, "Landmark End to Hispanic Suit on Bias in Housing," *New York Times*, August 8, 1997.

37 For further discussion of capital accumulation as a global phenomenon, see note 16 to chapter 2. For critical problematizations of the term *globalization*, see Harvey 2000, 53–72, and Holloway 1994.

38 Latino Institute Research, cited in Paral 1993.

39 See the related discussion of the thesis that African Americans are "displaced" by recent migrants in note 14 and the adjoining text in chapter 2.

40 Notably, the Illinois Legislative Investigating Commission report (1971, 6; and see 3–6, 13–17) specifically identified an industrial working-class suburb, Chicago Heights, to the south of the city, as having "a particularly serious problem" with undocumented Mexican migration.

41 Predictably, the report reductively equated the "illegal alien" status category with the act of "illegal entry" (1971, 1, 11, 43) and defined *illegal alien* as "any alien . . . who has not obtained permission from the United States Government to be admitted to this country" (Appendix 2, 43), thereby overlooking altogether the possibility of overstaying a visa, or working in violation of a visa, that otherwise would constitute undocumented labor in spite of having obtained "permission to

be admitted." This construction of migrant "illegality" is an effect of a long-established pattern of INS enforcement practices aimed disproportionately against "surreptitious entry" (the profile of Mexican undocumented migration in particular) rather than other manifestations of undocumented status (see chapter 6; see De Genova 2002).

42 Between January 1996 and June 1997, the INS arrested 1,562 undocumented workers in metropolitan Chicago, and could provide demographic information for 1,433. See Gordon 1997.

43 Prior to the imposition of a federal injunction prohibiting the practice, the INS could detain people on the street with impunity on the basis of their appearance or language, demand proof of citizenship or legal residency, and take the accused into custody until someone else provided documentation vindicating them.

44 For a more detailed discussion of Lozano's political career as well as the relationship of Latinos to the Democratic Party machine in Chicago, see De Genova and Ramos-Zayas 2003a, 39–41, 54–55.

45 Compare, for example, Carlos's narrative in chapter 6.

46 For a more detailed examination of Luisa's narrative, see De Genova and Ramos-Zayas 2003a, 137–42.

47 William Kornblum (1974, 9–10) makes these points quite eloquently, only then to regrettably reinscribe it all as an "ecology" of "ethnic provincialism."

48 Among the sixty most segregated U.S. metropolitan areas (PMSAs), Chicago tied for first for Black/Asian segregation and ranked first for Latino/Asian segregation, third for Black/Latino segregation, fifth for white/Black segregation, sixth for white/Latino segregation, and eighteenth for white/Asian segregation, according to measures of residential dissimilarity scores in U.S. cities, calculated from the 2000 Census by researchers at the Lewis Mumford Center. See Harrigan and Vogel 2000 and Squires et al. 1987.

49 Latinos comprised 26 percent of Chicago's total population, but the disproportionate preponderance of Mexicans among Chicago's Latinos has meant that Latinos are often conflated with, or simply presumed to be, Mexican. After Mexicans, the next largest Latino group, Puerto Ricans, constitute only 3.9 percent of the city's population, with all other Latino groups together comprising another 3.8 percent. As of the 2000 census, all Asian groups together constituted only 4.3 percent of the city's total population, with the largest three of these—Chinese, Filipinos, and Indians—each representing approximately 1 percent of the total.

50 The index of dissimilarity is a percentage; it indicates that percentage of the total population of a given group who would have to physically relocate in order for their group to be distributed across the particular geography's census tracts in the same way as members of the comparison group. The higher the value (on a scale from 0 to 100) reveals the degree to which the two groups compared tend to live in separate census tracts. These measures of residential dissimilarity scores in U.S. cities were calculated from the 2000 Census by researchers at the Lewis Mumford

Center. Whereas the overall segregation of Latinos from African Americans had ranked Chicago highest among all U.S. cities in 1980, and second highest in 1990, these figures ranked Chicago third highest for the year 2000. The comparative ranking among the sixty most segregated U.S. cities for overall segregation of Latinos from whites in Chicago had actually risen from ninth highest in 1990 to sixth highest in 2000.

51   Despite persistently severe levels of poverty, Latinos in Chicago have seldom shared housing or neighborhoods with African Americans in Chicago. Through very explicit policy prerogatives, large-scale subsidized public housing in Chicago was developed historically to deliberately reinforce and intensify the segregation of Black poverty from whites (Hirsch 1983; Squires et al. 1987) but has likewise served to exacerbate the separation of African Americans from Latinos. Indeed, according to a 1983 study, there were in fact more whites in Chicago's public housing than Latinos; of the total Chicago Housing Authority resident population, 2 percent were Latino, 3 percent were white, and the remaining 95 percent were African American (Orfield and Tostado 1983, cited in Squires et al. 1987, 110; see Ropka 1980, 125–26). In 1994, Latino housing advocacy organizations filed a class-action suit against the Chicago Housing Authority (CHA) and the U.S. Department of Housing and Urban Development (HUD), concerning discrimination against Latinos in federally assisted public housing in Chicago. The plaitiffs' forty-two-page report, "Latinos and Public Housing," indicated that as of 1992, Latinos occupied only 2.25 percent of the CHA's 42,000 housing units—including public housing complexes, elderly housing, and scattered-site subsidized housing—and only 1.56 percent of the city's 18,000 subsidized "Section Eight" units. See Nelson Soza, "Sins of Omission: Housing for Latinos May Be the CHA's Best Kept Secret," *Chicago Reader*, May 12, 1995.

52   This pedagogical dimension of Mexican/migrant reracialization emerges tellingly in an interview conducted by Víctor Espinosa in Guanajuato with a man who had worked as a migrant in Chicago, who recounts having gotten lost: "To top it off, it was in a Black neighborhood. As people had spoken very badly of the Blacks, well, I got scared. 'Oh my God! Don't let these fuckers [*cabrones*] kill me!'" (Durand 1996, 103; my translation). It was precisely because of what he had already been told about "the Blacks" that he became frightened. His fear was fostered by the fact that he had been tutored.

4. THE POLITICS OF PRODUCTION

1   As of the U.S. Census 2000, Marshall Park (a fictive name) was still 58 percent white, but had witnessed its Latino population grow to over 38 percent, of whom more than four out of five were Mexican.

2   For a discussion of time and motion studies as examples of the "scientific management" principles, usually identified as Taylorism, which seek to impose man-

agerial control over production processes through the supremacy of technical knowledge, see Braverman 1974, 85–138; Burawoy 1979 and 1985, 21–84; Peña 1997, 33–34, 342 nn38, 39.

5. BETWEEN AMERICANS AND BLACKS

1 For valuable contributions toward the ethnography of irony as a vital and pervasive force in everyday life, however, see, for example, Fernandez and Huber 2001 and G. Torres 1997.

2 This and all ensuing translations from the original are my own.

3 The familiar trope of disorder (itself another possible loose translation of *relajo*) supplies an important flashpoint where Portilla's "national character" discourse tends to resonate with anthropologist Oscar Lewis's "culture of poverty" thesis, originally elaborated in his research in Mexico (Lewis 1959 and 1970; see Díaz-Barriga 1997). For creative, ethnographic considerations of order, disorder, and ordering among Mexicans in the United States, see Cintrón 1997, 144, 154–55, and 182–85; and Limón 1989, 480–81, and 1994, 138–39.

4 Bartra ultimately contends that Portilla's conclusions ironically serve as the inadvertent indictment of his own complicity with the authoritarianism of hegemonic Mexican nationalism. By upholding *relajo* as an inherent pathology of the Mexican "national character," Portilla legitimizes a corrupt world in which oppressors and oppressed are united in meaninglessness (1992, 6, 140–42; see Lomnitz-Adler 1992, 251).

5 For critiques and/or further discussion of Paz's treatment of machismo, see Alonso 1995, 80–89, and Bartra 1992, 147–62.

6 For discussions of Mexican/Chicano joking, see Aguilar Melantzón and García Nuñez 1996; Limón 1977; 1994, 87–91; A. Paredes 1966; 1968, 49–72; and Reyna and Herrera-Sobek 1998.

7 Notably, Limón's account does not engage Portilla's treatment of *relajo* but rather follows Lauria 1964, which discusses *relajo* in Puerto Rico; thus, Limón does not address Portilla's specific argument that *relajo* subverts community (1966, 94–95). For a gendered critique of Limón's discussion, see Cummings 1991. Limón acknowledges Cummings' critique in the revised version of the essay (1994, 40).

8 Limón specifically focuses on the distinct genre of performative masculinist humor, known as *albures*, which relies upon lewd puns and playful verbal dexterity as a form of a verbal one-upmanship. *Albures* literally means "chances" or "risks." Cintrón 1997, 71–97 explicitly links *albures* to intermale sexualized domination; see Paz [1950] 1985, 39–40. Likewise, Schmidt (1978, 70, 114) notes the related practices of verbal one-upmanship associated with the verb *tantear* (literally, "to size up, to take the measure of," or somewhat more figuratively, "to test by trial and error"), which he links with notions of violent sexual domination. Similarly, A. Paredes 1971, 223, treats *albures* as "the Mexican equivalent of the

Dozens." Elsewhere, however, Paredes provides a broader contextualization for *albures*: "Insinuation and veiled language, for example, occupy a prominent place in greater Mexican verbal art. The use of indirect language has been refined in the wordplay of the *albur* to double and triple levels of meaning. Euphemism, circumlocution, and allusive language are employed, not to soften the force of an insult, but rather to heighten its effect" (1977, 84; see 1964, 115–16). This resonates remarkably with Rafaela Castro's discussion of euphemistic language and allusion in Mexican women's sexual joking (1982).

9   For an example of a "Stupid American" joke transposed as a "Stupid Anthropologist" joke, see A. Paredes 1993b, 74–75, 165n88.

10   Lancaster posits the same critical interpretive possibility: "It is precisely the 'gestic' or gestural element of jest that, in catching the *gist* of what it mimes, allows it to conceal so many obscure truths, so much manifold sobriety, such detailed and carnal knowledge of the world" (1997, 23–24; emphasis original).

11   The equation of Blackness with excessively drudging work, of course, has a long genealogy in the United States (see Roediger 1991, 144–50) as well as in Latin America (see Degler [1971] 1986, 245–46).

12   The term *chango* (monkey) was routinely used as a derogatory epithet for African Americans; also see note 23.

13   For discussions of the racialization of indigenous people in Mexico, see Friedlander 1975; Lomnitz-Adler 1992, 1996, and 2001; for other Latin American contexts, see Domínguez 1994; Gould 1998; Klor de Alva 1995; C. Smith 1997; Wade 1993, 29–47, and 1997.

14   Here (and wherever it appears in the ensuing text), the word *nigger* was uttered in English.

15   Despite important differences between post-Independence Mexico and the United States, this basic inside-outside distinction with regard to the respective racializations of Blackness and Indianness was not dramatically different in the racial order of Spanish colonial Mexico (Lomnitz-Adler 1992, 266–67).

16   However, the decline in the number of Latinos claiming *only* the "other race" option—from approximately 60 percent in 1990, to 51.5 percent in 2000—may indeed be explained by the possibility in Census 2000 to select multiple categories in combination.

17   For discussions of *huevos* (as related to masculinity), see Alonso 1995, 80–89, and Lugo 1995, 61–83. Lugo, in particular, treats masculinity and "laziness" in relation to labor discipline and subordination.

18   In the context of nineteenth- and early-twentieth-century Mexican campaigns of northern frontier colonization, Alonso assesses the meaning of *huevos* (but notably, *not* the related term *huevón*) in relation to work, as the premier expression of civilized and civilizing masculine honor. "Production itself was an education in maleness," in opposition to "laziness as a form of infamy [associated with barbarism and savagery] that had to be socially controlled," such that masculinized

work became "a sign of ethnic honor" (1995, 107–09). Furthermore, Alonso discusses the conflict between the value of work as a sign of "ethnic" and masculine honor and self-determination, on the one hand, and the servility of commodified wage labor as "emasculation," on the other (194–95). For parallel discussions of the United States, see Almaguer 1994, 32–38, and Bederman 1995.

19 For historical discussions of the *literal* coupling of racialized subjugation with a masculinity constituted through the demotion of one man by another to a gendered status analogous to that of a woman—through intermale rape by prostration and penetration, see R. Gutiérrez 1991, Trexler 1995, and Weismantel 2001, as well as Almaguer 1991, Beattie 1997, and Buffington 1997.

20 The racist stereotype of Black people as "lazy" has a tremendous currency throughout the Americas; for parallel ethnographic discussions, see Wade 1993, 13–14, 253–66, and B. Williams 1991, 49–69.

21 Paredes, in passing, acknowledges the existence and longevity of these tensions in Texas (1979, 11; see Foley 1997 and 1998).

22 Alonso points out that, still today, "to 'feel lazy' (*tener flojera*) is to be in a liminal state akin to illness" (1995, 109). For a discussion of *flojo* in terms of a colonial racial legacy that associated laziness with Indians, see Lugo 1995, 66–67.

23 The term *chango* (monkey) was most frequently used as a derogatory epithet for African Americans, but in the Czarnina and Sons factory (discussed later in this chapter) I also heard *chango* used to refer disparagingly to Southeast Asians, for whom Mexicans otherwise used the more generic, relatively "neutral" racial category *los chinos* [the Chinese]. In different contexts, however, *chango* could also refer—affectionately, but often in the diminutive form *changuito*—to children, as in *mis changos* ["my monkeys," to mean "my kids"]. Wade (1993, 240) discusses a parallel example for Colombia.

24 The term *mayate* (dung beetle), in my experience, was almost always used to refer derisively to African Americans; I heard it only once used to refer to male homosexuality. In the context of late-nineteenth- and early-twentieth-century Mexican criminological accounts of prison homosexuality, Buffington (1997, 120) describes how the term *mayate* was used to refer to the "active," (often) aggressive role in sex between men, coupled with the (sometimes) unwilling, "passive" (receiving) role, which was called the *caballo* (male horse), who is "ridden," so to speak, but perhaps more significantly, whose ass is penetrated by the dung beetle. Murray and Dynes (1995, 188) note that the term *mayate* also connotes "flashy dresser" and is used in U.S. Mexican/Chicano Spanish for "Black pimp."

25 Aguirre Beltrán ([1946] 1989, 173) suggests that *moreno* was used in colonial Mexico as a euphemism for *negro*, in order to circumvent racial prohibitions against the admission of "people of color" into the militia. In Colombia, the use of *moreno* is interpreted as an act of pity or condescension (Wade 1993, 264–65). In Brazil, both *preto* and *moreno* can be understood to serve a similarly euphemistic purpose (Degler [1971] 1986, 201; see Twine 1998).

26 Compare with the pedagogical aspect of Olivia's narrative, discussed in chapter 3.

27 For a related discussion of this joke, specifically in relation to the racialized politics of citizenship between Mexicans and Puerto Ricans, see De Genova and Ramos-Zayas 2003a, 76–78. For a discussion of Pancho Villa jokes as a distinct genre, see Reyna 1984. For discussions of the figure of Pancho Villa as a premier symbol of a heroic, popular-nationalist, Mexican masculinity, see Alonso 1995 and Paredes 1971, 234.

28 For an analogous discussion of the racialized juxtaposition of "Mexican"-ness and "American"-ness, see Foley 1997, 40–63; see Chabram-Dernersesian (1997, 120). For analyses of how white people construct their own whiteness as "American"-ness, see Frankenberg 1994 and Hale 1998. Frankenberg, however, is notably too quick to conclude that *American* is a name for whiteness only when it is whites who do the naming (4). For discussions of the racialization of Mexicans as "Mexicans," see Barrera 1979; D. Gutiérrez 1995, 24; Mirandé 1985, 76, and 1987, 3–9; Montejano 1987, 5, 82–85; Vélez-Ibáñez 1996, 19, 70–87; Vila 2000, 83–86.

29 Evangelina's usage of the term *Chicano* in this instance was fairly exceptional among Mexican migrants in Chicago.

30 It is possible to identify the same distinctions deployed fairly consistently by Mexican migrants in the interview transcripts compiled by Jorge Durand and his collaborators, and published in Spanish (1996). One encounters the phrase "americanos o negros" (217), as well as an operative mutually exclusive juxtaposition of "gringos" and "negros" (92–93, 106), or "gabachos" and "negros" (57). Notably, "moreno" is used to refer to an African American during an interview conducted in the United States (57), but in an interview that was conducted in Guadalajara, it is used to distinguish color differences among Mexicans (154).

31 For extended discussions of "Mexican American" antagonisms toward Mexican migrants, see Foley 1998, D. Gutiérrez 1995, Heyman 2002, and Vila 2000.

32 For critical perspectives on whiteness by Black writers, see Roediger 1998, editors of *Ebony* (1966), and hooks 1992, 165–78. For analogous Chicano perspectives, see Chabram-Dernersesian 1997; Paredes 1966.

6. THE LEGAL PRODUCTION OF ILLEGALITY

1 1st Cong., Sess. II; *Statutes at Large of the United States of America, 1789–1873* (17 vols., Washington, D.C., 1850–73), Ch. 3, 1 Stat. 103 (Act of March 26, 1790); see Haney López 1996.

2 However, it was indeed white U.S. citizens who were the original "illegal aliens" whose undocumented incursions into Mexican national territory had provided the prelude to the war; see Article 11 of Mexico's Decree of April 6, 1830 (Moquin and Van Doren 1971, 193; and see Acuña 1981, 3–5; Barrera 1979, 9; Mirandé 1985, 24; Vélez-Ibáñez 1996, 57–62).

3 The All-Asia Barred Zone remained in effect until the 1940s and 1950s (see Hing

1993; Lee 2003; Salyer 1995). Filipinos, having been designated as U.S. "nationals" due to their colonized status following the U.S. occupation after the Spanish-American War in 1898, were a notable exception to the all-Asian exclusion (Ngai 2004, 96–126).

4 Approximately 4.8 million contracts were issued to Mexican workers for employment as braceros over the course of the program's twenty-two years, and during that same period there were more than 5 million apprehensions of undocumented Mexican migrants (Samora 1971). It is a matter of speculation, of course, how many undocumented migrants succeeded for each of those caught. Both of these figures, furthermore, include redundancies and thus are not indicative of absolute numbers in any case; they are revealing nonetheless of the more general complementarity between contracted and undocumented migration flows.

5 There was a noteworthy resonance here between Javier's words and the title of María Patricia Fernández-Kelly's 1983 ethnography of Mexican maquiladora labor, *For We Are Sold, I and My People.*

6 This was true for all of the countries of the Western Hemisphere (excluding colonies) and so has implications for most countries in Latin America and the Caribbean, but none of these has ever had numbers of migrants at all comparable to those originating from Mexico. At the local level of U.S. consulates in Mexico, however, in the period prior to 1965, numerical restrictions of migrant visas were sometimes imposed unofficially (see Ngai 2004).

7 Partly in anticipation of unemployment pressures with the end of the Bracero Program and the return of migrant workers, the Mexican government introduced its Border Industrialization Program, which facilitated U.S.-owned, labor-intensive assembly plants (maquiladoras) to operate in a virtual free-trade zone along the U.S.-Mexico border. As a result, migration within Mexico to the border region accelerated; by 1974, one-third of the population of Mexico's border states was comprised of migrants (of whom a mere 3 percent were employed in the maquiladoras), intensifying circumstances in the region that might induce subsequent migration to the United States (Cockcroft 1986, 109).

8 Based on pooled estimates from the U.S. Census Bureau's Current Population Survey (March 1998, March 2000), 36.5 percent of the total Mexican population were "foreign-born" and 49.3 percent of the latter were "recent arrivals," having migrated during the 1990s (Logan 2001). The lower estimate is derived from U.S. Census Bureau data; the higher figure is an estimate by researchers at the Lewis Mumford Center, intended to adjust for Census undercounting (see Logan 2002).

9 This legalization procedure ultimately pertained to the undocumented parents of babies born between July 1, 1968 and December 31, 1976, due to the elimination of this clause by the 1976 immigration act.

10 Phyllis Chock (1991) provides a compelling discussion of the discursive production of an "illegal alien crisis" during the 1975 congressional debates that eventually led to the 1976 legislation. Unfortunately, Chock does not examine the

stipulations or material effects of that legislation itself and even appears in one passage to be incognizant of the very existence of the 1976 law—claiming inaccurately that "it would be more than a decade before Congress passed immigration legislation" (291).

11 In theoretical terms, Bach 1978, Burawoy 1976, Castells 1975, and Nikolinakos 1975 candidly and critically address the direct role of the state in the creation of "illegal" migrant vulnerability. Unfortunately, however, none extends this critique to an examination of the actual operations of the law. Coutin (1996, 1998, and 2000) argues precisely for a consideration of U.S. immigration law's production of "illegality" in its power to constitute individuals through its categories of differentiation, but despite her excellent, detailed, empirical treatment of immigration law for undocumented Salvadoran asylum-seekers, her discussion largely presupposes the extant legal regime that preceded the 1980s. Notably, Joppke (1999, 26–31) sustains the illegalization thesis through a considerably detailed, accurate, and sharply focused empirical account of the legal history. Yet, the remarkable irony here is that Joppke's own position is only a thinly veiled endorsement of this unprecedented illegalization of Mexican migration. Once "illegal immigration" was literally created, Joppke contends, seeking to control it more rigorously was a logically necessary and perfectly legitimate objective, inhibited only by the "client politics" of "pressure groups" who favored civil rights over the "national interest."

12 As a boon to agricultural employers' lobbies, the terms of legalization for undocumented agricultural workers were very lenient: migrants could adjust their status to temporary resident simply by proving that they had worked in perishable agriculture for at least ninety days during that prior year alone, and they could apply for permanent resident status after a year or two dependent upon how long they had been employed in agriculture. Otherwise, eligible for temporary resident status were those undocumented migrants who could establish that they had resided continuously in the United States since before January 1, 1982, and after a period of eighteen months, these newly legalized temporary residents would be permitted to apply for permanent resident status.

13 Employers could also elude the law by simply resorting to subcontracting, whereby a firm no longer directly employs its own undocumented workforce.

14 In strict legal terms, "the border" would include airports where migrants undergo inspection by immigration authorities, commonly with visas that later may be overstayed or violated (Bosniak 1996, 594n95). The Immigration Act of 1996 specified, however, that new Border Patrol personnel were to be deployed "along the border in proportion to the level of illegal *crossing*" (Title I, Section 101 [c]; emphasis added).

15 In what Josiah Heyman (1995) calls "the voluntary-departure complex," "deportable aliens" apprehended at the U.S.-Mexico border (who are, predictably, overwhelmingly Mexican) "are permitted (indeed, encouraged) to waive their rights

to a deportation hearing and return to Mexico without lengthy detention, expensive bonding, and trial," and then, upon release in Mexico near the border, "they can and do repeat their attempts to evade border enforcement until they finally succeed in entering" (266–67). The U.S. state thereby maximizes arrests while actually negating their efficacy, projecting the impression of "border control" while facilitating undocumented labor migration.

16 Before September 11, 2001, only four states—North Carolina, Tennessee, Utah, and Virginia—issued driver's licenses to any state resident who could pass the driving test, regardless of legal status (*New York Times*, August 4, 2001).

CONCLUSION

1 For discussion of more expanded excerpts of this interview, in relation to racialized formulations of "Latino" identity, see De Genova and Ramos-Zayas 2003a, 187, 194–95.

BIBLIOGRAPHY

Acuña, Rodolfo. 1972. *Occupied America: The Chicano's struggle toward liberation.* New York: Harper and Row.

——. 1981. *Occupied America: A history of Chicanos.* 2nd ed. New York: Harper and Row.

——. 1996. *Anything but Mexican: Chicanos in contemporary Los Angeles.* New York: Verso.

Agamben, Giorgio. 1998. *Homo sacer: Sovereign power and bare life.* Stanford, Calif.: Stanford University Press.

Aguilar Melantzón, Ricardo, and Fernando García Nuñez. 1996. La frontera narrativa y el humor. *Aztlán* 21:263–97.

Aguirre Beltrán, Gonzalo. [1946] 1989. *La población negra de México: Estudio etno-histórico.* Mexico City: Fondo de Cultura Económica.

Allen, Theodore W. 1994. *The invention of the white race, Vol. 1: Racial oppression and social control.* New York: Verso.

——. 1997. *The invention of the white race, Vol. 2: The origin of racial oppression in Anglo-America.* New York: Verso.

Almaguer, Tomás. 1991. Chicano men: A cartography of homosexual identity and behavior. *differences* 3(2):75–99.

——. 1994. *Racial fault lines: The historical origins of white supremacy in California.* Berkeley: University of California Press.

Alonso, Ana María. 1995. *Thread of blood: Colonialism, revolution, and gender on Mexico's northern frontier.* Tucson: University of Arizona Press.

Alvarez, Jr., Robert R. 1995. The Mexican-U.S. border: The making of an anthropology of borderlands. *Annual Review of Anthropology* 24:447–70.

Anaya, Rudolfo A. 1991. Aztlán: A homeland without boundaries. In Anaya and Lomelí 1991, 230–41.

Anaya, Rudolfo A., and Francisco Lomelí, eds. 1991. *Aztlán: Essays on the Chicano homeland.* Albuquerque: University of New Mexico Press.

Anderson, Benedict. [1983] 1991. *Imagined communities: Reflections on the origins and spread of nationalism.* Rev. ed. New York: Verso.

Andreas, Peter. 1998. The U.S. immigration control offensive: Constructing an image of order on the southwest border. In *Crossings: Mexican immigration in interdisciplinary perspectives*, ed. Marcelo M. Suárez-Orozco, 343–56. Cambridge, Mass.: Harvard University Press.

——. 2000. *Border Games: Policing the U.S.-Mexico Divide*. Ithaca, N.Y.: Cornell University Press.

Año Nuevo Kerr, Louise. 1975. Chicano settlements in Chicago: A brief history. *Journal of Ethnic Studies* 2(4):22–32.

——. 1976. The Chicano experience in Chicago, 1920–70. Ph.D. diss., University of Illinois at Chicago.

——. 1977. Mexican Chicago: Chicano assimilation aborted, 1939–1954. In *Ethnic Chicago*, ed. Melvin G. Holli and Peter d'A. Jones, 269–98. Grand Rapids, Mich.: William B. Eerdmans.

Anzaldúa, Gloria. 1983. La prieta. In *This bridge called my back: Writings by radical women of color*, ed. Cherríe Moraga and Gloria Anzaldúa, 198–209. New York: Kitchen Table Women of Color.

——. 1987. *Borderlands/la frontera: The new mestiza*. San Francisco: Spinster/Aunt Lute.

Appadurai, Arjun. 1990. Disjuncture and difference in the global cultural economy. *Public Culture* 2(2):1–24; reprinted as chap. 2 in Appadurai 1996.

——. 1991. Global ethnoscapes: Notes and queries for a transnational anthropology. In *Recapturing anthropology: Working in the present*, ed. Richard G. Fox, 191–210. Santa Fe, N.M.: School of American Research Press; reprinted as chap. 3 in Appadurai 1996.

——. 1996. *Modernity at large: Cultural dimensions of globalization*. Minneapolis: University of Minnesota Press.

——. 1998a. Dead certainty: Ethnic violence in the era of globalization. *Public Culture* 10(2):225–47.

——. 1998b. Full attachment. *Public Culture* 10(2):443–49.

Arias Jirasek, Rita, and Carlos Tortolero. 2001. *Mexican Chicago*. Chicago: Arcadia/ Tempus.

Aronowitz, Stanley. 1993. Paulo Freire's radical democratic humanism. In *Paulo Freire: A Critical Encounter*, ed. Peter McLaren and Peter Leonard, 8–24. New York: Routledge.

Arredondo, Gabriela F. 1999. What! The Mexicans, Americans? Race and ethnicity, Mexicans in Chicago, 1916–1939. Ph.D. diss., University of Chicago.

Arvizu, Steven F., ed. 1978. Chicano perspectives on decolonizing anthropology. *Grito del Sol* 3(1).

Asad, Talal. 1973a. Intro. to *Anthropology and the colonial encounter*, ed. Talal Asad, 9–19. Atlantic Highlands, N.J.: Humanities.

——. 1973b. Two European images of non-European rule. In *Anthropology and the colonial encounter*, ed. Talal Asad, 103–18. Atlantic Highlands, N.J.: Humanities.

——. 1991. Afterword: From the history of colonial anthropology to the anthropology of Western hegemony. In *Colonial situations: Essays on the contextualization of ethnographic knowledge*, 314–24. History of Anthropology, vol. 7. George W. Stocking, Jr., ed. Madison: University of Wisconsin Press.

Bach, Robert L. 1978. Mexican immigration and the American state. *International Migration Review* 12(4):536–58.

Baker, Anthony. 1995. The social production of space of two Chicago neighborhoods: Pilsen and Lincoln Park. Ph.D. diss., University of Illinois at Chicago.

Baker, Lee. 1998. *From savage to Negro: Anthropology and the construction of race, 1896–1954.* Berkeley: University of California Press.

Bakhtin, Mikhail M. 1981. *The dialogical imagination: Four essays.* Austin: University of Texas Press.

———. 1993. *Toward a philosophy of the act.* Austin: University of Texas Press.

Balderrama, Francisco E., and Raymond Rodríguez. 1995. *Decade of betrayal: Mexican repatriation in the 1930's.* Albuquerque: University of New Mexico Press.

Balibar, Etienne. 1991a. Is there a "neo-racism"? In Balibar and Wallerstein 1991, 17–28.

———. 1991b. Racism and nationalism. In Balibar and Wallerstein 1991, 37–67.

———. 1991c. The nation form: History and ideology. In Balibar and Wallerstein 1991, 86–106.

———. 1991d. Racism and crisis. In Balibar and Wallerstein 1991, 217–227.

Balibar, Etienne, and Immanuel Wallerstein. 1991. *Race, nation, class: Ambiguous identities.* New York: Verso.

Barrera, Mario. 1979. *Race and class in the Southwest: A theory of racial inequality.* Notre Dame, Ind.: University of Notre Dame Press.

Barrera, Mario, Carlos Muñoz, and Charles Ornelas. 1972. The barrio as internal colony. In *People and politics in urban society,* ed. Harlan Hahn, 465–98. Los Angeles: Sage.

Bartra, Roger. 1992. *The cage of melancholy: Identity and metamorphosis in the Mexican character.* New Brunswick, N.J.: Rutgers University Press.

Basch, Linda, Nina Glick Schiller, and Cristina Szanton Blanc. 1994. *Nations unbound: Transnational projects, postcolonial predicaments, and de-territorialized nation-states.* Langhorne, Pa.: Gordon and Breach.

Beattie, Peter. 1997. Conflicting penile codes: Modern masculinity and sodomy in the Brazilian military, 1860–1916. In *Sex and sexuality in Latin America,* ed. Daniel Balderston and Donna J. Guy, 65–85. New York: New York University Press.

Bederman, Gail. 1995. *Manliness and civilization: A cultural history of gender and race in the United States, 1880–1917.* Chicago: University of Chicago Press.

Belenchia, Joanne. 1977. The Latino communities. In *The political organization of Chicago's Latino communities,* ed. John Walton and Luis M. Salces. Evanston, Ill.: Center for Urban Affairs, Northwestern University.

———. 1982. Latinos and Chicago politics. In *After Daley: Chicago politics in transition,* ed. Samuel K. Gove and Louis H. Masotti, 118–45. Urbana: University of Illinois Press, 1982.

Berger, Mark T. 1995. *Under northern eyes: Latin American studies and U.S. hegemony in the Americas, 1898–1990.* Bloomington: Indiana University Press.

Berkhofer, Robert F. 1978 Jr. *The white man's Indian: Images of the American Indian from Columbus to the present*. New York: Vintage/Random House.

Betancur, John J., Teresa Cordova, and María de los Angeles Torres. 1993. Economic restructuring and the process of incorporation of Latinos into the Chicago economy. In *Latinos in a changing U.S. economy: Comparative perspectives on growing inequality*, ed. Rebecca Morales and Frank Bonilla, 109–132. Newbury Park, Calif.: Sage.

Blauner, Robert and David Wellman. 1973. Toward the decolonization of social research. In *The death of white sociology: Essays on race and culture*, ed. Joyce A. Ladner, 310–30. Baltimore: Black Classic Press, 1998.

Blea, Irene I. 1988. *Toward a Chicano social science*. New York: Praeger.

Bogardus, Emory S. [1934] 1970. *The Mexican in the United States*. Los Angeles: University of Southern California Press.

Bonefeld, Werner. 1995. Capital as subject and the existence of labour. In *Emancipating Marx: Open Marxism Vol. III*, ed. Werner Bonefeld, Richard Gunn, John Holloway, and Kosmos Psychopedis, 182–212. East Haven, Conn: Pluto.

Boruchoff, Judith A. 1999. Creating continuity across borders: Reconfiguring the spaces of community, state, and culture in Guerrero, Mexico and Chicago. Ph.D. diss., University of Chicago.

Bosniak, Linda S. 1994. Membership, equality, and the difference that alienage makes. *NYU Law Review* 69(6):1047–1149.

——. 1996. Opposing Proposition 187: Undocumented immigrants and the national imagination. *Connecticut Law Review* 28(3):555–619.

——. 1997. "Nativism" the concept: Some reflections. In Perea 1997, 279–99. New York: New York University Press.

Braverman, Harry. 1974. *Labor and monopoly capital*. New York: Monthly Review.

Brimelow, Peter. 1992. Time to rethink immigration? *National Review* 44 (June 22): 30–68.

——. 1995. *Alien nation: Common sense about America's immigration disaster*. New York: Random House.

Brodkin, Karen. 1998. *How Jews became white folks and what that says about race in America*. New Brunswick, N.J.: Rutgers University Press.

Buell, Frederick. 1998. Nationalist postnationalism: Globalist discourse in contemporary American culture. *American Quarterly* 50(3): 548–91.

Buffington, Rob. 1997. *Los jotos*: Contested visions of homosexuality in modern Mexico. In *Sex and sexuality in Latin America*, ed. Daniel Balderston and Donna J. Guy, 118–32. New York: New York University Press.

Bulmer, Martin. 1984. *The Chicago School of sociology: Institutionalization, diversity, and the rise of sociological research*. Chicago: University of Chicago Press.

Burawoy, Michael. 1976. The functions and reproduction of migrant labor: Comparative material from southern Africa and the United States. *American Journal of Sociology* 81(5): 1050–87.

——. 1979. *Manufacturing consent: Changes in the labor process under monopoly capitalism*. Chicago: University of Chicago Press.

——. 1985. *The politics of production*. New York: Verso.

Burnett, Christina Duffy, and Burke Marshall, eds. 2001. *Foreign in a domestic sense: Puerto Rico, American expansion, and the Constitution*. Durham, N.C.: Duke University Press.

Bustamante, Jorge A. 1992. Interdependence, undocumented migration, and national security. In *U.S.-Mexico Relations: Labor Market Interdependence*, ed. Jorge A. Bustamante, Clark W. Reynolds, and Raúl A. Hinojosa Ojeda, 21–41. Stanford, Calif.: Stanford University Press.

Cabán, Pedro. 1999. *Constructing a colonial people: Puerto Rico and the United States, 1898–1932*. New York: Westview.

Cabranes, José A. 1979. *Citizenship and the American empire*. New Haven, Conn.: Yale University Press.

Calavita, Kitty. 1982. California's "employer sanctions": The case of the disappearing law. Research Report Series, Number 39. Center for U.S.-Mexican Studies, University of California, San Diego.

——. 1984. *U.S. immigration law and the control of labor, 1820–1924*. New York: Harcourt Brace Jovanovich.

——. 1989. The immigration policy debate: Critical analysis and future options. In *Mexican migration to the United States: Origins, consequences, and policy options*, ed. Wayne A. Cornelius and Jorge A. Bustamante, 151–78. Center for U.S.-Mexican Studies, University of California, San Diego.

——. 1992. *Inside the state: The Bracero Program, immigration, and the I.N.S.* New York: Routledge.

——. 1996. The new politics of immigration: "Balanced budget conservatism" and the symbolism of Proposition 187. *Social Problems* 43(3):284–299.

——. 1998. Immigration, law, and marginalization in a global economy: Notes from Spain. *Law and Society Review* 32(3):529–66.

Cano, Gustavo. n.d. Political mobilization of Mexican immigrants in Chicago and Houston. Unpublished manuscript, Columbia University.

Cappetti, Carla. 1993. *Writing Chicago: Modernism, ethnography, and the novel*. New York: Columbia University Press.

Cárdenas, Gilbert. 1975. United States immigration policy toward Mexico: An historical perspective. *Chicano Law Review* 2:66–89.

——. 1976. Introduction: Who are the Midwestern Chicanos? Implications for Chicano Studies. *Aztlán* 7(2):141–152.

Cardoso, Lawerence. 1980. *Mexican emigration to the United States, 1897–1931*. Tucson: University of Arizona Press.

Carse, James P. 1986. *Finite and infinite games*. New York: Ballantine.

Caruso, Jorge, and Eduardo Camacho. 1985. *Hispanics in Chicago*. [Reprints from the Chicago Reporter.] Chicago: Community Renewal Society.

Castells, Manuel. 1975. Immigrant workers and class struggles in advanced capitalism: The Western European experience. *Politics and Society* 5:33–66.

Castillo, Ana. 1994. *Massacre of the dreamers: Essays on Xicanisma*. Albuquerque: University of New Mexico Press.

Castro, Rafaela. 1982. Mexican women's sexual jokes. *Aztlán* 13(1–2):275–93.

Chabram-Dernersesian, Angie. 1997. On the social construction of whiteness within selected Chicana/o discourses. In Frankenberg 1997, 107–64.

Chakrabarty, Dipesh. 1989. *Rethinking working-class history: Bengal, 1890–1940*. Princeton, N.J.: Princeton University Press.

Chatterjee, Partha. 1986. *Nationalist thought and the colonial world: A derivative discourse?* Minneapolis: University of Minnesota Press.

——. 1993. *The nation and its fragments: Colonial and postcolonial histories*. Princeton, N.J.: Princeton University Press.

Chávez, Leo R. 1988. Settlers and sojourners: The case of Mexicans in the United States. *Human Organization* 47: 95–108.

——. 1991. Outside the imagined community: Undocumented settlers and experiences of incorporation. *American Ethnologist* 18:257–78.

——. 1992. *Shadowed lives: Undocumented immigrants in American society*. Fort Worth, Tex.: Harcourt, Brace, and Jovanovich.

——. 1994. The power of the imagined community: The settlement of undocumented Mexicans and Central Americans in the United States. *American Anthropologist* 96(1):52–73.

——. 1997. Immigration reform and nativism: The nationalist response to the transnationalist challenge. In Perea 1997, 61–77.

——. 2001. *Covering immigration: Popular images and the politics of the nation*. Berkeley: University of California Press.

Chávez, Leo R., Estevan T. Flores, and Marta López-Garza. 1989. Migrants and settlers: A comparison of undocumented Mexicans and Central Americans. *Frontera Norte* 1:49–75.

Chilcote, Ronald H. 1997. U.S. hegemony and academics in the Americas. *Latin American Perspectives* 24(1):73–77.

Chock, Phyllis Pease. 1991. "Illegal aliens" and "opportunity": Myth-making in congressional testimony. *American Ethnologist* 18(2): 279–94.

——. 1995. Ambiguity in policy discourse: Congressional talk about immigration. *Policy Sciences* 28:165–184.

——. 1996. No new women: Gender, "alien," and "citizen" in the congressional debate on immigration. *PoLAR: Political and Legal Anthropology Review* 19(1): 1–9.

Churchill, Ward. 1992. *Fantasies of the master race: Literature, cinema, and the colonization of American Indians*. Monroe, Maine: Common Courage.

Cintrón, Ralph. 1997. *Angels' town: Chero ways, gang life, and rhetorics of the everyday*. Boston: Beacon.

Cisneros, Sandra. 1986. *The house on Mango Street*. Houston: Arte Publico.

———. 2002. *Caramelo*. New York: Knopf.

Clark, Victor S. [1908] 1974. *Mexican labor in the United States*. Bureau of Labor Bulletin 78. Washington, D.C.: Department of Commerce and Labor. [Reprinted in *Mexican labor in the United States*, ed. Carlos E. Cortés. New York: Arno.]

Clifford, James. 1983. On ethnographic authority. In Clifford 1988, 21–54.

———. 1986. Partial truths. In *Writing culture: The poetics and politics of ethnography*, ed. James Clifford and George E. Marcus, 1–26. Berkeley: University of California Press.

———. 1988. *The predicament of culture: Twentieth-century ethnography, literature, and art*. Cambridge, Mass.: Harvard University Press.

Cockcroft, James D. 1986. *Outlaws in the promised land: Mexican immigrant workers and America's future*. New York: Grove.

Cohn, Bernard S. 1980. History and anthropology: The state of play. In Cohn 1987, 18–49.

———. 1987. *An anthropologist among the historians*. New Delhi: Oxford University Press.

———. 1996. *Colonialism and its forms of knowledge: The British in India*. Princeton, N.J.: Princeton University Press.

Cohn, Bernard S., and Piya Chatterjee. n.d. Colonial knowledges/imperial outreach: World War II and the invention of area studies in the United States. Unpublished manuscript, Department of Anthropology, University of Chicago.

Cole, David. 2003. *Enemy aliens: Double standards and constitutional freedoms in the War on Terrorism*. New York: New Press.

Coniff, Richard. 1991. Chicago: Welcome to the neighborhood. *National Geographic* 179(5):50–77.

Cornelius, Wayne A. 1982. America in the era of limits: Nativist reactions to the "new" immigration. Working Papers in U.S.-Mexican Studies, Number 3. Center for U.S.-Mexican Studies, University of California, San Diego.

———. 1992. From sojourners to settlers: The changing profile of Mexican immigration to the United States. In *U.S.-Mexico relations: Labor market interdependence*, ed. Jorge Bustamante, Clark W. Reynolds, and Raúl Hinojosa Ojeda, 155–95. Stanford, Calif.: Stanford University Press.

Coutin, Susan Bibler. 1996. Differences within accounts of U.S. immigration law. *PoLAR: Political and Legal Anthropology Review* 19(1):11–20.

———. 1998. From refugees to immigrants: The legalization strategies of Salvadoran immigrants and activists. *International Migration Review* 32(4):901–25.

———. 2000. *Legalizing moves: Salvadoran immigrants' struggle for U.S. residency*. Ann Arbor: University of Michigan Press.

———. 2003. Suspension of deportation hearings and measures of "Americanness." *Journal of Latin American Anthropology* 8(2):58–95.

Coutin, Susan Bibler, and Phyllis Pease Chock. 1995. "Your friend, the illegal": Definition and paradox in newspaper accounts of U.S. immigration reform. *Identities* 2(1–2):123–48.

Cronon, William. 1991. *Nature's metropolis: Chicago and the Great West*. New York: W. W. Norton.

Cummings, Laura. 1991. Carne con limón: Reflections on the construction of social harmlessness. *American Ethnologist* 18(2):370–72.

Davalos, Karen Mary. 1993. Ethnic identity among Mexican and Mexican American women in Chicago, 1920–1991. Ph.D. diss., Yale University.

Davis, F. James. 1991. *Who is black? One nation's definition*. University Park: Pennsylvania State University Press.

Davis, Mike. 2000. *Magical urbanism: Latinos reinvent the U.S. big city*. New York: Verso.

De Genova, Nicholas. 2002. Migrant "illegality" and deportability in everyday life. *Annual Review of Anthropology* 31:419–47.

——. Forthcoming. Racial (trans)formations: Latinos and Asians at the frontiers of U.S. nationalism. Introduction to *Racial transformations: Latinos and Asians remaking the United States*, ed. Nicholas De Genova. Durham, N.C.: Duke University Press.

De Genova, Nicholas, and Ana Y. Ramos-Zayas. 2003a. *Latino crossings: Mexicans, Puerto Ricans, and the politics of race and citizenship*. New York: Routledge.

——. 2003b. Latino racial formations: An introduction. *Journal of Latin American Anthropology* 8(2):2–16.

Degler, Carl N. [1971] 1986. *Neither black nor white: Slavery and race relations in Brazil and the United States*. Madison: University of Wisconsin Press.

De León, Arnoldo. 1983. *They called them greasers: Anglo attitudes toward Mexicans in Texas, 1821–1900*. Austin: University of Texas Press.

Delgado, Richard. 1997. Citizenship. In Perea 1997, 318–23.

Desmond, Jane C., and Virginia R. Domínguez. 1996. Resituating American studies in a critical internationalism. *American Quarterly* 48(3):475–90.

Díaz-Barriga, Miguel. 1997. The culture of poverty as *relajo. Aztlán* 22(2):43–65.

di Leonardo, Micaela. 1998. *Exotics at home: Anthropologies, others, American modernity*. Chicago: University of Chicago Press.

Dinwoodie, D. H. 1977. Deportation: The Immigration Service and the Chicano labor movement in the 1930s. *New Mexico Historical Review* 52(3):193–206.

Dirks, Nicholas B. 2001. *Castes of mind: Colonialism and the making of modern India*. Princeton, N.J.: Princeton University Press.

Domínguez, Jorge I., ed. 1994. *Race and ethnicity in Latin America: Essays on Mexico, Central and South America: Scholarly debates from the 1950's to the 1990's, vol. 7*. New York: Garland.

Drinnon, Richard. 1980. *Facing west: The metaphysics of Indian-hating and empire-building*. New York: New American Library.

Du Bois, W. E. B. [1903] 1982. *The souls of black folk*. New York: Signet/Penguin.

Dunn, Timothy J. 1996. *The militarization of the U.S.-Mexico border, 1978–1992: Low-intensity conflict doctrine comes home*. Austin: Center for Mexican American Studies Books and University of Texas Press.

Durand, Jorge, ed. 1996. *El Norte es como el mar: Entrevistas a trabajadores migrantes en Estados Unidos*. Guadalajara: Universidad de Guadalajara.

Durand, Jorge, and Douglas S. Massey. 1992. Mexican migration to the United States: A critical review. *Latin American Research Review* 27(2):3–42.

———. 2003. The costs of contradiction: U.S. border policy, 1986–2000. *Latino Studies* 1(2):235–52.

Editors of *Ebony*. 1966. *The white problem in America*. Chicago: Johnson Publishing.

Elizondo, Sergio D. 1991. ABC: Aztlán, the borderlands, and Chicago. In *Aztlán: Essays on the Chicano homeland*, ed. Rudolfo Anaya and Francisco Lomelí, 205–218. Albuquerque: University of New Mexico Press.

Ellison, Ralph. [1953] 1964. *Shadow and act*. New York: Signet.

Evans-Pritchard, E. E. [1940] 1969. *The Nuer: A description of the modes of livelihood and political institutions of a Nilotic people*. New York: Oxford University Press.

Fabian, Johannes. 1983. *Time and the other: How anthropology makes its object*. New York: Columbia University Press.

———. 1990. Presence and representation: The other and anthropological writing. *Critical Inquiry* 16: 753–72.

Fanon, Frantz. [1952] 1967. *Black skin, white masks*. New York: Grove.

———. 1956. Racism and culture. In *Toward the African revolution: Political essays*, 29–44. New York: Grove Press, 1967.

Feagin, Joe R. 1997. Old poison in new bottles: The deep roots of modern nativism. In Perea 1997, 13–43.

Fernandez, James W., and Mary Taylor Huber. 2001. *Irony in action: Anthropology, practice, and the moral imagination*. Chicago: University of Chicago Press.

Fernández-Kelly, María Patricia. 1983. *For we are sold, I and my people: Women and industry in Mexico's frontier*. Albany: State University of New York Press.

Fitzpatrick, Peter. 1995. "We know what it is when you do not ask us": Nationalism as racism. In *Nationalism, racism, and the rule of law*, ed. Peter Fitzpatrick, 3–26. Brookfield, Vt.: Dartmouth Publishing.

Flores, William V., and Rina Benmayor, eds. 1997. *Latino cultural citizenship: Claiming identity, space, and rights*. Boston: Beacon.

Foley, Neil. 1997. *The white scourge: Mexicans, blacks, and poor whites in Texas cotton culture*. Berkeley, Calif.: University of California Press.

———. 1998. Becoming Hispanic: Mexican Americans and the Faustian pact with whiteness. In *Reflexiones 1997: New directions in Mexican American studies*, ed. Neil Foley, 53–70. Austin: Center for Mexican American Studies Books and University of Texas Press.

Foucault, Michel. 1977. *Discipline and punish: The birth of the prison*. New York: Random House.

Fragomen, Jr., Austin T. 1997. The Illegal Immigration Reform and Immigrant Responsibility Act of 1996: An overview. *International Migration Review* 31(2):438–60.

Frankenberg, Ruth. 1994. Whiteness and Americanness: Examining constructions of race, culture, and nation in white women's life narratives. In *Race*, ed. Steven Gregory and Roger Sanjek, 62–77. New Brunswick, N.J.: Rutgers University Press.

Frankenberg, Ruth, ed. 1997. *Displacing whiteness: Essays in social and cultural criticism*. Durham, N.C.: Duke University Press.

Freire, Paulo. [1968] 1990. *Pedagogy of the oppressed*. New York: Continuum.

———. 1978. *Pedagogy in process: The letters to Guinea-Bissau*. New York: Seabury.

———. 1985. *The politics of education: Culture, power, and liberation*. South Hadley, Mass.: Bergin and Garvey.

———. 1996. *Letters to Christina: Reflections on my life and work*. New York: Routledge.

Freire, Paulo, and Antonio Faundez. 1989. *Learning to question: A pedagogy of liberation*. New York: Continuum.

Freire, Paulo, and Donaldo Macedo. 1987. *Literacy: Reading the word and the world*. South Hadley, Mass.: Bergin and Garvey.

Friedlander, Judith. 1975. *Being Indian in Hueyapan: A Study of forced identity in contemporary Mexico*. New York: St. Martin's.

Fromm, Erich. 1994. *On being human*. New York: Continuum.

Fuchs, Lawrence H. 1990. The reactions of black Americans to immigration. In *Immigration reconsidered: History, sociology, politics*, ed. Virginia Yans-McLaughlin, 293–314. New York: Oxford University Press.

Fuller, John D. P. 1936. *The movement for the acquisition of all Mexico*. Baltimore: Johns Hopkins University Press.

Fusco, Coco. 1995. *English is broken here: Notes on cultural fusions in the Americas*. New York: New Press.

Galarza, Ernesto. 1964. *Merchants of labor: The Mexican Bracero story*. Santa Barbara, Calif.: McNally and Loftin.

Gamio, Manuel. [1930] 1971. *Mexican immigration to the United States: A study of human migration and adjustment*. New York: Dover.

García, Juan Ramón. 1980. *Operation Wetback: The mass deportation of Mexican undocumented workers in 1954*. Westport, Conn.: Greenwood.

———. 1996. *Mexicans in the Midwest, 1900–1932*. Tucson: University of Arizona Press.

García, Ramón. 1997. Patssi's eyes. *Aztlán* 22(2):169–80.

Geertz, Clifford. 1971. "From the native's point of view": On the nature of anthropological understanding. In *Meaning in anthropology*, ed. Keith H. Basso and Henry A. Selby, 221–37. Santa Fe: School of American Research/University of New Mexico Press.

Gilroy, Paul. 1990. One nation under a groove. In *Anatomy of racism*, ed. David Theo Goldberg, 263–82. Minneapolis: University of Minnesota Press.

———. 1993. *The black Atlantic: Modernity and double consciousness*. Cambridge, Mass.: Harvard University Press.

Giroux, Henry A. 1993. Paulo Freire and the politics of postcolonialism. In *Paulo Freire: A critical encounter*, ed. Peter McLaren and Peter Leonard, 177–88. New York: Routledge.

Glick Schiller, Nina, Linda Basch, and Cristina Szanton Blanc, eds. 1992. Towards a transnational perspective on migration. *Annals of the New York Academy of Sciences* 645.

Go, Jugrosfoguellian, and Anne L. Foster, eds. 2003. *The American colonial state in the Philippines*. Durham, N.C.: Duke University Press.

Goldberg, David Theo. 1993. *Racist culture: Philosophy and the politics of meaning*. Cambridge, Mass.: Blackwell.

——. 1997. *Racial subjects: Writing on race in America*. New York: Routledge.

——. 2002. *The racial state*. Malden, Mass.: Blackwell.

Gómez, Dante. 1999. Una poca de gracia . . . y otra cosita. In *La Bamba cultural: México en Chicago*, 248–52. Chicago: Instituto Mexicano de Cultura y Educación de Chicago.

Gómez-Peña, Guillermo. 1993. *Warrior for Gringostroika*. St. Paul, Minn.: Graywolf.

Gómez-Quiñones, Juan. 1977. *On culture*. Popular Series, UCLA Chicano Studies Publications, no. 1. Los Angeles: UCLA Chicano Studies Research Center Publications.

——. 1982. On culture. *Revista Chicano-Riqueña* 10(1–2): 290–308.

——. 1994. *Mexican American labor, 1790–1990*. Albuquerque: University of New Mexico Press.

González, Juan. 2000. *Harvest of empire: A history of Latinos in America*. New York: Viking/Penguin.

González, R. M., and R. A. Fernández. 1979. U.S. imperialism and migration: The effects on Mexican women and families. *Review of Radical Political Economics* 11(4):112–23.

González Baker, Susan. 1997. The "amnesty" aftermath: Current policy issues stemming from the legalization programs of the 1986 Immigration Reform and Control Act. *International Migration Review* 31(1):5–27.

González Baker, Susan, Frank D. Bean, Augustin Escobar Latapi, and Sidney Weintraub. 1998. U.S. immigration policies and trends: The growing importance of migration from Mexico. In *Crossings: Mexican immigration in interdisciplinary perspectives*, ed. Marcelo M. Suárez-Orozco, 79–105. Cambridge, Mass.: Harvard University Press.

Gordon, Danielle. 1997. INS aims at businesses, hits Mexicans. *Chicago Reporter*, July/August.

Goswami, Manu. 2004. *Producing India: From colonial economy to national space*. Chicago: University of Chicago Press.

Gould, Jeffrey L. 1998. *To die in this way: Nicaraguan Indians and the myth of mestizaje, 1880–1965*. Durham, N.C.: Duke University Press.

Gramsci, Antonio. [1929–35] 1971. *Selections from the prison notebooks*. New York: International Publishers.

Grenier, Guillermo J. 1988. *Inhuman relations: Quality circles and anti-unionism in American industry*. Philadelphia: Temple University Press.

Griswold del Castillo, Richard. 1990. *The Treaty of Guadalupe Hidalgo: A legacy of conflict*. Norma: University of Oklahoma Press.

Guerin-Gonzales, Camille. 1994. *Mexican workers and American dreams: Immigration, repatriation, and California farm labor, 1900–1939*. New Brunswick, N.J.: Rutgers University Press.

Guerra, Juan C. 1998. *Close to home: Oral and literate practices in a transnational Mexicano community*. New York: Teachers College Press.

Gupta, Akhil, and James Ferguson. 1992. Beyond "culture": Space, identity, and the politics of difference. *Cultural Anthropology* 7(1): 6–23.

Gutiérrez, David G. 1995. *Walls and mirrors: Mexican Americans, Mexican immigrants, and the politics of ethnicity*. Berkeley, Calif.: University of California Press.

Gutiérrez, Ramón A. 1991. *When Jesus came, the corn mothers went away: Marriage, sexuality, and power in New Mexico, 1500–1846*. Stanford, Calif.: Stanford University Press.

———. 2000. Chicano history: Paradigm shifts and shifting boundaries. In *Voices of a new Chicana/o history*, ed. Refugio I. Rochín and Dennis N. Valdés, 91–114. East Lansing: Michigan State University Press.

Gwaltney, John L. 1980. *Drylongso: A self-portrait of black America*. New York: Random House.

Habermas, Jürgen. 1998. *The inclusion of the other: Studies in political theory*. Cambridge, Mass.: MIT Press.

Hagan, Jacqueline Maria. 1994. *Deciding to be legal: A Maya community in Houston*. Philadelphia: Temple University Press.

Hale, Grace Elizabeth. 1998. *Making whiteness: The culture of segregation in the South, 1890–1940*. New York: Random House.

Handlin, Oscar. 1951. *The uprooted: The epic story of the great migrations that made the American people*. New York: Grosset and Dunlap.

Haney López, Ian F. 1996. *White by law: The legal construction of race*. New York: New York University Press.

Hannerz, Ulf. 1980. *Exploring the city: Inquiries toward an urban anthropology*. New York: Columbia University Press.

Harootunian, Harry. 1988. *Things seen and unseen: Discourse and ideology in Tokugawa nativism*. Chicago: University of Chicago Press.

———. 2000. *History's disquiet: Modernity, cultural practice, and the question of everyday life*. New York: Columbia University Press.

Harrigan, John J., and Ronald K. Vogel. 2000. *Political change in the metropolis*. 6th ed. New York: Longman.

Harris, Nigel. 1995. *The new untouchables: Immigration and the new world worker*. New York: I. B. Tauris.

Harrison, Faye V. 1991a. Anthropology as an agent of transformation: Introductory comments and queries. In *Decolonizing anthropology: Moving further toward an anthropology for liberation*, ed. Faye V. Harrison, 1–14. Washington, D.C.: Association of Black Anthropologists/American Anthropological Association.

———. 1991b. Ethnography as politics. In *Decolonizing anthropology: Moving further toward an anthropology for liberation*, ed. Faye V. Harrison, 88–109. Washington, D.C.: Association of Black Anthropologists/American Anthropological Association.

Harvey, David. 2000. *Spaces of hope*. Berkeley: University of California Press.

Hellwig, David J. 1982. Strangers in their own land: Patterns of black nativism, 1830–1930. *American Studies* 23(1): 85–98.

Heyman, Josiah McC. 1995. Putting power in the anthropology of bureaucracy: The Immigration and Naturalization Service at the Mexico–United States border. *Current Anthropology* 36(2):261–87.

———. 1998. State effects on labor: The INS and undocumented immigrants at the Mexico–United States border. *Critique of Anthropology* 18(2):157–80.

———. 1999. State escalation of force: A Vietnam/US-Mexico border analogy. In *States and illegal practices*, ed. Josiah McC. Heyman, 285–314. New York: Berg.

———. 2002. U.S. immigration officers of Mexican ancestry as Mexican Americans, citizens, and immigration police. *Current Anthropology* 43:479–507.

Hietala, Thomas R. 1985. *Manifest design: Anxious aggrandizement in late Jacksonian America*. Ithaca, N.Y.: Cornell University Press.

Higham, John. [1955] 1988. *Strangers in the land: Patterns of American nativism, 1865–1925*. New Brunswick, N.J.: Rutgers University Press.

Hing, Bill Ong. 1993. *Making and remaking Asian America through immigration policy, 1850–1990*. Stanford, Calif.: Stanford University Press.

Hirsch, Arnold R. 1983. *Making the second ghetto: Race and housing in Chicago, 1940–1960*. New York: Cambridge University Press.

Hoffman, Abraham. 1974. *Unwanted Mexican Americans in the Great Depression: Repatriation pressures, 1926–1939*. Tucson: University of Arizona Press.

Holloway, John. 1994. Global capital and the national state. *Capital and Class* 52:23–49.

———. 1995. From scream of refusal to scream of power: The centrality of work. In *Emancipating Marx: Open Marxism 3*, ed. Werner Bonefeld, Richard Gunn, John Holloway, and Kosmos Psychopedis, 155–81. East Haven, Conn.: Pluto.

Hondagneu-Sotelo, Pierrette. 1994. *Gendered transitions: Mexican experiences of immigration*. Berkeley, Calif.: University of California Press.

Honig, Bonnie. 1998. Immigrant America? How foreignness "solves" democracy's problems. *Social Text* 56:1–27.

———. 2001. *Democracy and the foreigner*. Princeton, N.J.: Princeton University Press.

hooks, bell. 1992. *Black looks: Race and representation*. Boston: South End.

Horowitz, Ruth. 1983. *Honor and the American dream: Culture and identity in a Chicano community*. New Brunswick, N.J.: Rutgers University Press.

Horsman, Reginald. 1981. *Race and manifest destiny: The origins of American racial Anglo-Saxonism*. Cambridge, Mass.: Harvard University Press.

Hutchinson, Edward P. 1981. *Legislative history of American immigration policy, 1798–1965*. Philadelphia: University of Pennsylvania Press.

Ignatiev, Noel. 1995. *How the Irish became white*. New York: Routledge.

Illinois Legislative Investigating Commission. 1971. *The illegal Mexican alien problem*. Springfield: State of Illinois Printing Office.

Jablonsky, Thomas J. 1993. *Pride in the jungle: Community and everyday life in Back of the Yards Chicago*. Baltimore: Johns Hopkins University Press.

Jacobson, Matthew Frye. 1998. *Whiteness of a different color: European Immigrants and the alchemy of race*. Cambridge, Mass.: Harvard University Press.

———. 2000. *Barbarian virtues: The United States encounters foreign peoples at home and abroad, 1876–1917*. New York: Hill and Wang.

Jennings, Francis. 1976. *The invasion of America: Indians, colonialism, and the cant of conquest*. New York: W. W. Norton.

———. 2000. *The creation of America: Through revolution to empire*. New York: Cambridge University Press.

Johnson, Kevin R. 1997. The new nativism: Something old, something new, something borrowed, something blue. In Perea 1997, 165–89.

Jones, Anita Edgar. [1928] 1971. *Conditions surrounding Mexicans in Chicago: A dissertation*. M.A. thesis, University of Chicago. [San Francisco: R and E Research Associates.]

Joppke, Christian. 1999. *Immigration and the nation-state: The United States, Germany, and Great Britain*. New York: Oxford University Press.

Joseph, Gilbert M., Catherine C. LeGrand, and Ricardo D. Salvatore, eds. 1998. *Close encounters of empire: Writing the cultural history of U.S.–Latin American relations*. Durham, N.C.: Duke University Press.

Kanstroom, Daniel. 1997. Dangerous undertones of the new nativism: Peter Brimelow and the decline of the West. In Perea 1997, 300–17.

Kaplan, Amy. 1993. *"Left alone with America"*: The absence of empire in the study of American culture. In Kaplan and Pease 1993, 3–21.

———. 2002. *The anarchy of empire in the making of U.S. culture*. Cambridge, Mass.: Harvard University Press.

Kaplan, Amy, and Donald E. Pease, eds. 1993. *Cultures of United States imperialism*. Durham, N.C.: Duke University Press.

Kearney, Michael. 1986. From the invisible hand to visible feet: Anthropological studies of migration and development. *Annual Review of Anthropology* 15: 331–61.

———. 1991. Borders and boundaries of states and self at the end of empire. *Journal of Historical Sociology* 4(1):52–74.

———. 1995. The effects of transnational culture, economy, and migration on Mixtec identity in Oaxacalifornia. In *The bubbling cauldron: Race, ethnicity, and the urban crisis*, ed. Michael Peter Smith and Joe R. Feagin, 226–43. Minneapolis: University of Minnesota Press.

———. 1996. *Reconceptualizing the peasantry: Anthropology in global perspective*. Boulder, Colo.: Westview.

———. 1998. *Peasants in the fields of value: Revisiting rural class differentiation in trans-*

national perspective. Unpublished ms., Department of Anthropology, University of California at Riverside.

Kennedy, David M. 1996. Can we still afford to be a nation of immigrants? *Atlantic Monthly* 278(5):52–68.

Kirschenman, Joleen and Kathryn Neckerman. 1991. "We'd love to hire them, but . . .": The meaning of race for employers. In *The urban underclass*, ed. Christopher Jenks and Paul E. Peterson, 203–34. Washington, D.C.: Brookings Institute.

Klor de Alva, Jorge. 1995. The postcolonization of the (Latin) American experience: A reconsideration of "colonialism," "postcolonialism," and "mestizaje." In *After colonialism: Imperial histories and postcolonial displacements*, ed. Gyan Prakash, 241–75. Princeton, N.J.: Princeton University Press.

Kornblum, William. 1974. *Blue collar community*. Chicago: University of Chicago Press.

Ladner, Joyce A., ed. [1973] 1998. *The death of white sociology: Essays on race and culture*. Baltimore: Black Classic.

Lancaster, Roger N. 1997. Guto's performance: Notes on the transvestitism of everyday life. In *Sex and sexuality in Latin America*, ed. Daniel Balderston and Donna J. Guy, 9–32. New York: New York University Press.

Lankshear, Colin, and Peter L. McLaren, eds. 1993. *Critical literacy: Politics, praxis, and the postmodern*. Albany: State University of New York Press.

Latino Institute. 1987. *Chicago's working Latinas: Confronting multiple roles and pressures*. Chicago: Latino Institute.

Lauria, Anthony, Jr. 1964. *Respeto, relajo*, and interpersonal relations in Puerto Rico. *Anthropological Quarterly* 3:53–67.

Lavie, Smadar. 1990. *The poetics of military occupation: Mzeina allegories of Bedouin identity under Israeli and Egyptian rule*. Berkeley: University of California Press.

Lee, Erika. 1999. Immigrants and immigration law: A state of the field assessment. *Journal of American Ethnic History* 18(4):85–114.

———. 2003. *At America's gates: Chinese immigration during the exclusion era, 1882–1943*. Chapel Hill: University of North Carolina Press.

Lefebvre, Henri. [1947] 1991. *Critique of everyday life*. Vol. 1. New York: Verso.

———. [1962] 1995. *Introduction to modernity: Twelve preludes, September 1959–May 1961*. New York: Verso.

———. [1974] 1991. *The production of space*. Cambridge, Mass.: Blackwell Publishing.

Lewis, Oscar. 1959. *Five families*. New York: Basic Books.

———. 1970. *Anthropological essays*. New York: Random House.

Liebowitz, Arnold H. 1984. The official character of language in the United States: Literacy requirements for immigration, citizenship, and entrance into American life. *Aztlán* 15(1):25–70.

Limerick, Patricia Nelson. 1987. *The legacy of conquest: The unbroken past of the American West*. New York: W. W. Norton.

Limón, José E. 1977. *Agringado* joking in Texas Mexican society: Folklore and differential identity. *New Scholar* 6:33–50.

———. 1989. Carne, carnales, and the carnivalesque: Bakhtinian batos, disorder, and narrative discourses. *American Ethnologist* 16(3):471–486.

———. 1994. *Dancing with the Devil: Society and cultural poetics in Mexican-American South Texas*. Madison: University of Wisconsin Press.

———. 1998. *American encounters: Greater Mexico, the United States, and the erotics of culture*. Boston: Beacon.

Lindsay-Poland, John. 2003. *Emperors in the jungle: The hidden history of the U.S. in Panama*. Durham, N.C.: Duke University Press.

Lipsitz, George. 1998. *The possessive investment in whiteness: How white people profit from identity politics*. Philadelphia: Temple University Press.

Logan, John R. 2001. *The new Latinos: Who they are, where they are*. Press conference advisory. Lewis Mumford Center for Comparative Urban and Regional Research, State University of New York at Albany.

———. 2002. *Hispanic populations and their residential patterns in the metropolis*. Press conference advisory. Lewis Mumford Center for Comparative Urban and Regional Research at the State University of New York at Albany.

Lomnitz-Adler, Claudio. 1992. *Exits from the labyrinth: Culture and ideology in the Mexican national space*. Berkeley: University of California Press.

———. 1996. Fissures in contemporary Mexican nationalism. *Public Culture* 9(1): 55–68.

———. 2001. *Deep Mexico, silent Mexico: An anthropology of nationalism*. Minneapolis: University of Minnesota Press.

Lowe, Lisa. 1996. *Immigrant acts: On Asian American cultural politics*. Durham, N.C.: Duke University Press.

———. 1998. The international within the national: American studies and Asian American critique. *Cultural Critique* 40:29–47.

Lubiano, Wahneema. 1997. Black nationalism and black common sense: Policing ourselves and others. In *The house that race built: Black Americans, U.S. terrain*, ed. Wahneema Lubiano, 232–52. New York: Random House.

Lugo, Alejandro. 1995. Fragmented lives, assembled goods: A study in maquilas, culture, and history at the Mexican borderlands. Ph.D. diss., Stanford University.

Lyman, Stanford M. 1994. *Color, culture, and civilization: Race and minority issues in American society*. Chicago: University of Illinois Press.

Macedo, Donaldo. 1994. Preface to *Politics of liberation: Paths from Freire*, ed. Peter L. McLaren and Colin Lankshear. New York: Routledge.

Maciel, David. 1981. *La clase obrera en la historia de México: Al norte del Río Bravo: Pasado inmediato, 1930–1981*. Mexico City: Siglo Ventiuno Editores/Instituto de Investigaciones Sociales de la UNAM.

Mackenthun, Gesa. 1996. State of the art: Adding empire to the study of American culture. *Journal of American Studies* 30(2):263–69.

Madrid-Barela, Arturo. 1973a. In search of the authentic *pachuco*: An interpretive essay. *Aztlán* 4(1):31–60.

——. 1973b. Towards an understanding of the Chicano experience. Aztlán 4(1):185–93.

——. 1976. *Pochos*: The different Mexicans, an interpretive essay, part I. *Aztlán* 7(1):51–64.

Mahler, Sarah J. 1995. *American dreaming: Immigrant life on the margins*. Princeton, N.J.: Princeton University Press.

Malcolm X. 1965. *Malcolm X speaks*. New York: Grove.

Malinowski, Bronislaw. [1922] 1984. *Argonauts of the western Pacific*. Prospect Heights, Ill.: Waveland.

Malkki, Liisa. 1992. National geographic: The rooting of peoples and the territorialization of national identity among scholars and refugees. *Cultural Anthropology* 7(1): 24–44.

Mamdani, Mahmood. 2001. *When victims become killers: Colonialism, nativism, and the genocide in Rwanda*. Princeton, N.J.: Princeton University Press.

Mannheim, Bruce, and Dennis Tedlock. 1995. Intro. to *The dialogic emergence of culture*, ed. Dennis Tedlock and Bruce Mannheim, 1–32. Chicago: University of Illinois Press.

Marcus, George E., and Dick Cushman. 1982. Ethnographies as texts. *Annual Review of Anthropology* 11:25–69.

Marcus, George, and Michael Fischer. 1986. *Anthropology as cultural critique: An experimental moment in the human sciences*. Chicago: University of Chicago Press.

Margon, Sarah. 2004. Naturalization in the United States. Washington, D.C.: Migration Policy Institute, Migration Information Source, May 1.

Martínez, George A. 1997. Mexican-Americans and whiteness. In *Critical white studies: Looking behind the mirror*, ed. Richard Delgado and Jean Stefancic, 210–13. Philadelphia: Temple University Press.

Martínez, Oscar J. 1994. *Border people: Life and society in the U.S.-Mexico borderlands*. Tucson: University of Arizona Press.

Marx, Karl. [1843] 1972. Open letter to Arnold Ruge. In *The Marx-Engels reader*, ed. Robert C. Tucker, 12–15. New York: W. W. Norton.

——. [1858] 1973. *Grundrisse: Foundations of the critique of political economy*. New York: Vintage/Random House.

——. [1867] 1976. *Capital: A critique of political economy*. Vol. 1. New York: Vintage/Random House.

Marx, Karl, and Friedrich Engels. [1848] 1967. *The communist manifesto*. New York: Penguin.

Massey, Douglas S. 1987. Understanding Mexican migration to the United States. *American Journal of Sociology* 92(6):1372–1403.

Massey, Douglas, Rafael Alarcón, Jorge Durand, and Humberto González. 1987. *Return to Aztlan: The social process of international migration from Western Mexico*. Berkeley, Calif.: University of California Press.

Massey, Douglas S., Jorge Durand, and Nolan J. Malone. 2002. *Beyond smoke and mirrors: Mexican immigration in an era of economic integration*. New York: Russell Sage Foundation.

Massey, Douglas S., and Zai Liang. 1989. The long-term consequences of a temporary worker program: The U.S. Bracero experience. *Population Research and Policy Review* 8:199–226.

McCaughey, Robert A. 1984. *International studies and academic enterprise: A chapter in the enclosure of American learning*. New York: Columbia University Press.

McClintock, Anne. 1995. *Imperial leather: Race, gender, and sexuality in the colonial contest*. New York: Routledge.

McLaren, Peter L. 1994. Postmodernism and the death of politics: A Brazilian reprieve. In *Politics of liberation: Paths from Freire*, ed. Peter L. McLaren and Colin Lankshear, 193–215. New York: Routledge.

——. 1995. Collisions with otherness: "Travelling" theory, postcolonial criticism, and the politics of ethnographic practice—The mission of the wounded ethnographer. In *Critical theory and educational research*, ed. Peter L. McLaren and James M. Giarelli. Albany: State University of New York Press.

Menchaca, Martha. 2001. *Recovering history, constructing race: The Indian, black, and white roots of Mexican Americans*. Austin: University of Texas Press.

Michaels, Walter Benn. 1995. *Our America: Nativism, modernism, and pluralism*. Durham, N.C.: Duke University Press.

Michaelsen, Scott. 1999. *The limits of multiculturalism: Interrogating the origins of American anthropology*. Minneapolis: University of Minnesota Press.

Mignolo, Walter D. 2000. *Local histories/global designs: Coloniality, subaltern knowledges, and border thinking*. Princeton, N.J.: Princeton University Press.

Miles, Jack. 1992. Blacks vs. browns: The struggle for the bottom rung. *Atlantic Monthly* 270(4):41–68.

Mirandé, Alfredo. 1985. *The Chicano experience: An alternative perspective*. Notre Dame, Ind.: University of Notre Dame Press.

——. 1987. *Gringo justice*. Notre Dame, Ind.: University of Notre Dame Press.

Monsiváis, Carlos. 1997. *Mexican postcards*. New York: Verso.

Montejano, David. 1987. *Anglos and Mexicans in the making of Texas, 1836–1986*. Austin: University of Texas Press.

Montiel, Miguel. 1970. The social science myth of the Mexican-American family. *El grito* 3(4): 56–63.

Moody, Kim. 1988. *An injury to all: The decline of American unionism*. New York: Verso.

Moquin, Wayne, and Charles Van Doren. 1971. *A documentary history of the Mexican Americans*. New York: Bantam.

Mora, Juan. N.d. A brief history of Chicago's Mexican community. In *Rudy Lozano: His life, his people*, 13–30. Chicago: Taller de Estudios Comunitarios.

Moraga, Cherríe. 1993. *The last generation: Prose and poetry*. Boston: South End.

Morawska, Ewa. 1990. The sociology and historiography of immigration. In *Immigration reconsidered: History, sociology, politics*, ed. Virginia Yans-McLaughlin, 187–238. New York: Oxford University Press.

Morrison, Toni. 1992. *Playing in the dark: Whiteness and the literary imagination*. Cambridge, Mass.: Harvard University Press.

———. 1994. On the backs of blacks. In *Arguing immigration: The debate over the changing face of America*, ed. Nicolaus Mills, 97–100. New York: Simon and Schuster.

Muñoz, Jr., Carlos. 1989. *Youth, identity, power: The Chicano movement*. New York: Verso.

Murray, Stephen O., and Wayne R. Dynes. 1995. Hispanic homosexuals: A Spanish lexicon. In *Latin American male homosexualities*, ed. Stephen O. Murray, 180–92. Albuquerque: University of New Mexico Press.

Nader, Laura. 1997. The phantom factor: Impact of the cold war on anthropology. In *The Cold War and the university: Toward an intellectual history of the postwar years*, ed. Noam Chomsky, 107–46. New York: New Press.

Necoechea Gracia, Gerardo. 1998. Customs and resistance: Mexican Immigrants in Chicago, 1910–1930. In *Border crossings: Mexican and Mexican-American workers*, ed. John Mason Hart, 185–207. Wilmington, Del.: Scholarly Resources.

Nelson, Dana D. 1998. *National manhood: Capitalist citizenship and the imagined fraternity of white men*. Durham, N.C.: Duke University Press.

Nevins, Joseph. 2002. *Operation gatekeeper: The rise of the "illegal alien" and the making of the U.S.-Mexico boundary*. New York: Routledge.

Ngai, Mae M. 2004. *Impossible subjects: Illegal aliens and the making of modern America*. Princeton, N.J.: Princeton University Press.

Nikolinakos, Marios. 1975. Notes towards a general theory of migration in late capitalism. *Race and Class* 17:5–18.

Nobles, Gregory H. 1997. *American frontiers: Cultural encounters and continental conquest*. New York: Hill and Wang.

Oboler, Suzanne. 1995. *Ethnic labels, Latino lives: Identity and the politics of (re)presentation in the United States*. Minneapolis: University of Minnesota.

Omi, Michael, and Howard Winant. 1986. *Racial formation in the United States: From the 1960's to the 1980's*. New York: Routledge.

Ong, Aihwa. 1999. *Flexible citizenship: The cultural logics of transnationality*. Durham, N.C.: Duke University Press.

Ong, Aihwa, and Donald Nonini, eds. 1997. *Ungrounded empires: The cultural politics of modern Chinese transnationalism*. New York: Routledge.

Orfield, Gary, and Ricard M. Tostado. 1983. *Latinos in metropolitan Chicago: A study of housing and employment*. Latino Institute monograph no. 6. Chicago: Latino Institute.

Orwell, George. [1947] 1956. Why I write. In *The Orwell Reader*, 390–96. New York: Harcourt Brace Jovanovich.

Page, Helán E. 1988. Dialogic principles of interactive learning in the ethnographic relationship. *Journal of Anthropological Research* 44(2): 163–81.

Paral, Rob. 1993. NAFTA and Chicago's Latinos. *Latino: A publication of the Latino Institute*, August, 1, 6.

——. 1997. *Public aid and Illinois immigrants: Serving non-citizens in the Welfare Reform era: A Latino Institute report*. Chicago: Illinois Immigrant Policy Project.

——. n.d. *Citizenship 2000: Illinois immigrants and naturalization needs. A report to the Fund for Immigrants and Refugees, and the Illinois Department of Human Services*. Chicago: National Center on Poverty Law.

Paredes, Américo. 1964. Some aspects of folk poetry. In Paredes 1993a, 113–27.

——. 1966. The Anglo-American in Mexican folklore. In *Literatura Chicana: Texto y contexto*, ed. Antonia Castañeda Shular, Tomás Ybarra-Frausto, and Joseph Sommers, 141–50. Englewood Cliffs, N.J.: Prentice-Hall.

——. 1968. Folk medicine and the intercultural jest. In Paredes 1993a, 49–72.

——. 1971. The United States, Mexico, and machismo. In Paredes 1993a, 215–34.

——. 1976. *A Texas-Mexican cancionero*. Urbana: University of Illinois Press.

——. 1977. On ethnographic work among minority groups: A folklorist's perspective. In Paredes 1993a, 73–110.

——. 1979. The folklore of groups of Mexican origin in the United States. In Paredes 1993a, 3–18.

——. 1993a. *Folklore and culture of the Texas-Mexican border*. Austin: Center for Mexican American Studies/University of Texas Press.

——. 1993b. *Uncle Remus con chile*. Houston: Arte Público.

Paredes, Raymund A. 1977. The origins of anti-Mexican sentiment in the United States. *New Scholar* 6:139–65.

Park, Robert E. [1914] 1980. Migration and the marginal man. In *The pleasures of sociology*, ed. Lewis A. Coser, 241–47. New York: New American Library.

——. 1929. The city as a social laboratory. In *Chicago: An experiment in social science research*, ed. T. V. Smith and L. D. White, 1–19. Chicago: University of Chicago Press.

——. 1950. *Race and culture: The collected papers of Robert Ezra Park*. Everett Cherington Hughes, ed. Glencoe, Ill.: Free Press.

Park, Robert E., and Ernest W. Burgess. 1924. *Introduction to the science of sociology*. Chicago: University of Chicago Press.

Park, Robert E., and Herbert A. Miller. 1921. *Old World traits transplanted*. New York: Harper.

Pashukanis, Evgeny B. [1929] 1989. *Law and Marxism: A general theory towards a critique of the fundamental juridical concepts*. Worcester, U.K.: Pluto.

Passel, Jeffrey. 2002. New estimates of the undocumented population in the United States. Migration Policy Institute, Migration Information Source.

Paz, Octavio. [1950] 1985. *The labyrinth of solitude*. New York: Grove.

Pease, Donald E. 1990. New Americanists: Revisionist interventions into the canon. *boundary 2* 17(1):1–37.

Pease, Donald E., and Robyn Wiegman, eds. 2002. *The futures of American studies*. Durham, N.C.: Duke University Press.

Peña, Devon G. 1997. *The terror of the machine: Technology, work, gender, and ecology on the U.S.-Mexico border.* Austin: Center for Mexican American Studies/University of Texas Press.

Perea, Juan. 2001. Fulfilling manifest destiny: Conquest, race, and the insular cases. In *Foreign in a domestic sense: Puerto Rico, American expansion, and the Constitution,* ed. Christina Duffy Burnett and Burke Marshal, 140–66. Durham, N.C.: Duke University Press.

Perea, Juan F., ed. 1997. *Immigrants out! The new nativism and the anti-immigrant impulse in the United States.* New York: New York University Press.

Persons, Stow. 1987. *Ethnic studies at Chicago, 1905–45.* Chicago: University of Illinois Press.

Piña, Francisco. n.d. His life. In *Rudy Lozano: His life, his people,* 45–73. Chicago: Taller de Estudios Comunitarios.

Pitt, Leonard. 1966. *The Decline of the Californios: A social history of the Spanish speaking Californians, 1846–1890.* Berkeley: University of California Press.

Porter, Carolyn. 1994. What we know that we don't know: Remapping American literary studies. *American Literary History* 6(3):467–526.

Portes, Alejandro. 1978. Toward a structural analysis of illegal (undocumented) immigration. *International Migration Review* 12(4):469–84.

———. 1995. Children of immigrants: Segmented assimilation and its determinants. In *The economic sociology of immigration: Essays on networks, ethnicity, and entrepreneurship,* ed. Alejandro Portes, 248–79. New York: The Russell Sage Foundation.

Portes, Alejandro, and Robert L. Bach. 1985. *Latin journey: Cuban and Mexican immigrants in the United States.* Berkeley: University of California Press.

Portes, Alejandro, and Rubén G. Rumbaut. 1990. *Immigrant America: A portrait.* Berkeley: University of California Press.

———. 2001. *Legacies: The story of the immigrant second generation.* Berkeley: University of California Press.

Portilla, Jorge. 1966. *Fenomenología del relajo, y otros ensayos.* Mexico City: Ediciones Era.

Preston, Michael B. 1982. Black politics in the post-Daley era. In *After Daley: Chicago politics in transition,* ed. Samuel K. Gove and Louis H. Masotti, 88–117. Urbana: University of Illinois Press.

Rabinow, Paul. 1986. Representations are social facts: Modernity and postmodernity in anthropology. In *Writing culture: The poetics and politics of ethnography,* ed. James Clifford and George E. Marcus, 234–61. Berkeley: University of California Press.

Radway, Janice. 1999. What's in a name? Presidential address to the American Studies Association, 20 November 1998. *American Quarterly* 51(1):1–32.

Rafael, Vicente L. 2000. *White love and other events in Filipino history.* Durham, N.C.: Duke University Press.

Ramos-Zayas, Ana Y. 2003. *National performances: The politics of class, race and space in Puerto Rican Chicago.* Chicago: University of Chicago Press.

Redfield, Robert. 1929. The antecedents of Mexican immigration to the United States. *American Journal of Sociology* 35:433–38.

———. 1930. *Tepoztlán: A Mexican village*. Chicago: University of Chicago Press.

———. 1931. Intro. to *The Mexican immigrant: His life story*, Manuel Gamio, v–ix. Chicago: University of Chicago Press.

———. 1956. *The little community: Peasant society and culture*. Chicago: University of Chicago Press.

Reimers, David M. [1985] 1992. *Still the golden door: The Third World comes to America*. 2nd ed. New York: Columbia University Press.

Reisler, Mark. 1976a. *By the sweat of their brow: Mexican immigrant labor in the United States, 1900–1940*. Westport, Conn.: Greenwood.

———. 1976b. *Always the laborer, never the citizen: Anglo perceptions of the Mexican immigrant during the 1920s*. In *Between two worlds: Mexican immigrants in the United States*, ed. David G. Gutiérrez, 23–43. Wilmington, Del.: Scholarly Resources.

Renda, Mary. 2001. *Taking Haiti: Military occupation and the culture of U.S. Imperialism, 1915–1940*. Chapel Hill: University of North Carolina Press.

Rendón, Armando B. 1971. *Chicano manifesto*. New York: Macmillan.

Reyna, José R. 1980. *Raza humor: Chicano joke tradition in Texas*. San Antonio: Penca Books.

———. 1984. Pancho Villa: The lighter side. *New Mexico Humanities Review* 7(1):57–62.

Reyna, José R., and María Herrera-Sobek. 1998. Jokelore, cultural differences, and linguistic dexterity. In *Culture across borders: Mexican immigration and popular culture*, ed. David R. Maciel and María Herrera-Sobek, 203–26. Tucson: University of Arizona Press.

Rich, Adrienne. 1986. *Blood, bread, and poetry: Selected prose, 1979–1985*. London: W. W. Norton.

Roberts, Dorothy E. 1997. Who may give birth to citizens? Reproduction, eugenics, and immigration. In Perea 1997, 205–19.

Rocco, Raymond A. 1976. The Chicano in the social sciences: Traditional concepts, myths, and images. *Aztlán* 7(1): 75–97.

Rodríguez, Clara, Aida Castro, Oscar García, and Analisa Torres. 1991. Latino racial identity: In the eye of the beholder? *Latino Studies Journal* 2(3):33–48.

Rodríguez, Néstor P. 1995. The real "new world order": The globalization of racial and ethnic relations in the late twentieth century. In *The bubbling cauldron: Race ethnicity and the urban crisis*, ed. Michael Peter Smith and Joe R. Feagin, 211–25. Minneapolis: University of Minnesota Press.

———. 1997. The social construction of the U.S.-Mexico border. In Perea 1997, 223–43.

Roediger, David R. 1991. *The wages of whiteness: Race and the making of the American working class*. New York: Verso.

———. 1994. *Toward the abolition of whiteness: Essays on race, politics, and working class history*. New York: Verso.

Roediger, David R., ed. 1998. *Black on white: Black writers on what it means to be white*. New York: Schocken.

Romano-V., Octavio Ignacio. 1968. The anthropology and sociology of the Mexican-Americans: The distortion of Mexican-American history. *El grito* 2(1): 13–26.

———. 1970. Social science, objectivity, and the Chicanos. *El grito* 4(1): 4–16.

Ropka, Gerald W. 1980. *The evolving residential pattern of the Mexican, Puerto Rican, and Cuban population in the City of Chicago*. New York: Arno.

Rorty, Richard. 1989. *Contingency, irony, and solidarity*. New York: Cambridge University Press.

Rosaldo, Renato. 1985. Chicano studies, 1970–1984. *Annual Review of Anthropology* 14:405–27.

———. 1986a. *When natives talk back: Chicano anthropology since the late sixties*. Renato Rosaldo Lecture Series, monograph number 2:3–20. Tucson: Mexican American Studies and Research Center/University of Arizona Press.

———. 1986b. Politics, patriarchs, and laughter. Stanford, Calif.: Stanford Center for Chicano Research, Working Paper Series, number 18.

———. 1986c. From the door of his tent: The fieldworker and the inquisitor. In *Writing culture: The poetics and politics of ethnography*, ed. James Clifford and George Marcus, 77–97. Berkeley: University of California Press.

———. 1989. *Culture and truth: The remaking of social analysis*. Boston: Beacon.

———. 1994. Cultural citizenship and educational democracy. *Cultural Anthropology* 9(3): 402–11.

———. 1997. Cultural citizenship, inequality, and multiculturalism. In Flores and Benmayor 1997, 27–38.

Rosaldo, Renato, and William Flores. 1997. Identity, conflict, and evolving Latino communities: Cultural citizenship in San Jose, California. In Flores and Benmayor 1997, 57–96.

Rosales, Francisco Arturo. 1978. Mexican immigration to the urban Midwest during the 1920's. Ph.D. diss., Indiana University.

———. 1999. *¡Pobre raza! Violence, justice, and mobilization among México Lindo immigrants, 1900–1936*. Austin: University of Texas Press.

Rosen, George. 1980. *Decision-making Chicago style: The genesis of a University of Illinois campus*. Urbana: University of Illinois Press.

Rosenfeld, Michael. 1993. Who killed Rudy Lozano? *Grey City Journal*, October 15, 1, 4–6.

Ross Pineda, Raúl. 1999. *Los mexicanos y el voto sin fronteras*. Chicago: Salsedo.

Rouse, Roger. 1991. Mexican migration and the social space of postmodernism. *Diaspora* 1(1): 8–23.

———. 1992. Making sense of settlement: Class transformation, cultural struggle, and transnationalism among Mexican migrants in the United States. In *Towards a transnational perspective on migration*, ed. Nina Glick Schiller. *Annals of the New York Academy of Sciences* 645: 25–52.

———. 1995. Thinking through transnationalism: Notes on the cultural politics of class relations in the contemporary United States. *Public Culture* 7(2): 353–402.

Rowe, John Carlos. 1998. Post-nationalism, globalism, and the new American studies. *Cultural Critique* 40:11–28.

———. 2000a. *Literary culture and U.S. imperialism: From the Revolution to World War II*. New York: Oxford University Press.

Rowe, John Carlos, ed. 2000b. *Post-nationalist American studies*. Berkeley: University of California Press.

Rumbaut, Rubén G., and Alejandro Portes, eds. 2001. *Ethnicities: Children of immigrants in America*. Berkeley: University of California Press.

Ruiz, Vicki L. 1998. *From out of the shadows: Mexican women in twentieth-century America*. New York: Oxford University Press.

Said, Edward W. 1989. Representing the colonized: Anthropology's interlocutors. *Critical Inquiry* 15: 205–25.

Saldaña-Portillo, Josefina. 2001. Who's the Indian in Aztlán? Re-writing mestizaje, Indianism, and Chicanismo from the Lacandón. In *The Latin American subaltern studies reader*, ed. Ileana Rodríguez, 402–23. Durham, N.C.: Duke University Press.

Saldívar, José David. 1991. *The dialectics of our America: Genealogy, cultural critique, and literary history*. Durham, N.C.: Duke University Press.

———. 1997. *Border matters: Remapping American cultural studies*. Berkeley: University of California Press.

Salyer, Lucy E. 1995. *Laws harsh as tigers: Chinese immigrants and the shaping of modern immigration law*. Chapel Hill: University of North Carolina Press.

Samora, Julian. 1971. *Los mojados: The wetback story*. Notre Dame, Ind.: University of Notre Dame Press.

Sanadjian, Manuchehr. 1990. From participant to partisan observation: An open end. *Critique of Anthropology* 10(1): 113–35.

San Juan, Jr. E. 2000. *After postcolonialism: Remapping Philippines–United States confrontations*. New York: Rowman and Littlefield.

Sassen, Saskia. 1988. *The mobility of labor and capital: A study in international investment and labor flow*. New York: Cambridge University Press.

———. 1989. America's immigration "problem." *World Policy Journal* 6(4):811–32.

———. 1991. *The global city: New York, London, Tokyo*. Princeton, N.J.: Princeton University Press.

———. 1994. *Cities in a world economy*. Thousand Oaks, Calif.: Pine Forge.

———. 1996a. Whose city is it? Globalization and the formation of new claims. *Public Culture* 8(2): 205–223.

———. 1996b. Rebuilding the global city: Economics, ethnicity, and space. In *Representing the city: Ethnicity, capital, and culture in the twenty-first century metropolis*, ed. Anthony D. King, 23–42. New York: New York University Press.

Sassen-Koob, Saskia. 1984. The new labor demand in global cities. In *Cities in trans-*

formation: Class, capital, and the state, ed. Michael Peter Smith, 139–71. Urban Affairs Annual Review 26.

Saxton, Alexander. 1971. *The indispensable enemy: Labor and the anti-Chinese movement in California*. Berkeley: University of California Press.

———. 1990. *The rise and fall of the white republic: Class politics and mass culture in nineteenth-century America*. New York: Verso.

Schmidt, Henry C. 1978. *The roots of* lo mexicano*: Self and society in Mexican thought, 1900–1934*. College Station: Texas A & M University Press.

Schneider, Dorothee. 1998. "I know all about Emma Lazarus": Nationalism and its contradictions in congressional rhetoric of immigration restriction. *Cultural Anthropology* 13(1):82–99.

Schuck, Peter H., and Rogers M. Smith. 1985. *Citizenship without consent: Illegal aliens in the American polity*. New Haven, Conn.: Yale University Press.

Sepúlveda, Ciro. 1976. La colonia del harbor: A history of Mexicanos in East Chicago, Indiana, 1919–1932. Ph.D. diss., University of Notre Dame.

Shankman, Arnold. 1977. "Asiatic ogre" or "desirable citizen"? The image of Japanese Americans in the Afro-American press, 1867–1933. *Pacific Historical Review* 46(4):567–87.

Shor, Ira. 1993. Education is politics: Paulo Freire's critical pedagogy. In *Paulo Freire: A critical encounter*, ed. Peter McLaren and Peter Leonard, 25–35. New York: Routledge.

Short, Jr., James F. 1971. *The social fabric of the metropolis: Contributions of the Chicago School of urban sociology*. Chicago: University of Chicago Press.

Simmel, Georg. [1908] 1980. The stranger. In *The pleasures of sociology*, ed. Lewis A. Coser, 235–40. New York: New American Library.

Simon, Jonathan. 1998. Refugees in a carceral age: The rebirth of immigration prisons in the United States, 1976–1992. *Public Culture* 10(3):577–606.

Simpson, David. 1986. *The politics of American English, 1776–1850*. New York: Oxford University Press.

Singh, Nikhil Pal. 1998. Culture/wars: Recoding empire in an age of democracy. *American Quarterly* 50(3):471–522.

Skirius, John. 1976. Vasconcelos and México de afuera (1928). *Aztlán* 7(3):479–97.

Slayton, Robert A. 1986. *Back of the Yards: The making of a local democracy*. Chicago: University of Chicago Press.

Slotkin, Richard. 1973. *Regeneration through violence: The mythology of the American frontier, 1600–1860*. Norman: University of Oklahoma Press.

———. 1985. *The fatal environment: The myth of the frontier in the Age of Industrialization, 1800–1890*. New York: Harper-Collins.

———. 1992. *Gunfighter nation: The myth of the frontier in twentieth-century America*. New York: Harper-Collins.

Smedley, Audrey. 1993. *Race in North America: Origin and evolution of a worldview*. Boulder, Colo.: Westview.

Smith, Carol A. 1997. The symbolics of blood: Mestizaje in the Americas. *Identities* 3(4):495–521.

Smith, Raymond T. 1984. Anthropology and the concept of social class. *Annual Review of Anthropology* 13:467–94.

———. 1996. *The matrifocal family: Power, pluralism, and politics.* New York: Routledge.

Smith, Robert C. 1996. Mexicans in New York: Membership and incorporation in a new immigrant community. In *Latinos in New York: Communities in transition,* ed. Gabriel Haslip-Viera and Sherrie L. Baver, 57–103. Notre Dame, Ind.: University of Notre Dame Press.

Smith, Rogers M. 1997. *Civic ideals: Conflicting visions of citizenship in U.S. history.* New Haven, Conn.: Yale University Press.

Smith, T. V., and Leonard D. White. 1929. *Chicago: An experiment in social science research.* Chicago: University of Chicago Press.

Solbakken, Lisa C. 1997. The Anti-Terrorism and Effective Death Penalty Act: Anti-immigration legislation veiled in anti-terrorism pretext. *Brooklyn Law Review* 63: 1381–1410.

Squires, Gregory D., Larry Bennett, Kathleen McCourt, and Phillip Nyden. 1987. *Chicago: Race, class, and the response to urban decline.* Philadelphia: Temple University Press.

Stavenhagen, Rodolfo. 1971. Decolonizing applied social sciences. *Human Organization* 30(4): 333–44.

Stefancic, Jean. 1997. Funding the nativist agenda. In Perea 1997, 119–35.

Steinberg, Stephen. [1981] 1989. *The ethnic myth: Race, ethnicity, and class in America.* Updated and expanded ed. Boston: Beacon.

———. 1995. *Turning back: The retreat from racial justice in American thought and policy.* Boston: Beacon.

Stewart, Kathleen. 1996. *A space on the side of the road: Cultural poetics in an "other" America.* Princeton, N.J.: Princeton University Press.

Stocking, Jr., George. 1968. *Race, culture, and evolution: Essays in the history of anthropology.* Chicago: University of Chicago Press.

Suárez-Orozco, Marcelo M., ed. 1998. *Crossings: Mexican immigration in interdisciplinary perspectives.* Cambridge, Mass.: Harvard University Press.

Suttles, Gerald D. 1968. *The social order of the slum: Ethnicity and territory in the inner city.* Chicago: University of Chicago Press.

Takaki, Ronald. 1979. *Iron cages: Race and culture in nineteenth-century America.* New York: Oxford University Press.

Tatalovich, Raymond. 1997. *Official English as nativist backlash.* In Perea 1997, 78–102.

Taylor, Paul S. 1932. *Mexican labor in the United States.* University of California Publications in Economics, vol. 7. Berkeley: University of California Press.

Thomas, William I., and Florian Znaniecki. 1927. *The Polish peasant in Europe and America.* Boston: Knopf.

Torres, Gabriel. 1997. *The force of irony: Power in the everyday life of Mexican tomato workers.* New York: Berg.

Trexler, Richard C. 1995. *Sex and conquest: Gendered violence, political order, and the European conquest of the Americas*. Ithaca, N.Y.: Cornell University Press.

Trouillot, Michel-Rolph. 1991. Anthropology and the savage slot: The poetics and politics of otherness. In *Recapturing anthropology: Working in the present*, ed. Richard G. Fox, 17–44. Santa Fe, N.M.: School of American Research Press.

Turner, Terence S. 1991. Representing, resisting, rethinking: Historical transformations of Kayapo culture and anthropological consciousness. In *Colonial situations: Essays on the contextualization of ethnographic knowledge. History of Anthropology, vol. 7.*, ed. George W. Stocking Jr., 285–313. Madison: University of Wisconsin Press.

Twine, France Winddance. 1998. *Racism in a racial democracy: The maintenance of white supremacy in Brazil*. New Brunswick, N.J.: Rutgers University Press.

U.S. Department of Labor. 1991. *Employer sanctions and U.S. labor markets: Final report*. Washington, D.C.: Division of Immigration Policy and Research, U.S. Department of Labor.

Vaca, Nick C. 1970a. The Mexican-American in the social sciences, 1912–1970. Part I: 1912–1935. *El grito* 3(3):3–24.

——. 1970b. The Mexican-American in the social sciences, 1912–1970. Part II: 1936–1970. *El grito* 4(1):17–51.

Valdés, Dennis Nodín. 1991. Al Norte: *Agricultural workers in the Great Lakes Region, 1917–1970*. Austin: University of Texas Press.

——. 2000. Region, nation, and world-system: Perspectives on midwestern Chicana/o history. In *Voices of a new Chicana/o history*, ed. Refugio I. Rochín and Dennis N. Valdés, 115–40. East Lansing: Michigan State University Press.

Vargas, Zaragoza. 1993. *Proletarians of the North: Mexican industrial workers in Detroit and the Midwest, 1917–1933*. Berkeley: University of California Press.

Vasconcelos, José. [1925] 1983. *La raza cósmica*. Mexico City: Associación Nacional de Libreros.

Vélez-Ibáñez, Carlos G. 1996. *Border visions: Mexican cultures of the southwest United States*. Tucson: University of Arizona Press.

Vila, Pablo. 2000. *Crossing borders, reinforcing borders: Social categories, metaphors, and narrative identities on the U.S.-Mexico frontier*. Austin: University of Texas Press.

Villar, María de Lourdes. 1989. From sojourners to settlers: The experience of Mexican undocumented migrants in Chicago. Ph.D. diss., Indiana University.

——. 1990. Rethinking settlement processes: The experience of Mexican undocumented migrants in Chicago. *Urban Anthropology* 19(1–2):63–79.

——. 1999. The amnesty reveals intra-ethnic divisions among Mexicans in Chicago. *Urban Anthropology* 28(1):37–64.

Vološinov, V. N. [1929] 1986. *Marxism and the philosophy of language*. Cambridge, Mass.: Harvard University Press.

Wade, Peter. 1993. *Blackness and race mixture: The dynamics of racial identity in Colombia*. Baltimore: Johns Hopkins University Press.

——. 1997. *Race and ethnicity in Latin America*. Chicago: Pluto.

Wald, Priscilla. 1993. Terms of assimilation: Legislating subjectivity in the emerging nation. In *Cultures of United States imperialism*, ed. Amy Kaplan and Donald E. Pease, 59–84. Durham, N.C.: Duke University Press.

Waldinger, Roger. 1996. *Still the promised city? African-Americans and new immigrants in postindustrial New York*. Cambridge, Mass.: Harvard University Press.

Wallerstein, Immanuel. 1991. The construction of peoplehood: Racism, nationalism, ethnicity. In Balibar and Wallerstein 1991, 71–85.

——. 1997a. The unintended consequences of cold war area studies. In *The cold war and the university: Toward an intellectual history of the postwar years*, ed. Noam Chomsky, 195–232. New York: New Press.

——. 1997b. Eurocentrism and its avatars: The dilemmas of social science. *New Left Review* 226:93–107.

Weber, David S. 1982. Anglo views of Mexican immigrants: Popular perceptions and neighborhood realities in Chicago, 1900–1940. Ph.D. diss., Ohio State University.

Weiler, Kathleen. 1994. Freire and a feminist pedagogy of difference. In *Politics of liberation: Paths from Freire*, ed. Peter L. McLaren and Colin Lankshear, 12–40. New York: Routledge.

Weismantel, Mary J. 2001. Cholas *and* pishtacos*: Tales of race and sex in Andean South America*. Chicago: University of Chicago Press.

Williams, Brackette F. 1991. *Stains on my name, war in my veins: Guyana and the politics of cultural struggle*. Durham, N.C.: Duke University Press.

Williams, William Appleman. 1955. The frontier thesis and American foreign policy. *Pacific Historical Review* 24:379–95.

——. 1959. *The tragedy of American diplomacy*. Cleveland: World.

——. 1980. *Empire as a way of life*. New York: Oxford University Press.

Winant, Howard. 1994. *Racial conditions: Politics, theory, comparisons*. Minneapolis: University of Minnesota Press.

Wirth, Louis. 1928. *The ghetto*. Chicago: University of Chicago Press.

——. 1964. *On cities and social life: Selected papers*. Chicago: University of Chicago Press.

Young, Robert J. C. 1990. *White mythologies: Writing history and the West*. New York: Routledge.

——. 1995. *Colonial desire: Hybridity in theory, culture, and race*. New York: Routledge.

Zamudio, Patricia E. 1999. Huejuquillense immigrants in Chicago: Culture, gender, and community in the shaping of consciousness. Ph.D. diss., Northwestern University.

Zavella, Patricia. 1987. *Women's work and Chicano families: Cannery workers of the Santa Clara Valley*. Ithaca, N.Y.: Cornell University Press.

Žižek, Slavoj. 1994. How did Marx invent the symptom? In *Mapping Ideology*, ed. Slavoj Žižek, 296–331. New York: Verso.

Zolberg, Aristide R. 1990. Reforming the back door: The Immigration Reform and

Control Act of 1986 in historical perspective. In *Immigration reconsidered: History, sociology, politics*, ed. Virginia Yans-McLaughlin, 315–39. New York: Oxford University Press.

Zorbaugh, Harvey Warren. 1929. *The Gold Coast and the slum: A sociological study of Chicago's Near North Side*. Chicago: University of Chicago Press.

INDEX

Absurdity: and machismo, 170–71; mediation of, 168; in Paz, 170–71; and "race," 168–69, 186; social power of, 169. *See also* Humor; Irony; *Relajo*; Surrealism

Acapulco, 149

Acuña, Rodolfo, 97

Addams, Jane, 114

Addison, Illinois, 270 n.36

Adelita, figure of, 148

Adult education, 23. *See also* English as a Second Language; Pedagogy; Workplace literacy

Affirmative action, 70

Africa, 65, 178

African Americans, 5, 70–77, 114, 115, 117, 118, 124, 179–82, 196–98, 208–9, 220, 263–64 n.17; as "aliens," 208, 263–64 n.17; as "American," 77; birthright U.S. citizenship of, 200, 262 n.10; and Blackness, 182, 192, 197–98, 255 n.1; as "criminal," 139–40; as "dangerous," 139–41, 272 n.52; and "deindustrialization," 124–26; as "displaced" from employment by migrant workers, 73–74, 262 n.11, 262–63 n.14; as disqualified from "American"-ness, 199–200, 208–9, 263–64 n.17; employer discrimination against, 125–26; erasure of centrality to U.S. history, 208; figured as nemesis of "immigrants," 208–9; figured as privileged vis-a-vis Mexicans, 193–95; and language, 182; as "lazy," 165, 190, 192–97, 199–200; as

"native," 70–77; rebellion of, 125–26, 138, 232; relations with Mexicans, 114, 140–41, 159, 165, 193–95, 209; as replacements for unionized Mexican workers, 159, 165; segregation in Chicago, 138–39, 271 n.48, 272 nn.50–51; and slavery, 187, 198; subordinate citizenship of, 208; as "welfare-dependent," 193–95, 199–200, 206; West Side communities of, 139. *See also* Blackness

Africans, 64; enslaved, 187; as "monkeys," 178

Afro-Mexicans, 198, 220

Agriculture, 221, 224

Agriculture, Department of (U.S.), 224

Aguascalientes, 3

Aguirre-Beltrán, Gonzalo, 275 n.25

Alamo, Battle of the, 226

Albures, 273–74 n.8

"Alien," 59, 89–91, 115, 200, 208, 216, 263–64 n.17; deportable, 59, 91, 93; as opposed to the iconic "immigrant," 90; as spatialized sociopolitical status, 95. *See also* "Illegal alien"

Alien Nation: Common Sense about America's Immigration Disaster, 64–68

All-Asia Barred Zone, 221, 222, 230, 276–77 n.3

Allen, Theodore, 168

Alonso, Ana, 274–75 n.18

"America," as United States, 64–66, 101

America First, 64

"American Dream," 32, 94

Carse, James, 173

Cass, Lewis, 218

Castillo, Ana, 265 n.7

"Caucasian," as racial category, 222–23

Census data, 114–20, 138, 222, 268–70 nn.26–28, 30–32, 34, 36, 271 nn.48–49, 272 n.1; Latinos and "race" in Chicago, 188; Mexican migrants in United States, 229, 277 n.8; Mexicans in Chicago, 114–117, 268–69 nn.26–28, 269 nn.30–32, 270 n.34; Mexicans in Chicago metropolitan region, 117, 268 nn.26–27, 270 n.36

Census, U.S. Bureau of the, 198; designation of "Mexican" as racial category, 221; as producing racial order, 188; racial categories of, 187–88; responses of Latinos to, 188, 198

Center for Autonomous Social Action, 97

Chango, 196, 274 n.12, 275 n.23

Chatterjee, Partha, 19

Chávez, Leo, 87–88, 92, 264 nn.20–21

Chiapas, 49, 164

Chicago, xvi, 3–5, 95–143 (passim); as "city of neighborhoods," 137–38; de-industrialization of, 123; as "global city," 123; as industrial center, 113, 123; Latino communities on North Side of, 119; Mexican neighborhoods on South Side of, 114, 117–20, 179–80; as railroad metropolis, 113; in relation to Chicano studies, 105–8; in relation to North American capitalism, 113; racial segregation in, 138, 271 n.48, 272 nn.50–51. *See also* Mexican Chicago

Chicago Heights, Illinois, 270 n.40

Chicago Housing Authority, 272 n.51

Chicago School of sociology, 79–80, 111, 267 nn.19–20

Chicago Tribune, 116

Chicana feminism, 105–6

"Chicana/o" (term): as new identity asserted by Chicano Movement, 104; as politicized, 109–10; usage of, 3, 109–10, 265 n.6. *See also* "Mexican" (term)

Chicana/os: civil rights concerns of, 127; as colonized, 77, 106–8; as disqualified from "American"-ness, 201–2, 205; as distinct from Mexicans, 107–109, 201–2, 204–5; farmworkers' movement of, 233; figured as abject derivative of "American"-ness, 205; figured as "immigrants," 75; figured as "native," 107; historical claims of, 75–76, 105; as hybrid, 106; as "lazy," 241; and *mestizaje,* 266 n.13; as Mexican, 267 n.17; relations with Mexican migrants, 107–10; as undeserving, 240–41; as U.S.-citizen "minority," 107–8, 201; as "welfare dependent," 240–41

Chicanismo, 108. *See also* Chicano Movement; Chicano nationalism

Chicano Manifesto, 107–8

Chicano Movement, 104, 265 n.7, 266 n.12

Chicano nationalism, 104; feminist critiques of, 105–6, 266 n.11; obsessions of, with "purity" and "authenticity," 106; spatial politics of, 104–110

Chicano studies, 96–97, 104–111, 220, 266 n.14, 268 n.24; as anti-assimilationist, 104, 110; as anti-imperialist, 103–5, 110, 267 n.17; as anti-racist, 104, 110; defined, 104–5; erasure of historical claims of, 97; geographical orientation to U.S. Southwest, 104–110, 266 n.8; indigenist claims of, 105; institutionalization of, 104; omission of Chicago in, 105, 107, 265 n.7, 266 n.8; as politically oriented to the United States, 108–11; reconceptualization of, 7, 96, 106; as self-representation, 110; spatial presuppositions of, 104–110

172, 180; *relajo* in, 171–74; as research practice, 13, 19–21; self-reflexive, xvi; seriousness in, 172–73, 180; as signature methodology in sociocultural anthropology, 168; surrealism in, 167–68, 197; as text, 20–21, 258 n.10; textualist critique of, 167–68; in urban sociology, 111, 267 n.18. *See also* Anthropology; Dialogue

Eurocentrism, of Mexican elite, 110

Europe, 222, 230

Europeans, 65, 71, 101, 203, 222

Evans-Pritchard, E. E., 257 n.4, 258–9 n.14

Everyday life, xvi, 112, 120, 142, 145, 147, 196, 254; critical knowledge of, 252–53; critical perspectives on white supremacy in, 208; "illegality" effect in, 245–47; insubordinate spatial practices of, 98; and racialization, 137, 142, 169, 198, 220; *relajo* in, 173; surrealism as discursive strategy in, 168–69; surveillance in, 246–47

Fabian, Johannes, 38

Family reunification provisions, 232–34, 236

Fanon, Frantz, 22, 48, 253

Feminism. *See* Chicana feminism

Fenomenología del relajo, 169–70

Ferguson, Colin, 67–68

Ferguson, James, 136

Field Museum of Natural History (Chicago), 15

"Fieldwork": as disciplinary myth, 18–22. *See also* Ethnography

Filipinos, 233, 277 n.3

Flojo, as laziness, 193, 195, 275 n.22. *See also Huevón,* as laziness; Laziness

Foley, Neil, 218

"Folk-urban continuum," idea of, 111–12, 267 n.20

Fordism, 32

"Foreign"-ness, 60, 67, 76, 86, 88–89, 260–61 n.3; comprising an outside of the nation, 89, 216; of the "illegal alien," 215; as problem for nationalism, 76–78; as reinvigorating democracy, 88

Fourteenth Amendment (U.S. Constitution), 262 n.10

Frankenberg, Ruth, 276 n.28

Freire, Paulo, 23–30, 175, 257 nn.6–8, 258 nn.11–12, 258–9 n.14, 259 nn.15–16, 260 nn.21–22

Fromm, Erich, 259 n.16

Gamio, Manuel, 267 n.20

Gangs, 131, 180, 205, 247

García, Ramón, 168

Gender, 81, 93, 133–34, 191, 195–96, 264 n.21. *See also* Masculinity

Gendered Transitions: Mexican Experiences of Immigration, 264 n.21

Genocide, 89

Gentrification, 269 n.32

Global capital accumulation, 122–23, 263 n.16; articulation with established social inequalities, 137; class politics of, 57. *See also* Capitalism

"Globalization," 31–33, 57, 96, 122–23, 125; articulation with established social inequalities, 137; as euphemism, 122

Gómez-Peña, Guillermo, 99, 101

González, Juan, 75

Good Neighbor Policy, 100

Gramsci, Antonio, 147

Great Depression, 115, 224

Greater Mexico, idea of, 99

Greeks, 209

Guadalajara, 246

Guadalupe Hidalgo, Treaty of, 218–221

Guanajuato, 3, 4, 46, 190, 204–5, 272 n.52

Guatemala, 164

Guatemalans, 176, 181, 183

Güero, 184, 193, 198–99, 253. *See also, Blanco; Indio; Moreno; Negro; Prieto*

Guerrero, 3, 4, 129–30, 134, 251

Gupta, Akhil, 136

Gutiérrez, David, 266 n.14

Gutiérrez, Guillermo, 173

Gutiérrez, Ramón, 266 n.14, 266–67 n.15

Gwaltney, John, 173

Handlin, Oscar, 85, 88

"Hard work": as masculine virility, 195; as virtue, 32, 35, 165, 193, 195, 207. *See also* "Laziness"

Harris, Nigel, 262 n.14

Hart-Celler Immigration Act. *See* Immigration Act of 1965

Hegwisch, 117, 268–69 n.28

Heyman, Josiah, 278–79 n.15

Hidalgo, 3

Higham, John, 60, 260 n.3

"Hispanic": as "ethnic" category in U.S. Census, 187; as homogenizing strategy of erasure, 256 n.7; as a racial category, 41–42, 44, 46, 187, 199 (*see also* "Latino," as a racial category; "Spanish," as a racial category)

"Hispanic whites," 198

Hispano elite (New Mexico), 219

Historicity, 1, 22, 24, 25–28, 52, 211, 213, 252

Holloway, John, 228

Homeland Security, Department of (U.S.), 248

"Homeland security," discourse of, 63

Hometown associations (Mexican), in Chicago, 4

Hondagneu-Sotelo, Pierrette, 264 n.21

Honduras, 14

Honig, Bonnie, 88–90

Huasteca Potosina, 179

Huazteco, 179

Huevón, as laziness, 189–91, 195. *See also Flojo*, as laziness; "Laziness"

Huevos (testicles), 190, 274–75 n.18

Hull House, 114, 118,

Humboldt Park, 119

Humor, 169–205 (passim), 252; as articulation of critical perspectives, 173, 252; in Chicano culture, 171–72; in Díaz-Barriga, 173; and insinuation, 178; in Lancaster, 171; and machismo, 170; and masculinity, 176; in Paredes, 172; in Paz, 170–71; and performance, 172, 178; and racialization, 169, 174–88; as resistance, 171–73; in Rosaldo, 171. *See also* Irony; *Relajo*

Hutchinson, Edward, 223

Hyde Park, 17

Identity, politics of, 60–62, 66, 69, 81, 261 n.5. *See also* Nativism, as identity politics; Nativism, as pluralist

"Illegal alien," 90, 91–94, 126–27, 214, 248, 270–71 n.41; as affront to national sovereignty, 90, 91; as heterosexual male, 93; as incorrigible for "Americanization," 93, 215; Mexicans as iconic, 2, 8, 91, 200; as preoccupation of nativism in the 1990s, 62–63; as racialized figure, 91; as racialized and spatialized status, 245; in Schuck and Smith, 90; as "sojourner," 93; as subverting national sovereignty, 215; as synonymous with "Mexican," 91–94, 202, 231; as undermining liberal consent, 90; white U.S. citizens as original, 276 n.2. *See also* "Illegality"

"Illegal immigration." *See* Undocumented migration

Illegal Immigration Reform and Immigrant Responsibility Act of 1996, heightened workplace raids following, 126, 206, 241–42, 278 n.14

"Illegality," 223–49, 255 n.2: and deportability, 215; as effect of discursive formation, 228; effects of, 214; in everyday life, 245–47; as feature of racialization of Mexicans, 8, 14, 91–94, 124, 126–27, 142, 203, 215, 226, 245; figured as exclusively Mexican, 200; figured as status of *all* migrants, 201; historical specificity of, 227; as identity, 238–39; the legal production of, 2, 8, 93, 202, 213–49 (passim); naturalization of, 214, 228, 242, 248; relation to labor, 8, 30, 54, 133, 215, 246–47; rendered visible through border policing, 242; as spatialized social condition, 8, 215, 245; and surveillance, 246–47; and undeservingness, 202. *See also* Citizenship, the politics of; Deportability; Undocumented migration

Illegalization. *See* "Illegality," the legal production of

Illegal Mexican Alien Problem, The, 126

Illinois, 115, 116, 126, 175, 235, 239

Illinois Legislative Investigating Commission, 126, 270 n.40

Illinois State Register, 103

"Immigrant America," myth of, 32, 88–89, 90, 204. *See also* Xenophilia

Immigrant essentialism, 71–73, 80

"Immigrant," figure of, 56–94 (passim), 111; as ambivalent, 80–82; as fetish of U.S. nationalism, 55, 85–89, 90; as having no past history, 87; as hybrid, 80–82; as masculine individual, 86–87, 264 n.19; as non-question, 83–85; as object of suspicion, 81–82; as problem, 79–85; as question, 79–85; as racialized, 64–68; as spatialized sociopolitical status, 95; as teleological, 98; as transhistorical, 71; as transplant,

80–82; as window onto "American"-ness, 79. *See also* Migrant, terminological usage of

"Immigration," 56–94 (passim); liberal discourse of, 69, 75, 87–88; in public debate, 55, 56, 58, 83, 86–87, 206; as racialized figure, 64–68; as teleological, 2–3, 7, 56–58; as transhistorical, 71, 87. *See also* Migration(s)

Immigration Act of 1917, 221

Immigration Act of 1924, 222

Immigration Act of 1965, 63, 124, 217, 229–33; figured as liberal reform, 230

Immigration Act of 1976, 233–34

Immigration Act of 1978, 234

Immigration Act of 1990, 236

Immigration and Nationalities Act (1952), 63, 217, 230

Immigration and Naturalization Service, 14, 91, 126–27, 230–31, 235, 243–44, 247–48, 271 nn.42–43. *See also* Border Patrol

Immigration complex. *See* Immigrant essentialism

Immigration law (U.S.), 8, 62–63, 64, 90–91, 213–49 (passim); as crisis management, 227–28; definition of border in, 278 n.14; as inclusion through illegalization, 234; as tactic of labor discipline, 228; and racism, 72, 221–23. *See also* "Illegality," the legal production of

Immigration Reform (1996). *See* Illegal Immigration Reform and Immigrant Responsibility Act of 1996

Immigration Reform and Control Act of 1986, 63, 235–36, 259 n.19, 278 n.12

Imperialism, 122–23, 263 n.16. *See also* Colonialism

Imperialism (U.S.), xv–xvi, 74–75, 86, 89, 98, 100, 103, 105, 122, 125, 217–18, 248,

and division in workplace, 159; and ethnographic literalism, 172; and performance, 172; racialization of, 45–48, 185; and social control, 179. *See also* English (language); Spanish (language)

La Raza, terminological usage of, 109, 266–67 n.15

"Latin," as marker of otherness, 101

Latin America, 15, 75, 106, 178, 188, 230, 256 n.7; dominant spatial ideologies of, 95–104; conceptualized as outside of the United States, 101, 103–4; as "Latin," 101; relation of Chicago to, 120 (*see also* Mexican Chicago); relevance of anti-Mexican racism to, 103

Latin American studies, 96–104, 110; anti-imperialist scholarship in, 100, 104; U.S. imperialist epistemology of, 96, 100, 103–4; reconceptualization of, 7, 96;

Latina/os (or Latin Americans), 16, 17, 40, 44, 46, 64, 71, 75, 103, 118, 127, 148–49, 174, 175, 181–82, 186, 187–88, 256 n.7, 264 n.20, 271 n.44; and Asians, 202; and Blackness, 186–88, 202; discrimination against, 54, 127, 270 n.36; as disqualified from "American"-ness, 200, 202; and "Indian"-ness, 188; intermediacy of racial locations of, 187–88, 202; labor-force participation of, 124; neighborhoods of, as racial "buffer zones," 138–39; and police, 246; racialized as "brown," 230; responses to U.S. Census "race" question, 188, 198; segregation in Chicago, 112, 138, 271 n.48, 272 nn.50–51; and whiteness, 198

"Latino": as "ethnic" category in U.S. Census, 187; as a racial category, 46–47, 187–88, 199; terminological usage of, 256 n.7 (*see also* "Hispanic," as a racial category; "Spanish," as a racial category)

Latinoamericano, terminological usage of, 256 n.7

Latino studies, and the politics of representation, 17–18

La Villita. See Little Village

Law, 227–29; as conflicted and contradictory, 227; employer disregard for, 160; historicity of, 227–28; instrumentality of, 228; and legislation, 227; as naturalized in scholarship, 228; practical materiality of, 227–28; productivity of, 227–28; treated as transhistorical, 228; as undetermined struggle, 228. *See also* Immigration law

"Laziness," 165, 177, 179, 189–96, 207, 240–41, 275 n.22; as masculine self-determination, 190–91; and whiteness, 191. *See also* "Hard work"

Lefebvre, Henri, 95, 113, 137, 145, 147, 211, 213, 215, 254

Legalization, 225, 232, 235, 239, 248–49, 277 n.9, 278 n.12. *See also* Amnesty

"Legal permanent resident," immigration status of, 239

Lewis, Oscar, 173, 273 n.3

Limerick, Patirica Nelson, 98

Limón, José, 171–72, 273 nn.7–8

Little Village, 41, 118–19, 139–40, 269 n.32; community organizing in, 127

Logan Square, 119

Lomnitz-Adler, Claudio, 179

Los Angeles, California, 4, 238, 243, 270 n.35; "zoot suit" riots in, 268 n.25

Lowe, Lisa, 75, 86

Lower West Side. *See* Pilsen

Lozano, Rudy, 127, 271 n.44

Machismo, 41–42, 44; and humor, 170; in Paz, 170–71, 273 n.5. *See also* Masculinity

category, 3, 8, 46–48, 102–3, 138, 140–
41, 187, 198–99; 221; and racial intermediacy, 5, 6, 8–9, 138–39, 169, 174–
209 (passim); as racialized transnationality, 4, 9, 96, 115, 199–206; in
relation to African Americans, 193–
96, 199–200, 209; in relation to
"American"-ness, 6, 8, 95, 102–3, 115,
142, 199–200, 203, 209, 215, 224; in
relation to Blackness, 139–41, 193–96;
in relation to Puerto Ricans, 199–200;
as "sojourner," 88, 91–94; as synonymous with "illegal alien," 2, 8, 14,
91–94, 124, 126–27, 200, 202, 203, 215,
232; and undeservingness, 200; and
U.S. Census, 221; and whiteness, 209,
219–21. *See also* "American"-ness, as
U.S. national identity
Mexican Revolution, 148, 199, 222
Mexico, 75–76, 97, 99, 100, 131, 193, 224–
26; and migrant organizations, 265
n.4; race and racism in, 139, 175, 178–
79; relation to United States, 97, 102–
3, 107; as threshold to Latin America,
103; and U.S.-Mexico border, 277 n.7;
U.S. war against, 75, 97, 102–3, 217–18,
221, 226
Mexico City, 37, 46, 97, 139, 149, 176, 218,
226
México de afuera, idea of, 99
México, 3, 149
Michaels, Walter Benn, 60–61
Michoacán, 3, 4, 28, 183
Mignolo, Walter, 266 n.9
Migrant, terminological usage of, 2–3.
See also Immigrant essentialism;
"Immigrant," figure of
Migrant "illegality." *See* "Illegality"
Migration(s), 91; historical specificity of,
56, 71, 227; as movement, 2, 56, 83, 251;
post-1965, 64; relation to imperialism,
74. *See also* "Immigration"

Miles, Jack, 262 n.13
Miscegenation, 80, 103. *See also* Purity,
racial (ideology of)
Mojado, 196, 201, 239. *See also* "Wetback"
Monterrey, 150
Moraga, Cherríe, 106, 108, 109, 266 n.12
Morelia, Michoacán, 28
Morelos, 3, 13
Moreno, 165, 193, 196–99, 244, 253, 275
n.25, 276 n.30. *See also Blanco; Güero;
Indio; Negro; Prieto*
Morrison, Toni, 208–9
Multiculturalism, 83, 85
Muslims, nativism against, 63
Mutual aid associations, 115

Nader, Laura, 173
Nation, 61, 69, 77, 87, 89; contingency of,
7, 61–62; as "extended family," 66–68;
and internal "minorities," 76–78; and
race, 68, 77–78; as requiring limits, 61,
89; as simulacrum of inclusiveness, 86.
See also Nationalism
"National character" (Mexican), 170–71,
273 nn.3–4
"National economy," idea of, 73, 74, 263
n.16
National identity, 216
Nationalism: critique of, 7, 94; and inter-
nal "minorities," 76–78; and nativism,
7, 60–62, 69; as politics of space, 95;
and problem of foreignness, 76–78.
See also Chicano nationalism; Nation,
U.S. nationalism
Nationalism (U.S.). *See* U.S. nationalism
National origins quota system, 222–23,
230
"Native": as a political identity, 58–59; as
spatialized sociopolitical status, 95
Native Americans, 218, 220, 264 n.17
"Native's point of view," 7, 58–60, 78, 85,
91, 94. *See also* Nativism

Racism (*continued*)
240; as central problem of working-class consciousness and action, 137; as dehumanizing, 253; of ethnographer, 172; in Latin America, 188; and Manifest Destiny, 217; in Mexico, 139, 178–79; as premise of Chicano studies, 105; systemic mediation of U.S. everyday life by, 169; and Welfare Reform, 206. *See also* Nativism; Race; White supremacy

Racist hegemony. *See* White supremacy

Radway, Janice, 56, 58, 59, 260 n.2

Raids, in workplaces (by INS), 63, 126, 236, 243

Railroads, 113–118, 221, 224

"Reconquista," discourse of, 238

Redfield, Robert, 267 n.20

Refugee Act of 1980, 234

Reimers, David, 233

Relajo, 169–203 (passim); as articulation of critical perspectives, 169, 172, 173; in Bartra, 169; definitions of, 169–70; as dialogical, 173; in Díaz-Barriga, 173; in ethnography, 171–74; in everyday life, 173; in Limón, 171–72; as nihilism, 170, 171; in Portilla, 169–71, 173; as producing solidarity, 171–72; and seriousness, 170, 173, 180, 183, 184; as subversive, 171. *See also* Humor; Irony; Surrealism

Remittances, 128–29, 134, 204

Rendón, Armando, 107–8, 110, 265 n.6, 266 n.13

Repatriation, 115–16, 224

Republican Party, 64, 184

Reracialization, 4, 8–9, 67, 139–142, 169, 196–99, 203; and ambiguity, 180–81, 198; and irresolution, 203; transnational repercussions of, 141–42; and white-Black binary, 202; and whiteness, 203. *See also* Racialization

Revolving-door policy, 8, 133, 223, 225, 226, 231, 242, 248

Rich, Adrienne, 95

Río Bravo, 97

Rio Grande, 97, 218

Rodríguez, Ricardo, 221

Roediger, David, 203, 209, 255 n.1

Roosevelt, Franklin, 100

Rorty, Richard, 174

Rosaldo, Renato, 171, 174, 267 n.16

Ross Pineda, Raúl, 128

Rouse, Roger, 265 n.3

"Rule of law, the," 91, 237; as a figure for "the nation," 237

Said, Edward, xv, 13, 15, 19,

Saldívar, José David, 56

Salvadorans, 181, 183

San Clemente, California, 244

San Luis Potosí, 3, 4, 176, 179, 240

Santa Anna, Antonio López de, 226

"Save Our State" ballot initiative (California), 55. *See also* Proposition 187

Schuck, Peter, 90, 93

"Second generation," 72, 83–85; as hybrid, 84–85.

Segregation, racial, 5, 103, 118, 138–40, 162, 271 n.48, 272 nn.50–51; dissimilarity indices for Mexicans in Chicago, 138; in suburbs, 162

Settlement, 81, 83–85, 87–88, 98, 264 n.21; equated with families, 93, 206; equated with women, 93, 206; of Mexican migrants, 91–94, 206. *See also* "Americanization"; "Assimilation"

Shadowed Lives: Undocumented Immigrants in American Society, 87–88

Sharecropping, 131

Shor, Ira, 258 n.12

Simmel, Georg, 81

Simpson, Alan, 237

Slavery, 70–71, 89, 187, 198; as feminized,

191–92; as metaphor, 160, 165, 183, 189–92, 196; in Mexico, 198; as racialized metaphor (equated with Blackness), 177, 178, 181, 189, 191–92, 197–98

Smith, Raymond T., 262 n.9

Smith, Rogers, 90, 93

Soccer teams (Mexican), in Chicago, 256 n.2

Social science, 22, 259 n.15; and the politics of representation, 18, 92–94. *See also* Anthropology; Ethnography

Sociology, 79, 87, 109, 111, 137, 264 n.18. *See also* Chicago School of sociology

"Sojourner," figure of, 81, 87–88, 91–94, 264 n.20; gendered as male, 93; as heterosexual, 93; as nativist stereotype of Mexicans, 88

South Chicago, 117, 268 n.28

South Deering, 117, 268–69 n.28

Southeast Asians, 200, 275 n.23

South Lawndale. *See* Little Village

South Side, 114, 117–20, 179–80

Southwest (U.S.), 104–7, 114, 115, 217–18, 223, 224, 266 n.12; legacy of conquest and colonization in, 5, 75–76, 97, 221, 238; nativist alarm over Mexican "Quebec" in, 237–38

Sovereignty, 63, 65, 69, 216, 237; as authoritarianism in immigration and naturalization regime, 237; "illegal alien" as affront to, 90, 91, 215, 237; and "national culture," 237

Space, 95–143 (passim); annihilation of, 122; differential, 100, 123, 142; in Freire, 175; of nation-state, 95; and pedagogy, 175; policing of public, 245–47; politics of, 7; and race, 136–41; social production of, 111, 113, 120, 123, 137; urban, 111, 113, 137–41

"Spanish," as racial category, 185–86,

219–220. *See also* "Hispanic," as a racial category; "Latino," as a racial category

Spanish (language): as deficiency or "lack," 45, 50, 174, 185–86; discrimination against, 45–48; in ESL classes, 50–51; as racialized, 45–48, 185–86; as sign of traditionalism, 42; subordinate status of, 46. *See also* English as a Second Language

Special Committee on Importation of Mexican Labor, 224

State federations (Mexican), in Chicago, 4

State formation, 228, 263 n.16

Steel (industry), 114, 117

Steinberg, Stephen, 70–77, 262 nn.11–13, 262–63 n.14, 263 n.15

Stockyards (Union), 114, 117

Stone Park, Illinois, 270 n.35

Strikebreaking, 114, 116

Sullivan, Othman, 173

Supreme Court (U.S.), 221

Surrealism: and Chicano identity, 168; as discursive strategy in everyday life, 168–69, 201; ethnographic, 167–68; and "race," 168, 174, 181, 186, 188. *See also* Irony; *Relajo*

Taylorism, 163–64, 272–73 n.2

Tejana/os, 240

"Terrorism," suspicions of, 63

Terror of the Machine, 257 n.7

Texas, 106, 107, 116, 128, 149, 175, 176, 219–21, 226, 246, 269–70 n.33, 275 n.21

Texas–Santa Fe expedition, 102

Thanksgiving, 204

Theory, social, 252

Tijuana, 243

Total Quality Management, 33–34, 40, 158

Transnational corporations, 31–32

Transnationalism, 122–23, 128–43, 267
n.21; articulation with established
social inequalities, 137; and critique of
nationalism, 7, 59, 96; interrelation of
United States and Mexico, 5, 97–98,
107, 142; as racialized, 141–43; in relation to imperialism, 122–23; as theoretical paradigm, 7, 57–58
Transnationalization of labor, 57, 75, 123,
252; as central to Mexican Chicago, 111
Transnational migration, 2, 6, 74, 95, 112,
123, 141–42; as labor recruitment strategy, 161–62; and rural poverty, 131–33
Treaty of Guadalupe Hidalgo (1848),
218–221
Trouillot, Michel-Rolph, 40
*Turning Back: The Retreat from Racial
Justice in American Thought and Policy,* 70–76
Tyler, Stephen, 258 n.10

Unamuno, Miguel de, 259 n.16
Undeservingness, 200, 202, 224, 240–41
Undocumented migrants, 54, 58–59, 90,
97, 116, 142, 192–93, 194, 196, 203, 224–
25, 256 n.1, 268 n.23, 277 n.4; allegations of "abuse" of social services by,
206; apprehensions of, 126–27, 230–31,
242–44, 271 n.42, 277 n.4; approximate
number of Mexicans in United States,
229; children of, 90, 93, 238; border-
crossing narratives of, 132–33, 243–44;
and deportability, 247–48; as "deportable aliens," 59, 91; employment insecurity of, 207; fertility of women, 93;
as fiscal "burden," 206; and labor, 124,
247–48; recruited by Border Patrol,
225; as "temporary," 247–48
Undocumented migration, 126; absence
of, as a topic during legislative debate
prior to 1965, 233; during Bracero Program era, 224–25; equated with un-

authorized border-crossing, 231–32,
235, 270–71 n.41; as explicit "problem"
of legislative debate after 1968, 233, 235;
and labor, 54, 133, 192, 196; as object of
immigration law, 213–49 (passim); as
permanent importation of labor, 242;
as preoccupation of nativism, 63; as
premise of immigration law enforcement, 247–48. *See also* "Illegality"
Unions, 31, 52, 126, 148–65, 176, 224; as
"trouble making," 126, 155; and
workers' self-organization, 151
University of Chicago, 14–16, 17, 79
University of Illinois, 118
"Urban renewal," 118
U.S. imperialism. *See* Imperialism (U.S.)
U.S. nationalism, 57–59, 64, 65, 74–75,
79, 96, 248, 252–53; and American
studies, 260 n.2; ethnographic critique
of, 7, 59, 96, 253–54; figured as cos-
mopolitan, 252–53; figured as egalitarian, 253; figured as inclusive, 86,
252–53; as parochial, 248; as a racial
formation, 8, 78, 102, 260 n.1; relegitimation projects of, 89; as xenophilic,
85–90; *See also* "American"-ness, as
U.S. national identity
U.S. Steel, 117

Valdés, Dennis, 266 n.8
Valdés de Villalva, Guillermina, 257 n.7
Vasconcelos, José, 99, 128, 266 n.13
Vietnamese, 32, 200, 202
Villa, Francisco (Pancho), 148, 199–201,
276 n.27
"Voluntary departure complex," idea of,
278–79 n.15
Vološinov, V. N., 258 n.13
Voting rights, 218–21, 240

Washington, D.C., 62
Waukegan, Illinois, 270 n.36

Wisconsin, 116

Welfare, 16, 17, 135; "abuse" of, 240–41; and "dependency," 16, 194, 199–200; and "laziness," 193–95, 199–200; in public debate, 206–7; as substantive entitlement of U.S. citizens, 193, 200

Welfare reform (1996). *See* Personal Responsibility and Work Opportunity Reconciliation Act (1996)

Western Hemisphere, 223, 230–34, 277 n.6

West Indies, 230

West Town, 119

West Virginia, 34

"Wetback," 196, 201, 203, 205, 225, 239; "drying out" of, 225; as synonymous with "Mexican," 196, 203. *See also Mojado*

"White flight," 5, 117, 118, 125, 138, 269 n.30

White nationalism, 217

Whites, 32, 40–46, 125, 158, 181, 185–86, 190, 198, 218, 240, 247; class differences among, 186; as "lazy," 190; as police, 162, 246; and politics, 184; relations with Latinos, 46, 185–86; relations with Mexicans, 114, 162, 174; segregation in Chicago, 138, 271 n.48, 272 nn. 50–51; and whiteness, 186. *See also* "White flight"; Whiteness

Whiteness, 8–9, 64–68, 71–72, 101–3, 115, 186, 201, 209, 217, 253; and categorical opposition to Blackness, 187; and citizenship, 218–21; claims to, 181, 186, 198; as destructive ideology, 209; and eligibility for naturalization, 216–17; and European-origin migrants, 203; and "immigration," 209; and labor, 177–178; and luxury, 174, 177–78, 185; in Naturalization Act of 1790, 216–17; as oppressive and false, 255 n.1; performances of, 181; and power, 198; and

privilege, 174, 177–78, 185–86, 198; as racialized status of anthropologist, 167, 180–81; and reracialization, 203; in Roediger, 209, 255 n.1. *See also* "American"-ness, as U.S. national identity; Blackness; White supremacy

White supremacy (U.S.), xv, 71, 77, 102–3, 174, 184, 187, 197, 254; and "American"-ness, 208–9; and Manifest Destiny, 217; as both national and imperial project, 103; produced through polarity of whiteness and Blackness, 187, 202. *See also* Racism; Whiteness

Williams, William Appleman, 74, 264–65 n.2

Wilson, Pete, 184

Winant, Howard, 168

Workplace literacy, 23, 30–39, 45, 48–52, 165; as exemption from labor process, 139–40, 185–86. *See also* English as a Second Language; Pedagogy

World Trade Center, attacks on, 62–63

World War I, 113, 222

World War II, 100, 115, 116, 224

Xenophilia, 85–89, 90. *See also* "Immigrant America"; Nativism; Xenophobia

Xenophobia, 60, 69, 261 n.4. *See also* Nativism; Xenophilia

Xicote, 196

Yugoslavia, 65

Zacatecas, 3, 4, 16, 175, 190, 192

Zapatistas (*Ejército Zapatista de Liberación Nacional*), 49, 164

Zavella, Patricia

Žižek, Slavoj, 170

Zolberg, Aristide, 230

"Zulus," 65–66, 78, 81

Nicholas De Genova is an assistant
professor in the department of
anthropology and the program in Latina/o
studies at Columbia University.

Library of Congress Cataloging-in-Publication Data
De Genova, Nicholas.
Working the boundaries : race, space, and "illegality" in
Mexican Chicago / Nicholas De Genova.
v. cm.   Includes bibliographical references and index.
ISBN 0-8223-3626-x (cloth : alk. paper)
ISBN 0-8223-3615-4 (pbk. : alk. paper)
1. Mexican Americans—Illinois—Chicago—Social conditions.
2. Mexicans—Illinois—Chicago—Social conditions.
3. Immigrants—Illinois—Chicago—Social conditions.
4. Illegal aliens—Illinois—Chicago—Social conditions.
5. Chicago (Ill.)—Race relations.
6. Chicago (Ill.)—Emigration and immigration.
7. Mexico—Emigration and immigration.
8. Nationalism—United States.
9. Emigration and immigration—Political aspects—United States.
10. Mexican Americans—Study and teaching.
I. Title.
F548.9.M5D425 2005   305.868'720977311—dc22
2005004621